Praise for the plays of Mark Jackson

American $uicide

"Fast, funny and densely satiric..."
— SAN FRANCISCO CHRONICLE

"A truly transcendent comedy... But writer/director Mark Jackson has more up his sleeve than easy yuks... America's obsession with fame and fortune spins absurdly, riotously out of control. Along the way, Jackson pokes fun at every American archetype... Altogether, this show is a delight."
— SAN FRANCISCO EXAMINER

"A perceptive commentary on American society's fascination with the media... This sardonic farce is unlike anything you have ever seen."
— TALKINBROADWAY.COM

BANG!

"BANG! is brilliant [and] pretty damn funny."
— SF WEEKLY

"A farce of hilarious proportions."
— WWW.FESTONLINE.CO.UK

"A hugely funny and melodramatic exploration of the purpose and value of theatre..."
— WWW.THREEWEEKS.CO.UK

Brave

"This is bright, ambitious stuff."
— SAN FRANCISCO BAY GUARDIAN

"All three stories deal baldly with private and national identity; together they give an interesting impression of a country in flux. Art Street Theatre has somehow managed, again, to make itself entertaining without being straightforward..."
— SF WEEKLY

The Death of Meyerhold

"An ambitious new work by brilliant playwright/director Mark Jackson... In three acts that are alternately funny, chilling, poignant, and starkly dramatic – and never less than consummately entertaining – Jackson traces the theatrical life of Vsevolod Meyerhold. ...Stunning, and a must see."
— BACK STAGE

"Mark Jackson's The Death of Meyerhold *is a play on the march, a bristling, witty phalanx of old Russian poses advancing, at its best, with the force of a tank... It's fast and funny... The writing is expansive and sophisticated, with humor that keeps pompousness at bay.*"
– WASHINGTON POST

"*Playwright Mark Jackson is not one to shy away from big subjects...* [The Death of Meyerhold] *is a play that demands the audiences' attention in order to be understood and appreciated. And, along the way, it is a great deal of fun with some terrific humor and insightful dialogue...*"
– CURTAINUP.COM

Faust Pt1

"*An exhilarating experience... Intellectually stimulating, startlingly bloody and emotionally gripping... Stark, funny, sobering and provocative, this is a* Faust *for our times.*"
– SAN FRANCISCO CHRONICLE

"*Dazzling... This is a disciplined, intentional piece of theatre... A script that crackles with poetry, comedy and terror.*"
– THEATERDOGS.NET

"*Tightly written and beautifully constructed... There are moments of stark beauty and incomparable emotion... Huge praise must go to Jackson... His adaptation leaves many of the story's conclusions to the audience. And that may be what works best of all in this story – it plays across the mind for quite awhile after the final blackout.*"
– CONTRA COSTA TIMES

The Forest War

"Mark Jackson's The Forest War *weaves a tale that's as old as the trees and still somehow feels like a spring sapling... Jackson drives his epic plot along with prose that's as muscular as it is bewitching. Swaggering political speeches melt into lines of lyrical sweetness...*"
– SF WEEKLY

"*When art speaks truth, it hurts, and it never hurts so much as in Mark Jackson's stylish new play* The Forest War*... Written and directed with imaginative flair... the imagery is power-packed, and worthy of a story that looks like it will already be the stuff of legend.*"
– KQED.ORG

"This is a gutsy show... It's beautiful and powerful... A bold undertaking that uses ancient forms to tell a modern story of love, politics, and needless bloodshed."
— EAST BAY EXPRESS

I Am Hamlet

"A rare dose of fresh and engaging cutting-edge theatre."
— SAN FRANCISCO MAGAZINE

"A hilarious show with flashes of brilliance. Jackson shapes his speeches and scenes like an expert craftsman..."
— SF WEEKLY

Messenger #1

"It's dark, damning, graceful, and funny as hell."
— SF WEEKLY

"Veering from word-drunk paeans of justice to sharp one-liners, Jackson knows how to weave the poignant and the scatological, the contemporary and the classical, together in an accessible and entertaining way that adds to the power of the original [Oresteia] in a sometimes startling manner."
— BACK STAGE WEST

"A profound and moving piece..."
— SAN FRANCISCO EXAMINER

R&J

"This hallucinatory response to Romeo & Juliet is an inspired piece of work... A rich meditation on a magical story and the nature of love, bristling with imagination and intelligence."
— SAN FRANCISCO BAY GUARDIAN

"It's both quirky and dense, arty and absurd, stylized and entertaining..."
— SF WEEKLY (1997)

"Startlingly alive and eerily dreamy... The familiarity of the text brilliantly serves Mark Jackson's methodology of fragmentation. The action moves steadily from quirky irony to senseless tragedy to heartbreaking silence at an astonishing rate... As full and complete as any of the more traditional versions I've seen. And, on the whole, vastly more entertaining."
— SF WEEKLY (1996)

Mark Jackson

TEN PLAYS

Ten Plays
Copyright © 2010 by Mark Jackson
All rights reserved

Published by EXIT PRESS
Assistance for this publication was provided by the San Francisco Study Center and The Ambassador Program of the Philanthropic Ventures Foundation.
Cover design by Kevin Clarke
Front cover photo by Benjamin Privitt, from *Faust Pt1*, produced by Shotgun Players, Berkeley, CA.
Back cover photo by Clayton Lord, from *American $uicide*, produced by Encore Theatre Company and Z Space Studio, San Francisco, CA.

First Edition: June 2010

CAUTION: Professionals and amateurs are hereby warned that the plays represented in this book are subject to a royalty.

All rights of every kind to the plays included in this collection belong to their author, Mark Jackson. These plays are protected by United States and international copyright law. These laws ensure the author is rewarded for his work and protected against theft or abuse of that work. The author encourages you to produce the plays, to option them for other mediums, or to make other public use of them. But you must pay him for the right to do so. This is true for academic, amateur, professional or any other producers.

Securing rights for theatrical production or any other public use of these plays is very simple. Go to www.artstreettheatre.org where you will find contact information for the author, Mark Jackson. Contact him to negotiate a legal contract with all relevant details, among them rights and payment of royalties.

If you produce or in any other public way use one of these plays, in part or in whole, without going through this simple procedure, you will be stealing the livelihood of the author, breaking the law, and will be prosecuted under the full extent of that law.

In addition to not performing or otherwise publicly using these plays without obtaining prior written permission from the author and without paying the requisite royalty, please do not photocopy, scan, or otherwise duplicate any part of this book as such actions also constitute a violation of the law.

For additional information about U.S. copyright laws, go to www.copyright.gov.

For additional information about EXIT PRESS, go to www.theexit.org.

For additional information about Mark Jackson, or to contact him for any reason, go to www.artstreettheatre.org.

Some of the plays in this collection contain stage directions suggesting the use of specific works of music. EXIT PRESS has not obtained permissions for the use of these works of music. Any producer of these plays electing to use these works of music in production is advised to obtain the necessary permissions, and, toward that end, to consult the above listed U.S. Copyright Office website, as well as that of ASCAP (www.ascap.com), BMI (www.bmi.com), or NMPA (www.nmpa.org) as applicable.

ISBN: 978-0-9843964-0-5

EXIT PRESS
156 Eddy Street
San Francisco, CA 94102-2708

Life or death, only not sleep.
— *Vsevolod Meyerhold*

Contents

Preface	xi
Foreword	xiii
Introduction	xvii
American $uicide	1
BANG!	73
Brave	111
The Death of Meyerhold	157
Faust Pt1	231
The Forest War	277
I Am Hamlet	331
little extremes	365
Messenger #1	383
R&J	423
Notes on the Plays	455
Other Plays By Mark Jackson	467
About The Author	470

Preface

EXIT Theatre is pleased to inaugurate EXIT PRESS with the publication of TEN PLAYS by Mark Jackson. Since our beginning in 1983 we have been dedicated to collaborating with playwrights in support of new work. For decades talented theatre artists have been contributing to the new American theatre on the EXIT stages. We hope EXIT PRESS will help this important work find a home on many other stages in the future. Through art we can change the world.

Christina Augello
EXIT Theatre

Foreword

I first encountered the work of Mark Jackson in the spring of 2000. I had just left both graduate school and the 20th century for something new, exactly what I hadn't yet discovered. Two friends with a small theatre company of their own had a strong professional interest in following Jackson's Art Street Theatre, then already five years old. They urged me to join them over at EXIT Theatre's tiny Stage Left black box, on Eddy Street in San Francisco's chancy Tenderloin district: Art Street was mounting Jackson's "new ancient Greek tragedy," *Messenger #1,* and I wouldn't want to miss it.

The first thing I noticed, passing from Eddy Street into the comparatively serene lobby of the then three-stage EXIT Theatre complex (where Art Street was in residence), was the director-playwright himself. A tall upright 30ish fellow with a serious forehead rising from thick auburn eyebrows into a thatch of ruddy hair, Jackson loomed over a small table with a roll of tickets, a cash box, and fresh copies of his self-published title, *THEATREWORK*. In those days, as my friends explained, Art Street's artistic director was given to distributing broadsheet manifestos at shows. *THEATREWORK* was a culmination of his ideas on process developed over Art Street's first five years.

Here, I thought, was a serious man with a serious operation, tucked into the most unlikely of venues. Later I realized how misleading my first impression was. Not that Jackson isn't serious. More dedicated and sure an artist working on the margins of professional theatre would be hard to find. But that forthright intellectualism I spied in the lobby in no way prepared me for the abounding playfulness, curiosity, dexterity, intuition and humor that emerged as soon as the house lights went down. I have been an enthusiastic follower of Jackson's work ever since.

But my first impression was mistaken too in failing to grasp how natural a fit, in fact, Jackson and his eccentric and committed company were for a place like EXIT Theatre. Since more than half of the plays amassed here under EXIT's new imprint were incubated under its own roof, it is worth saying something about the incubator.

For newbie artists in the ecology of Bay Area theatre, Christina Augello and Richard Livingston's EXIT Theatreplex – established in 1983 and today including a fourth 66-seat venue around the corner as well as a forthcoming Studio Theatre adjacent to the Eddy Street storefront – is more than a place to perform. It's a wild and weedy campsite, a meeting ground, a low-rent oasis where itinerant artists with little more than their own talent and inspiration can develop work, skills, an aesthetic, and (not least) an audience.

It's also the sponsor and epicenter since 1992 of the lottery-based San Francisco Fringe Festival, an invigorating annual blast of non-curated democratic bedlam that delivers adventurous audiences a range of surprises – and hands hard-working DIY performers the full take of the box office. EXIT's annual DIVAfest, meanwhile, serves as yet another platform, this one for work by and about women.

This amounts to an essential seedbed for new theatrical life in the Bay Area and beyond. There are few places as inviting and supportive – while also as unperturbedly hands off – where the early artistic vision of a playwright/director-driven outfit like Art Street can nurture itself over multiple productions. Operating obscurely if contentedly a short walk from the city's official theatre district, the EXIT has quietly served as a launching pad for some of San Francisco's most dynamic artists. Indeed, several of these – Jackson among them – have propelled themselves into theatrical orbit from the circus cannon of the Fringe.

Would these artists be the same otherwise? Would they be doing theatre at all? With Jackson's work, both as playwright and director, you get the feeling he is doing what he was born to do. It takes an insouciance, a bravery – to summon just one of the themes and titles running through this collection – to commit as fully to the theatre. It arguably also takes places like the EXIT.

As you embark on the wonderful plays in this volume, you'll find certain thematic threads winding throughout often inspired by, and in tension with, classic texts ancient and modern. For here is work that flouts convention, laughs at reverence, and yet finds forward motion in constantly cycling back through our dramatic and literary inheritance, constantly asking questions about its meaning, relevance, realities, possibilities. Far from a hermetic exercise, these questions invariably bring the contemporary world along with them. For Jackson, an ironical proposition like a "new ancient Greek tragedy" contains too a very earnest hope.

If these plays tend to straddle the line between the stage and the street, they retain an inherent theatricality in even the most barebones productions. Rigorously styled and kinetic in performance, they naturally reach for the full range of resources and potentialities of the stage while making canny use of its limits – demanding much of the actor and design team in the process. (To this end, Jackson, an able actor himself, has benefited from excellent collaborators, including stalwarts Beth Wilmurt, Kevin Clarke, and Jake Rodriguez.)

Perhaps just as strongly, you'll register the productive dance between form and content running through the plays. Among the most ambitious works here, *American $uicide, The Forest War,* and *The Death of Meyerhold* all throw form and content into a sometimes manic dialogue, refusing to resolve the contrasts that arise but making keen use of them all the same. These three plays, hearkening back to real or imagined pasts, also strongly resonate with our own cultural, political moment – while refracting it enticingly, provocatively through another time and another set of historical actors wildly unlike, but then also similar to ourselves.

Much more could be said about these plays, of course, and no doubt deservedly will now that they are readily available to the public. Whatever unevenness and teeth-cutting register across work spanning more than a decade, it's fair to call all of these plays youthful in the best sense of asking "why?" to everything – even their own theatrical urge – and deeply mature too, also in the best sense, in not always needing to have an answer.

Rob Avila
Theatre critic, *San Francisco Bay Guardian*
June 2010

Introduction

I've always liked the feel of a single collection of some author's plays in my hand, a little paperback coffer of related thoughts, feelings, impulses, characters, stories and themes that I can sift through at my leisure. And so it goes without saying that I'm very pleased to see these ten of my own plays, written between 1993 and 2009, gathered together between two covers. I am particularly proud for them to be presented thus by EXIT PRESS, since EXIT Theatre is where six of these plays were born and where I cut my professional theatre-making teeth.

I've arranged the plays alphabetically, not chronologically – a small attempt to disrupt the orderly idea of Time's linear arc with another orderly idea. But despite this minor effort to trip up artistic assumptions of chronology, no matter in what order the plays are read I nevertheless hope that by the end one gleans a sense of a continuum of work. Why I have included these particular plays and not others that I've written until now has to do with a combination of my fondness for variety and the fact that the publication of a play typically gives the impression that the playwright is done working on it.

With regard to variety, but also this notion of a continuum, I look at these ten plays collected together and see a range of styles, genres and tones – farce, satire, tragedy, epic, intimate, political, personal, physical, verbal, classical, contemporary, dark, light, grotesque, even occasional splashes of realism and naturalism. I also see common thematic threads – a questioning of history and our evolving relationship to it; the theme of maturation; violence and other severe attempts at control; the connection between individuals and the world outside of themselves; personal struggles with politics; searches for hope and meaning.

With regard to the impression of finality given by plays in print, those plays *not* included here I felt maybe I'd like to tinker with a bit more extensively should future productions permit me the opportunity. Of these, those that remain as-of-yet to be performed I of course expect I'll be tinkering with aplenty when production eventually teaches me their ropes.

But even the plays included here I might mess with a bit further. Writing never feels totally finished to me. *Brave*, for example, is a script I'd like to dig into again and retool. And I'm obsessively curious about how different audiences react to different things. Their own lives and the life of the world can have an incredible, unforeseeable impact, even from night to night. Once, with *The Death of Meyerhold*, I rewrote a line mid-run to accommodate a change of world events because an actor noted the line quite suddenly no longer jived. A couple of weeks after the historic moment had passed, things were such that we thought the old line should be reinstated and so we did. And when *American $uicide* was running in the early spring of 2007, we changed certain lines and even sound cues weekly according to the latest headlines.

All of this is to say that, as far as I'm concerned, a play is only a seemingly fixed entity that inevitably changes once it's up on certain actors' feet in certain spaces at certain times, directed and designed in certain ways and played to certain audiences. This inevitable change is exciting and particular to writing for the live theatre. Like most playwrights I take pleasure in discovering what other people – actors, directors, designers and audiences – hear and see in a script I wrote, things that I did or didn't hear or see in quite the same way myself.

Some of these plays are longer, some shorter. But all were lucky to receive the benefit of longer than usual rehearsal and performance periods, which is great for any play but especially new plays. In general I agree that the American theatre, both its process and its "product" (hate that word), is far too rushed. While developing a script through rehearsal and performance I find that I resist the infanticide of any artistic impulse, small or large, that seems even yet indefinably worthy of time and attention. I put my trust in both the original impulse and in Time itself to help me understand what something is or isn't, and have greatly appreciated the actors, designers, producers, stage managers, directors and theatre companies that have put their trust in my trust and seen these plays through with me. These people and organizations all contributed in one way or another to making the plays better. It is with immense gratitude that I thank them, and they are:

Christina Augello, Andy Alabran, American Conservatory Theater, Rob Anderson, Drew Anderson, Joan Arhelger, David Babich, Nina Ball, Kehren Barbour, Raquel Barreto, Heather Basarab, Tammy Bates, Zehra Berkman, Chris Black, Gillian Brecker, Chris Broderick, Cassidy Brown, Dan Bruno, Fontana Butterfield, Michael Cano, Denise Balthrop Cassidy, Gillian Chadsey, Kathryn Clark, Kevin Clarke, Valera Coble, Ashley Costa, Temple Crocker, Reid Davis, Sarah Deutsch, Djerassi Resident Artists Program, Patrick Dooley, Encore Theatre Company, EXIT Theatre, James Faerron, Lukas Ferreira, Jody Flader, Jordon Flato, Caroline Ford, Blythe Foster, Michael Patrick Gaffney, Christie Gilmore, Tonya Glanz, Karen Hallock, Ryan Hodgkin, Sara Huddleston, Caroline Hewitt, Anna Ishida, Richard James, Melpomene Katakolos, Rhonda Kerr, Chris Kuckenbaker, Richard Livingston, Phil Lowery, Lisa Maher, Dave Maier, Delia MacDougall, Eric Miller, Bricine Mitchell, Lorraine Olsen, Isabelle Ortega, PCPA Theaterfest, Carla Pantoja, Marty Pistone, The Play Café, Benjamin Privitt, Karl Ramsey, Rich Reinholdt, Jason Ries, Jake Rodriguez, Peter Ruocco, Shotgun Players, Rick Simas, Michelle Smith, Elizabeth Spreen, Andrew Sproule, Marilyn Stanley, Lisa Steindler, Erin Stuart, The Studio Theatre, Christopher Studley, Ambra Sultzbaugh, Michelle Talgarow, Ryan Tasker, Frank Torrano, Thu Tran, Liam Vincent, Jud Williford, Clive Worsley, Dara Yazdani, Z Space Studio and the one and only Beth Wilmurt. Thank you!

One other thing. The quote that appears on the page prior to the table of contents. It is something that Vsevolod Meyerhold, before he had become

MEYERHOLD, wrote in his diary during the first days of the twentieth century. "Life or death, only not sleep." I will never forget it. Though writing plays is not a matter of life and death for me given I live in a relatively free society, I do find the plays are inevitably *about* life and death, or circumstances the characters at least feel are a matter of these two forces. And despite our free American society, alongside our pleasures we have our share of problems, some of them quite deep and pressing. I wouldn't make a good politician. But I don't want to sit back and swallow what the nightly news feeds me, either. I don't want to sleep. And so I write plays, hoping that they will keep the audience and me awake and moving forward in life as we strive to understand ourselves, one another, our various problems (which I'd rather call our various possibilities), and even our happiness, before death inevitably comes to either end it all or open up the next set of possibilities.

I hope you enjoy the plays.

Mark Jackson
June 2010

American $uicide

Freely adapted from *The Suicide* by Nikolai Erdman

American $uicide

American $uicide was commissioned and developed by Z Space Studio and The Magic Theatre / Z Space Studio New Works Initiative, San Francisco, CA. The world premiere of *American $uicide* was presented by Z Space Studio and Encore Theatre Company at Thick House, San Francisco, CA, on February 12, 2007. The production was directed by the author, with the following cast and staff:

SAM SMALL	Jud Williford
MARY SMALL	Beth Wilmurt
ALBERT PRICE	Marty Pistone
MARGARET	Denise Balthrop Cassidy
GIGI BOLT / BARBARA NORTON	Delia MacDougall
MAX MAXWELL	Michael Patrick Gaffney
CHLOE BANKS	Jody Flader
THE MYSTERIOUS MEN	Liam Vincent
Set	James Faerron
Lights	Christopher Studley
Costumes	Raquel Barreto
Sound	Sara Huddleston
Choreography	Chris Black
Stage Manager	Michael Kano

Cast of Characters

> Sam Small, an unemployed man.
> Mary Small, his wife and a waitress.
> Albert Price, their self-employed neighbor.
> Margaret, his mistress and a bartender at a club.
> Gigi Bolt, executive director of Theatre Communications Group.[1]
> Barbara Norton, a casting agent.
> Max Maxwell, a washed-up film director.
> Chloe Banks, a film actress, half Valley Girl and half Norma Desmond,

---

[1] *This is an entirely fictional Gigi Bolt, and not based on the real Gigi Bolt in any way whatsoever. As of the world premiere production, Bolt was the interim executive director of TCG. The name of this character should be changed to that of the actual person holding this position at TCG at the time of production. Should that person be male, any text in [brackets] should be either substituted for the text preceding it or included, accordingly.*

in her early twenties and so already a fading star.
Mysterious Foreign Man, likely from the Middle East.
Mysterious American Man, likely from Washington, D.C.

Note

A slash in the dialogue (/) indicates that the next actor should start their line, creating overlapping speech.

Productions should update references to Internet, digital and other technologies as needed to make them current.

Time, place and design

The time is now. The place is a big American city. In it we see Sam and Mary's apartment, the hall outside, a casting office, a bench in a city park, a montage of these locations, and a throbbing dance club. To depict all of this, the design should make use of what theatre does best and what current technology has to offer. Old school and new school elements should be allowed to clash against and to blend harmoniously with one another. In other words, don't pretend it ain't theatre and don't ignore the fact that it's being produced right now.

Preshow

Music selected and edited with the overall production in mind. Or maybe the audio track of the latest Fox News broadcast, complete with commercial breaks.

Act One

Episode One

Sam and Mary's studio apartment (#86, incidentally), which includes a main room, a separate kitchen and a separate bathroom. It is night and SAM and MARY are in bed.

SAM Mary. Mary, are you asleep? Mary.
MARY Ah! / Ah! Ah!
SAM What? What's the matter? What's the matter? It's me! It's me!
MARY Is that you Sam?
SAM Yes! It's me!

MARY Oh. What do you want?

SAM Well. I just wanted to ask you. Mary? Mary, are you asleep again? Mary.

MARY Ah! / Ah! Ah!

SAM What? What's the matter? What's the matter? It's me! It's me!

MARY Is that you Sam?

SAM Yes! It's me!

MARY Oh.

SAM Who do you think it would be?

MARY I would expect it to be you. Who else do I know that would wake me up in the middle of the night when I'm trying to sleep?

SAM I want to ask you something.

MARY Well what is it?

SAM Do we have any leftover sausage?

MARY Oh! Sausage! I have had it with your sausage. You're always waking me up with your sausage. Why can't you handle your sausage yourself and stop bothering me with it. It's bad enough I have to serve sausage and eggs and bacon and hamburgers and milkshakes and grease and FAT all day every day. You ask me to bring it home, too, and then you have to wake me up for it. I need to sleep, Sam. I need to sleep and to dream about more than sizzling meat and whether or not strange people would like "fries or potato salad with that." When I hang up my apron at the end of the day, I want to leave it hanging there. Am I wearing an apron to bed? No, I'm wearing a nighty. I'm not your waitress, Sam, I'm your wife. You might not do anything all day but I do. And if you can't sleep at night I'm sorry but that doesn't mean you have to wake other people up, Sam. Sam? Sam, are you asleep? Sam.

SAM Ah! / Ah! Ah!

MARY What? What's the matter? What's the matter? It's me! It's me!

SAM Is that you Mary?

MARY Yes! It's me!

SAM Oh. What do you want?

MARY I said, just because you're not asleep doesn't mean you have to wake other people up.

SAM Then what are you waking me up for?

MARY You wanted sausage.

SAM Oh, did you get it? Thanks.

MARY No I didn't get it.

SAM Well then what are you waking me up for?

MARY Sam, the only reason either of us are awake right now is because you wanted sausage. I am not going to be woken up in vain. Go get it.

SAM Now wait a minute.

MARY Why don't you eat when you're supposed to, Sam? It's bad enough that after a long day at work slinging hash I have to come home and sling it for you too. You're not working. You have all day. You could make us a gourmet meal. With vegetables! They're good for you, Sam. But no, we can't afford vegetables, and all you want is sausage, which is weird; nobody eats sausage at home. It's diner food. And I hate it. It's bad enough that I have to steal food from work so that we can have something on the table for dinner, the least you could do is eat it when I serve it to you.

SAM You know why I don't eat it when you serve it to me? Because by the time it's put in front of me I'm already filled up to here with a heaping Sermon Appetizer. "Get a job Sam. Get out of the apartment Sam. Do something Sam." Just because I'm unemployed doesn't mean you can boss me around. I'm your husband.

MARY Yeah, some husband. I have to sneak home the bacon AND fry it up, too. This isn't the life I wanted, Sam.

SAM Yeah well the life you wanted ended when Mary Tyler Moore started working for Mister Grant. Times have changed, Mary. Men don't do all the work now.

MARY You don't do any work.

SAM You think that makes me happy? Look. Look at this. You just look. Now watch this.

> *Sitting on the edge of the bed, SAM crosses his leg and taps his knee and the leg kicks in reflex, as it should.*

SAM See that?

MARY What's that?

SAM A nervous tic. I have developed a nervous tic.

MARY Sam.

SAM I'm depressed Mary. I'm depressed. Do you understand? No, you don't. You're a woman with a job. You have no idea what it's like to be an unemployed man. It means you're nobody. When people meet you, they don't ask what you believe in. They ask what you do. Your job. It's who you are. You're a waitress.

MARY Pop the champagne.

SAM At least it's something. What do I have to pop the champagne about? How easy I've got it? Unemployed and living off my wife's greasy tips? It's embarrassing.

MARY Then do something. *(for the thousandth time:)* Go to a temp agency.

SAM Oh, forget I said a word. I don't know why I even bother talking to you. You WANT to be unemployed.

MARY What I want is to have at least one dress that isn't either a waitress uniform or some thrift store rag, a NEW dress from an actual store with shoes that match. I want to get my hair done for once in my life. I want to come in from a day in the garden and put my feet up. I want to relax on weekends. I want normal things, Sam. I have been working since I was ten years old.

SAM Oh, here we go with the biography.

MARY I took the paper route to the frozen food aisle and ended up stuck in a greasy spoon. THIS is the last Twenty-Five Years of my life, Sam. I DO want to be unemployed. I want to win the lottery. I want to kick my shoes off for good. I want to go on vacations. I want to sit on a porch. I want to stay at home all day. I want to cook a chicken for my husband and two kids. I want to be a wife and that's it, just like wives used to be.

SAM Yeah well that kind of wife died out a long time ago, Mary. But men are still men. When I talk to Albert about it HE understands. As an unemployed man himself, he understands.

MARY Yes but Albert's trying to do something about it. He's an entrepreneur.

SAM Albert picks up garbage at flea markets and out of people's trashcans and sells it on eBay. That's not employment. That's desperation.

MARY It's something.

SAM It's a hobby.

MARY He's making money at it.

SAM Pff!

MARY You shouldn't be bothering Albert with your troubles anyway. The man is grieving.

SAM Oh come on, his wife died a month ago and he's already got some new lady hangin' around.

MARY Well there you go. Albert's moved on. He got fired, lost his wife, now he's already got a hobby and a new girlfriend.

SAM Oh forget it forget it just FORGET IT. I might as well KILL myself. I'm reading.

MARY Sam, don't talk like that.

SAM I can read if I want to.

MARY What are you going to read?

SAM *(for the thousandth time:)* Hamlet.

MARY That morbid BOOK?

SAM It is not a morbid book, it's Shakespeare. Don't you know anything?

MARY Every time you read that you get more depressed. You shouldn't read that.

SAM Mary. I can't sleep. Just let me read.

MARY Count sheep.

SAM Mary, I'll shoot myself! I swear to God!

MARY Sam, now be quiet, you're in no condition to shoot yourself.
SAM Mary, I have a nervous tic!
MARY Stop it Sam.
SAM You're pushin' me!
MARY Sam!
SAM Mary–!

The power sputters and goes out.

SAM Oh. Great. Now they've turned our lights out. We can't even afford to see anymore. You see, I might as well blow my own lights out!
MARY Now Sam, I told you, no. They didn't turn our lights out, I paid the bill. *I* paid the bill. …What's happening to us? No one should have to live like this. …Okay, I'LL get the flashlight. Jeez. It's under the bed isn't it? Or in the kitchen? Do you know where it is, Sam? Ow. I'm not finding it here. I think we have some candles in the bathroom.

We hear a door close.

MARY Sam. Did you hear that? I heard the bathroom door close. I think someone's in the apartment. Sam I'm scared. Sam? Sam where are you? Sam!

The power flickers back on.

MARY Ah! Ah!

SAM is gone. The bathroom door is closed and locked.

MARY Sam? Sam, are you in there? Sam, come out. What are you doing? Hamlet. Oh no, Sam. Sam! It's okay! Open the door! I'll get you your sausage, Sam! And no sermon appetizer, I promise! I'm sorry about your nervous tic, I know you're depressed. I know it's hard for you not having a job. You'll find one, Sam! Sammy? …Sam!

MARY throws her shoulder against the door.

MARY Ow. Okay. Help. Help. Who. Albert. Help. Sam?! Albert.

Episode Two

MARY runs out into the hall and bangs on the door across from hers

(#69, incidentally). SHE looks back through her own door, then bangs again.

MARY Albert! Albert I need you!

The door opens and MARGARET steps out, dressed like a porn star in mid-shoot.

MARGARET Who are you?
MARY Oh. Hello. Where's Albert?
MARGARET Why do you want Albert at this time of night dressed like that?
ALBERT *(unseen)* Margaret, who is it?
MARGARET That's what I want to know.

ALBERT arrives in the doorway, also dressed as a porn star in mid-shoot and with a video camera in his hand.

ALBERT Oh, hello Mary.
MARY Oh, Albert!
MARGARET You know her?
ALBERT No Margaret. Well yes.
MARGARET Is she that other slut you've been with?
ALBERT No, Margaret, you're the only one. She's not a slut, she's my neighbor. This is Mary. Sam's wife. Mary, this is Margaret.
MARY Nice to meet you.
MARGARET I see Sam all the time. I never see you with him.
MARY I work all day.
MARGARET What do you want with Albert? The man's grieving, don't you know?
ALBERT Shhh, Margaret, she doesn't want anything with me.
MARY No, Albert, I need you.
MARGARET Ah HA. What for?
ALBERT Nothing Margaret. Mary. Need me? What is it? What do you need?
MARGARET At this time of night.
ALBERT At this time of night.
MARY I need a man.
MARGARET You need a cold shower.
ALBERT Margaret. What for, Mary?
MARY It's Sam.

ALBERT What about him?
MARY I need you to break the bathroom door down and help me talk to him.
ALBERT Break the door down? Talk to him? About what? What's going on?
MARY He's not in his right mind. He's locked himself in the bathroom. And while we were in bed he showed me his tic.
ALBERT Isn't that normal between a husband and wife?
MARY Tic, Albert, tic. A nervous tic.
ALBERT Oh, oh.
MARY He's very depressed. He reads *Hamlet*. I think he might do something desperate.
ALBERT What am I supposed to do about it?
MARY You can talk to him. He'll listen to you. You're an unemployed man.
ALBERT A self-employed man, thank you.
MARY See, that's what I told him but he doesn't believe me. He's been unemployed almost a year already and he's ashamed to be living off his wife. Now please Albert come and get him out of the bathroom. He's desperate! He's libel to swallow a bottle of pills or slit his throat or shoot himself or god knows / what else!
ALBERT Alright, alright. I'll talk to him. Stay here. Here, take this.

ALBERT hands the video camera off to MARGARET and then goes into Mary and Sam's apartment. MARY and MARGARET stay behind in the hall.

Episode Three

ALBERT knocks at the bathroom door in Mary and Sam's apartment.

ALBERT Sam? Sam, it's me, Albert.
SAM *(in the bathroom)* What do you want?
ALBERT I want you to come out of there and talk to Mary.
SAM Leave me alone! It's none of your business.
ALBERT Mary asked me to get you out of there, now come on out or I'm gonna break the door in.
SAM Break the door in?
ALBERT Don't do anything desperate Sam.
SAM Go away!
ALBERT Sam I'm gonna count to three.
SAM Count as high as you like.
ALBERT One.

SAM Stop it.
ALBERT Two.
SAM Just leave me alone, will yuh?
ALBERT Three!

> *ALBERT busts in the door. We can hear SAM and ALBERT struggling and yelling at one another. MARY and MARGARET remain huddled in the front doorway.*

MARY Oh!
SAM What the–?! Jesus Albert you broke the door!
ALBERT Sam, what are you doing? Put that down!
SAM Hey, get your own! It's mine! Leave me alone! Hey!
ALBERT It can't be worth it, I tell yuh, whatever it is! Now just let me talk to you!

> *SAM flies into the room with ALBERT holding on to him.*

MARY Sam!
SAM Did you tell him to do this?!
ALBERT Close the door Mary! I'll handle it!
SAM What's the matter with you?
MARY I couldn't do it myself!
SAM Well what's the big idea?
ALBERT Would you just close the door and let me handle it, Mary?

> *MARY closes the door. SAM breaks away from ALBERT.*

SAM Now listen Albert!
ALBERT No you listen, Sam!
SAM Back off, I tell yuh, / just back off!
ALBERT Okay okay! Okay. Just listen to me a minute will yuh?
SAM What do you want?
ALBERT I want you to hand it over.
SAM Hand what over?
ALBERT Come on, I saw you sticking it in your mouth and I know you've got it in your pocket, now hand it over.
SAM No, get your own. It's mine. Is THAT why you busted in the door? For god's sake!

ALBERT Mary told me what you were up to and I didn't believe it. Really, Sam, it can't be worth it.

SAM Exactly! So what are you breaking down the door for? For god's sake!

ALBERT Look, I know exactly what you're going through. My dot com dream was about to come true and then all of a sudden, boom, it popped like bubblegum. Now my job is floating down the Ganges in India, but did I let that get me down? No!

SAM What's India got to do with me?

ALBERT We're living in the twenty-first century, Sam. Things change like THAT. You'll see. They'll change for you too. It's the technological age, Sam, the age of enlightenment.

SAM Oh yeah? And when they turn your lights out, then what age is it? The dark age.

ALBERT Mary's right.

SAM About what?

ALBERT You have been reading *Hamlet*.

SAM So what?

ALBERT So, you're thinking too much Sam. Too much but not too well. Don't think, Sam. Work.

SAM I can't work. I don't have a job. Nobody will hire me.

ALBERT Nobody has to hire you. I told you. It's the twenty-first century. Regular guys like us can make something out of life. I'm doing it. I got the eBay thing going, me and my new lady are starting up a website, I'm making my own life.

SAM Even though your wife died a month ago? You're not depressed?

ALBERT (*shrugs, then:*) No use crying over what's dead and buried. You have to move on, Sam. You can too. Find something you want and do it, Sam.

SAM …I know what I want. But I can't do it by myself.

ALBERT What is it?

SAM No, you'll just laugh.

ALBERT Try me.

SAM I'd like to be an actor.

ALBERT An actor?

SAM Yeah. Everybody likes you, and those actors make huge money. One big movie and you're set for life. You never have to work again.

ALBERT Well, yeah, but Sam you can't just–

SAM Oh, oh, oh, yeah, okay, here it comes. "It's not that easy Sam. Be sensible Sam! You're no <u>NAME OF CURRENT HOT MEDIOCRE ACTOR</u>, Sam!" If I had a little encouragement maybe I COULD make it! You know how much I'd like to be an actor? So much my insides bust just thinking about it. Why if

I were a great actor, a great big star… But stars don't shine on me. No sir. Any star hanging over my head prob'ly died out a hundred years ago, and all I got left is a few thin beams of light just waiting to fade out, the end.

ALBERT Oh come on, Sam, it can't be that bad. Certainly not worth shooting yourself.

SAM Who's shooting himself?

ALBERT You.

SAM Me? Why?

ALBERT Don't you know?

SAM I'm asking you.

ALBERT Because you've been unemployed for almost a year and ashamed to be living off your wife. Really now isn't that stupid, Sam? It's the twenty-first century.

SAM Mary told you that?

ALBERT Now don't get upset.

SAM How dare she! That was a private matter between husband and wife. You're not her husband! And you're certainly not my wife! Now get out of here and leave me alone!

ALBERT Not until you give me that gun.

SAM What gun?

ALBERT I saw you sticking it in your mouth.

SAM Oh that. If you don't leave me alone I'll stick it in YOUR mouth.

ALBERT Now Sam.

SAM Get out of here Albert!

ALBERT Sam just listen to me one more minute.

SAM I'm tired of listening to you. This time I'M gonna count to three and when I'm done you better bust through THAT door or I'll pop you wide open!

ALBERT Sam, think about what you're saying!

SAM *(sticks his hand in his pocket)* One!

ALBERT Sam, don't!

SAM *(braces himself)* Two!

ALBERT Okay! I'm going! I'm going!

SAM Three!

> ALBERT *exits out the front door and slams it behind him. And on that SAM whips out a sausage from his pocket, pointing it like a gun at the door. SAM pretends to blow smoke from the barrel of his "gun" before biting the tip off.*

Episode Four

As the dialogue of this episode commences, SAM stands thinking for a long moment. HE picks up his copy of Hamlet *and stares at it. HIS expression furrows. HE gets a pen and paper and sits down to write something. The pen does not work. SAM digs up another pen, which doesn't work either. HE digs up a third pen, also out of ink. SAM throws things aside looking for another pen and can't find one. HE goes to the front door and listens to the others in the hall, thinks, looks at the kitchen doorway, then exits into the kitchen.*

Meanwhile, out in the hallway:

MARY What's going on?
ALBERT He's off his rocker. He's dangling over the edge. There's just no talking to him.
MARY Dangling over the edge? Where?
ALBERT In there.
MARY …WHAT'S he doing in there?
ALBERT I don't know, but he threatened to shoot me.
MARY Shoot you? With what?
ALBERT His gun.
MARY His gun? He has a gun?
ALBERT I thought you knew that.
MARY No. I thought he might take pills or cut himself, I didn't know he actually had a gun.
ALBERT Well he does and it's in there with him.
MARY Well we have to go in there.
ALBERT Where the gun is? Think, Mary, think!
MARY But he's going to shoot himself and we have to stop him! I can't do that by myself! You have to help me! He may already have done it and he could be lying in a pool of blood right now and we're just standing here in the hallway doing nothing! Oh! Catch me!

MARY faints.

MARGARET She's fainted. Some neighbor.
ALBERT Great. Now what do we do?
MARGARET What about Sam?
ALBERT The man has a gun, I'm not going back in there.

MARGARET Well what are we going to do about her?

ALBERT Oh Jesus! Alright, look, you deal with her. Here, give me that. Stay back.

> *ALBERT takes the video camera from MARGARET, who tends to the wilted MARY. ALBERT slowly cracks open the front door to Mary and Sam's apartment and quietly slips the camera in so that he can see in the room. SAM has by now disappeared into the kitchen.*

MARGARET Can you see anything?

ALBERT I don't see him. But the place is a mess. ...Sam, you in there? It's me, Albert. I'm coming back in. Just don't SHOOT ME, okay? ...Sam, you hear me? Mary's very upset and she's fainted. We're going to bring her in, okay? ...Sam?

> *ALBERT bursts through the doorway. Using the camera as his own "gun," he checks under the bedspread as a cop might – ready to defend himself with his weapon – then, in the same manner, the bathroom, and finally the kitchen.*

ALBERT Sam?

MARGARET Is he dead?

ALBERT He's not here.

MARGARET What do you mean he's not there?

ALBERT Looks like he slipped out the kitchen window and down the fire escape. Put her down there, will yuh?

> *MARGARET drags MARY to the bed.*

MARGARET Well. Here's a familiar scenario. Why do I always have to carry the body?

ALBERT Margaret.

MARGARET Anything for you, Albert.

> *MARGARET throws MARY down on the bed.*

MARGARET So what do we do now?

ALBERT *(looking at Mary)* I don't know. Say...

> *Looking at MARY spread out on the bed, ALBERT raises his camera to film her.*

MARGARET Albert!

ALBERT You never know, it might come in handy. Ask any filmmaker worth his salt, he'll tell you: be sure to get enough coverage.

MARGARET You have plenty of coverage already. Of me.

ALBERT I'm just gonna get a couple of shots.

MARY Oh. Where am I?

ALBERT Don't worry, Mary, we're all friends here.

MARY What's going on?

ALBERT You fainted, that's all, just lay back.

MARY What? I fainted?

MARGARET Yes, and woke up just in time.

MARY Just in time? For what? Where's Sam? Is he dead?

ALBERT Not yet. He slipped out the kitchen window.

MARY Slipped out the kitchen window? But his pants are right here. He wouldn't go out without his pants.

ALBERT He doesn't care about his pants, he's suicidal.

MARGARET Albert.

MARY Oh! Now what am I going to do?

ALBERT You're going to encourage him to be an actor, that's what you're gonna do.

MARY An actor?

ALBERT He wants to be an actor. That's what he said. It's his big dream. Good luck to him. But if you encourage him and it lifts his spirits, great.

MARY He'd be a terrible actor.

ALBERT Well you just tell him he'd be great. By the way, have you ever considered acting? I was just thinking while you were passed out on the bed–

MARGARET –Albert.

MARY That's why he's been reading "Hamlet." Because he wants to be an actor.

ALBERT Can't hurt to humor him. He could use a good joke. And what have you got to lose?

MARY I hope you're right. But first I have to find him. Ah! There he is!

SAM has entered through the front door. Caught off guard, ALBERT impulsively aims his camera like a gun.

SAM You're still here?

MARY Sam!

ALBERT What'd you do with that gun?

SAM I ate it.
MARGARET Oh come on, Albert, let's leave them alone.
ALBERT You'll be alright, Mary?
MARY Yes Albert.
ALBERT Okay.

> *ALBERT and MARGARET exit, ALBERT with his camera at the ready should SAM actually not have eaten his gun.*

Episode Five

MARY Albert said you have a gun.
SAM It was a sausage.
MARY Ah. Where'd you go?
SAM The corner store.
MARY Ah. What for?
SAM All our pens are out of ink.
MARY Ah. You gonna write something?

> *SAM has sat down to write with a pen from a new box of cheap pens.*

SAM Yep.
MARY What are you going to write?
SAM A letter.
MARY Ah. To who?
SAM To the world, Mary.
MARY Ah. What are you gonna say?
SAM Mary? I'm trying to write.
MARY I'm sorry I nagged at you Sam. I know you're unhappy. I think maybe we need to spend some quality time together. Go on a date. Maybe see a movie or something. How about I look in the paper and see what's playing, okay?

> *SAM is doing his best to write and ignore MARY, who picks up a newspaper and turns to the entertainment section. The movie titles and weekend grosses she reads should come from whatever the most current highest grossing movies at the time of performance happen to be.*

MARY So, let's see. Oh look, <u>MOVIE TITLE #1</u> made <u>$$$$</u> last weekend, so that sounds like it might be good. <u>MOVIE TITLE #2</u> made <u>$$$</u>, that might be good too. Oh, here we go. <u>MOVIE TITLE #3</u> has made <u>$$$$$</u> to date! Can't argue with that. That's sure to be a good one. What do you think, Sam?

>   SAM crumples up his paper and starts afresh.

MARY   We haven't been to a movie in a long time. Might be fun. Go to the movies? See some good acting? …Sam. Albert told me how you want to be an actor.
SAM   He told you?
MARY   Yes. And I think you'd be a great actor.
SAM   Well nobody asked you. I can't believe he told you that. Do you two tell each other everything?
MARY   No.
SAM   Can't I have any privacy? Can't you go to the bathroom and let me write in peace?
MARY   But I don't have to go to the bathroom.
SAM   Mary, please, just go to the bathroom for five minutes. You can do it. I know you've got it in you.
MARY   I'll go to the kitchen!
SAM   Fine!
MARY   …I love you, Sam.
SAM   *(looks at her)* I love you too.

>   MARY goes to the kitchen and stops in the doorway.

MARY   If you really wanted to be an actor, I'd encourage you.

>   SAM and MARY stare at one another. MARY disappears into the kitchen. SAM stares after her, then looks out, then looks at his paper, then writes, then reads what he wrote, then writes again:

SAM   "No one… is… to blame…"

>   SAM reads what he just wrote, then adds:

SAM   "Love… Sam."

>   SAM holds up the letter, looks at it, looks after MARY, looks out thinking, then neatly folds up the letter.

Act Two

Episode Six

> *Sam and Mary's apartment. A few days later. SAM enters with a book and sits down to read it. MARY is offstage in the kitchen.*

MARY What took you so long, Sam? I thought you were going to the corner.
SAM I was, but I ran into this nice lady [fellow].
MARY What nice lady [fellow]?
SAM Bolt Something. A traveling salesperson, I think. Like the Avon Lady. Lives out of her car. [*LAST NAME* Something. A traveling salesman, I think. Lives out of his car.]

> *MARY enters from the kitchen.*

MARY Where does she [he] live?
SAM Halfway down the block right now, but around the country I gather.
MARY What's she [he] selling?
SAM Books, for one. Sold me this book here. Exactly what I needed.
MARY What kinda book is it?
SAM It's called *How To Act*, by Mister Gus Harold.
MARY Oh!
SAM Yeah, listen to this. *(the back cover)* "In *How To Act*, Gus Harold reveals his brilliant techniques that have worked miracles for the millions of stage and screen actors he has coached, beginners and stars alike." That's me. A beginning star. "Instead of yet another acting method, Harold offers a strategy based on the radically refreshing idea that acting is very simple. Just follow the advice in these pages, and your dreams of stardom can come true."
MARY Oooo!
SAM "To become the actor you want to be tomorrow, read *How To Act* today."
MARY Great, Sam!
SAM There you have it. *How To Act*. Now it says it's simple, but simple and easy are two different things, Mary. If I'm going to be a big movie actor I'm going to need to take this seriously.
MARY That's right.
SAM Do my research. So let's see what I have to do. *(opens the book) How To Act*. Chapter One… Don't act. Hear that? I was wrong. Simple IS easy! Mary, hang up that apron once and for all; your hash slinging days are as good as over. We're gonna be rich. Pretty soon you're gonna be reading my weekend grosses in the paper.

MARY But Sam, you haven't really learned how to act yet.
SAM Oh come on it's easy, you don't even have to do anything, it says right here.
MARY But that's just the title of the first chapter. You haven't even read it yet.
SAM Mary. It's a summation.
MARY But maybe you should take a little more time to–
SAM –More time? I don't have time to take more time. This is the technological age, Mary. You take more time and someone else is gonna beat you to it in half a double click.
MARY But that's computers and things, Sam, this is acting.
SAM Acting's come a long way, too, Mary. This is the twenty-first century. You gotta catch up.
MARY I just think that maybe–
SAM Are you trying to discourage me from being an actor?
MARY No!
SAM I just started, Mary! Give me two seconds, at least!
MARY No, Sam, of course.
SAM Or maybe you don't want me to become a big movie star because then I'LL be bringing home the bacon, and you won't be able to fry it up in your marinade of martyrdom, is that it?
MARY No, Sam.
SAM It's not as if I've never contributed anything. Who bought this bed? And that chair? And look, look.

SAM runs into the kitchen and returns with a cereal bowl.

MARY Sam, you're overacting.
SAM Who bought these fancy cereal bowls? Huh? I did. And when they're all broken will you have the means to buy a new set of fancy cereal bowls?
MARY Of course, Sam.
SAM Oh really?

SAM throws down the cereal bowl and it shatters. HE immediately darts into the kitchen and returns just as quickly with a coffee cup.

MARY Sam! Look what you did!
SAM And what about coffee cups? Will you have enough to buy more coffee cups?
MARY Yes, Sam, of course.

> SAM *throws down the coffee cup and it shatters. HE immediately darts into the kitchen and returns just as quickly with a plate.*

MARY Sam! What are you–?

SAM And how about these plates, Mary? Will you have enough to buy these?

MARY No, I won't!

SAM I thought not. That means there's just one thing for me to do. Now get out of here and give me some peace so I can do it.

MARY No! Don't do it, Sam.

SAM DON'T do it?

MARY Please don't do it!

SAM Ah, so now it comes out, plain as day. Don't do it, she says. Just don't do it. Well I am going to do it, you'll see, but I need some peace and quiet, so you take a walk.

MARY No, Sam, please, you'll be a great actor.

SAM Yeah yeah yeah! Too late for that missy!

MARY I didn't mean to discourage you, Sam, really I didn't!

> *But SAM has now succeeded in shoving MARY out the door and into the hallway. HE locks the door.*

MARY Please don't do it Sam!

SAM I'll do it. I'll show her. Wait'll she sees me up in lights.

MARY Sam?

SAM Let's see. *How To Act.* (*opens the book*)

MARY Sam, can you hear me?

SAM Oh! *(to himself:)* Yes. Me and the neighbors both.

> *SAM exits into the bathroom.*

MARY Sam? I think you'll be a really great actor. Don't do anything rash, Sam. Sam?

> *SAM returns from the bathroom with big wads of cotton in his ears. HE picks up his acting book again.*

SAM Okay. So. "Exercises for Acting Shakespeare." *(flips to it)* Ah. "Exercise One. To develop a clear understanding of Shakespeare's text, try putting it into your own words." Oh. Good idea.

MARY Sam?

SAM picks up his copy of Hamlet *and flips to a certain page. SAM holds the book up to the side where he can refer to it while also striking an actorly pose and trying to act out to an audience. When SAM speaks, he projects as he assumes he should. MARY can hear him somewhat and listens desperately through the door.*

SAM Should I, or shouldn't I? That's my question.

MARY What? Sam? What'd you say?

SAM Is it really such a good idea to put up with stuff? Or should I do something to end it? Dying might simply be like sleeping – and by that I mean taking a break from depression and hard knocks. Boy I sure do wish for that! Death!

MARY Oh!

SAM The big sleep!

MARY No Sam.

SAM The big dream! Ah HA. There's the kicker! When I'm dead what kind of crazy nightmares will I have then? Huh? That's the bit that makes a tragedy of living. I mean, why would anyone put up with life's trials and tribulations, with oppressive people, proud men's costumes, lost love, the justice system that takes forever, rude office workers, and insults against the poor, when he could just slit his own throat?

MARY Oh! Sam, no!

SAM Why carry all that baggage and get all sweaty trying to live life? I'll tell yuh why. Because we're scared. We're scared of what might happen after death, that unknown land. No one ever comes back. It's confusing. Better to live with what I got than take on God knows what. I'm a coward. I think too much and don't do anything. And those big hopes, those dreams, get washed away by all this thinking, and they never come true.

MARY *(crying)* Sam, Sam, Sam...

MARY sinks down to the floor outside. SAM pulls the cotton out of his ears.

SAM Albert said it. "Don't think. Work." I have to do something. I have to make it happen. My life.

SAM sits down, mesmerized by his revelation.

Episode Seven

Out in the hallway, ALBERT comes home to find MARY crying on the floor.

ALBERT Mary, what are you doing on the floor? It's filthy.

MARY Oh Albert, I discouraged Sam. It was an accident. Now he's locked himself in there and he's really going to do it, if he hasn't already.

ALBERT Do what?

MARY Kill himself!

ALBERT Again? Listen Mary, I've been thinking about this and I've got an idea that just might work.

MARY You do?

ALBERT He'll never be an actor. He needs to shoot for something more realistic. Let me talk to him. Sam? Sam, you in there? Open up, it's me, Albert. I got an idea that I think you'll like.

SAM What is it?

ALBERT Let me in and I'll pitch it to you.

Episode Eight

SAM opens the door and ALBERT and MARY come in. MARY runs to SAM and hugs him.

MARY Oh! Sam! You're alive! You're alive!

SAM Of course I am, Mary.

ALBERT Now just listen, Sam, and don't give me any trouble about it this time.

SAM What is it?

ALBERT I was thinking about what you said the other night.

SAM I was just thinking about what you / said.

ALBERT Now hear me out, Sam. You need a purpose.

SAM Yes!

ALBERT You need to do something.

SAM Exactly!

ALBERT And I think I can help you.

SAM You can?

ALBERT That's right. Now, you know how I sell things on ebay.

SAM Yeah.

ALBERT I make out pretty good.

SAM Sure.

ALBERT Enough to get by, anyway. And I bought all that new video equipment, too.

MARY You see, Sam.

SAM Yes / Mary.

ALBERT Now listen, Sam. I was thinking about you wanting to commit suicide, and that got me thinking about suicide in general, and how romantic people think it is until they go and try it themselves.

SAM Well you don't have to / worry about–

ALBERT Now just hear me out, Sam. If you really are serious about this suicide business, you might as well make it a business. Now my first thought was, auction it off on eBay.

SAM Auction it off?

ALBERT Yeah. Commit your suicide in the name of the winning bidder.

MARY What?

ALBERT But I looked into it and that sort of thing just wouldn't fly with the ebay people. A guy tried to auction off a kidney once and it didn't go down too well. So then I got to thinking. We don't need eBay. We can do up our own website.

SAM A website?

ALBERT Yeah. Pictures of you. A daily suicide note blog. Maybe some links to a Mary page. You know, make it personal. And: instead of an auction, we make it a raffle. People get to know you, they begin to feel invested, like they've got a stake in you, a real connection. They start buying raffle tickets, and the price shoots up in half a double click.

SAM The price of what?

ALBERT Your big moment! Your Grand Finale! We set a date and a time, you see. Let's say midnight on a particular day. As the time draws near we keep upping the price. So the earlier you buy the better. As the tension mounts, it gets more expensive. Then, at midnight on the appointed day, we announce the lucky winner!

SAM And I commit suicide.

ALBERT If you're gonna to do it anyway, why not put it to good use? Give Mary a nice big nest egg? Some security? A good future, Sam. One that you earned.

MARY looks at SAM. SAM looks at MARY, then back to ALBERT.

SAM I don't know Albert. It sounds a little funny.

ALBERT It's a website. Everybody has a website. And people around the world are clicking through them all night long. And if they work in an office, all day too. It's a huge audience. Bigger than any theatre can hold, Sam. Reach more people, make more money.

MARY How much money?

ALBERT Sky's the limit long as we do it up right.

MARY thinks about that, looks at SAM. SAM stands uncertainly.

SAM Well. I don't know. What about my acting career?

ALBERT Oh come on, Sam! You know how long it can take for an actor to make it? Five, ten years sometimes. Most never make it at all, just pound the pavement 'til they drop. Acting's a tough business. But technology, Sam. We'll make a celebrity of you like THAT! Think of it as e-theatre. With you playing out the story of your life, your LIFE, for all the world to see. They'll eat it up like popcorn, I guarantee it. An average Joe. Someone we can all identify with. A pretty wife. Then suddenly: stardom! Drama! And a spectacular end! That's ancient stuff. Shakespearean. Greek, even. Sam. It's the role of a lifetime!

SAM thinks. MARY and ALBERT wait in anticipation.

SAM I'll try Hamlet first. See how that goes. I have to at least give it a shot.

ALBERT I understand. Gotta get it out of your system. Well, just an idea. A million more where that came from. But if you change your mind, you know where to find me.

MARY Thank you, Albert.

ALBERT Talk to him Mary. This could be big.

MARY You really think so?

ALBERT Of course.

MARY You don't think it's a little weird?

ALBERT Mary, people want to see something spectacular. And they want it to be real. We'd just be giving them what they want, that's all.

MARY Right.

ALBERT Good luck.

ALBERT is gone. MARY turns and looks at SAM. SAM looks at her. MARY smiles. SAM picks up his copy of Hamlet *and begins to practice his acting.*

SAM Should I, or shouldn't I. That's my question.

As SAM begins his soliloquy, MARY noisily sweeps up the dishes, then exits.

Epsiode Nine

> *A casting office. As the set changes, SAM is still delivering his monologue. BARBARA, a casting director, and MAX are watching him. BARBARA should cut him off once the set has fully changed; i.e. the actor playing SAM need not complete the monologue.*

SAM Whether 'tis nobler in the mind to suffer the slings and arrows of outrageous fortune, or to take arms against a sea of troubles and by opposing end them. To die – to sleep, no more; and by a sleep to say we end the heartache and the thousand natural shocks that flesh is heir to: 'tis a consummation devoutly to be wish'd. To die, to sleep; to sleep, perchance to dream – ay, there's the rub: for in that sleep of death what dreams may come, when we have shuffled off this mortal coil, must give us pause – there's the respect that makes calamity of so long life. For who would bear the whips and scorns of time, th' oppressor's wrong, the proud man's contumely, the pangs of dispriz'd love, the law's delay, the insolence of office, and the spurns that patient merit of th' unworthy takes, when he himself might his quietus make with a bare bodkin? Who would farts bear, to grunt and sweat under a weary life, but that the dread of something after death, the undiscover'd country, from whose bourn no traveler returns, puzzles the will, and makes us rather bear those ills we have than fly to others that we know not of? Thus conscience does make cowards of us all, and thus the native hue of resolution is sicklied o'er with the pale cast of thought, and enterprises of great pitch and moment with this regard their currents turn awry and lose the name of action.
BARBARA Thank you, Sam.
MAX Yeah thanks Sam. That was terrible. Do you have anything more contemporary?
SAM Contemporary?
MAX Yeah, you know, new? Not four hundred years old?
SAM Was it really that terrible?
MAX Sam, you called us, so I know you read the ad. "Independent film." "Contemporary drama." "Modern young man who speaks like an actual person." Does that say Shakespeare to you?
SAM Shakespeare's language is actually very modern. He's our contemporary.
MAX Look, I don't want to debate Bardology with you. I'm making a movie, okay? That means real people who speak a lingo that other real people can actually comprehend.
SAM I could do it again and put it in my own words.
MAX I don't think so.
SAM You don't understand. This could be my big break. Just give me a chance. I really want to be an actor, Mister Maxwell. Was I really that bad?

MAX Don't take it so hard. But take my card. In my spare time I offer private acting lessons. Right now you're terrible, but I see something in you that I'd like to help bloom.

SAM Really?

BARBARA Max, you're not allowed to do that.

MAX The kid needs help, I'm helping the kid out.

BARBARA You can't sell acting lessons to actors you don't hire. I could get in trouble with the unions, Max. You want to help this kid out, help him out the door.

MAX Barbara relax. Don't worry about Barbara. She used to be an actress, now she's a casting agent. You can imagine the bitterness. Gimme a jingle and I'll see if I can squeeze you in.

SAM I gotta be honest with you, I can't afford acting lessons.

MAX We'll work something out.

SAM That's why I need this job.

MAX Well I'm sorry Sam but you're a terrible actor. And I need someone who can carry his own against Chloe Banks.

SAM Who?

BARBARA See.

MAX Chloe Banks! She's the next big thing!

BARBARA She flashed her thing in the pan a long time ago.

MAX A year ago.

BARBARA In Hollywood years that's a lifetime.

MAX She's making a comeback.

BARBARA She's making a mistake.

MAX Barbara, darling, you know how much I love you. But on this point you are wrong. This picture is gonna rocket Chloe Banks back into the firmament.

BARBARA I thought Chloe Banks was supposed to rocket this picture into the Weinteins' peripheral vision.

MAX *(stressed)* Barbara!

BARBARA You don't have a producer, Max.

MAX I'm workin' on it!

BARBARA You don't even have a screenplay.

MAX It's all up here, baby.

BARBARA If I didn't feel sorry for you, you wouldn't even have a casting agent.

MAX Baby, be sweet to Daddy. Need I remind you how far we go back?

BARBARA Too far.

MAX Not too far for me to forget cleaning up your puke when you were still a drunken actress screwing every producer who still never gave you job.

BARBARA Much appreciated. So what can you do for me now?

MAX Plenty. I know everybody who knows somebody.

BARBARA Which means you're nobody.

MAX Barbara! I gotta get this picture done if I have to kill myself doin' it. What else have I got? Now come on, Barbara, who's next?

BARBARA He's it.

MAX What do you mean he's it? He called us! Who'd you call?

BARBARA My entire Rolodex. Nobody's interested.

MAX What? Did you tell them that Max Maxwell was directing this picture?

BARBARA Yep.

After a beat, MAX puts his face in his hands.

SAM What am I gonna do? I failed. How am I gonna tell Mary?

MAX Why are you still here?

SAM I might as WELL kill myself.

MAX Ah jeez. Method actor.

Suddenly CHLOE BANKS sails into the room.

CHLOE BANKS Max?

MAX Chloe! Baby! What a surprise. What happened to later this week?

CHLOE BANKS You said later this week months ago, Max. If you really want me to sign on to this picture I need some guarantees. I'm fielding offers left and right and you know how it goes when opportunity knocks.

BARBARA Opportunity's knocking?

CHLOE BANKS Let's just say my window's open but I'm getting chilly.

MAX Chloe, with your name on this picture we're gonna incite us a bidding war, trust me.

CHLOE BANKS And who's my leading man?

MAX You're leading man?

CHLOE BANKS Hello! A leading man! As far as I'm aware I'm still the only other person besides you signed on to this picture. Now have you found me a leading man or haven't you?

MAX Now, Chloe–

CHLOE BANKS –Because if you haven't I've got those other offers I'm fielding left and right and though I'd sure like to help you out and give something back to the Indies, I've got a big career to think about. You show me my leading man or I'm walking!

MAX bursts with hysterical laughter to cover hysterical panic, then:

MAX Don't lace up your pretty boots just yet, baby. Your timing is too good. Through the genius of Barbara Norton, casting agent to the gods, we have just found and signed THE leading man of leading men. Chloe Banks, it is my pleasure to introduce you to Sam…?
SAM Yes? Yes! Sam! Sam Small. Very nice to meet you.
CHLOE BANKS Charmed. I've never heard of you.
SAM Oh that's okay, I've never heard of you / either
MAX Sam is a big fan of your work, Chloe, a big big fan.
CHLOE BANKS But who is he? You said he was the leading man of leading men, why have I never heard of him?
MAX He's the next big thing.
CHLOE BANKS The next big thing?
BARBARA He's making a comeback.
MAX He's done a lot of work in the theatre, haven't you Sam. That's why you've never heard of him. But you drop his name on Broadway and a thousand stage door Jennies will fall all over themselves trying to pick it up. He's hot stuff I tell yuh. And we're getting to him first.

CHLOE BANKS looks at SAM. SAM smiles nervously.

CHLOE BANKS What plays have you appeared in on Broadway, Sam?
SAM What plays? On Broadway? Oh, there've been so many I can't remember.
CHLOE BANKS Do you have a website? Or do they not have websites in the theatre?
SAM Website? Oh, yeah, of course. I've had a website for years.
CHLOE BANKS WWW dot…?
SAM Oh. I don't know. My people take care of it for me.
CHLOE BANKS Your people?! Well. Then I'll just have to Google you.

CHLOE BANKS flirtatiously pokes SAM in the stomach and HE laughs just a bit too hard.

MAX Okay well I'm glad we were able to get you two kids together. I don't want to keep you from that important lunch date, Sam.
SAM Lunch date?
MAX Sam's always having lunch with one director or another these days. But guess who got to him first? Huh? Huh?

MAX and SAM laugh together as MAX pokes chummily at SAM.

MAX Okay, bye now Sam, we'll call you.
SAM Oh. Oh! Okay! Thanks! Thanks so much! Bye. Goodbye Miss Banks.
CHLOE BANKS Goodbye Sam. Can't wait to click on you.
SAM Oh, the website. Yeah. Have fun with that. Bye.
MAX Bye bye now.

MAX closes the door, shutting SAM out, then turns to CHLOE BANKS, smiles broadly with his arms outstretched. SAM, meanwhile, dashes home.

Episode Ten

The hallway between Sam and Albert's apartments. SAM dashes up to ALBERT'S door and knocks on it repeatedly.

ALBERT *(unseen)* Alright alright I'm coming!

ALBERT opens the door wearing another porn outfit, a cop with leather pants, and with his video camera in hand.

SAM Oh!
ALBERT Jesus!
SAM Albert!
ALBERT Where's the fire, Sam?
SAM *(thrown)* What? Fire?
ALBERT What do you need so badly that you're knocking my door down? Margaret and I are trying to work.
SAM Oh. I'm sorry to interrupt. I gotta big favor to ask of you Albert.
ALBERT What is it?
SAM You remember that website idea you had?
ALBERT Yeah.
SAM And how you said you could do it up?
ALBERT Yeah.
SAM Well I just got signed on to a big motion picture only I told them I have a website and now the leading lady is gonna Google me so I need that website up as soon as possible can you do it?
ALBERT Whoa, back up, you got signed on to a what?

SAM A movie, a movie, Albert! That audition, I got it. I'm playing opposite Chloe Banks.

ALBERT Who?

SAM Chloe Banks! She's the next big thing, AND she's making a comeback. I'm her leading man. But she's gonna Google me and I told her I had a website so I need one, fast. She could be Googling me right now.

ALBERT So you want a fan site, like for an actor.

SAM Yes.

ALBERT But you've never acted in anything. What am I supposed to put on it?

SAM I don't know, make something up. The director of the movie, Max Maxwell, have you heard of him? Max Maxwell? He told her I'd acted in a bunch of theatre plays on Broadway. So just make up a list of plays I've done. *Hamlet*. Put *Hamlet* on it. Everyone's heard of that. Please say you'll do it, Albert. This is my big chance.

ALBERT I don't know; it's a lot of work Sam.

SAM I'll pay you.

ALBERT With what?

SAM With all the money I'm gonna make from the movie.

ALBERT Uh-huh. Did you say that was an audition you went to or a cocktail bar?

SAM An audition, which I got, so now I'm starring opposite Chloe Banks the next big thing and I need a website. Everyone's got a website, Albert, you said so yourself. And you said you could do it now I'm asking you, / please.

ALBERT Alright alright I'll do it.

SAM You will? You will! Oh! Great! Great! Thanks so much, Albert. Of course I can't pay you right away, but I will, I will Albert, when those weekend grosses start rolling in!

ALBERT Okay, Sam.

SAM Okay, you get started, I gotta go wait by the phone. Mister Maxwell said he'd be calling me and I don't want to miss that call.

SAM hugs ALBERT and leaves.

SAM Thank you Albert!

ALBERT Okay, good enough.

SAM runs into his apartment and ALBERT closes his door.

ALBERT Jeez.

ALBERT turns to exit into his apartment, revealing that he's wearing butt-less chaps.

Episode Eleven

Sam and Mary's apartment. SAM is sitting, staring at the phone expectantly. He looks at the clock, the dial of which is rotating in time-lapse, then back to the phone. SAM begins to slouch with worry. And finally he falls to a very dejected place. There is a knock at the door.

SAM   Albert.

SAM goes to the door and opens it.

SAM   Did you finish it? Oh. Hello.
GIGI BOLT   Hello, Sam, remember me? Gigi Bolt, executive director, Theatre Communications Group.
SAM   Yeah, the Avon Lady [traveling salesman].
GIGI BOLT   I suppose that's one way to put it.
SAM   Theatre Communications Group?
GIGI BOLT   I represent the American theatre.
SAM   Oh. Say, do you know the names of any Broadway plays?
GIGI BOLT   A few.
SAM   Maybe you could write them down for me.
GIGI BOLT   Of course. Mind if I come in? Tell me, how's that acting career coming along?
SAM   Pretty well. At least I think so. I'm actually waiting for a call about an audition.
GIGI BOLT   Ah, the life of the actor. It's a tough profession, the theatre. Why do we do it, Sam?
SAM   To make money.
GIGI BOLT   No. We do it because we have to. We MUST. I travel all over the country, Sam, speaking to government officials, boards of trustees, Elks lodges and other rich people. And I tell them. The theatre is as vital as blood and oxygen. The theatre is like a heart and lungs giving life to the soul. I believe that, Sam. And yet I come to you today as a dying woman [man]. I come to you in the name of the American theatre.
SAM   Oh. Why me?
GIGI BOLT   Just after we met the other day, I found this note in the gutter next to my car.

SAM What note? Oh, that note.
GIGI BOLT "No one is to blame. Love, Sam." Oh Sam. Is that Sam you, Sam?

GIGI BOLT hands SAM the note.

SAM Sam. I am. It is. It was. But like I said I'm waiting for a phone call about this audition I had for a movie.
GIGI BOLT A movie! Oh Sam, not you as well.
SAM What?
GIGI BOLT Another actor lost to the dream factory. It's true, Sam, there is a lot of money to be made in movies. But in the end, is it really worth it? Is life really about money?
SAM Yeah.
GIGI BOLT Sam, I wonder if you fully comprehend your situation. Permit me, in the name of the American theatre, to explain it to you, you, who came to me so hopeless, so ignorant, so filled with despair. And what did I give you?
SAM A book.
GIGI BOLT An education. About what?
SAM Acting.
GIGI BOLT That sacred art! That priesthood. That noble profession so easily perverted by greed and ambition. What has our world come to, Sam? Why you, even you, an average Joe in pursuit of happiness, how quick you were to charge down Macbeth's bloody path of ambition, desperate for fame and fortune.
SAM Yes!
GIGI BOLT Yet what are fame and fortune, Sam, but the fleeting image of a swollen apple dangling from the silver screen, or flickering for a few seconds across five hundred of the same channel. Just an illusion. Life today is projected, transmitted, downloaded, but no longer lived. We have forgotten how to live. This is why you want to take your life.
SAM It is?
GIGI BOLT Yes! So tear up that note, Sam, and write another. Write it with the blood of your heart and the wind of your lungs. Write it to set your soul free. Write that you take your life in the name of the American theatre, that temple of the soul. And like a bright light in the dark you will awaken that great slumbering audience–

GIGI BOLT steps to the edge of the stage and addresses the audience, an action that seems to perplex SAM greatly.

GIGI BOLT –the American people, who between fistfuls of popcorn and onslaughts of ad campaigns have sold their souls to the dream factory. Your death will be the drum that calls them out of their lonely multiplexes and flickering living rooms and back to the theatre, where they can experience life as it was meant to be: live!

SAM What are you doing?

GIGI BOLT I'm breaking the fourth wall, Sam.

SAM *(confused)* The what?

GIGI BOLT It's a theatrical convention, Sam, don't worry about it.

SAM Well it totally pulled me out of what you were saying.

GIGI BOLT grabs SAM by the shoulders.

GIGI BOLT Sam, I envy you.

SAM You do?

GIGI BOLT I'd kill to make such a dramatic final exit as yours. But I've got my own part to play.

SAM What part is that?

GIGI BOLT Think of me as Horatio to your Hamlet. And after your death, I'll sum up your tragic tale to all the bit players in a soliloquy worthy of their tax dollars. I will explain to them why the American theatre is central to their lives.

SAM Well, if you have to explain it to them–

GIGI BOLT Not just have to, Sam. I MUST. Right now, in fact. I'm speaking to the Association of Wealthy Widows at a luncheon across town and I've got to go. So what do you say, Sam? If you'd like I can write the note for you. I'll even have it printed in *American Theatre* magazine, with your photograph featured on the cover.

SAM My photo on a magazine cover?

GIGI BOLT How does that grab you?

SAM Well that grabs me good.

GIGI BOLT Grand! Well, I don't want to keep those wealthy widows waiting. I'll write up that note and be in touch. Oh, you don't have any extra change do you? I have to feed the meter.

SAM Oh, sure. It's my wife's, but, she won't mind.

SAM gives GIGI BOLT some change.

GIGI BOLT Tell her it's a donation. I'll see if I can have her name put on the passenger seat. Sam, in the name of life, the soul, and the American theatre, I applaud you.

GIGI BOLT applauds SAM. For a long time. Too long. Then SHE exits, still applauding. SAM closes the door behind her.

SAM Gosh. My photo on the cover of *American Theatre* magazine. That would be good publicity. And the soul is important. I wonder if anyone reads *American Theatre* magazine.

Episode Twelve

SAM Oh! I forgot to get the names of those Broadway plays!

SAM runs to the door and opens it, revealing CHLOE BANKS.

SAM Miss Bolt! Oh. Chloe Banks.
CHLOE BANKS Hello Sam.
SAM Hi.
CHLOE BANKS May I come in?
SAM Sure. Uh, what are you doing here?
CHLOE BANKS I need to talk to you, Sam.
SAM You Googled me didn't you? I can explain.
CHLOE BANKS I didn't Google you Sam. Max came clean. He told me that you're a terrible actor and a nobody and very desperate.
SAM He did?
CHLOE BANKS Yea-uh. He told me you had even said you might as well kill yourself, is that right?
SAM I did say that.
CHLOE BANKS *(smiling)* Mmm. Well don't you worry, Sam. I told Max that you are the only leading man for me.
SAM You did?
CHLOE BANKS Of course. You're very handsome. One look and I knew, you're just what I need.
SAM *(awkwardly)* Thanks.
CHLOE BANKS I'll be honest with you, Sam. Max Maxwell is so washed up. Years ago he made a splash at *(mildly French:)* Cannes.
SAM Where?
CHLOE BANKS *(very French:)* Cannes.
SAM Where?
CHLOE BANKS *(entirely American:)* Cannes. For his next picture he commanded the biggest budget in town, and it sucked. Then it was just one gobble gobble after another. Now even the operator won't answer his calls. I only agreed to star in his little picture to help the poor man out and give something back to the Indies.

SAM Well that's very nice of you. Especially considering all those other offers you're fielding.

CHLOE BANKS Uh huh.

CHLOE BANKS bursts in sobs.

SAM What's the matter? What happened?

CHLOE BANKS You see right through me, don't you?

SAM No, no.

CHLOE BANKS There are no other offers. No offers, no magazine covers, no trespassing paparazzi. I agreed to do Max Maxwell's picture because I was desperate. I'd have taken anything. I used to be somebody. You should have seen me back then, Sam. I was so young, so naive. So full of promise. Twenty-one years old and I was the next big thing. Everybody said so. Now I'm twenty-two and just another falling star.

SAM Oh.

CHLOE BANKS No no, don't try to kiss me, Sam.

SAM Oh, no, I wasn't–

CHLOE BANKS It would be so easy, wouldn't it, so romantic, I know, to fall into one another's arms and kiss each other madly through my tears.

SAM It would, yes.

CHLOE BANKS I need you, Sam.

SAM You do?

CHLOE BANKS There's something that binds us, Sam, something we both want. Do you feel it?

SAM I think I do.

CHLOE BANKS Try to feel what you want, Sam.

SAM Really?

CHLOE BANKS Yes.

SAM grabs CHLOE BANKS, his hands grappling her butt. SHE is a bit surprised, but goes with it.

CHLOE BANKS Oh! Sam. Careful. That's three thousand dollars you're feeling.

SAM Oh, sorry.

CHLOE BANKS Three thousand dollars needs to be handled very carefully.

SAM I'll be careful.

SAM continues to squeeze CHLOE BANKS' butt with greater care.

SAM'S hands move on to her hips:

CHLOE BANKS Mmm, five thousand.

Her stomach:

CHLOE BANKS Seven thousand.

Her breasts:

CHLOE BANKS Ten thousand.

Her face:

CHLOE BANKS Twenty thousand!

SAM dives into HER neck and hair with his lips.

CHLOE BANKS Oh Sam! I knew I was right. There is a bond between us! All I want is to be loved. That's what you want too, don't you?
SAM Yes.
CHLOE BANKS To be loved?
SAM Yes.
CHLOE BANKS Adored!
SAM Yes.
CHLOE BANKS By millions!

HIS hands running all over CHLOE BANKS:

SAM Millions and millions!
CHLOE BANKS Then do it Sam!
SAM I'm doing it!
CHLOE BANKS Yes, do it! Do it, Sam! Kill yourself!
SAM What?
CHLOE BANKS Kill yourself over me! Leave only your final words behind! Tell the world that your small life wasn't worth living without Chloe Banks burning up the big screen!
SAM You want me to kill myself over you?
CHLOE BANKS I knew you would help me, Sam. We do share a bond, you see? Beneath the surface we're not so different you and I. I'm a beautiful

actress and you're a terrible actor. I was somebody, and you're nobody. You're desperate, and so am I. Alone, we're lost out there in the dark. But together, we can shine. You, like a firework. And me like a star. Make me the next big thing, Sam! I'm ready for my comeback.

CHLOE BANKS kisses SAM and he embraces her body madly.

Episode Thirteen

MARY opens the door and sees SAM and CHLOE BANKS.

MARY Oh, I'm so sorry. How embarrassing. *(starts to leave, but:)* Wait a minute. Sam! What's going on?
CHLOE BANKS Who is this?
MARY Who is this?
SAM Uh, Chloe this is my wife, Mary. Wife Mary, this is Chloe Banks.
MARY Who?
SAM Chloe Banks. She's the next big thing.
MARY The next big thing?
SAM Well, she's making her comeback.
MARY I can see that.
SAM No, Mary, it's not what you think. She's just an actress.
MARY What's she doing here? Acting?
SAM Yes! Remember that movie I auditioned for?
MARY Yeah?
SAM Well, I got the part!
MARY You did?
SAM Yes. And Chloe and I were just rehearsing our big scene together.
CHLOE BANKS The climax.
MARY Really. You got the part?
SAM Isn't that great?
MARY Yay! Sam! Congratulations!

MARY and SAM embrace and bounce.

CHLOE BANKS So I'll call you later, Sam, and we'll work on your monologue.
SAM My monologue?
CHLOE BANKS Your final monologue?
SAM Oh, yes. Yes, we'll work that out.

CHLOE BANKS Good. *(kisses SAM on the cheek)*
SAM Oh! Friends.
CHLOE BANKS *(to MARY)* Very nice to have met you.
MARY You too.
CHLOE BANKS Ciao.
SAM Goodbye, Bye…

CHLOE BANKS exits.

MARY She's pretty.
SAM Oh, if you like that sort of thing.
MARY Sam! It's so exciting! Your very first audition, and you won!
SAM Isn't that something?
MARY You see, Sam? You wanted it, you went for it, and you got it.
SAM Yes.
MARY I'm so proud of you. Oh! And guess what I brought home?
SAM What?
MARY Your favorite sausages!
SAM Oh!
MARY And you can eat as many as you want. It's a celebration!
SAM Yay.
MARY Are you happy, Sam?
SAM I am.
MARY No more depression?
SAM No.
MARY And no more suicide attempts?
SAM Nnno.
MARY Good. Well, I'm going to take a shower, and then I want to hear all about your audition and the movie and your big climax with Chloe Banks.
SAM *(laughs awkwardly on:)* Okay.

MARY blows SAM a kiss and disappears into the bathroom to take a shower. SAM listens for a moment, and when he hears the water turn on he dashes out the front door and down the hall, leaving the door ajar.

SAM What have I gotten myself into? Chloe? Chloe! I'll go the back way and try to cut her off at the pass.

Episode Fourteen

> *MARY starts to sing ridiculously in the shower. After a moment, MAX pokes his head in through the door.*

MAX Hello, anybody home? Sam?

> *MAX hears MARY singing in the shower and sneaks over to peep through the keyhole. ALBERT taps on the open door and steps in, dressed in a very tacky tux.*

ALBERT Knock knock, who's there?
MAX –Oh!
ALBERT Who are you?
MAX Hello there.
ALBERT What do you think you're doing? You some kind of pervert, looking through a keyhole while the lady's trying to take a shower?
MAX No, no, I was only looking from a cinematic angle. Max Maxwell, film director, pleased to meet you.
ALBERT Film director, huh? What are you trying to do, get a close-up? Where's Sam?
MAX So I have come to the right place. You know Sam?
ALBERT Sure I know Sam. What do you want with him?
MAX Well, due to an unforeseen circumstance I've just recently cast him in my latest picture opposite Chloe Banks.
ALBERT Who?
MAX Chloe Banks. She's the next big thing. Well, she's making a comeback. Look, whatever! So I need to talk to Sam. Do you know where he is?
ALBERT Ah, so you must be the director of that film Sam auditioned for this morning. I just stopped by to talk to him about that myself.
MAX Really, and you are?
ALBERT Albert Price. I'm Sam's agent.
MAX His agent? Didn't know Sam had an agent.
ALBERT Well he does and I'm it. So any business you have with Sam needs to go through me.
MAX Alright then. It's very important that I get Sam's signature on this contract right away.
ALBERT What's the hurry?
MAX It's just very important that I get him signed on, because, well, production schedules being what they are.

ALBERT Well. You don't think you're the only director with a production schedule interested in Sam these days?

MAX I just assumed.

ALBERT Are you kidding? Sam's whatcha call an overnight sensation. I've been fielding offers left and right. But I'll look this contract over alongside the rest and see if it's worth Sam carving some time out of his schedule for.

MAX Just so yuh know, this picture is gonna be big, a huge hit, a Blockbuster.

ALBERT Is it now? I'll review your offer with that in mind and get back to you.

MAX Look, Al – May I call yuh Al? – I'll be honest with you. Sam's a terrible actor. As his agent I'm sure you're already aware of that. But it's alright, we'll fix it in post-production, they can do anything with CGI these days. Point is, Chloe Banks wants Sam as her leading man. And as you might guess, what Chloe Banks wants, Chloe Banks gets.

ALBERT I've never heard of Chloe Banks.

MAX What do you mean you've never–?! She's Chloe Banks! Look, okay, OKAY! Granted: Chloe Banks may be over the hill – I mean the woman's twenty-two years old for god's sake – but she's the only card I got up my sleeve, and if I loose her I may never get this picture up, never, do you understand?

ALBERT Sounds like you need our Sammy pretty bad.

MAX Look Mac: I've put everything I got left into this picture! Every last dollar, every last drop of sweat, every last ounce of my dignity! I ain't got nothing left! If this picture doesn't get the green light god help me– …I don't know what I'll do…

ALBERT Well I'll take that into consideration. In the meantime–

MARGARET enters, dressed as a bride.

MARGARET Albert, for Christ sake, how long can it take to borrow a bottle of Wesson oil? I'm getting cold.

ALBERT Margaret, may I introduce you to Max Maxwell. Max is that film director Sam auditioned for this morning.

MARGARET Really.

MAX Nice to meet you.

ALBERT Margaret's my uh, secretary. Max and I were just discussing the big movie deal that he's offering Sam. An agent's work is never done, you know.

MARGARET An agent's work?

ALBERT Yes. Especially Sam's agent.

MARGARET Oh that's right. Yes, Albert here's a regular agent provocateur. Best in the business.

ALBERT Ha! Secretary humor. Bitter to the core. Well Max it was nice to

meet you and like I said I'll look this over and get back to you.
MAX When, do you think?
ALBERT A-S-A-P.
MAX Can't you look it over any sooner than that?
ALBERT Lots of contracts to go through, as I said, but I'll do my best. Bye now.

And ALBERT has ushered MAX out the door, closing it behind him.

MARGARET Sam's agent?
ALBERT Quick thinking, huh?
MARGARET And that sucker bought it?
ALBERT Hook line and stinker.
MARGARET Where are Sam and Mary?
ALBERT I don't know where Sam is off to, but Mary–

Just then MARY opens the bathroom door, a towel around her body and another around her hair, and strikes a pose as well as a high note. Her high note is fairly quickly cut off by the realization that it's not Sam but rather ALBERT and MARGARET standing before her.

MARY Oh! Albert, Margaret! I didn't realize you were here. Where's Sam?
ALBERT He must have stepped out. I just stopped by to borrow some Wesson oil and I ran into this fellow who said he's the director of that movie Sam auditioned for.
MARY The director was here?
ALBERT Yup. Came by to drop off Sam's contract.
MARY Oh! His contract? How exciting!
ALBERT I told him I was Sam's agent and that I'd be looking the contract over on Sam's behalf.
MARY Oh, well that's awful sweet of you, Albert.
ALBERT Happy to help. Of course I'll have to take a small percentage of Sam's wages. Agent's fees, you know.
MARY Oh I'm sure Sam won't mind. All big movie stars have agents, after all!
ALBERT That's right!
MARY Eeeee!

MARY claps her hands gleefully.

ALBERT Well. Looks like I better go get started on that website.

MARGARET Right now? I guess we're done shooting for the day, then.

ALBERT If Sam is going to be a big movie actor the man needs a website.

MARGARET Took you long enough to put our website together, how fast do you think you're gonna get Sam's up.

ALBERT Easy. Sam needs an actor's website. I've got a porn site. Couple of minor adjustments and voilà.

MARGARET You're going to convert our porn site into Sam's actor website? What about all our plans? What about all these outfits we bought?

ALBERT Now Margaret–

SAM enters, frazzled.

SAM Oh! Hello everyone.

MARY Sam, you'll never guess who stopped by!

SAM Who?

MARY Tell him, Albert. Your director!

SAM My director?

ALBERT Max Maxwell. He dropped off this contract for you. I'll admit I didn't quite buy it when you came bangin' at my door earlier, but you weren't joking. That Max Maxwell wants you bad. But don't worry, I played it real cool. We'll squeeze the big bucks out of him.

SAM We will?

MARY Albert's your agent.

SAM He is?

MARY *(indicating that SAM should say "thank you")* Isn't that nice?

SAM Oh, well sure. Thanks Albert.

ALBERT Happy to help.

MARGARET Albert, I want to talk to you.

ALBERT Oh, that's right, I almost forgot. Sam, I'm gonna get to work on that website right away. It won't take long, the foundation's already been laid. Oh! No pun intended. *(laughs)*

MARGARET Albert, that porn site was supposed to be our nest egg. What about all that money we were going to make, you and me, together? We made a commitment, Albert.

ALBERT Don't you worry, Margaret, we're gonna make money alright. We're gonna make a killing!

MARGARET But Albert–

ALBERT Time to get to work!

With a wave to SAM, ALBERT exits. MARGARET stands stunned with thought.

SAM Bye Albert. And thanks again!
MARY Oh Sam! You're going to be a big, rich movie star! I think this is just the beginning! Tell you what. Forget the sausages. Let's go out and celebrate!
SAM Out? Okay!

> *MARY kisses SAM joyfully and disappears into the bathroom where she can be heard singing again. SAM pulls his suicide note out of his pocket.*

SAM You just never know how things are gonna turn out.
MARGARET What's that?
SAM This? Just a bad idea I had.

> *SAM crumples up the note and tosses it triumphantly. It lands near MARGARET'S feet.*

SAM I think I'll go join my agent and look over that contract! Ooo, and the website! You know what? I think Mary's right. This is only the beginning!

> *SAM exits. MARGARET picks up SAM'S note and uncrumples it. SHE reads it, looks after SAM, looks after MARY, then thinks hard before tucking the note away in her outfit and making an exit herself. Intermission.*

Act Three

Episode Fifteen

> *A few days later. In the hallway between Sam and Albert's apartments. SAM enters with some pseudo-trendy shopping bags and whistling "Hooray For Hollywood." At his door, HE fumbles repeatedly with his keys and the bags. MARGARET comes out of Albert's apartment, dressed to bartend rather than for a porn shoot.*

MARGARET Sam.
SAM Oh hi Margaret. Time to go to work?
MARGARET Yes.
SAM Bouncing or bartending tonight?
MARGARET Bartending.
SAM Well, pour one for me, will yuh?

MARGARET I will. Sam?

SAM Darn these keys. Yes?

MARGARET Do you have a minute?

SAM Sure.

MARGARET There's something I've wanted to talk to you about, since Albert became your agent and put up your website.

SAM Okay.

MARGARET That website was my future, Sam. Albert's and mine. We were going to make our bundle and retire together to some beautiful paradise. The things I did for a world of sickoes to click on. Not to mention– Well. Let's just say I made my commitment to Albert with actions that speak much louder than any marriage vow.

SAM Okay.

MARGARET And everything I did, I did for love. Commitment. A future worth living for. Because I'm sick of this empty, aching life.

SAM Okay.

MARGARET I don't hold anything against you, Sam. It was Albert who abandoned our future and dumped our website for yours. But the way I see it you do owe me one. And so I'm hoping that when that final moment comes, I'll be your lucky winner.

SAM My what?

MARGARET When you kill yourself, whoever you're supposed to do it for, do it for me instead.

SAM Oh. No, I'm going to be an actor now.

MARGARET stares at SAM.

SAM I just bought all these new clothes. I've got an agent, the website. I'm gonna be an actor.

MARGARET *(beat)* I think you need to talk to Albert. After which I believe you'll see things my way. And it will be our little secret. Our: "surprise finale." Do it Sam, but not just for me. Do it for commitment. Real commitment. Show Albert that in the end it's love that's worth dying for, not greed.

SAM But–

MARGARET You're a good kid, Sam. I know you'll do the right thing. *(checks her watch)* I have to go. I've got alcoholics to encourage. We'll speak again. But remember, we never spoke.

MARGARET exits down the hall.

SAM I am so confused. I guess I SHOULD talk to Albert.

Episode Sixteen

> *SAM is about to knock on Albert's door when GIGI BOLT enters down the aisle of the theatre.*

GIGI BOLT Sam!
SAM Miss Bolt? What are you–
GIGI BOLT I'm glad I caught you before you left.
SAM Oh, no, I'm just getting home. How–?
GIGI BOLT Good, then I'm not keeping you from anything.
SAM Well, no–
GIGI BOLT Do you have a moment?
SAM Sure.
GIGI BOLT Well! Your plot has twisted since last we spoke. You certainly have raised the stakes, Sam.
SAM Raised the stakes?
GIGI BOLT Very dramatic indeed. So I thought I'd drop by personally and reaffirm my own interest in that final bow of yours.
SAM Final bow?
GIGI BOLT I drafted that note for you, as we discussed. And the front cover of *American Theatre* magazine's next issue has your name written all over it.
SAM Oh, well, Miss Bolt–
GIGI BOLT But that's not all, Sam. Listen to this. I had a conversation with this hot young playwright and director, Mark Jackson.
SAM Who?
GIGI BOLT Mark Jackson. He's the next big thing. Anyway, then I put in a call to the folks over at the National Endowment for the Arts and I think we can get Jackson lined up for a nice fat grant to write and direct a new play about your life. Jackson's a sucker for grand finales and when I explained yours to him he just couldn't wait to get to work. I even picked up the phone again and got a handful of big regional theatres on board, so the play's guaranteed at least a four-city tour. Then who knows, maybe Broadway. How does that sound?
SAM Wait a minute, slow down. Miss Bolt–

> *MAX enters from down the hall.*

MAX Sammy baby!
SAM What! Mister Maxwell!
MAX How's tricks?

SAM Who?

MAX I'm sorry, am I interrupting anything?

SAM Uh, no.

MAX Max Maxwell, film director.

GIGI BOLT Gigi Bolt, executive director, Theatre Communications Group.

MAX Theatre? Well, good luck to yuh. Listen, Sam, I know Albert wants to hold off on that contract until the "big moment." And I'll admit I was a bit miffed at first. But then I got to thinkin'. And then I got to talkin' on my cellular phone. And I have a pretty good feeling we can get some big money interested in your story.

SAM Big money?

MAX I'm thinkin' Miramax.

GIGI BOLT Excuse me.

MAX Sure, hold on. Picture this, Sam: <u>NAME OF SAME CURRENT HOT MEDIOCRE ACTOR USED IN EPISODE THREE</u> plays you, and Chloe Banks plays your girlfriend.

SAM Wife.

MAX Whatever. <u>NAME OF CURRENT HOT MEDIOCRE ACTOR</u> and Chloe Banks will burn up the screen. And you know how people love to gawk at a true story with a tragic ending. It can't miss! What do you say?

GIGI BOLT Excuse me, but I was talking to Sam.

MAX What about?

GIGI BOLT A life in the theatre.

MAX A life in the theatre? The kid's got what, a week to go?

SAM A week?

MAX What's he want to waste it in a theatre for?

GIGI BOLT Hold on to your soul, Sam, hold on to your soul.

MAX Oh, yeah, that'll sell tickets. Theatre people. They got no business sense. I got it all worked out, Sam.

SAM Mister Maxwell–!

CHLOE BANKS enters from down the hall.

CHLOE BANKS Sam!

SAM & MAX Chloe!

CHLOE BANKS Max! What are you doing here?

MAX Just talkin' shop with our handsome tearjerker.

GIGI BOLT I was talking to him first.

CHLOE BANKS And who are you?

GIGI BOLT Gigi Bolt, executive director, Theatre Communications Group.
CHLOE BANKS Oh theatre. Interesting.
MAX Chloe baby, let's leave the hoofer [busker] alone. Sam is very busy.
SAM Actually–
MAX I know you're very busy Sam. But perhaps the three of us could step inside for just a moment and I'll give you my hundred-word elevator pitch on the new picture.
CHLOE BANKS The NEW picture?
MAX Same picture, baby, just a face-lift. You know how that goes.
CHLOE BANKS Max, I came to talk to Sam. Alone.
GIGI BOLT So did I.
MAX Alone, eh? Well, are you two pumping for tabloid fuel already?
CHLOE BANKS Now listen, / Max!
GIGI BOLT If you / would please!

ALBERT opens his door with his cell phone in hand.

SAM Would everybody just–
SAM & ALBERT Be quiet!
SAM Albert!
MAX Albert baby.
ALBERT Hey, I told you: I'D call YOU. And who are these people?
GIGI BOLT Gigi Bolt, executive director, Theatre Communications Group.
ALBERT Oh right, I got your telegram.
CHLOE BANKS I'm Chloe Banks.
ALBERT Who?
MAX Chloe Banks!
ALBERT Oh right, I got your text message. And I got all of your emails and phone calls and faxes but I'm sorry you're just gonna have to wait like everybody else.
SAM Albert, what is going on?
ALBERT Don't you worry, Sam, I'll take care of them. These your bags?
SAM Yeah. No wait the lock / is jammed.

ALBERT opens the door to SAM'S apartment easily.

ALBERT Go on in, I've got a few updates for you.

ALBERT shoves the bags into SAM's arms, and SAM into the apartment.

SAM How did you–? Updates?
CHLOE BANKS, MAX & GIGI BOLT Sam? Sam! Etc...
ALBERT And you people hit the road before I call the police and have you arrested for stalking a celebrity. I told you, if you want to talk to Sam you gotta go through me. Now beat it!

As ALBERT closes the door:

CHLOE BANKS / Sam, don't forget that final monologue! Our big climax!
MAX / It's gonna be a block buster, Sam, a real blockbuster!
GIGI BOLT A four-city tour, Sam! And then straight to Broadway!

Episode Seventeen

Inside SAM'S apartment.

ALBERT Jesus. Vultures, all of 'em.
SAM What is going on, Albert?
ALBERT Hold that thought just one second, Sam. Hello sorry to have kept you waiting. So where were we? Right, well, as I said, I got a flood of offers pouring in so you just sail that pitch on over and I'll take a look-see. Okay. Alright. Ciao.
SAM And who was that?
ALBERT Sam we need to talk.
SAM You bet we do.
ALBERT Do you know who that was?
SAM Who?
ALBERT That, was one of many.
SAM Who?
ALBERT Offers Sam. They're pouring in left and right.
SAM Acting offers?
ALBERT Well you see that's the thing.
SAM What is?
ALBERT Nobody was interested in you as an actor.
SAM What do you mean?
ALBERT Oh come on, Sam, I told you, there are a million actors out there. Two million. You were just one more trying to hop on the back of the heap and nobody cared. And yet, as your agent whose job it is to look after your interests, I have managed to secure for you, to forge from the very ether of

imagination and technology, THE money making media performance art reality entertainment gig of the century.
SAM What's that?
ALBERT You remember that idea I had about raffling off your suicide?
SAM Yeah.
ALBERT And how on a certain date we throw a big party and announce the lucky winner.
SAM Yeah.
ALBERT Well, I took the liberty of putting a link on your website.
SAM A link? To what?
ALBERT WWW dot American dash suicide dot com.
SAM What? And people are calling left and right?
ALBERT Calling, emailing, faxing, text messaging, coming out from under rocks, slipping through the cracks, you name it. That phone call I just wrapped?
SAM Yeah?
ALBERT Well THAT was Fox Television. They want to do a reality TV show on you. Follow you around and stuff. I also got a call from Michael Moore, wants to make a documentary about you, something about how the conservative right and unemployment created by big business are driving average Americans to despair. And just yesterday I get a call from that European film director? What's his name. Lars Von Trier! Wants to make a trilogy of films based on your suicide and what it says about the American character. And those are just three drops in a bucket of thousands of people hoping to win their fifteen minutes of YOU! YOU Sam, are gonna be big!
SAM After I'm dead.
ALBERT Now, Sam, don't think of it that way. Death. What is death? It's just a concept. Besides, it's not the dead man himself that counts. It's what he leaves behind. And you, my shooting star, will leave behind a glittering trail, I'm talkin' history, a legend, and more money than you and Mary ever dreamed of. Do you understand the magnitude of this thing? This is going to be the most spectacular, dramatic, and poignant venture in the history of Internet commerce, not to mention the media event of the year if not the decade and the century!
SAM You really think so?
ALBERT Yes! Sam! Okay look, you just wait here, and let me show you the LIST of people who want a piece of YOU. People who are gonna make you the biggest, richest celebrity ever invented.
SAM But Albert–
ALBERT Just hang on one minute. I'll be right back.

ALBERT runs out.

Episode Eighteen

> SAM *stands stupefied for a moment. HE thinks. HE picks up his copy of* Hamlet *and looks at it, fans through its pages quickly, then holds it up as if to see whether it is or isn't much of anything. MARY enters from her long day at work.*

MARY Hello.
SAM Oh. Mary.
MARY What? What's wrong? Has something happened? Sam, have you been reading *Hamlet* again?
SAM No. But it looks like I might be through with acting.
MARY Why is that?
SAM Well. I kinda got another job.
MARY Really. A temp job?
SAM No, it's pretty permanent.
MARY Well what is it, Sam?

> ALBERT *bursts in with a long list in hand.*

ALBERT Okay Sam now look at this. Oh, hi Mary. Sam tell you the big news?
MARY Some kind of job?
ALBERT If you call living on Easy Street a job.
MARY (!) What do you mean? Sam, what does he mean?
ALBERT ...Well don't break the good news to her gently, Sam. Go ahead.
SAM It looks like we might be rich, Mary.
MARY Oh! How? Wha'd you do?
SAM Albert did it.
MARY Wha'd you do?
ALBERT As Sam's agent, I did the thinking for him, and went ahead with that website I told you about.
MARY I thought you said you were through with acting.
ALBERT Not THAT website. The other one.
MARY Oh.
ALBERT And it's a HUGE HIT!
MARY Oh!
ALBERT Yeah, look at this. We got nightly news programs, daytime talk shows, late night talk shows, national magazines and newspapers all wanting exclusive interviews. The downtown Hilton Hotel wants to offer "last days"

luxury suites, paid in advance. The city of San Francisco wants you to do it on the Golden Gate Bridge, help boost tourism. The Museum of Modern Art wants to videotape it and sell it as performance art. Then we got the Earth Liberation Front, they want you to do it in protest over environmental pollution. PETA wants you to dress in animal skins and do it as a gesture of atonement for all the furry critters that have died to keep us warm. The National Right To Life Committee wants you to do it as a sacrifice in penance for all the innocent unborn dead. Pro Choice America wants you to talk about the hard times you've had and that you're doing it because you can see now it WOULD have been better had you never been born – which is probably true anyway, right, I mean how did this whole idea come about in the first place? And then an endless list of wives and girlfriends wanting to prove they're worth dying for, husbands and boyfriends hoping to impress their sweethearts, friends wanting to get something for that friend who's got everything, people wanting to be a part of something, people with money to burn, people with nothing better to do, it just goes on and on. We have already sold close to a million dollars in raffle tickets alone!

MARY / Oh my god!

SAM A million dollars?

ALBERT Meanwhile I'm brokering between the big wigs to nail down the highest bidders for brand name placement and post-mortem rights to this and that. *(beat)* It's just nuts!

MARY I can't believe it!

ALBERT Mary, you are never gonna have to work another day in your life, and you can thank Sam for that.

MARY Eeeee! Thank you thank you thank you thank you!

ALBERT And we are planning a mega party at Margaret's club for the big announcement. Oo, which reminds me, I gotta open up ticket sales for that. There's just so much to do!

SAM Say, when IS the big announcement?

ALBERT Uh, week from tomorrow.

SAM Really. That soon?

> *ALBERT looks directly at SAM, then makes a noticeably focused beeline to him. The focused calm in his voice is a striking change.*

ALBERT Yuh gotta move fast on these things, Sam. It's all about momentum. We keep things rolling and a week from tomorrow when that old clock strikes midnight, your ship is comin' in. Are you ready to set sail?

> *ALBERT offers SAM his hand. MARY looks at SAM. SAM looks down at ALBERT'S hand, at MARY, at ALBERT again, then shakes ALBERT'S*

hand.

SAM Okay, I'm ready!

MARY Yay! Oh my goodness what am I gonna wear to the party? I don't have a dress.

ALBERT Well you get shoppin' little missy. I'll work up a final speech for you, Sam, and Mary we need to talk about the reveal.

MARY Ooo the reveal what's that?

ALBERT "It's the moment everyone's been waiting for," when you in your beautiful dress step forward to read Sam's note, and we find out "Who will be the lucky winner?"

MARY Ooo, how exciting!

ALBERT Now Margaret is arranging everything down at the club, but Mary if I could get your help with the funeral arrangements, / picking out flowers, that sort of thing.

MARY Oh. …Right.

ALBERT And Sam, we gotta get YOU an outfit.

SAM I just bought / a few things.

ALBERT Oh, and Mary, people are going to want to interview you too, so we'll set up a day for that, get everybody done at once, boom boom boom, which means we gotta get you an appointment with a hairdresser.

MARY Yes!

ALBERT And don't worry, I'll write up a few things for you to say.

MARY Yeah because I get nervous.

ALBERT Exactly. Oo, and let's talk about that dress because people are bound to ask who you're wearing and we want to make sure you're wearing the right person, so lemme call around and see *(writing)* who is interested in designing Mary's dress.

MARY Eeeee!

ALBERT Okay so I'm on that. Oh, and lemme get you the catalogue of the florist I picked out so you can take a look. We want everything to be spectacular…!

Episode Nineteen

MARY, ALBERT, and the apartment have receded into the background as SAM'S mind has wandered off in thought. Very quietly, a MYSTERIOUS FOREIGN MAN places a park bench behind SAM. SAM does not notice this due to some birds twittering on a branch somewhere above him that have caught his attention. Without looking at the bench, SAM sits down on it, still taking in the birds. HE smiles. SAM stares out contemplatively. The MYSTERIOUS FOREIGN MAN eventually sits on the bench next to SAM. Now SAM notices him. A small exchange of nods. The MYSTERIOUS FOREIGN MAN stares at SAM. A small exchange of eyebrow lifts. More staring. Eventually:

SAM Howdy.

MYSTERIOUS FOREIGN MAN How-dee.

SAM Oh, where're you from?

MYSTERIOUS FOREIGN MAN Here.

SAM No, I meant before.

MYSTERIOUS FOREIGN MAN Before what?

SAM Before you– arrived. On these shores. *(remembers the word:)* Immigrated. Oh, maybe you're on vacation.

MYSTERIOUS FOREIGN MAN No. It is no vacation. I came here to speak to you.

SAM Me?

MYSTERIOUS FOREIGN MAN That is right.

SAM …You came all the way here to talk to me.

MYSTERIOUS FOREIGN MAN *(impatiently)* I have been here, in America, for many years now. I came here, to this park, to speak to you. I am speaking your English. Do you understand me, *(making a point that he knows his name:)* Sam?

SAM Hey. How do you know that?

MYSTERIOUS FOREIGN MAN I told you. I came here to speak to you.

SAM stares blankly. After a pause, the MYSTERIOUS FOREIGN MAN notes what he would think would be obvious:

MYSTERIOUS FOREIGN MAN WWW dot American dash suicide dot com.

SAM Oh. Oh, right. Well, what, do you want an autograph or–

MYSTERIOUS FOREIGN MAN I do not want your autograph. I want your signature. Your name. On a note to the American people that, like your website says, your beautiful wife will read aloud when you have sacrificed yourself.

SAM Well, –sacrifice? Uh, no, I'm, heh! I'm just doin' it for the money.

MYSTERIOUS FOREIGN MAN I am prepared to provide you twice the highest price for your sacrifice of blood to be drawn in the name of a great and holy cause.

SAM What cause is that?

MYSTERIOUS FOREIGN MAN Have you heard the one about the chicken and the ducks?

SAM There's a chicken and duck cause?

MYSTERIOUS FOREIGN MAN No, that is not the cause.

SAM Oh it's a joke. No, I haven't heard that one.

MYSTERIOUS FOREIGN MAN It is not a joke either! It is an allegory.

SAM An allegory?

MYSTERIOUS FOREIGN MAN I will tell it. Some duck eggs were set upon by a certain chicken who was afraid of a bear. For many years she set upon the duck eggs, keeping them warm, helping them grow strong in their shells. Eventually the chicken's job was complete. The ducks broke through the eggshells, crawled triumphantly from under the chicken, and drove away the bear. When the ducks turned back, they saw that the chicken was still there. So the ducks said, "Thank you, kind chicken. Now, leave us to our pond." But the chicken said, "Not so fast. I need your pond for water to drink. I will stay here now." "No," said the ducks. "You set upon us, and we thank you, but this is our pond, and now you must go." "No," said the chicken," I will not leave. And what's more, you ducks will stop now from swimming and flying freely, and instead feed on the droppings I leave upon your shores and learn to roost in a barn like chickens." "But no," said the ducks, "this is not our way of life!" "No," said the chicken, "but it will be!" And they go back and forth like this for a long time. You understand the allegory.

SAM No. Not really.

MYSTERIOUS FOREIGN MAN Then I continue. Maybe in time it becomes clear to you. "No," said the ducks, "leave us to swim and to fly!" "No," said the chicken, "I will not leave! I will drink from your pond and you will learn to roost like chickens!" And so the ducks grabbed the chicken by the throat and dragged her to the pond! The chicken screamed, "Wait! I hatched you. What are you doing?" "Swim," said the ducks! "I do not swim!" cried the chicken. "Then fly!" said the ducks. "I do not fly!" cried the chicken. "Ah, you want to drink from our pond," said the ducks, "but you do not bother to understand our way of life! Too bad for you!" And so the ducks took to the sky, flew themselves into the chicken's great barn, and scattered it in pieces to the wind, al-Hamdulillah! …Do you understand the allegory?

SAM I think so. It's not very funny.

MYSTERIOUS FOREIGN MAN I told you, it is not a joke. I come to you in great seriousness, to ask that you make your sacrifice in the name of our cause. Show the American people that there are those among them who understand the truth. Show the American people that the chickens at roost in Washington are crushing their own eggs when they set too long on other's.

SAM …What?

MYSTERIOUS FOREIGN MAN Oh! You Americans have no feeling for poetic speaking! It is no wonder you now export your thinking jobs since you have not bothered to educate anybody for the past twenty years! So now you sit back and enjoy surfing the benefits of your innovation, and you are having such a good time that you do not notice how stupid you have become! While you were busy being so surprised by 9/11, and waving your flags in front of your eyes, a few backwards foreigners were setting up shop. Now an ex-comrade in Moscow can quietly make eighty thousand dollars a year working for a company in your Palo Alto. A Kathakali dancer in New Delhi can give you tech support on your shiny new laptop. Not that you would notice what a foreigner is doing, so long as he does not interrupt your high-speed connection!

> *The MYSTERIOUS FOREIGN MAN spits on the ground near SAM'S feet.*

SAM Why do you hate me so much?
MYSTERIOUS FOREIGN MAN I apologize for the spitting. It was a bit much. Please believe me, we do not hate YOU, Sam. It is just that we are not terribly fond of your UNCLE Sam. For its crimes against us, we cannot make your government surrender to our own laws of punishment. And so, we have goaded its people to surrender to their own fascist politicians. And you have. You have punished yourselves. You had already lost your silly "War on Terror" before it had been declared. Even YOUR God would agree. For over half a century, you sowed the wind, and now, you reap the whirlwind.
SAM I don't get it.
MYSTERIOUS FOREIGN MAN That is right. But if you give your life to it, Sam, then you will understand. Give your life to this great cause, make of yourself a sacrifice for your fellow chickens, and everything will become clear – to you, and to them.

> *SAM looks up at the chirping birds.*

SAM I have always wanted a cause. Some, greater purpose.
MYSTERIOUS FOREIGN MAN Now you have it.
SAM ...I'll think about it.
MYSTERIOUS FOREIGN MAN Don't think, Sam. Die. For the chickens, the ducks, and all the birds. And for twice the highest price, guaranteed.
SAM Thank you. I'll talk to my agent.
MYSTERIOUS FOREIGN MAN Tell him I said hello.
SAM You've spoken to Albert already?

> *The MYSTERIOUS FOREIGN MAN leaves, taking the bench with him.*

SAM Hey. *(stands)* Hey!

Episode Twenty

SAM alone.

SAM Jeez Louise! I can't even take a moment to sit by myself on a park bench and listen to the birds!

We hear the birds suddenly chirp in angst and flutter off. As SAM speaks, time passes, people and locations come and go. There is something dreamlike about what unfolds.

SAM The sun is gonna rise tomorrow morning and that old clock is gonna strike midnight before I know it. Things just move so fast. Tick tock and you're taking your first breath. Tick tock and you're old. Tick tock and it's all over. I remember that time when I was a kid, walking with my mother across the parking lot outside the mall, and I kept looking up at the sky. My mother asked me what I was looking for. I said, "I'm looking for the big zipper in case I need to get out of this world quick." I guess I've found it. I'm gonna be a star, Mary. And I'M finally gonna look after YOU. Very soon you will never have to put on that apron again.
MARY Oh, Sam.
SAM Tick tock.
MARY Tell me what you think.
SAM Now tick I understand. But tock?

MARY holds up a dress and a pair of shoes.

MARY Do you think they go together?
SAM That I don't know.
MARY I think they're beautiful.
SAM Tick. And here I am alive.
MARY The color matches the flowers, too.
SAM Tock. And I don't know where I'll be.
MARY *(hugs SAM)* Oh, Sam. Everything's going to work out alright, isn't it?
SAM Tick. And I feel my wife next to me.
MARY I'm sick of this dull, boring life.
SAM Tock.
MARY Thank you, Sam. *(looks at him)*
SAM And she's gone.

MARY Thank you so much.

> *MARY kisses SAM, then leaves as ALBERT arrives with papers for SAM to sign, which SAM does distractedly.*

SAM What if at the last moment I can't do it? People will be upset.

ALBERT Yes they will.

SAM What do you think they'll do?

ALBERT Turn against you. But don't worry about it. We'll get you on Saturday Night Live, you'll make jokes about yourself, and all will be forgiven.

SAM Really?

ALBERT Sure. People love to watch other people do penance. Especially if it's funny. *(exits)*

SAM Maybe I do need a cause. Maybe it's not enough to do it for myself and for Mary. Maybe it is better to give my life to some greater good.

GIGI BOLT Do it for the American Theatre, Sam.

MARGARET Do it for commitment, Sam.

CHLOE BANKS Show the world I'm still worth adoring.

MAX Give the world a blockbuster, Sam! A real blockbuster!

GIGI BOLT Do it for something worthy of the soul!

MARGARET Do it for someone worth loving!

CHLOE BANKS Worth remembering forever!

MAX Worth the price of admission!

SAM I'm just not sure what that would be! And I need to know. I need some purpose. I'm sick of this endless, confusing life! What do I need this life for anyway if I've never had happiness? But what do I get when it's over? What am I dying for?! …God? I'm not a praying man. But if you're up there I sure wish you'd tell me so. A lot of people down here are counting on me. And I'd just like to know that someone's gonna be up there to greet me when I come knocking. Tick, when I put that gun to this machine. Tock, and bust it wide open. Will my soul come flying out and have something, somewhere to fly to? Or will a big bang echo into nothing, nowhere. …What happens to us? What's the answer? Someone give me a sign!

Episode Twenty-one

> *At the sound of a massive electrical switch, SAM is suddenly caught in a harsh spotlight from upstage. It is bright enough that both SAM and the audience can only barely make out the MYSTERIOUS AMERICAN MAN who is standing behind it.*

MYSTERIOUS AMERICAN MAN Sam Small.

SAM Aw, jeez that's bright. Yes, that's me. Who are you?

MYSTERIOUS AMERICAN MAN Who I am doesn't matter. It's whom I represent that counts.

SAM Okay. Who's that?

MYSTERIOUS AMERICAN MAN You, Sam.

SAM Me? Oh, no, I'm sorry, I already have an agent.

MYSTERIOUS AMERICAN MAN Albert Price.

SAM So you know about him.

MYSTERIOUS AMERICAN MAN We know everything about everyone.

SAM Who's we?

MYSTERIOUS AMERICAN MAN The people I represent.

SAM And that's me.

MYSTERIOUS AMERICAN MAN *(impatient)* No, by you, Sam, I meant the American people. By we, I mean the party whose candidate will give the American people hope and a renewed sense of purpose.

SAM Oh yeah? Which party is that?

MYSTERIOUS AMERICAN MAN The right party, Sam.

SAM *(clarifying:)* The RIGHT, party?

MYSTERIOUS AMERICAN MAN Does the name Senator McPatsy mean anything to you?

SAM Oh yeah, didn't he get in trouble with that woman or do drugs or something?

MYSTERIOUS AMERICAN MAN *(That again!)* Yes, that's him. That mud dried up and flaked off a long time ago, Sam. Senator McPatsy made his peace, and now he's fighting for your future.

SAM Is he?

MYSTERIOUS AMERICAN MAN And he needs your help.

SAM Oh! Of course! I shoulda known. Well if he wants my help, first he needs to turn off that light, then he needs to talk to my agent.

The light goes out. The stage is pitch black.

SAM Hey. I can't see.

The light comes on again, brighter, from a different angle.

SAM Aw! Say, what's the big idea?

MYSTERIOUS AMERICAN MAN Senator McPatsy needs your help, Sam.

SAM Oh he does, does he? What for?

MYSTERIOUS AMERICAN MAN It used to be, Sam, that people had ideas they were willing to die for. Nowadays people with ideas just want to live. Never has there been a greater need for dead ideologists. Tomorrow when the clock strikes midnight, you are going to kill yourself.

SAM That's right I am.

MYSTERIOUS AMERICAN MAN You are going to kill yourself because, like so many of your fellow Americans, you despair the terrible state to which your great nation has come – particularly due to the policies backed by Senator McPatsy's opponent. And so you took your life. Senator McPatsy will then campaign in your name, to right the wrongs that have driven good American citizens like Sam Small to such desperation.

SAM What wrongs are those, exactly?

MYSTERIOUS AMERICAN MAN Well, it's complicated.

SAM Well can you sum it up? If I'm gonna die for some Senator I need to know why, don't I?

MYSTERIOUS AMERICAN MAN Have you heard the one about the chicken and the ducks?

SAM Oh! Is it gonna be funny this time?

MYSTERIOUS AMERICAN MAN Some duck eggs were set on by a certain chicken. For many years she set on them, keeping them warm, until finally her task was complete. The ducks broke through the eggshells, crawled happily from under the chicken, then grabbed her by the scruff of the neck and dragged her towards the pond. The chicken screamed, "Wait! I hatched you! What are you doing?" "Swim," said the ducks. "I don't know how to swim!" cried the chicken. "Then fly!" said the ducks. "I don't know how to fly!" cried the chicken. "Then sit there," said the ducks, "and do nothing." …Do you understand the allegory?

SAM I'm sorry, Sir, I'm really not very good at this allegory stuff.

MYSTERIOUS AMERICAN MAN Who are the ducks, Sam?

SAM I don't know.

MYSTERIOUS AMERICAN MAN The other party. And who is the chicken?

SAM Uh…

MYSTERIOUS AMERICAN MAN The American people. Or?

SAM Or? You mean I get a choice about what it means?

MYSTERIOUS AMERICAN MAN Sure. It can mean whatever you want it to mean.

SAM Well that's handy. Look, let's just cut to the chase. How much money are YOU offering?

MYSTERIOUS AMERICAN MAN One million dollars and your wife will never pay taxes again.

SAM Woah! Say, that's pretty good.

MYSTERIOUS AMERICAN MAN Do it, Sam! Do it: for America.
SAM Mmmaybe but I need to think about it.
MYSTERIOUS AMERICAN MAN Do it for all Americans who work hard and deserve a fair shake.
SAM Like my wife. Mary.
MYSTERIOUS AMERICAN MAN That's right! Do it for Mary, Sam. Do it for her. And the baby.
SAM The baby? What do you mean the baby?
MYSTERIOUS AMERICAN MAN You need to talk to your wife.
SAM Wait a minute!
MYSTERIOUS AMERICAN MAN Goodnight, Sam.
SAM How do you know about a baby?
MYSTERIOUS AMERICAN MAN And God bless America.
SAM Did Mary tell you that before telling me? Why am I always the last to know everything?! Hey!

> *The spotlight goes out with the sound of a massive electrical switch. Darkness.*

SAM I can't see anything!

Act Four

Episode Twenty-two

> *At the sound of another massive electrical switch, heart-pounding dance music explodes into the air. The theatre flares up in a frenzy of colored lights and has suddenly transformed into a raging dance club, packed to the gills with a hundred party hungry clubbers. EVERYONE pounces on SAM, rips off his clothes and forcibly dresses him in his hip new outfit. During this, SAM is by turns startled and excited. In the end, when he sees how hip he looks, SAM joins in with the bouncing, throbbing, sweaty, desperately energetic dancing. Then...*

SAM Albert!
ALBERT Sam! What do you think? Quite a party isn't it?
SAM Yeah!
ALBERT Margaret sure set the place up real nice. Here, have a drink!
SAM Oh, thanks!
ALBERT Having a good time?

SAM Sure. Say, do you know what time it is?
ALBERT Don't you worry about a thing, I'll let you know when it's time. You just enjoy yourself, Sam! This is your night!

MARY joins them. ALBERT slips away.

MARY Oh! I haven't danced this much since high school!
SAM Mary!
MARY Are you having a good time, Sam?
SAM Sure!
MARY How do I look? *(takes SAM's drink)*
SAM You look great! How do I look?

MARY swigs from SAM's drink.

MARY Mmm, you look great!
SAM *(taking the drink away)* Mary, do you think you should be–?
MARY Don't think, Sam! Dance!

MARY pulls SAM back out onto the dance floor. Dancing. (Throughout the scene, MARGARET's assignment from ALBERT is to be there to hand SAM another drink whenever he runs dry.) Then...

CHLOE BANKS So do you travel often?
MYSTERIOUS FOREIGN MAN Yes. I have been to Germany and London. Oh, and Paris, too, but it was vacation.
CHLOE BANKS Tell me. What kind of breasts are popular in Paris these days, big ones or small ones?
MYSTERIOUS FOREIGN MAN I would not know. Excuse me.

The MYSTERIOUS FOREIGN MAN moves off after ALBERT, who has just passed by, and THEY disappear together. A brief flare up of dancing. Then CHLOE BANKS catches sight of SAM.

CHLOE BANKS Sam! There you are, darling!
SAM Oh, hi, Chloe!
CHLOE BANKS I haven't forgotten about our big climax, Sam.
SAM Oh?

CHLOE BANKS slips a folded note into SAM's pants pocket.

CHLOE BANKS And here's that final monologue. I wrote it myself, just for you.
SAM Oh, you did?
CHLOE BANKS Don't let me down, Sam. I'm counting on you.
SAM Chloe, I think–
CHLOE BANKS Don't think, Sam. Drink!

SAM drinks. Dancing. Then...

MAX Sammy baby!
SAM Oh, Mister Maxwell.
MAX I've been talkin' on my cellular phone again, Sam.
SAM Oh yeah?
MAX I've got all of Hollywood on hold, just waiting for that green light. You know the one I mean.
SAM Look, Mister Maxwell, you've got to go through my agent, Albert.
MAX Don't you worry, Sam, I've been in the business a long time, I know the drill. I'll talk to Albert, alright. But I want you to know that with me it's not just business. It's personal.

MAX slips a folded note into SAM'S pocket.

SAM Mister Maxwell, I really think–
MAX Don't think, Sam. Drink!

SAM drinks. Dancing. Then...

GIGI BOLT Sam!
SAM Hello Miss Bolt.
GIGI BOLT I'm sure you've got a lot on your mind, Sam.
SAM What?
GIGI BOLT I said I'm sure you've got a lot on your mind. But I just want to remind you what you could do for the American Theatre tonight! The soul of our culture is counting on you, Sam!

GIGI BOLT slips a folded note into SAM'S pocket.

SAM Oh, my head is spinning. Look, I'm tired of you people. It's too much to think about. Too many ideas and not enough reason to pay attention to them.

GIGI BOLT You shouldn't say that, Sam!

SAM But it's true!

GIGI BOLT Yes, but you shouldn't say it!

SAM Why not?

GIGI BOLT Because if the critics don't like this play they might take that line and use it against the playwright, and then maybe HE'D kill himself! Could you live with THAT?

SAM What? The playwright? Miss Bolt, I don't think–

GIGI BOLT Don't think, Sam! Drink!

SAM drinks. Dancing. Then, at the bar...

CHLOE BANKS I've totally considered the possibility of doing a little theatre.

GIGI BOLT Really? Did you get your start in the theatre?

CHLOE BANKS No, I just thought it might help boost my image as a serious actress.

GIGI BOLT I see.

MARGARET Do you know anyone who actually goes to the theatre? What's it ever about, anyway?

GIGI BOLT What's it about? It's about everything!

MARGARET Really. Everything? Well I'm a bartender. Is there any theatre about bartenders?

GIGI BOLT Certainly. Eugene O'Neill?

CHLOE BANKS Dude, I've heard of him. Didn't he die or something?

GIGI BOLT Yes.

CHLOE BANKS How?

GIGI BOLT A bartender killed him.

MARGARET Excuse me. Sam! Sam.

MARGARET moves away from CHLOE BANKS and GIGI BOLT and takes SAM by the arm.

SAM Margaret. Boy, the club sure looks great!

MARGARET Thanks. You remember what we spoke about, Sam. Our surprise finale?

SAM Yes, I remember.

MARGARET puts a folded note into SAM's pocket.

MARGARET Good. Now I wrote this speech for you.

SAM Oh, you did?

MARGARET I'm counting on you Sam. Don't think all these pretty lights are for Albert.

ALBERT *(arriving)* Margaret, the club's a knockout. You really transformed the place.

MARGARET Anything for you, Albert.

ALBERT Say, do you mind giving Sam and I a minute?

MARGARET Sure. Goodbye Sam.

MARGARET leaves.

ALBERT Listen to this one, Sam. You'll just die laughing.

SAM Oh, no, I gotta hold out 'till midnight.

ALBERT I was just talking to this guy from the NRA. He asked if I'd do him "a favor" and slip the NRA the winning ticket.

SAM You mean rig the raffle?

ALBERT Yeah. He had a big fancy statement he wanted Mary to read and everything.

SAM A statement? What did it say?

ALBERT Oh, the right to bear arms, from my cold dead hand, yadda yadda yadda. But get this. He hands it to me and he says, "Here's the statement, signed by thirty-five thousand voters."

SAM Thirty-five thousand people signed it?

ALBERT That's what I asked.

SAM Wha'd he say?

ALBERT He said, "No, I signed it." So I say, "But you just said thirty-five thousand voters." "Yeah," he says, "that's my pseudonym." *(laughs)* Can you believe that? *(looks around:)* What people won't stoop to these days. Aaanyway. *(back to SAM:)* Feast your eyes on this piece of work.

ALBERT produces a super cool, gleaming handgun. It's a little scary, actually.

SAM Wow! What's that?

ALBERT That is for you. Had it made special.

SAM Really? It's very shiny.

ALBERT It's even got silver bullets. Just in case.

SAM What?

ALBERT I'm joking, Sam. I wanted you to hold it in your hand before the big moment, so you wouldn't be surprised or anything.

SAM It sure is heavy.
ALBERT Yeah, but it delivers the goods light as a feather. Now just remember what we talked about. Plant your feet, hold this baby in one hand like this, and hold up the other hand like this.

ALBERT holds up a fancy, sealed envelope.

SAM What's that?
ALBERT The lucky winner.
SAM So who IS the lucky winner, anyway?
ALBERT Patience! You deliver your speech, press the magic button, and then Mary reads the note. Just like we talked about. Okay?
SAM How can I tell them what I'm dying for when I haven't even read my own suicide note?
ALBERT Don't worry about it, Sam. Everything's been taken care of. And didn't I write a great speech for you?
SAM Sure, but don't you think–
ALBERT Ehp! Don't think, Sam!
SAM & ALBERT Drink!

SAM drinks. Dancing. Then, at the bar...

MARY Hey Margaret! How 'bout another round?
MARGARET You bet.
MARY This is some party.
MARGARET Sure is. How're you holding up?
MARY Oh, fine.

MARY downs her drink.

MARY I'm a very lucky girl.
MARGARET I bet. Listen it's none of my business but did you ever sign a contract with Albert? About the proceeds?
MARY Contract? No, I trust Albert. "Set for life," that's what he said.
MARGARET Uh huh. Sam doesn't have a life insurance policy on him does he?
MARY No.
MARGARET *(beat)* Well, those things don't always turn out to be worth as much as you'd hope they would anyway, believe me. ...You want another?
MARY Okay.

MARGARET turns away to get a fresh bottle. MARY thinks. SHE spots ALBERT and goes to him.

MARY Albert.
ALBERT Yeah, Mary.
MARY I'm nervous.
ALBERT Why? You look fabulous!
MARY Well. What if at the last minute, I get sad, and I can't read the note?
ALBERT You'll be fine. Just think of it like a game show and you're Vanna White. It's just a show.
MARY Right.
ALBERT And after that curtain comes down, you are gonna be the luckiest girl in America.
MARY / Right.
MAX Albert baby!
ALBERT Max!
MAX And the winner is?

MAX is pulling a plump envelope from his coat. ALBERT stops him.

ALBERT Only time will tell, Max, only time will tell.
MAX Tick tock.
ALBERT Max, you know Mary, Sam's wife.
MAX Hello, doll. Say, who is THAT you're wearing?
ALBERT Doesn't she look great? Huh? Now you keep dancing, Mary, while I have a little chat with Max here.
MARY Okay.
ALBERT You just have a good time. And don't worry!
MARY Okay!

ALBERT moves off with MAX. Dancing. MARY's dancing is eventually overcome by thought, and she finds her way to a side room of the club to collect herself. SAM stumbles in.

MARY Oh! Sam!
SAM There you are, Mary.
MARY How are you feeling, Sam?
SAM I feel great!

MARY Really?

SAM Yeah. You know why? Because I just realized: when you KNOW you're time is up, it gives you such freedom! Think about it. I can do anything. I can do whatever I want. And if someone doesn't like it, what are they gonna do? Kill me? I'm the king of the world. In fact, watch this. Gimme that phone.

SAM whips out a fancy new cell phone.

MARY Oh! Who are you calling?

SAM I'm calling the White House.

MARY The White House? Sam!

SAM dials 411 on his cell phone.

SAM Shh, yes, what city please? I'll tell you what city please. Washington, D.C., that's what city please. …Mm-hm, the White House. …You heard me: the White House. …Well I don't know which number. Gimme the president's number. …*(to MARY:)* Not listed. *(to operator:)* Well then give me whatever that number is that people can call in and say what's on their mind. …You know the number I mean. That number people can call up and say what's on their mind. You can't tell me I'm the first person ever to speak his mind in Washington. Now look that number up. …Thank you. …It's ringing. …Ah, hello? Hello! …It's a machine. Nobody's home. Nobody's near the phone at the White House. What am I paying my taxes for if they don't even have someone to pick up the phone when they're not home? Alright, I'll leave a message. Press three? Here yuh go: three! …Hello. This is Sam Small. And I have something I wanna say. I just wanna say…

Elsewhere, CHLOE BANKS has stopped dancing and stares out into a terrible void. MAX is nearby dancing obliviously.

SAM Uh… I just wanna say…

After a pause, SAM lowers the phone from his ear, then hangs up.

MARY What is it Sam? Sam, what is it?

CHLOE BANKS I'm sick of this fast, exciting life.

MAX has heard CHLOE BANKS, but either doesn't comprehend her or doesn't want to. Either way, HIS dancing is now altered by the intrusion of introspection.

MARY …Sam?

SAM looks at MARY.

SAM Hey. Ain't nobody here but us chickens.

MARY smiles. SAM steps closer to MARY. HE looks down at her stomach. A romantic pop ballad starts to play in the distance beneath the techno beat.

SAM Mary? Is there anything you want to tell me?
MARY *(innocently)* No. …? …Sam. …Do you think you should–?
SAM Don't think. Dance…?

MARY takes SAM's hand. Despite the throbbing beat that continues to pulse beneath their pop ballad, SAM and MARY's dancing remains slow and romantic. The MYSTERIOUS AMERICAN MAN appears behind his harsh spotlight, which passes over CHLOE BANKS who turns her head to look at Sam and Mary, MAX dancing his guts out, MARGARET standing alone and already looking at Sam and Mary, MARY and SAM slow dancing, GIGI BOLT imagining her final bow, and ALBERT counting a thick stack of money. The spotlight dims and the MYSTERIOUS AMERICAN MAN disappears. The beat of the techno music begins to grow stronger again, gradually overwhelming the pop ballad. EVERYONE begins to get caught up in it again if they weren't already, and soon their dancing bounces to its most desperate, exhausted, and treacherous height!

Episode Twenty-three

The music explodes to a halt. ALBERT steps up to a microphone. The CROWD punctuates his speech vocally throughout. The MYSTERIOUS AMERICAN MAN is tucked somewhere off to the side, unseen and listening.

ALBERT Ladies and gentlemen! It's that time! The moment you have all been waiting for! Who will be the lucky winner? …But before I turn the microphone over to the man of the hour, let me say just a few words. As Sam's agent, his neighbor, and friend, I am deeply touched by the interest shown to him by all of you, and people around the globe. I want to personally thank my right hand lady, and your favorite barmaid, who has stood by my side and single handedly transformed this joint into the hippest club in town, let's give a big hand to

Margaret! ...And of course I must introduce the woman behind the man: the most gorgeous ex-waitress in town, Mary Small! ...Now Sam has a few words to say, and then after he bids us all farewell, the lovely Mary will personally take this envelope from his hand, open it, and announce the LUCKY WINNER! ...And now, it is my pleasure, and my honor, to introduce to you the man of not just the hour but the decade and the century, you know him, you love him, you spent your last dollar on him, please give a big hand for Mister Sam Small!

> *Huge applause! SAM steps up to the microphone, smiling nervously. ALBERT gives SAM the gun and fancy envelope, then steps away. SAM pulls a folded note out of one pocket, then another out of another pocket, and a third out of a third pocket, a fourth, and a fifth. For a moment, SAM is not sure what to do.*

ALBERT Uh, heh! You need some help there, Sam?

> *SAM drops all of the papers but one, which he unfolds and holds up. HE looks at the gun. Another pause, and SAM drops the paper. ALBERT quickly picks it up and tries to hand it to SAM.*

ALBERT Ope... Here you go... Right here, Sam... Would you like me to read it for you, Sam?
SAM No it's alright. I can do it. ...Uhm. Ladies and gentlemen. ...Uh. Ever since I was a little kid I wanted to be a genius, but my parents were against it.

> *EVERYONE laughs tentatively and nervously, which SAM didn't expect. Then he continues...*

SAM So what have I lived for since then? To be a number? No sir. ...All these years life has done nothing but mock me. ...Well I'll show life what's what! Life isn't going to take ME for a ride anymore! I'm taking LIFE! My life! And I'm gonna ride Hell's hand basket straight to Heaven! Nobody's gonna drag Sam Small down again! I will make a difference! If not in life, then in death!

> *By this time EVERYONE has already been punctuating SAM's speech with rousing cheers, but that last line puts them over the top. SAM is fully in the game.*

SAM What's that old clock on the wall say Albert?
ALBERT We got fifteen seconds, Sam!
SAM Fifteen seconds!

Drum roll. The crowd is going wild. SAM kisses MARY, says something to her that we can't hear and she nods to, and then takes his position with the gun and fancy envelope in hand. MARY, clenching back tears, puts on her best Vanna White.

ALBERT Let's count him down everybody! Ten!
EVERYONE Nine! Eight! Seven! Six! Five! Four! Three!! Two!!! One!!!!

On top of "one" MARY screams. But even this isn't as loud as:

EVERYONE Yeah!!!!!

SAM doesn't pull the trigger. There is a tense silence. SAM lowers the gun.

ALBERT Uh, just a little nervous everybody. It'll just be a moment. Sam. Sam, what's the matter?
SAM What am I doing?
ALBERT That's what I want to know? Everybody's waiting for you Sam.
SAM …I want to live.
ALBERT No you don't, you want to die.
SAM No. I want to live.

ALBERT turns to the crowd and laughs awkwardly, waving his hands and shaking his head "no."

ALBERT Heh heh! Huhhh. *(to SAM:)* What do you think you're doing? Do you know how much money you're blowing away? Think about Mary. Do you know how much all of this cost?
SAM I'm sorry, Albert, I can't do it.
MARY *(uncertainly)* Sam?
SAM I'm sorry, Mary.
MAX Is he going to do it or not?
MARGARET What are you waiting for Sam?
GIGI BOLT Do it for the soul Sam!
MARGARET Do it for commitment!
CHLOE BANKS Do it for me Sam!
MAX No, do it for me! / My career!
EVERYBODY BUT MARY You promised me, Sam! Do it for me! Do it for…

SAM points the gun in the air. EVERYONE goes silent.

SAM …No.
ALBERT You bastard, I'll kill you!
CHLOE BANKS He strung us along, the dirty fake!
GIGI BOLT The filthy liar!
MAX He's a fraud!
MARGARET You stole my future from me, Sam!
ALBERT I'm gonna sue! I'm gonna squeeze you for every last dime I SPENT on yuh!
GIGI BOLT You coward!
MARGARET You chicken!
CHLOE BANKS Chicken!
MARGARET, ALBERT & GIGI BOLT Chicken!!
SAM Fine, fine, I'll be the chicken! I'll run around with my head cut off, I don't care! But I want to live!
MAX Somebody grab the gun!
CHLOE BANKS Shoot him!
ALBERT Kill yourself!
EVERYBODY BUT MARY Kill your/self! *(or:)* Shoot / him! *(or:)* Do / it! *(or:)* Now!
SAM Wait! …You all want so badly for me to kill myself? You want me to die for your causes? For love? Money? Fame? To prove some point? If it's so important to you, here's the gun, go ahead, do it yourself. Come on, take it. Shoot yourself, please. Go ahead.

> *SAM goes about the room holding the gun by the barrel and offering the handle to different people, who each back away. MARGARET even leaves the room when SAM approaches her. SAM then looks out into the audience and offers the gun to a few of them. HE turns back to the stage and makes one final sweep, holding out the handle of the gun for anyone to take…*

SAM Here chic chic chic! Here chic chic!

> *…but THEY all back away again.*

SAM You're all afraid. And what was it you were just accusing me of? What was my crime? That I chose life over a lucrative death? What kind of people are you? What kind of COUNTRY is this? What kind of WORLD? You all wanted me to die! But what am I guilty of? Nothing! I've never hurt anyone in my life! No one can say otherwise! And none of YOU can say as much! I might not be the smartest man, I might not have a job, I might not even be worth the shoes I'm standing in! But none of you, not one, can say that I am responsible for hurting a single person on this earth!

> *MARGARET bursts in.*

MARGARET Everybody listen, I just heard on the radio in the kitchen, it's all over the news!
EVERYBODY What? What is it? Sam? Am I on the news? etc…
MARGARET Shhh! …Right at midnight, thousands of people across the country and all over the world–! …committed suicide.

> *EVERYONE turns and looks at SAM. MARY faints. CHLOE BANKS, MAX, and GIGI BOLT each walk out in different directions – GIGI BOLT up the theatre aisle, of course. The MYSTERIOUS AMERICAN MAN slips away as well. ALBERT and MARGARET stare at SAM, who is stunned. With a sputtering buzz, the lights flicker. Then at the sound of a massive electrical switch they go out.*

The end.

BANG!

a backstage fringe comedy

BANG!

The world premiere of *BANG!* was presented by Art Street Theatre at EXIT Stage Left, San Francisco, CA, on March 5, 1999. The production was directed by the author, with the following cast and staff:

ELEANOR	Caroline Ford
SHELLY	Beth Wilmurt
JIM	Chris Kuckenbaker
KATE	Karen Hallock
BENNY	Eric Miller
JOAN	Kathryn Clark
Sound	Jake Rodriguez
Set, lights and costumes	Ana Hashimoto
Dramaturgy	Gillian Brecker and Kathryn Clark
Stage Manager	Kathryn Clark

BANG! was subsequently produced by The Play Café at the 2004 Edinburgh Festival Fringe. The production was directed and designed by Joan Grinde, with the following cast and staff:

ELEANOR	Elizabeth Daly
SHELLY	Miranda Calderon
JIM	Thor Aagaard
KATE	Lily Oglesby
BENNY	Warden Lawlor
JOAN	Joan Grinde
Composer	Karole Langlois
Movement	Lauren Steiner

Cast of Characters

Eleanor, an audience member who once was mute but now can speak.
Shelly, an actress who cannot decide.
Kate, an actress on the go.
Jim, an actor slash playwright, caught between panic and conviction.
Benny, a director and ardent quoter of life.
Joan, a stage manager, period.

Time and Place

Now, onstage and then backstage.

Note

Indented dialogue is to be spoken simultaneously with the dialogue immediately following until the point indicated by ***, at which point both sections of dialogue should come to their conclusion.

A slash in the dialogue (/) indicates that the next actor should start their line, creating overlapping speech.

Preshow

Upstage there are fifty empty chairs grouped on risers in a few rows. The front row is flanked on the left and right by the backs of flats or curtains. Downstage, the clutter of a dressing room.

ELEANOR is sitting in one of the chairs with a program in hand, her mind a million miles away. Eventually, BENNY enters and passes ELEANOR to stand as far back into the corner behind the rows of chairs as he can possibly squeeze.

Scene One and Only

Suddenly, the play begins and the actors – SHELLY, KATE and JIM – pounce the stage. Light cues flicker rapidly and the sound hurdles forward through the loudspeakers as the actors scramble about enacting the entire show in a matter of moments. It is evidently an intense and complicated play with quite an absurd range of elements and emotions. It should appear somewhat ridiculous. Suddenly the ACTORS screech to a halt for the last scene.

SHELLY Go ahead. Surprise me.
JIM I'm all out of surprises. The last of 'em went out with the garbage yesterday, didn't it? Ask some other sucker; I'm not moving.
SHELLY You have to do something. ...*Do something*. The country won't cave in, Jim. Love her. Love me. It doesn't matter.
KATE No, Shelly, it matters. It matters to me. I know this now. It's not that I have to be with him for the rest of my life; It's that I can't not be with him. ...It's almost an unfortunate situation, being in love.
SHELLY What do you know about it? After all that's happened? Secrets!

Bombings! Murdering that innocent child before it had the chance to cry out at the first sight of your lousy world! What do you know about love? It was never you that he needed, Kate!

KATE He loves me!

SHELLY You used him!

KATE I'm not that tricky.

SHELLY You need to believe in that, don't you?

JIM Do you two hear what you're doing? Again? You talk as if I'm not in the room well I have been in the room all night! I have been in the room all my life! A statue. A crowbar maybe. The man who nods when a nod is required. I have done everything that was asked of me.

SHELLY And that is your choice.

JIM My choice?

KATE Jim, don't listen to her.

SHELLY There's no gun to your head. Nobody ever made you shut your trap. Nobody forced you to join her line. Tell me I'm wrong and I'll cry uncle! … Nothing. God, sometimes I wish you would slap me, spit on me, throw a chair at me from across the room, anything to let me know you are alive in there, that you can feel something!

KATE No. Jim, you are a good man. Please. Though you think so I have never taken you for granted. I never meant for things to get so thick. I can't bring the baby back but if you will forgive me that I will forget anything. The Cause. Her. Everything!

JIM Don't you see? It's not about that! Wake up! Wake up the world! I wake up! Every night! I wake up and my hand is reaching out. But I can never remember why. It's as if my dreams are held from me, *(he reaches out)* just out of sight. Every night there I am and I know that if when the sun rises I could still reach out, if I could only *reach out*, then someone, *someone* would take my empty hand and fill it! …Someone would! …At some point!

> *JIM has been reaching out his hand in such a way that it is blatantly obvious he hopes ELEANOR will take it. Now, she reluctantly complies.*

JIM And like rain filling an empty desert, that palm filling my palm would bring new life! And I would know that I am not just between the two of you, or one cause and the other, but the sky and the earth, and that I am alive! *(lets ELEANOR's hand go)* I am alive!

> *Pause. Blackout. Pause. Lights up. ELEANOR applauds as the ACTORS bow. BENNY applauds as well. The ACTORS exit the stage as post-show music plays. BENNY scrambles past ELEANOR and runs after them. ELEANOR remains in her chair, clearly in a mix of emotion. Soon,*

JOAN shuffles in and out executing her various duties. But now we hear the actors as they enter the dressing room. They are bristling with post-performance electricity.

KATE That was the most embarrassing experience of my entire life! This show is a turd!

BENNY The worst is not, so long as we can say "this is the worst."

KATE Shut up, Benny.

BENNY *King Lear.*

KATE The rule is that if the actors out number the audience, the show does not go on.

BENNY "The show must go on." That's how the saying goes.

KATE I don't care how The Saying goes. Being out there tonight was worse than diarrhea.

BENNY One person is better than none.

KATE No no: Benny: none would be perfect. None would be what I have prayed for. Tonight was hideous! It was like death! Death, do you hear me?!

BENNY How do you think I felt standing out there?

KATE No you get to do your squirming in the dark. We have to do it up on the stage in front of everybody! Or one body, as the case might be! *We* didn't like it, *she* didn't like it, *no* one liked it! It's crap!

BENNY How do you know? She may have liked it.

KATE How do I know?! Benny, she was the only one out there! Nobody can enjoy a play when they're the only person in the audience! It is not possible. It is the ultimate distraction!

JIM I don't understand it. It makes no sense whatsoever. How could only one person show up?!

SHELLY At least she took your hand.

JIM Well who else was going to do it?

SHELLY That moment always makes me feel weird anyhow.

JIM *(stops)* It's the best part.

SHELLY I don't know.

JIM It's the whole show. Without it the whole thing would be meaningless.

SHELLY It's too pushy.

JIM Exactly! That's the whole struggle of my character. That's every one's struggle: Pushing our limits!

SHELLY You're right, you're right, you wrote it, you're right.

JIM …No it's crap, you're right its crap. Every time I'm out there waiting with my hand out my bowels sweat.

SHELLY Well then cut it.

JIM No. That would negate the whole show. We need to call more rehearsals. I don't care about the money.

SHELLY I don't think anyone wants to rehearse anymore.

JIM *(obviously)* But the show needs it.

SHELLY What the show needs is an audience!

JIM That's not funny. You're right! But that's not funny. We're in trouble. I don't understand why nobody showed up. One person!

***

JIM Benny!

BENNY Jim!

KATE Excuse me.

JIM Benny what is happening? Where is everybody?

> **SHELLY** Okay, I'm going to change my clothes everybody, so don't look. Don't look. Don't look. Don't look. Don't look. Don't look. Don't look. Don't look. Don't look… *(continues…)*

BENNY The beauty of the soul shines out when a man bears with composure one heavy mischance after another.

JIM What?

BENNY Aristotle.

JIM Benny! Where are the people?

BENNY I am as mystified as you are.

JIM Well you never seem very concerned, Mister Director.

BENNY To be unable to bear an ill is itself a great ill.

JIM What?

BENNY Bion, philosopher second century B.C.

JIM Benny! We are scandalous! We should be turning people away in droves!

BENNY I know.

JIM This play should piss people off. The Pro-choicers. The Right-To-Lifers. ACT UP. The NRA, the N double ACP. …Triple A.

BENNY It is inflammatory, yes.

JIM Only if there is an audience to see it.

BENNY That is true.

JIM …Well respond please!

BENNY Fate has no reprieve.

JIM What?
BENNY Euripides.

***

        KATE Why are you saying that? Nobody is looking at you.
        SHELLY I just want to be courteous.
        KATE It's a dressing room. Jesus.
BENNY Look, Jim, we can only do what we're already doing. It's not that bad. So we had another slow night.
JIM A slow night?!
BENNY Calmness.

***

JIM One out of fifty seats sold! Those are bad figures Benny.
BENNY If we were doing it for the money, yes. But *we're* not doing this for the *money*.
JIM Yeah well it sure would be nice to make some of it back! Money *is* important! But I'm not even talking about the money! The money is not important! I want people to *see my play!* I mean the houses haven't been great but they haven't been empty. *(suspicious)* Then suddenly, on a _____ night, nobody shows up?
KATE *(to herself, a realization)* Shit!
JIM That is very peculiar, don't you think?
KATE Excuse me. *(exits quickly)*
BENNY Well, maybe it is too offensive.
JIM Oh come on if you put on a play that offends everybody you get an audience. It's math, Benny, its two plus two equals four. It's ____*night* for cryin' out loud!

    JOAN, the stage manager, enters the dressing room. SHELLY sings to herself as she goes about her business, somewhat distractedly.

        JOAN Benny.... Benny.... Benny.... Benny.... Benny.... Benny.... *(etcetera)*
BENNY Jim, it's out of our hands. There is nothing we can do about it now. We're listed in all the papers. We took out ads we have posters up we sent out postcards. We rehearsed for three months. You wrote a very interesting play.
JIM Interesting?
BENNY Yes.

JIM Interesting is a friendly word for terrible.
BENNY That is not what I meant.
JIM *(dawning)* You *do* hate it.
BENNY No I do not!
JIM I knew you hated it! And you're right! / I failed! Oh god I failed! Oh my god! Its *not* working!
BENNY No, Jim, it's poetic, it's funny, it's meaningful. It's got a few problems, of course, it's a new play. Maybe I staged it wrong!
JIM Benny.
BENNY What?
JOAN Benny.
JIM *(pointing)* Joan.
BENNY *(to JOAN)* What?!
JOAN Now that I have your undivided.
BENNY Sorry, Joan, yes.

> *After a pause, JIM dashes for his script and begins to thumb through, looking at specific passages and analyzing them with intense scrutiny. SHELLY eventually stares at herself in a mirror, lost in pre-marital thought.*

JOAN Tonight is the night I have to leave early, recall? We talked about this.
BENNY Yes, give me the keys and I will lock up.
JOAN I would turn everything off myself but the *audience still hasn't left her seat.*
BENNY Why not?
JOAN I don't know, she's reading the program.
BENNY Do you think she liked it? I mean, could you judge her reaction from the booth?

> *KATE soon enters the dressing room looking miffed and secretive.*

JOAN I'm not judgmental. Here are the keys. Double check everything. Make sure all the equipment is off and the lights are out. Lock every door that locks. I don't want the one night I break protocol and leave first to be the night something bad happens.
BENNY Everything will be fine, just go.
JOAN You have to be the last one out that door.
BENNY I understand. I'll take care of everything, now go have a good time.
JOAN I'm going to the airport on a _____ night so I can fly to Vegas and

watch my mother get *married* again, not to have a good time.
BENNY Welllll make the best of it.
JOAN I'll make a gin and tonic. Goodbye actor people!

The ACTORS drop what they are doing and all chime in...

ACTORS Thank you Joan!

...JOAN signals and THEY continue on as before.

JOAN *(to BENNY)* Enjoy your meeting.
BENNY Look, Joan, could you check on that woman again as you leave
>   **BENNY** and let her know we're trying to close up shop so we can have our meeting.
>   **JOAN** Don't say I never did you a favor.
>   **BENNY** And be polite with her please.
>   **JOAN** Of course. *(exits)*

JIM Forget it! Forget it! Just forget it!
SHELLY What's wrong?

JIM has crossed into an aisle amidst the real audience and is momentarily confused, then returns to the stage proper.

JIM What am I doing? I have to change my clothes. What? Oh. The play is crap and its all my fault!
SHELLY Oh no.
JIM Yes it is, it's terrible.

***

>   *BENNY approaches KATE happily. KATE attempts to keep her irritation, and so also the conversation, at low volume.*
>
>   **BENNY** So, Kate, about that rain check. We should pick a night to go get dinner this week.
>   **KATE** It's a busy week for me, Benny.
>   **BENNY** Okay, well, do you think you'll have some time?
>   **KATE** I don't know, I really... I don't know. Can we wait? Do we have to figure this out now?
>   **BENNY** No, we don't have to figure it out. Should we make a

plan to make a plan?
KATE Benny, I'm sorry, I want to go out, I do, I've just got a lot to do this week, okay?
BENNY Okay, maybe next week then. How's next week?
KATE You know I don't like to plan that far ahead.
BENNY Amid a multitude of projects, no plan is devised.
KATE Look.
BENNY Publilius Syrus.
KATE I'm sorry, I did not enjoy tonight, okay, so could you just give me a moment to deal with that, please, so that I do not strangle you.
BENNY Certainly.
KATE Thank you.
BENNY Don't forget we're having a meeting.
KATE Yes, Dear.

BENNY busies himself with cleaning up. KATE busies herself with getting changed and ready to go, etcetera.

SHELLY It's not that bad. It's political theatre.
JIM Well what does that mean?
SHELLY Well. *You* know.
JIM Just because a play says something doesn't automatically make it bad.
SHELLY You're right, I know, I'm sorry. You're right. I was just, nn-nn-nn. …Listen do you think the meeting tonight will take long?
JIM What?
SHELLY I said do you think tonight's meeting will take long?
JIM I don't know.
SHELLY Because my fiancé is coming to meet me tonight.
JIM Who?
SHELLY My fiancé. We're madly in love.
JIM Oh, him, yeah, I don't know, I can't imagine it taking too long. Have you two, uh, set a wedding date yet?
SHELLY That's why we're going out tonight. We're going to go get a drink and set a date. A wedding date.
JIM You need a drink first?
SHELLY Not a *drink*, we're not going to *get drunk*. A glass of wine. Something romantic.
JIM That should be nice.

SHELLY Yes. If you like that sort of thing.

JIM What, romance?

***

> *JOAN has entered the house to speak with ELEANOR.*

JOAN Excuse me, we're trying to go home, do you mind?

> **ELEANOR** Oh, well, I'd like to meet the cast if that's alright.
>
> **JOAN** You can wait for them out in the hall. They'll show their faces eventually.
>
> **ELEANOR** Oh alright.
>
> **JOAN** My pleasure.

> *JOAN shows ELEANOR out and then closes the curtains and exits.*

JIM *(180 degrees)* Why can't a play be political? Huh? What is wrong with politics? Politics fill the news! It's what people talk about everyday! Clinton this, Wall Street that! Everywhere you look there's politics! But no, not on stage! –Oh! unless of course it's fashionable. I could write a play about being a woman molested as a child and that would be just fine. I could strip to my skivies and say I'm a black gay man and proud of it and what's left of the NEA would give me a grant. But get up there and say you're a socialist, or that having only two political parties represented in Washington is killing democracy in America, or that we're popping out too many babies and maybe Jonathan Swift was on to something when he made that Modest Proposal, and everybody gets annoyed!

***

SHELLY Have you seen my blue eyeliner?

KATE So are we having that meeting or what?

BENNY Yes.

KATE Good. Let's get to it, shall we?

BENNY We shall sooner have the fowl by hatching the egg than by smashing it.

KATE What?

BENNY Abraham Lincoln. Patience.

SHELLY Will this take long? My fiancé is coming to meet me soon.

BENNY Who?

SHELLY My fiancé. We're madly in love.
KATE Oh, do we finally get to meet this allusive fiancé?
SHELLY *(laughs awkwardly)*
BENNY Kindness it is that brings forth kindness always.
KATE Benny.
BENNY Sophocles. Be nice.
KATE Let's go!
BENNY So. …Thank you all for agreeing to stay late. I don't pretend to know *your* exact thoughts – that's why were here, to give everyone a chance to openly speak her or his mind – but I feel that it is pretty clear that the show is not going as well as one might hope.
KATE Turds float better than this shit!
JIM Thank you! / Thank you, Kate! I'm only sitting right over here! Hello, here I am!
SHELLY / *(ears covered and singing)* Wheh eh eh eh ere, is love?
BENNY Kate. Jim. Alright. Thank you. Thank you Shelly. Thank you. …Now: Jim has expressed his conviction that we might need to call more rehearsals.
JIM Yes!
BENNY And I would agree that it wouldn't *hurt*… How do you two feel about that?
KATE I think my opinion on that is known throughout the land.
BENNY Okay, thank you. Shelly?
SHELLY Well. Uh. Sure– I mean: if everyone else wants to.
KATE What? Shelly. Tell them what you told me yesterday.
SHELLY Kate.
KATE Because I think it's about time someone did something to help flush this turd down the toilet.
BENNY Kate, would you please cut the turds.
JIM No she's right! It stinks!
KATE Even the playwright agrees.
JIM *(definite)* We need to call more rehearsals!
KATE I think this is your cue, Shelly.
SHELLY Kate!
BENNY What is it, Shelly?
SHELLY Kate, that was my business!
JIM Just say it Shelly what is it?
SHELLY Nothing, it's nothing, I'll tell you later.
KATE *(gruff, as to a dog)* Come on, Shelly.
SHELLY Kate! It's nothing it's nothing. Everyone just go back to what you

were doing.
KATE This is what we're doing. Now say it.
JIM What's going on?
SHELLY Nothing.
KATE Shelly.
SHELLY It's nothing.
KATE She's quitting the show.
SHELLY God!!! Kate!!!
JIM What?
BENNY Shelly, why?
SHELLY …It grates on my stability. I don't agree with the idea of having an ideology… Has anyone seen my blue eyeliner?
BENNY Shelly. You can't just quit, we don't have an understudy. Besides, we only have ____ weekend(s) left.
SHELLY *(making light of it)* I know, I know.
JIM I am shocked.
SHELLY Jim it's not your script, your script is- -great. It's just not for me.
JIM Not for you?
SHELLY I- I don't agree with it.
JIM You're an actress! You don't have to agree with it!
BENNY Shelly, please reconsider.
SHELLY I know, you're right. *(making light)* I'm not quitting, you're right, I was just- talking aloud you know, the magic "what if." Where's my eyeliner! But I want to. Quit, I mean.
JIM She wants to quit.
SHELLY I'd like to.
JIM It *is* a turd.
SHELLY No no.
JIM A hot steaming turd!
SHELLY Ew.
BENNY Now let's calm down; The show- is not- a turd.
SHELLY I don't like that word.
JIM It's a stinking soapbox!
KATE It's embarrassing.
BENNY Kate.
KATE I'm *glad* only one person had to see me up there tonight!
BENNY Nay, come, Kate, come; you must not look so sour.
KATE Would you stop quoting.
BENNY Though old the thought and oft exprest, 'Tis his at last who says it

best.

KATE Stop that!

JIM I have something to say!

JOAN *(having entered)* But before you do, just know that your entire audience is waiting outside in the hall to meet you.

BENNY ...She is?

JOAN She enjoyed herself. Go figure.

BENNY Well, that's great!

JOAN Yes it is. We're a hit.

BENNY She really liked it?

JOAN She's been talking my ear off for the last ___ minutes. Now I'm deaf. And I've got a plane to catch. Good night everybody.

ALL Thank you Joan.

JOAN exits.

BENNY You see everyone, she liked it.

KATE She must be a retard.

BENNY Uh– Jim, what were you going to say?

JIM *(stunned)* She liked it? ...No, *she* didn't like it! She's lying! I have nothing to say. I don't even know why I bothered writing this damn play. I don't have anything to say to anybody. But I will say this! I know we're not making any money. But we've worked long and hard and the least we can do is hold out until the end. It cant be *that* bad?

KATE It is sooo *bad*.

JIM What!?

KATE It is excruciating. It's like bamboo torture. I like you Jim, believe it or not, I still do. But it is so painful–

JIM –Oh!– Why?! Why is it so painful for you?

KATE Eh– There's too much exposition, we stand around talking about something the audience never saw, it's self referential, it's preachy, it's way too political–

JIM –Here we go again!: What is wrong with politics! If Clifford Odets were alive today–

KATE –Clifford Odets is not alive today and there's a reason for that.

SHELLY He had a heart attack.

JIM In 1935 *Waiting For Lefty* got a forty-five minute, hysterical, standing ovation. Clifford Odets was back stage vomiting he was so overwhelmed. That could never happen in the theatre today–

KATE –Exactly my point!–

JIM –and it's wrong! It's wrong! It *should* happen! People *should* care! People *should* yell "strike" with the characters onstage! People should get up and scream and go crazy and riot in the streets!

KATE If people get up because of this show, Jim, they'll be getting up to leave. The gutsy ones will yell rubbish as they go.

JIM That would be great!

KATE Wrong, / wrong, wrong!

JIM It would be a reaction! That's the whole purpose!

KATE Jim, the purpose is to entertain them, not to annoy them!

SHELLY Can we not fight?

KATE You can't just stick your finger in people's faces.

JIM Well what would you stick in their face?

KATE Nothing.

> *KATE bends over to pick something up, thus sticking her butt in the face of the front row of the real audience.*

JIM I state what I believe to be the truth. And what I believe happens to be political. That in and of itself shouldn't be a problem in life. But: say something blatantly political on stage and everybody complains: "Oh it's the author's voice! Ew!" What about a big blatant *love* story? Why isn't that ever the author's voice? Love, no, that's just fine, but politics, heaven forbid we talk about the *very thing that makes us who we are!*

KATE Why am I even trying? It's too late, anyway.

BENNY If everyone would just sit down.

> *SHELLY sits.*

BENNY Thank you, Shelly.

KATE Look, tomorrow I have to go to work after my morning spinning class which means I'm up at six AM and after work I have an audition, a chiropractic appointment, and a prescription to pick up before I come *here* again so please call me if luck has it and you cancel the rest of the run. Good night.

BENNY Kate, you're not helping company morale.

> *During the following explosion of argument, ELEANOR enters and observes from a distance.*

KATE What company morale?! We've all hated this for weeks!

JIM *You've* hated this for weeks!

BENNY Yes don't speak for other people, Kate.

KATE Did you not just hear what Shelly said? / She wanted to quit!

SHELLY I took it back I took it back!

BENNY / This is not helping our situation.

JIM You have done nothing but fight this show from the beginning, which is very peculiar given that you were sooo excited to be a part of it *before* you got cast!

KATE / I *was* excited about it! It was exciting!

> **SHELLY** Peace. Peace now. No fighting! No confleect! No conefleectomundo! You guys! Stop it! *(singing a la Carmen)* I don't like it, when people fight, I do not like it when they fight like this! *(speaking)* You guys! My fiancé is coming to pick me up any minute! You better stop! I'm gonna have to leave! You guys! *(singing again)* I don't like it, when people fight, I do not like it when they fight like this! When people fight, I do not like, I do not like it when the people fight! etcetera…

JIM "Oh the script is great Jim! Oh it's so timely Jim! It's gonna be a great show! I'm so excited!"

KATE / Oh come on, Jim.

JIM Then once you get cast suddenly it's turd this and turd that! Everything's a problem! You wouldn't even be here in the first place if Benny weren't in love with you!

KATE That is not true!

BENNY / Now, Jim, let's be fair!

JIM Oh come on Kate! You're not that dumb! He's in love with you, / that's why you're here!

BENNY Jim, I think we're straying from the purpose / of this meeting. Kate, it's alright.

KATE Our relationship is none of your business / and you don't know a thing about it!

JIM I'm sorry I said that out loud Benny / but I have had it with her mediocre attitude! *(to KATE)* It's mediocre!

BENNY That's okay.

KATE / Don't take that from him Benny.

JIM If you weren't always running around / with your head cut off doing a million things at once maybe you'd finally be able to make a commitment to something!

BENNY Kate, we can talk about it later. / I cast you because you're a good actress.

KATE He's insulting you left and right. *(to JIM)* Wait a minute what? What are you saying?

JIM / What are you doing?!
BENNY / Shelly would you please!
KATE Would you shut up Shelly!

***

ELEANOR Excuse me! …Excuse me. I'm sorry to interrupt.
BENNY Hello.
ELEANOR I was in the audience tonight?
BENNY We noticed you there, yes.
ELEANOR I'm sorry to interrupt… *(excitedly)* Were you just rehearsing?
BENNY No. No we were just having little a meeting. May I help you?
ELEANOR Well I just wanted to say what a wonderful job I thought you all did tonight, / it was a very powerful experience.
BENNY Oh, well thank you. … Really?
ELEANOR Very powerful.
BENNY *(to the CAST)* That's great.
JIM Thank you.
ELEANOR *(to KATE)* You were sooo sweet! My heart just dropped for you.
KATE Thanks.
ELEANOR *(to SHELLY)* And you were very dramatic. Such powerful words.
SHELLY *(smiles awkwardly.)* huh–uh…
ELEANOR *(JIM and KATE)* And the way the two of you first met, ah! So touching.
JIM Thank you.
ELEANOR Very moving.
JIM Thank you very much.
ELEANOR You also wrote it, correct?
JIM Yes I did.
ELEANOR And you're the director?
KATE Ha!
BENNY …Yes I am.
ELEANOR Well it was just terrific. All of you.
JIM Thank you.
BENNY Thank you.
ELEANOR Oh! I'm rude, my name is Eleanor.
JIM / Very nice to meet you, Eleanor.
ALL Hi. Hello. Etc.

ELEANOR *(waving program)* I know all of your names.

KATE May I ask: why you came tonight– how you got in?

ELEANOR I saw the sign.

KATE You *saw* the sign.

ELEANOR Well, poster, in the window of that corner store.

KATE Oh. …But you came in the front door?

ELEANOR Yes. …I should explain. You see I'd been walking aimlessly all day – all my life, actually, but that's a whole 'nother drama. *(chortles)* …Anyway, I was walking and walking and I was about to flag down a cab to get to the Golden Gate Bridge so that I could– well, you know, throw myself into the ocean, –when I saw your poster! And I thought to myself: *Ah,* I have never seen a play before. In all my life I'd never gone to the theatre. Isn't that odd? I saw that the theatre was just down the block and I thought: here I am, as they say there is no time like the present, I might as well see a play before I jump. I'm not on anyone's schedule anymore. I quit my job today. –Well, I called in sick. But I know that I quit… Anyway– Now, mind you, I was in a terrible state. My make-up was running down my face from crying and I just looked awful. I had come early so I bought my ticket and went into the ladies room to sit down and collect myself. Then eventually I came in and found a seat– I was a million miles away; I didn't even glance at the program. I was still feeling just pathetic. And then the play! *Oh,* the play! I am so glad I decided to stop and see it. You were just so inspiring to me. I don't exactly have the words quite yet, but I've been thinking about it while I've been waiting in the hall and, something about it– …it has changed my life.

KATE …Right, and you didn't find it odd that you were the only person in the audience?

ELEANOR No. I didn't think much about it, actually. As I said, I've never been to the theatre before.

JIM *(stunned)* It has changed your life.

ELEANOR Oh yes. I feel– different somehow.

BENNY *(doubtful)* Really.

JIM That is great!

KATE Lovely. Benny? Could you…?

BENNY Yes. Uh, well, thank you very much for your comments, we appreciate them highly–

JIM –It is always gratifying to hear that one's work is appreciated. Thank you very much.

BENNY Yes. Thank you. But: we are in the middle of a meeting at the moment, actually, that we need to finish, so, uh, thank you for coming tonight, aaaand please tell your friends.

ELEANOR Are you discussing the play?

BENNY Yes, we are.
ELEANOR Oh I would love to listen in! If that's okay.

BENNY looks to KATE. Her opinion is clear.

BENNY Eeeeeeewell, actually, I'm afraid it's a private company meeting.
ELEANOR …I was going to shoot myself in the head and fall off the Golden Gate Bridge into the Pacific ocean tonight but after watching your play I have found a reason to live… *(pure enthusiasm)* And I'd really like to stay!
BENNY Oh. Uhm. Well, I'm glad we were able to- -give you a reason to live, but-
JIM That is wonderful!
ELEANOR You don't even know!
JIM What was it, exactly, that made you feel that way?
KATE Benny, / dear, may I have a moment?
BENNY / Yes.

BENNY and KATE whisper heatedly to the side.

ELEANOR Oh, many things. You're relationship with Kate. And what she said about how the common person is rendered silent by the modern societal machine. If I understood that correctly, that's me! My childhood, my job, my entire life. The way you spoke with each other so openly, I have never been able to do that myself, and when she said to you that one voice can be heard I thought, that is right, it can!
JIM That is great!
SHELLY Why were you going to shoot yourself and jump off the bridge? Oh! I'm sorry, that was rude.
ELEANOR Oh, that's alright. I brought it up, I suppose.
SHELLY It's just that you seem so happy. I can't imagine why would you. Jump, I mean.
ELEANOR Well, the usual reasons. …I live alone… But enough about *me*, let's talk about *the play!*

KATE shoves BENNY back toward the group.

BENNY I'm! sorry to interrupt. Jim, Shelly, we really should be getting back to the meeting. It is late.
ELEANOR Please may I stay I won't be a bother! I'll just sit off to the side.
BENNY Well I don't think our meeting would really be of much interest to

you.

ELEANOR Oh!

JIM Actually, I think we have a rare opportunity to get some feedback from a member of our audience.

KATE *The* member, if you will.

JIM Maybe we should have her stay and ask her some questions.

ELEANOR Oh I would love that. Please! Please!

JIM What do you say, Benny?

BENNY Uh… …That would probably be beneficial–

KATE –Oh!

JIM Great! Here, let's get you a chair.

SHELLY This means the meeting is going to go longer?

BENNY *(to KATE)* We'll just ask her a few / questions. It'll be good.

SHELLY Because my fiancé is coming to meet me and…

ELEANOR Oh how exciting! Now, as I said, this was my first play. So I'm no expert but I'll do my best… *(pause. Then, thrilled)* So!

JIM So. Benny, ask her a question.

BENNY Oh, okay. Uh–

JIM –You were saying about the common person, and being heard.

ELEANOR *Yes!*

JIM …Well– …what about it?

ELEANOR Oh! It's wonderful!

JIM …Okay, uuuh, by "it" do you meannn–? …What do you mean?

ELEANOR Well. Kate. And Shelly. And you. You made me want to stand up for *my*self too. I've never been able to protest or– no not complain– to *defend* myself out loud. But I feel it inside. To see each of you fight so hard for what you wanted. And that you *went* through so much. It was your personal or, your emotional battles that touched me, really, and that you would share them with me so openly. I could never do that before but now I think–

JIM –Okay, but how did you feel about the political aspects of the play? About how we handled them?

ELEANOR …Well… They were explicit. I didn't really pay much attention to that, actually.

KATE Ha!

ELEANOR Am I wrong? Did I miss something? Am I wrong?

JIM No, no, whatever you experienced is what we want to hear.

ELEANOR It is my first play.

JIM That's fine. We want to hear what *you* think.

ELEANOR Okay, well, I didn't think much about those political things. But as

I said I've never been much of a revolutionary, of *any* kind. I just loved–

JIM –So– …So, you didn't feel that by placing the love story in a greater political context, the petty concerns of love were elevated to a more substantial level, and that, by the same token, the social-political world of the play was juxtaposed against the lesser love story so that, just as the personal is made meaningful by the social, the social-political was made acceptable to you as an audience member by the comparatively inconsequential personal conflicts between the characters.

ELEANOR I'm sorry?

BENNY Did the politics bother you?

ELEANOR Oh. Well, again, I'm no expert. But my mind did tend to wander during those, I guess you're saying, political scenes. I just don't follow much of that sort of thing. It's all so… far away. But it was heartbreaking how that, uh, "The Cause," got between the three of you, so in that sense I suppose you do need to have all that political talk in order to explain things. I'm still not exactly certain what The Cause was. …But you're so brave to share your story. That is what I found inspiring.

KATE What did you think about our names?

ELEANOR …They're nice names.

JIM Did it make you, I mean, knowing that the character's names were our names as well, did that– …do anything for you?

ELEANOR Well, you are the characters. *I mean,* they're you. It's about you.

JIM Right– well, they're just characters but we chose– *I* chose– to use our real names.

ELEANOR …You mean–? *(to KATE)* …So you've never had an abortion?

KATE No.

ELEANOR That didn't happen? The three of you aren't in love?

KATE No.

ELEANOR *(to JIM)* And you never fought for those causes?

JIM Well no, not personally. But I believe in them. No, I just used the same names because– well, my intent: was to heighten the sense that this stuff is Real.

ELEANOR …Well that's very disappointing. I thought you *actually* cared about those things.

JIM Well I do. About the themes. But the story is made up.

SHELLY You thought it was autobiographical?

KATE You see? It implies that we all have some sort of direct, literal connection to our characters. *Which* we do not.

SHELLY Yeah.

JIM *(corrective)* Yes you do.

KATE They're characters, Jim, that *You Wrote*.

JIM How many times do we have to go through this, Kate? You have to believe in what your character believes.
KATE Tell him, Benny.
BENNY An actor who believes that he really is King Lear is emotionally ill.
JIM Benny.
BENNY Sonia Moore.
JIM Obviously I don't mean it like that. But you have to *believe in what you're doing* if you expect other people to– I mean, you don't have to *actually* believe it or, go blow up a catholic church or abort a baby or– I mean, obviously you don't have to actually believe– I mean, if I were playing Macbeth I certainly wouldn't go out and stab a– you know, I mean, just to– …Line!
JOAN *(from the real tech booth)* What am I even talking / about.
JIM What am I even talking about? You know this, it's acting! Jesus it's acting!
ELEANOR Well then why did you lie about your names?
JIM …Those are our real names.
ELEANOR What I mean is, if you never actually did those things in the play, why did you use your names? That's lying.
SHELLY I never understood the name thing either.
JIM As I said: I wanted it to be real, and personal. It's not *lying*. I thought it would make it seem more convicted. I never thought anyone would really think that we did the things our characters do, I mean, that would be crazy, I mean, no, we're not King Lear, of course. …You thought that *we actually* did those things.
ELEANOR It seemed like you meant it.
SHELLY Told you! That's what I was saying but nobody would listen to me. That's what I was trying to *tell* you guys in the beginning. They're characters, they should have their own names. I'm not *Shelly*. I mean, I, Shelly, don't act like Shelly my character. I don't– *do* that kind of stuff. It's like you sneak up with our real names and put 'em on the program and try to make everyone think that we all really did this stuff. I don't believe in everything this play says.
JIM But we want them to *think* that you do. Ahg! Benny, would you help me please. This should be so simple.
BENNY She makes a good point.
SHELLY Good point, Shelly!
JIM What? You said the names were a good idea.
BENNY Yes. Yes I did. But.
JIM –But you didn't *actually* think so!
BENNY No, now– …You seemed to think it would work and I didn't want to say No to something just because at first it didn't seem like a good idea to *me*. What if I were wrong?

JIM You're the director; you're supposed to be weeding out the bad ideas.

BENNY Where there is an open mind, there will always be a frontier.

JIM What?

KATE It's one of his favorites.

BENNY Charles F. Kettering. Where there is an open mind, there will always be a frontier.

JIM Okay, well, eventually you settle the frontier. I mean isn't that what happens? You make a decision Benny! You do know what a decision is don't you?

KATE Don't attack Benny. He *went* with the names, he went with *your* decision. True, he could try making some decisions of his own once in a while. But you *fought* for the name thing, Jim, come on. "It's the most important part! It's the whole show!" Just like the hand.

JIM Ah! What about the hand?

ELEANOR The hand.

SHELLY Not the hand!

JIM The hand, at the end, where you took my hand.

ELEANOR Oh. Yes. Actually. I wanted to ask you about that.

JIM Please.

ELEANOR …Why did you do that?

JIM Well, what do *you* think?

ELEANOR …I hated it.

JIM …Benny she hated it. You told me that was a good idea too.

BENNY Jim, you wanted to keep it in.

KATE Yeah, that was "The Whole Show" too, remember?

JIM *(to ELEANOR)* …You didn't feel that by taking my hand, by breaking the barrier between audience and actor, that you had a greater sense of the power of contact, the immediate and present need for contact in modern society, that we can't just pretend, like actors do, to make commitments to one another but that we must actually make actual contact if we hope to improve our lives!

ELEANOR No. Until that moment I was enjoying myself. When you made me take your hand it burst my bubble.

KATE / Ah HA!

SHELLY Yeah!

ELEANOR I'm not an actor.

JIM You could have chosen not to take my hand.

KATE Oh come on Jim you were practically slapping her in the face! She had no escape.

JIM She could have resisted. That would have been just as meaningful.

KATE You are such a hypocrite.

JIM *(serious)* Don't! call me that.

ELEANOR So you *don't* really love each other, do you?

KATE ...No. We played characters in a play. Theatre, play, illusion... You've seen a *movie* before, haven't you?

BENNY Kindness, Kate.

ELEANOR Yes but movies are fake.

KATE The play: is fake, okay?

ELEANOR Then why don't you make a movie? Why are you getting up there and doing it in front of people?

KATE You know I ask myself that all the time and I have no idea.

ELEANOR Well. That's not very good. I mean if you're going to go to the trouble of doing all of that in front of people night after night one might assume you would have a real reason.

JIM There we go! Hear that? That is what I'm talking about!

ELEANOR I mean it's embarrassing, after all, to get up in front of people.

JIM Yes! It is embarrassing! And that's what makes it great! Because it's embarrassing but you get up there anyway and you do it in front of people! Theatre is proof that we are mortal!

KATE Well I wouldn't go that far. But it is proof that we can look like idiots. If it were a book at least you could snap it shut and hurl it across the room; at the movies the actors aren't really there. But in the theatre you have to sit there and face these poor fools who are *actually* up there, *actually* being bad, and they know it's bad, and they know you know it's bad, and it's just *excruciating waiting for the whole thing to the end!*

JIM Theatre is the poetry of the performing arts.

KATE Well that's pretty, Jim. But you can count on your hands how many people actually read poetry anymore.

JIM There is still a poetry section at every Barnes & Noble in every mall across this country.

KATE Yeah, and it's bigger than the theatre section. And all the theatre section has is Shakespeare and those big Andrew Lloyd Webber books. We will never make a living doing *this,* Jim! Nobody wants it. This is America and Clifford Odets is dead. If you plan on making any money at all, ever, with this kind of play, which I assume you would like to do, then you've got to reinvent the entire history of this country, which is short, has all to do with money and very little to do with theatre, or art in general beyond old *habits dragged over from the Mother Country.*

JIM So then, Miss Americana, what are *you* doing here?

KATE I thought this was going to be good. It *sounded* good.

JIM Why? You don't like politics.

KATE No, Jim, no, you have never understood this. I do not oppose your politics. Or you. I oppose your play.

JIM What's the difference? I *am* my politics. They are my beliefs and make me who I am. And my play is my expression of that and therefore to reject my play is to reject both me and my politics.

KATE You and your politics are confused.

JIM I don't think so.

KATE *(to ELEANOR)* Okay: The Ending. What did you think about the ending?

ELEANOR I told you, I didn't like it.

KATE I don't mean the hand thing, I mean before that, the whole last scene. Did you know what was happening there?

ELEANOR Well–

JIM Obviously it sums up the whole–

KATE Ehp! Let her answer! Go ahead. What happened at the end?

ELEANOR Well. Shelly wanted Jim to abandon your Cause and go with her. And you were willing to give up the Cause if Jim would stay with you.

KATE And then Jim, what did he do?

ELEANOR …He stuck his hand in my face.

KATE Right, but what was he talking about?

ELEANOR Well I don't know exactly; I was very distracted by the hand. But he said something about not choosing either of you, or The Cause, and– being alive.

KATE That's it. *(to JIM)* What does that mean?

SHELLY It means we should cut the hand. *(covers her mouth)*

ELEANOR Yes, cut the hand.

KATE Besides that. What does that ending *mean*, Jim?

JIM It means– …I mean it's obvious.

KATE She doesn't know what it means.

JIM Because of the hand.

KATE Okay so let's say we cut the hand. Same dialogue. No hand. What does it mean? What's the last line?

JIM Uh. Tsch. Okay, I'm holding her hand–

SHELLY We cut the hand.

JIM Okay well I'm holding my hand out! and I say, uh, "that palm filling my palm would bring new life. And I would know that I am not just between the two of you, or one cause and the other, but the sky and the earth, and that I am alive. I am alive."

KATE Pause. Blackout. What does that mean?

JIM …Benny, would you explain this to her?

BENNY How much he gains who does not look to see what his neighbor says or does or thinks, but only at what he does himself.

JIM Jesus Christ.

BENNY Marcus Aurelius.

KATE *You* don't know what it means! You never decided. You don't choose me over Shelly. You don't choose love over politics or politics over love. You're hand is out there, and you're waiting. You choose to wait. You choose nothing. And then you say you're *alive?* What does that mean?

BENNY That's right, she's right.

SHELLY Yeah, what's up with that ending?

JIM Well, obviously, I choose politics.

KATE You, Jim, choose politics. But what does Jim the character choose?

JIM The whole play is about the politics. The love story is just something to help the medicine go down. It's a device. I mean who cares about two people sitting on a bench somewhere being in love, next to the U.S. Military accidentally inventing AIDS and calling it the Homo Cancer, or the inherent injustices built into American capitalism, or evil Catholic hypocrites who blow up abortion clinics. The only reason anyone cares about the love story is because of the politics. People cared about Leo DiCaprio and Kate Winslet because the Titanic *sank,* not because their love story was so great. It's the boat that mattered, *and the lower classes being locked up in the basement!*

KATE No, no, the whole last scene of your play is about love. Do you love me or do you love Shelly? That's what everything eventually boils down to. Love, not politics.

JIM But you and Shelly represent politics and love. You're symbols. It's clever.

KATE Okay, so why don't you choose? You wrote a love story. *That's* what you wrote. That's all she cared about.

ELEANOR Actually–

JIM She cared about being heard.

BENNY But not politically.

ELEANOR What I–

KATE Thank you.

JIM Don't put words in her mouth.

SHELLY No wonder nobody likes it!

JIM She's an adult, Kate, she can speak he own mind.

ELEANOR What I–

JIM As I recall, aside from the hand thing she loved the play.

ELEANOR But only because I thought–

KATE Jim she's never been to the theatre before!

JIM Well that's a bit elitist, don't you think?

KATE I didn't mean it like that.

JIM Oh how else could you have meant it? You just insulted her. Apologize.

BENNY All Kate meant is that maybe she enjoyed the experience but not the play.

ELEANOR I–

SHELLY She thought it was autobiographical.

ELEANOR Yes!

BENNY It was the experience.

JIM What are you talking about? The play *is* the experience! Have you gone crazy? Am I going out of my mind? Suddenly I have to define plays and acting to people who supposedly studied this stuff?

BENNY Listen, Jim, she sees a play for the first time and she gets caught up in the experience of a live – and rather lively – performance.

JIM Rather lively.

BENNY Okay provocative.

JIM No: You said: "rather lively."

KATE God, Jim, you know what he meant.

JIM I thought I knew what he meant when he said several months ago that the play was Exciting. Now it's Rather Lively.

KATE So?

JIM So that was a covertly condescending remark. An insult really. If you had meant provocative you would have said provocative. And if you didn't like the play from the beginning you should have said as much and saved us all the "embarrassment" of "doing it in front of people!" *Sorry* that I *dragged* everyone through such an *agonizing experience!*

BENNY Jim.

JIM It's not like I put a gun to your heads! You all agreed to do it! You must have had a reason!

SHELLY I just wanted to be in a show.

KATE That's the only reason I did it.

JIM Why!

KATE Because it's theatre and it's what I want to do.

JIM Then why this show? You're not getting paid! It's not a stepping stone to boost your career! You don't even like it! Why did you agree to do it?

KATE Maybe you're right! Maybe I should quit right now!

ELEANOR No!

KATE *Shelly's* quitting!

SHELLY I'm not quitting! I *wanted* to!

ELEANOR No, you can't quit. You mustn't quit. Just like you said in that first scene where you *(KATE)* wanted him to join that group and, and you *(SHELLY)*

wanted him to run away with you, *(to KATE)* what did you say?
KATE I don't remember.
ELEANOR Jim said, "I won't say a word. But I do have a voice." That was it. Then you *(KATE)* said, "You don't know *what* you have." You don't know what you *have*. Even if it wasn't real – I didn't know that at the time – feelings are important. You need to stick to them. You can't just Quit.
KATE I am not quitting, okay. I was just talking. I do not quit.
BENNY *(bitterly)* No, you don't.
JIM But you'd love it if Shelly would quit.
SHELLY I'm not quitting!
JIM I know, Shelly, I'm just saying, she hates the show and she wanted you to quit because then *she wouldn't have to!*
KATE You are ridiculous, do you know that?
BENNY It's true, Kate.
KATE Shut up Benny!
JIM Ah, suddenly Benny's back on your black list. How the tides turn!
KATE I told you to leave our relationship out of it.
JIM Who said anything about your relationship?
KATE Nothing. No one! Never mind. Alright, you want to know why nobody showed up tonight, *Jim?*
JIM Yes, why Kate? Why? You tell me why. Why did nobody show up?
KATE Because I have come to hate performing this thing so much that I put up a sign on the front door– apparently after Madam Suicide here slipped in and hid away in the bathroom– I put up a sign, on the door, that said "Show Canceled." Show! Canceled! That's how desperate I was to pinch this turd!

> *Pause. JIM suddenly lunges at KATE. He throws her against the wall. She immediately does the same to him. They take turns for a moment. SHELLY dances around in fevered and vocal denial. Then JIM slaps KATE, spits on her, and picks up a chair with which to smash her. BENNY snatches the chair from JIM's hands and KATE pounces JIM, pinning him to the floor. BENNY pulls her off and JIM springs up. BENNY holds him back.*

JIM You hideous wench! You hag! You fiendish harpy!

> *BENNY slaps JIM once.*

BENNY Oo! Sorry! Did that hurt?
JIM …Oh my god. What did I do? I've gone insane. How could I lose control

like that? I'm a pacifist.

KATE You're a hypocrite.

> *Pause. JIM suddenly lunges at KATE and throws her against the wall. She immediately does the same to him, and again he grabs her, slaps her, spits on her, and picks up the chair before BENNY pulls HIM away.*

JIM You put up a sign?! How could you *do* that? How could you even conceive of that idea without being totally insane and then actually do it?! You are an animal!

BENNY Calm down, Jim!

JIM What are you doing here when you should be off hopping around some carcass in the desert?!

BENNY Jim!

JIM "Show canceled," Benny! "Show canceled!"

BENNY I know.

JIM ...You knew?!

BENNY No! No! I had no idea!

JIM Oh Benny how can you *love that woman?*

BENNY Jim.

JIM Sabotage! Deliberate and cold-blooded! I am floored. I am– *(gains control)* I am very moved. This is unprecedented; I have never felt such anger. How could you hate me that much? It's a *play!* ...Show Canceled?!

> *JIM has a brief fit of rage with clawing fingers but immediately contains it where he stands, clutching his face with his hands. Then:*

JIM I'm leaving. I quit. Ha! There! How do you like that? *I* quit. "Not a quitter," Ha! You quit a long time ago. You just couldn't say it out loud because what you really are is a coward! I am the only person in this room who has had the guts to make a commitment. You never committed to this show because you're too committed to too many things day and night to really be committed to anything, much less a play, much less *Benny* how do you think he feels? And you, Benny, you've never committed to a single thought of your own: "So-and-so said this, so-and-so said that!" And you, *you*, Missy, can't commit to Anything! Ever!

SHELLY Me?

JIM Yes you!

SHELLY I'm not quitting!

JIM But you'd like to!

SHELLY Well, yeah.

JIM So *do* it! *Do* it for god's sake! *Make a decision!* Do *something!* If Benny hadn't made all you're choices for you you never would have even *moved* in this show! You would have just stood there, stupidly! That is pitiful! …Oh my god!

JIM collapses in a heap on the floor. SHELLY is frozen by an epiphany.

SHELLY …He's right. I can't get married.

BENNY What?

SHELLY I can't get married. I've never wanted to marry that man.

KATE Shelly what are you talking about?

SHELLY That fiancé. He doesn't let me do what I want to do. He doesn't like my wanting to be an actress. He *hates* theatre. I don't want to marry him.

KATE *(sincerely)* Oh my god, Shelly.

SHELLY You're right. I never make a decision. I never even decided to marry him, *he* decided. "We're getting married," he said. "It's been decided." Just like that. I can't marry him. How am I going to get out of this marriage? …Will you marry me?

JIM What?

SHELLY Will you marry me?

BENNY Shelly, maybe you should sit down.

SHELLY I can't sit down, I need to get out of my marriage.

KATE Just tell him you don't want to marry him.

SHELLY I can't do that. He'd be crushed. Shoot, he's gonna to be here any minute. What am I going to do?

JIM Shouldn't he have been here a long time ago?

KATE He always makes her wait.

SHELLY He could walk through that door at any moment, Jim, you have to marry me!

JIM No.

SHELLY I have to break my engagement!

JIM No Shelly!

BENNY Shelly? Why don't you sit down?

SHELLY I need to stand. I need to leave. I need to quit the show. –No, I need– I need to– …I need to think for a second.

SHELLY goes to a chair and sits, completely involved in her spinning mind. SHE does not even appear to register ELEANOR.

ELEANOR Honey? Sweetie, now, I don't know anything about your relationship with this man, so I can't comment on that. But you can't quit this play, dear. Jim needs to fiddle with that ending, yes, but you're doing something that is wonderful. *(to KATE)* And you too. You made me think that someone like me can stand up and be heard, that I could have meaning. I believed you. And I have to admit that it is very disappointing to realize you're actually a quitter.

KATE Look, I am not quitting, alright. Don't call me a quitter! You don't know about everything that has happened before tonight. Life is different on the hot side of the footlights, *Lady*.

ELEANOR It's Eleanor. My name is Eleanor.

KATE I cannot believe that *this play* changed your life!

ELEANOR Well it did.

KATE It did not!

ELEANOR How would you know?

KATE It's not even what you thought it was. And who are you to call me a quitter? Who are you period? You just walk in here. You were going to go blow your brains out and topple off the Golden Gate Bridge tonight and you're calling *me* a quitter?

BENNY Kate.

JIM Jesus Kate.

KATE A normal person does not share that kind of information!

ELEANOR I wanted you to understand how much you affected me.

KATE You wanted pity you liar! If you really wanted to kill yourself tonight you wouldn't have stopped to see a show! You would have gone and done it! You were going to commit the ultimate Quit! And you couldn't even follow through on that! So don't *you* call *me* a quitter!

ELEANOR Alright then! Watch me! You don't believe me? You think I'm a quitter? Watch me!

ELEANOR pulls a gun from her purse and puts it to her head.

KATE Go ahead! Pull the trigger!

JIM Jesus Christ Kate!

BENNY Maybe we should all sit down! Or sing!

KATE She's not going to do it! She was never going to do it!

ELEANOR I'll do it right now and splatter my brains all over your face! Then you'll wish you had been more polite!

KATE Oh! Will that be your Big Statement? Will you have been *heard?* You'll make me, one person, feel bad for being mean! Will that be the Grand Legacy you leave behind?

A pause. Then ELEANOR takes the gun from her head and aims it at

KATE.

ELEANOR ...I've always lived alone. I don't have any children. And I've never created any work of art. Who's going to remember me? I'm just the audience... ...And you are very inconsiderate.
KATE I'm sorry.
ELEANOR *(sarcasm)* Why? What's changed?
KATE *(sarcasm returned)* The stakes.
BENNY Kate–
KATE –Sorry. I see your point, I'm sorry, I was wrong.
ELEANOR I'm not putting this away until you apologize to each person in this room for your bad behavior.
BENNY Eleanor it's okay, we like Kate.
ELEANOR Well I don't like her. She's rude. And that's not right. You have to live in this world with other people. They give you meaning. Which I've never had. But at least I know what I don't have.
BENNY Maybe you should put the gun down, Eleanor.
JIM Yeah, don't be crazy, Eleanor. *(making light)* I'm not really mad at Kate.
ELEANOR Yes you are. What do you mean you're not really mad at Kate, you tried to throw her through the wall?! ...She's right about you, you know. You are a hypocrite! When the going gets tough, huh? ...I'm not crazy. And I don't know what your play means. I thought I did but now I don't! You lied about your names, you took my hand, you don't believe in what you say you believe, and the ending *is* a mess!
BENNY Eleanor, we'll cut the ending!
JIM We're not cutting the ending!
BENNY Jim!
JIM It's the most important part!
KATE Jim would you focus please on the matter at hand!
JIM I am not wrecking my play because of some blue hair with a gun!
ELEANOR Pardon me! I am *not!* A blue! Hair!

> *KATE grabs for ELEANOR's gun. BENNY and JIM join the tussle. The gun flies across the room and lands at SHELLY's feet. As JIM lets into ELEANOR, SHELLY slowly picks up the gun in a daze.*

JIM Good! Great! You're a nut! Grab that Shelly! I can't believe I ever thought you're opinion would have mattered for anything! You're crazy! Pulling a gun? What do you think this is? It's a play! You don't pull out a gun! You boo! You hiss! You walk out maybe! You could pick up a chair and throw it at us if you really felt riled! That would be great! But you don't pull a gun on people! And you said *Kate* was rude? I am going to go call the police right now and you're gonna be in trouble! Hold on to her Benny!

JIM makes for the door. But SHELLY is aiming the gun at him.

SHELLY Jim get away from that door.
JIM Shelly what are you doing?
SHELLY Are you going to marry me or not?
BENNY …Shelly?
JIM I told you, Shelly, no. Put that down, you're not thinking straight.
SHELLY Don't tell me what I'm thinking! I know what I'm thinking!
KATE Shelly, honey, put it down, don't be stupid.
SHELLY You be quiet, traitor!
KATE Shelly!
SHELLY You told them I was going to quit.
KATE You were.
SHELLY Well it was *my business!*
ELEANOR She's crazy.
BENNY Shelly, give Kate the gun.
SHELLY What's it gonna be Jim?
JIM Shelly you can't be serious.
SHELLY I have to get out of my marriage! It's been decided! By me! …B-but I- But I can't do it by myself.
JIM Shelly this isn't the best way to go about it.
SHELLY I don't want to end up like her. That woman is me in thirty years. I don't want to end up alone and meaningless like her! -Sorry, sorry! I didn't mean it like that I, I just, I was going to marry him so that I wouldn't be alone. I'd still be alone only I'd be married! Married to a man who makes me wait. Look, he's not even here yet! That's not a marriage: *Waiting!* If he walked through that door right now I'd say: "You're Late!" And blow his head off! …He said this play was stupid.
JIM Wwwhat?
SHELLY He said I was stupid for doing it.
JIM Bastard.
SHELLY He doesn't respect me. He doesn't make time for me. God, you have to marry me, Jim, please!
JIM But- -why me, Shelly?
SHELLY Well… We both like theatre.
JIM But I'm not in love with you.

SHELLY I can't tell him I'm not going to marry him without having a good excuse to back it up, *Jim!* I'll say I'm marrying you instead. I'll say you asked me first!

JIM But *he* asked you a long time ago.

SHELLY I'll say I forgot! Jim, I'm not going to go through my life letting other people decide things for me, things like Getting Married. I'm not going to always make time for other people. Now *I've* made a decision. Someone is going to make time for *me!* I'm *not* going to marry him. A decision's a decision! I'm making something *happen!*

JIM But Shelly!

SHELLY You will marry me right now!

> *On sudden impulse, BENNY grabs the gun in SHELLY's hands and there is a tussle. SHELLY ends up falling to the floor.*

BENNY Oh! I'm sorry! Are you okay? Are you hurt?

SHELLY Yeah. I'm okay.

> *Pause. SHELLY stays on the ground. SHE cries. BENNY stands, holding the gun, looking at SHELLY intently. KATE is looking at SHELLY as well. There is a pause. Then–*

KATE Benny?

BENNY What? ...What Kate?

KATE I don't like the way you quote all the time and I'd like you to stop.

BENNY ...Can we talk about that later?

KATE No. You're always quoting. You never tell me what *you* think and I need you to do that. I've never known what you want.

BENNY You know what I want.

KATE No I don't. We always do what I want. N–now I want to do what you want.

BENNY Well okay if that's what you want.

KATE No Benny!

BENNY Kate. Please.

KATE What do you want?

BENNY Kate– Eh– The personal life of every individual is based on secrecy,

KATE Benny.

BENNY and perhaps it is partly for that *reason* / that civilized man is so nervously anxious that personal privacy should be respected!

KATE Benny. Stop it Benny!

BENNY Anton Chekhov!!
KATE I left you because I never knew what you wanted!
BENNY Privacy, Kate!
KATE You never demand anything! It's maddening!
JIM Uh, you guys?
BENNY I want what you want.
KATE No, you don't!
BENNY Okay.
KATE If that's true, why did you decide to leave me.
ELEANOR I thought you left him.
KATE Be quiet, it's complicated! Why did you leave me after I came back?
BENNY *(growing agitated)* I thought it was what you wanted.
KATE I wanted you to express something yourself!
BENNY Kate, can we talk about this later. Shelly is very upset.
KATE Benny–!
BENNY –Kate. I do not want to talk about this in public.
KATE You never want to talk about it!
BENNY *(unleashed)* How would you *know*? You're never *around*!

> *BENNY is now standing in such a way that the gun is incidentally pointing at KATE. Incidentally. But pointing, nonetheless.*

KATE I'm sorry. Is that it?
BENNY …What do you mean is that it? …Are you okay?

> *SHELLY shrugs BENNY off and pulls herself up and onto a chair. BENNY turns to the others. HE is still holding the gun and, incidentally, it is still pointing.*

BENNY Now I think it's about time we called an end to this meeting. Thank you, Eleanor, for your comments. They were very helpful. Thank you Jim. And Kate. For being so honest–
KATE –Benny–
BENNY *(sharply)* –What.
KATE You haven't answered my question.
BENNY Kate, how can I be more clear. I want you: to drop it.
KATE And?
BENNY And that's it.
KATE And what else?

BENNY And go home.

KATE And then what?

BENNY And then nothing!

KATE And after another round of nothing, then what, Benny? What are we going to do?

BENNY Okay you want to know what I want? I want you to respect other people's privacy, and other people's beliefs. Just because you don't like something doesn't mean you have the right, or the obligation, as you seem to think, to say so! I want you to relax! I want you to stop filling up every hour of every day with things you "must" do before finding one hour at the end of the week to spend on me! I want you to devote some of your time to me! …Oh, god you see I hate this. This is nobody's business. You goaded me into saying this and I didn't want to. It's private. It's between you and me and if you ever would have penciled me in I'd have told you as much! You never want me to leave but you never give me any of your time! You don't give you! I want you! "Love is above all the gift of ones self," Jean Anouilh!

KATE If you quote one more time I'm gonna slap you!

BENNY …Kiss me, Kate.

KATE slaps BENNY.

ELEANOR Oh Kate! You are terrible.

KATE *(taking the gun)* And don't point that at me.

ELEANOR You are awful!

KATE Stay out of this!

JIM Can we put that thing down?

ELEANOR He just opened his heart to you!

KATE And it's none of your business!

ELEANOR You just won't admit that it's true. It is true, isn't it! It makes complete sense!

SHELLY What is going on?

KATE We are all going to go home now.

ELEANOR *(mocking)* "And then what?" "And then what?"

KATE Don't make fun of me!

JIM Can we put the gun away please?

KATE I am going home and I am calling the police and they're going to arrest you and lock you up in an insane asylum! And I am not performing this show ever again! This show is canceled!

JIM You stick that gun in your mouth and pull that trigger!

BENNY I think we all need to take a deep breath *right* now!

SHELLY What is going *on?!*
KATE This is the worst night of my life and it's your fault!
JIM Stop waving that around!
KATE Don't tell me what to do!
JIM You're insane!
KATE You're a terrible playwright!

> *JIM grabs for the gun. There is a tussle. It is a wild one. EVERYONE else moves about calling out. SHELLY is practically banging her head against the wall in an utter, frazzled frenzy. Suddenly JIM has maneuvered the gun into a position against the front of KATE's forehead and pushes her backwards across the room, much to the concern of BENNY and ELEANOR. KATE grabs the gun and the struggle hits its peak! The gun is aimed straight out above the audience and the trigger is squeezed and–*
>
> Click!
>
> *Everything stops. Together, JIM and KATE, with perplexed expressions, pull the trigger twice. Click. Click. THEY relax their grip on one another and look at the gun.*

JIM It's empty.
ELEANOR Empty? Let me see that.
JIM Yeah, look, it's empty.

> *JIM casually aims at KATE's head and pulls the trigger. Click. KATE suddenly realizes what HE is doing and slaps the gun away. ELEANOR takes it and checks it out.*

KATE Stop that.
ELEANOR I don't believe it. I swore it was loaded. It's been sitting on my nightstand for weeks, waiting there for me to work up the courage. I swore it was loaded.
KATE An empty gun? You are sooo stupid.

> *Pause. ELEANOR looks at KATE, dumbfounded. ELEANOR looks around at everybody.*

ELEANOR I can't believe you people… What are you all doing here? …I loved your play because I thought you were sharing your real feelings with me. That was it. And that was enough for me. As it turns out you're all a bunch of frauds.

You don't *know* anything. You're not *committed* to anything. Who are you? You're actors! You can't do some weird play where you grab people's hands and rant about things you don't really know anything about and then call it a day! "There, I've done my part!" You've never fought for Causes! You've never had an abortion! And if what I've witnessed here tonight means anything then you can't know what love means! You're hypocrites and quitters! Your play is worth nothing, I don't care if it *is* Art! If you loved what you were doing at least you could say that! But you all want to *quit!* You can't quit! What does that do? You can't reach out and grab people without knowing why! You can't fight to have the last word and leave it at that! You can't just pretend to change the world, you have to go out and do it!

>*Beat. ELEANOR looks out. Epiphany. Then, abruptly, she exits and is gone.*
>
>*Pause.*
>
>*SHELLY picks up her bags and exits.*
>
>*KATE, BENNY, and JIM are alone. THEY glance at one another.*
>
>*Pause.*
>
>*BENNY sits down.*
>
>*Music. Lights fade slowly to black. Though still dazed, THEY notice the lights are fading.*
>
>*The end.*

Brave

an American play

Brave

The world premiere of *Brave* was presented by Art Street Theatre at EXIT Stage Left, San Francisco, CA, on May 7, 1998. The production was directed by the author, with the following cast and staff:

ANDREW	Mark Jackson
ANNE	Lisa Maher
ANNIE	Bricine Mitchell
ANDRE	Jordon Flato
ANA	Beth Wilmurt
ANDY	Jake Rodriguez
Sound	Jake Rodriguez
Set, lights and costumes	Ana Hashimoto
Dramaturgy	Jordon Flato and Kathryn Clark
Stage Manager	Kathryn Clark
Conceived by	Jordon Flato and Mark Jackson

Brave was subsequently presented as a part of Interplay, a festival of new plays produced by PCPA Theaterfest, Santa Maria, CA, in January, 2003, directed by Jeremy Mann, with the following cast and staff:

ANDREW	Jeff Evan Clarke
ANNE	Gillian Chadsey
ANNIE	Erin Ayala
ANDRE	Chris Leuenberger
ANA	Kathleen Mary Mulligan
ANDY	Andy Wilson
Lights	Margaret Hartmann
Stage Manager	Lisa Marie Black-Meller

Cast of Characters

> *Andrew, a right wing lecturer.*
> *Anne, a left wing activist.*
> *Annie, a young traveler.*
> *Andre, a young man with a mission.*
> *Ana, a young single mom.*
> *Andy, her ten-year-old son.*

Notes

A slash in the dialogue (/) indicates that the next actor should start their line, creating overlapping speech.

In the original production, Andy was played by an adult actor. Also, nobody ever left the stage. This created opportunities for further character and story development through tableaux and simple actions carried out by characters during other characters' scenes.

Time and Place

Spring, 1998. San Francisco, California, USA.

Preshow

Music of an American nature is playing.

Prologue

As "This Land Is Your Land" draws to its rousing conclusion, the stage suddenly flares up brightly like an epiphany and a group of people are all moving about quickly. The effect resembles a street swarming with people. We catch snippets of the evening to come, patterns and relationships. Then...

Scene 1 – Definition #1

...the music ends. ANDREW is for all intents and purposes alone on stage, though we can see the others only dimly in the background seated as at a lecture. ANNE had entered to speak, but stopped when she saw that ANDREW already had taken the floor. Eventually, having heard enough, she quietly sets up a bomb igniter and waits, poised to blow ANDREW's ideology to bits.

ANDREW I would like to begin this evening with some definition of who we are. I beg your pardon if that seems a bit too bookish or dry. But I think it is necessary and will eventually sound its resonance.

I offer you this definition: that we are a group of people in a particular country at a particular time, all squinting into the distance to witness that Millennium as it rolls over the horizon into the twenty-first century – our Eden or our Armageddon, depending on who you talk to.

This horizon, our future, is nothing mystical. It is nothing fated. It is ours to invent. But *we* approach the Millennium and we are interested in angels, in UFOs, horrifying natural disasters, and near-death experiences caught on tape. We have more faith in these things than we do in the Social Security System. We are afraid of what might lurk ahead. And the more we give up our power to the unknown, the more we *will be* afraid. There is ignorance in letting go of one's certainty, and that *is* something to fear.

We in America have reason to be certain, not to fear. For we have our American History. We *have* our definition:

We have been, we are, and we will always be, in deed and in spirit: Pioneers. In its two hundred twenty odd years, The United States of America has experienced the most rapid ascent to maturity of any major nation in the history of the planet. Not because we have sat about fingering our chins and pondering the possibilities. But because we have gone West. We have set out to discover. We have built. We have invented. We have stood and we have taken action. We have dared to do what no nation has done before: we have created a country where every man and woman of every race and religion is welcome to be born within our borders with equal rights to life, liberty, and the pursuit of happiness. Our industries and corporations web the planet. The reach of our philosophies and material achievements extends beyond our coastlines around and back again, and our strength is undeniably internationally Certain.

So, now you think I have come here to talk to you about America. Well that is partly true, and then only as a matter of context, but it is hardly my primary concern. And having said that I might assume you are wondering again as you were when I first stepped up to exercise my lips who I am and why I am up here spouting at you.

We have been coursing through troubled times. From the arrival of English speaking colonists in 1607 until 1965, there was one continuous civilization built around a set of commonly accepted legal and cultural principles. From the Pilgrims up to Norman Rockwell there was a clear sense of what it meant to be an American. The intellectual nonsense propagated since 1965 – in media, on university campuses, even amongst our religious and political leaders – now threatens our Definition of, and our ability to define, who we are.

We have split atoms. We have touched the moon. Yet our schools have decayed into corrals, we are dooming to exile a growing list of words and names branded politically incorrect rendering even basic communication more and more precarious, and we cannot get through the week without our well cared for protective shell of cynicism. We used to have friends and neighbors to tell us who we are, now we have therapists, self-help books, Hollywood, and doubt.

There is something fundamentally wrong. We risk, by our own hand, not being able to understand the world we have invented.

It is time to decide. It is time for conviction. It is time to remember our History. I am not talking about America. I am talking about you, each of you, each of us, reclaiming our Definition of who we are.

Scene 2 – The Takeover

> *BOOM! There is a tremendous explosion. The figures who have been in the background are suddenly thrust into disarray. ANDREW is apprehended by ANNE.*
>
> *As the noise subsides we hear someone singing to a guitar, played by ANDRE. Others eventually join in. The song is "Worried Man." Over the course of a few verses, ANDREW is placed in a chair and his hands taped behind him, his mouth taped over. His captor, ANNE, remains just out of sight so she cannot be seen clearly by him. The song is over.*

Scene 3 – The Information Desks

> *ANNIE at an airport in Scotland. ANA at a Muni station in San Francisco. Both dealing with unhelpful Information Booth workers. ANDY at home alone.*

ANNIE Excuse me?
ANA Excuse me.
ANNIE May I ask you a question?
ANA I have a question.
ANNIE Do you think I could–?
ANA I need to know–
ANNIE Could you tell me if–?
ANA If you could just tell me–
ANNIE Do you have a minute?
ANA I only need one second of your time.
ANNIE Am I in the right line?
ANA I'm not certain where to go.
ANNIE Am I okay?
ANA I've been waiting here forever.
ANNIE Because if–
ANA Hey–
ANNIE Sorry–?
ANA Excuse me.
ANNIE Where am I *now*?

ANA The sign *says* "Information" and I need some information from–
ANNIE Excuse me?
ANA I–I didn't hear you, repeat that please.
ANNIE Could you say again?
ANA No I was still talking when you answered.
ANNIE Could you speak a little–?
ANA You have to speak louder.
ANNIE What did you *say*?
ANA Yes louder than silent please!
ANNIE I'm sorry?
ANA Sorry.
ANNIE Sorry?
ANA Sorry.
ANNIE Look–
ANA It's just that–
ANNIE I just don't want to miss my flight.
ANA I just want to get home.
ANNIE What? Pardon me what?
ANA Someone–
ANNIE Wait? For *what* announcement?
ANA Someone announced that my regular bus was cancelled and I just need to know what other bus to take.
ANNIE Can't you just tell me now?
ANA Look if you can't help me, then–
ANNIE I can't miss my flight; I need to go home.
ANA Something is fundamentally wrong.
ANDY Dad?
ANNIE Who? …Hello?…
ANA …Never mind.

Scene 4 – Definition #2?

> *ANDY takes a test at school. ANDREW is still taped in place. ANNE delivers a rapid onslaught of questions, some to the audience, some to ANDREW, and all to both.*

ANNE Comfy? Thank you for being patient. Now that I have your attention, I would like to ask you a few questions. I'll give you a brief moment following each question to: select your answer in the case of a multiple choice question, or else to respond in complete sentences. If your answer is Yes or No, please do elaborate. But remember, the time in which you complete this test does effect your over all scoring. Why is that? A, time is money. B, money is power. Or C, power is choice.

Next question.

Are you comfortable?

What makes you comfortable?

When in life are you most comfortable?

Does being comfortable make you more comfortable?

Does being comfortable make you hungry?

If asked, how would you define comfort?

Which of the following best defines *you*? A, comfy. B, uncomfy. Or C, undecided.

What is your definition of the American character? Please be brief.

What is your definition of Rebel?

What makes a Pioneer a pioneer?

When people ask you who you are, do you answer with your job description?

Let's go back a little farther, shall we, to your childhood. When the early American colonists, in protest against tax hikes, dumped British tea into the Boston Harbor were they acting out as A, pioneers. B, rebels. Or C, hoodlums.

When those same colonists dumped said tea into said Harbor did they disguise themselves as A, Indians. B, Native Americans. Or C, Indigenous persons.

Do cowboys still roam the American west?

Do you consider your country your home?

Speaking of which, did Norman Rockwell paint pictures of A, scenes from American life. B, political promises. Or C, revolution.

Which American president said that every several years the tree of Liberty must be watered with the blood of patriots and tyrants?

Have you fought in any American wars, past or present– no you haven't– in which case do you wish you had?

When the Persian Gulf War broke out were you glued to your television?

When it ended a few days later were you slightly disappointed?

Would you pin a medal on the chest of someone who looked you in the eye?

Would you ever pin a medal on your *own* chest?

What *did* Lewis and Clark discover?

Were *they* hungry?

Do questions make you angry?

Do you fight against your instincts?

Does *fear* inspire you?

Does *my* vote count?
Do *you* dump tea overboard?
Would you like to ask *me* a question?
When you were young did you resist the temptation to cry?
When do you feel most free? Alone? Or *with others?*
When did you discover that you can be the cause of an effect?
Why do I have to blow the room up to get your attention?
What *is it* you plan to *do* with your one, wild and precious life?!

>*ANNE touches ANDREW'S shoulder.*

ANNE Time's up.

>*ANDREW bursts from his bonds, startling ANNE tremendously. It is a sudden and violent moment. Then...*

ANNE ...What.

Scene 5 – Day After Day

>*ANA finally arrives home from work. ANDY is sitting alone.*

ANA I'm home.
ANDY Hello.
ANA It was a struggle getting here. When you grow up, Andy, I want you to go away and become someone big enough to make our lives run smoothly.
ANDY Okay.
ANA Let that be your mark on this world.
ANDY Mom?
ANA Yes.
ANDY How was your day?
ANA Busy.
ANDY I had a test at school.
ANA That's good.
ANDY I found a book today about where we came from.
ANA And where is that?
ANDY All over the place. Different countries.
ANA The great American melting pot.
ANDY That's what my book says.

ANA I'm beat.
ANDY Are you hungry?
ANA I'll make dinner later.
ANDY Can I ask you a question?
ANA You have before.
ANDY Are you too tired to be hungry?
ANA Maybe that's it.
ANDY I'd really like to know.
ANA Well, you always have been a curious kid. I said, later.
ANDY "Curiosity killed the cat."
ANA So they say.
ANDY Who are "They?"
ANA Grown-ups.
ANDY Are "They" you?
ANA *(leaving the room)* Unfortunately.
ANDY Where are you going?

> *At this point they are in the same place as when the scene started, and in fact the scene does start again. The same score is repeated a second time, with ANA more frustrated but ANDY playing the scene exactly as before.*

ANA I'm home.
ANDY Hello.
ANA It was a struggle getting here. When you grow up, Andy, I want you to go away and become someone big enough to make our lives run smoothly.
ANDY Okay.
ANA Let that be your mark on this world.
ANDY Mom?
ANA Yes.
ANDY How was your day?
ANA Busy.
ANDY I had a test at school.
ANA That's good.
ANDY I found a book today about where we came from.
ANA And where is that?
ANDY All over the place. Different countries.
ANA The great American melting pot.
ANDY That's what my book says.
ANA I'm beat.

ANDY Are you hungry?
ANA I'll make dinner later.
ANDY Can I ask you a question?
ANA You have before.
ANDY Are you too tired to be hungry?
ANA Maybe that's it.
ANDY I'd really like to know.
ANA Well, you always have been a curious kid. I said, later.
ANDY "Curiosity killed the cat."
ANA So they say.
ANDY Who are "They?"
ANA Grown-ups.
ANDY Are "They" you?
ANA *(leaving the room)* Unfortunately.
ANDY Where are you going?

> *The scene repeats a third time, but without ANA's physical score. We can hear the frustration mounting in her voice. She remains standing in the doorway. ANDY performs his score exactly as before.*

ANA I'm home.
ANDY Hello.
ANA It was a struggle getting here. When you grow up, Andy, I want you to go away and become someone big enough to make our lives run smoothly.
ANDY Okay.
ANA Let that be your mark on this world.
ANDY Mom?
ANA Yes.
ANDY How was your day?
ANA Busy.
ANDY I had a test at school.
ANA That's good.
ANDY I found a book today about where we came from.
ANA And where is that?
ANDY All over the place. Different countries.
ANA The great American melting pot.
ANDY That's what my book says.
ANA I'm beat.
ANDY Are you hungry?

ANA I'll make dinner later.
ANDY Can I ask you a question?
ANA You have before.
ANDY Are you too tired to be hungry?
ANA Maybe that's it.
ANDY I'd really like to know.
ANA Well, you always have been a curious kid. I said, later.
ANDY "Curiosity killed the cat."
ANA So they say.
ANDY Who are "They?"
ANA Grown-ups.
ANDY Are "They" you?
ANA Unfortunately.
ANDY Where are you going?

> *And a fourth time. ANDY's score still hasn't changed one bit. ANA cuts out shortly, and her gaze eventually slips outward. She can barely stand it.*

ANA I'm home.
ANDY Hello.
Okay.
Mom?
How was your day?
I had a test at school.
I found a book today about where we came from.
All over the place. Different countries.
That's what my book says.
Are you hungry?
Can I ask you a question?
Are you too tired to be hungry?
I'd really like to know.
"Curiosity killed the cat."
Who are "They?"
Are "They" you?
Where are you going?

> *Beat.*

ANA I have to get out of here. *(she does)*
ANDY *(calling after her)* When's dinner?!

Scene 6 – Bus #1

> *On a bus. ANNIE enters with her suitcase. ANDRE is already there. He watches, moves from seat to seat, getting closer to her. ANDREW and ANNE are passengers; they do not appear to know each other in this instance. ANA is also a passenger. ANDY sits on the floor at home with a toy bus in his hands.*

ANDRE Hey there. Hi… Hellooo, hello… Tough day behind the plow, eh? …People sure are quiet on this bus. You know when animals notice it's quiet they get very alert as it could mean a potential for danger. Right now everybody is thinking about how I'm talking at a normal volume, saying to yourselves "that's just not done."

> *ANDRE finally makes it to ANNIE and notices her suitcase.*

ANDRE Where yuh been?
ANNIE I'm sorry?
ANDRE You've been traveling.
ANNIE Yes.
ANDRE Where to?
ANNIE …Scotland.
ANDRE Ooo, what'd you go there for? It's cold, isn't it?
ANNIE It's very beautiful though.
ANDRE Got any pictures?
ANNIE They're not developed yet.
ANDRE Well I bet we could find a one-hour place. They're all over.
ANNIE That's okay. But thank you.
ANDRE How did you find Scotland?
ANNIE Well, the pilot took care of that.
ANDRE No, I mean how did you like it?
ANNIE I know, I was making a joke–
ANDRE –You were making a joke! Good, Good. I get it the pilot I get it. So anyway I didn't mean to interrupt. You were saying.
ANNIE Uh I'm not sure that I was.
ANDRE You were telling me about Scotland.
ANNIE And that it was very beautiful.

ANDRE Right. Why'd you go there? Why Scotland?

ANNIE Well, I was going to stay but… I changed my mind. It wasn't what I wanted so I came back.

ANDRE You were going to move there? For good?

ANNIE Actually yes, I thought I was going to, yes. I was *going* to. But– it *is* very cold, as you said… Part of my family is from Scotland.

ANDRE They live there now?

ANNIE No my, my old family. Originally. On my father's side. His parents came over from Scotland. So, my ancestors are from Scotland.

ANDRE Ancestors. They sound old.

ANNIE Well, I'm sure they were. Everyone in Scotland is old. It's rough over there. And cold. Being there really made the United States clear to me.

ANDRE Oh of course. How so?

ANNIE Scottish people are cynical. But they're also very friendly. Americans are friendly but you don't always believe them; you wonder what they're selling. And we don't know anything about our country; in Scotland they're very aware of what goes on. But Scotland is small; we've got way too much space to know what's going on. …Anyway. I met a lot of people.

ANDRE And you stayed with family while you were there?

ANNIE No, I couldn't find any, actually. They're all gone. I don't know where. I was hoping to find them, that's why I went.

ANDRE That's too bad. How long were you there?

ANNIE About a year.

ANDRE A year?! Wow. You just picked up and went? That's very gutsy.

ANNIE Well. No.

ANDRE I think so. You just picked up and *moved to Scotland?*

ANNIE I guess that is what I did, yes.

ANDRE *(to ANDREW)* You'd never do that… *(to ANNIE)* So you didn't find anyone. So, but, why didn't you stay? You know they've got those Findhorn people over there that talk to the plants and rocks, you could have stayed with them.

ANNIE That would have been interesting.

ANDRE Well I'm glad you went. Even if you don't know why now, that experience will unfold in you for the rest of your life.

ANNIE Maybe.

ANDRE Oh yeah, everyone should have that experience. It's like the tribes who send their young men out into the jungle for a week. That's the doorway to maturity. Alone in the world. But you did it without a tribe. Not everyone is willing to do that.

ANNIE Well, as it turns out, neither am I.

ANDRE What do you mean? You went!

ANNIE But I came back.

ANDRE But you went.

ANNIE True.

ANDRE And you found things you have yet to discover… Where do you live now?

ANNIE Oh, now, I can't tell you that.

ANDRE Oh I bet you could if you tried.

ANNIE Mom taught me not to talk to strangers. Sorry.

ANDRE …There was this old guy I met once, I don't know where *he* is now either. But I met him on a bus and he kept giving me advice and saying things like "One day" or "in my day" or "young people these days" except that he wasn't like what you might think for a guy who says things like that, he actually seemed very understanding of time and change and generations, there was nothing cantankerous about him… Except he hated it when people were impolite… *(looks at Andrew)* Anyway so he talked to me the whole ride home from work. It was like he was a wrapped package unfolding. But we never asked each other's names. Didn't matter. We were just Two Guys Who Knew Each Other On The Bus. For most people on a bus the last thing they will do, the most terrifying thing they can imagine: is to even make eye contact with someone else. I mean are you kidding, come on, look someone in the eye? No, sir. Out of the corner of an eye, maybe. But if two normal people actually made eye contact, or worse, struck up a conversation about something, that'd be the end of the world. I'd look at my watch and say is this thing working? I'd swear it was the year two thousand twelve and all of theology had it wrong: Judgement Day isn't Doom's Day or Armageddon, it's two strangers in 1998 making contact on a bus over more than how irritated they are with the Bus Driver! The only thing strangers on a bus are capable of bonding over is their collective anger! That's just wrong!

ANDREW Would you please shut up!

ANDRE I feel for you man. I do. *(to ANNIE)* I'm sorry if I've embarrassed you. A person should be able to talk… Ah! Now I've ruined it. …Well, it was nice to have met you. You've taken on one adventure so that means: you're in for more. I admire you. Good luck. But don't be scared of people who break the silence.

> *ANDRE gets off the bus. ANNIE exchanges a look with ANDREW, then stares out.*

ANNIE Where to now?

Scene 7 – Q vs. A

We see fragments of ANA and ANDY's previous scene and something of what they think about that. We see ANNIE get off the bus and wander. We see ANDRE hopping from seat to seat. We see ANDREW and ANNE in conflict with one another. Eventually it is ANDREW and ANNE who have taken the stage. It is a wild and physically exhausting fight as they literally wrestle their arguments, each trying to gag the other from speaking or else escape the other's gagging to push their respective messages on the audience.

ANDREW I am amazed every time I hear reports of teen suicide or stories about people who despair because of boredom or because they have nothing left to look forward to. We are on the verge of enormous frontiers of knowledge and opportunity, except that our elite and entertainment cultures are so negative and cynical, and so scientifically and technologically ignorant, that you would never know it.

ANNE Why is it that artists are attacked whenever a government needs not to be questioned?

ANDREW We are on the threshold of great achievements. Our lives are going to be enriched and expanded by discoveries of which we now have only the vaguest ideas.

ANNE Who does the research? Who writes the checks? Who asks the questions? And who publishes the answers?

ANDREW On Thomas Jefferson's two hundred and fiftieth birthday not a single mention of his life was made at the Organization of American Historians. There were, however, seminars about radical history, labor history, gay and lesbian history, multicultural history, and all the other pet obsessions of contemporary academia. As a consequence, our children are being cheated. They have a legacy that comes from they know not where, paid for at a price they cannot comprehend by men whose names they scarcely know– or, if they do know them, it is as slaveholders, imperialists, Daddy Warbucks, or Doctor Strangelove. Given this academic bias, it is no wonder American civilization and its values are not being transmitted to the next generation. They must know our past if they are to be our future.

ANNE What makes a buzzword buzz the way it does?

ANDREW All this would be laughable if it weren't destructive of America's future.

ANNE Are you comfortable?

ANDREW Ideas do have consequences.

ANNE When in life are you most comfortable?

ANDREW Having a generation brainwashed with a distorted version of reality is dangerous for our civilization!

ANNE Which of the following best defines *you*? A, comfy. B, uncomfy. Or C, undecided!

ANDREW Curiosity killed the cat!

ANNE Where are you? Where did you come from? And where are you going?

Scene 8 – What about Dad?

> *ANDY at home. He enters the bathroom and washes his hands. Then he looks in the mirror. He does silly things in the mirror. Then...*

ANDY Hi, my name is Andy. Do you reco'nize me?... ...Hello, you don't know me, but you should... ...Does the name Andy mean anything to you?... ...Hi. I'm your son. Whayuh think about that?

> *ANDY washes his face. Washed, he looks at his face, plays with it a bit. Then...*

ANDY Why can't I ask you anything? You never– No. ...Why can't you just tell me now? We never get to "later", when is "later?" You say that all the time so I looked that word up, and it means... n–nnext. Like, it's gonna happen next. That's what I thought it meant only you keep using it like it means never. You don't know what things mean. No. You don't know what things mean. Y– You– You don't know what things mean.

> *ANA comes home, as usual. At first she does not appear to notice that ANDY isn't in his usual spot.*

ANA I'm home.

ANDY Hello.

ANA It was a struggle getting here. When you grow up, Andy, I want you to go away and become someone big enough to make our lives run smoothly.

ANDY Okay.

ANA Let that be your mark on this world.

ANDY Mom?

ANA Yes.

ANDY Where did I come from?

ANA Busy.

ANDY Mom?

ANA That's good. –What?

ANDY Where did I come from?

ANA *(trying to get back on track)* Uh– The great American melting pot.

ANDY That's what my book says.

ANA I'm beat.

ANDY Why don't I look just like you since you're my only parent?

ANA Uh. That's a complicated question.

ANDY I'd really like to know.

ANA Well you always have been a curious kid. I said, later.

ANDY No you didn't, not yet.

ANA *Now* I've said later. Look it up: Later means later.

ANDY *(caught yuh)* Or *does* it!

ANA Talking back. Interesting.

ANDY Where did I come from?

ANA *(leaving the room)* Stop asking that.

ANDY Where are you going?

ANA *(reels on him)* I'm home, Andy, I'm home! You're lucky I even come home! You don't know how much I'd like to take that bus straight on to the airport, fly away and live my life somewhere else but I come home and I do what I can! Now when I get here I'm tired and I need to rest before I start answering ridiculous questions… Yes, my little latchkey child, Mommy is a person too. We're people. You like to do things by *yourself.* So does Mom… It doesn't mean that I don't– love you. Andy. I love you Andy. But when you ask a lot of questions right when I get home from work I wanna slug yuh.

ANDY You could ask me questions.

ANA I know everything about you, I'm your mother.

ANDY You don't know everything about my life.

ANA I *gave* you life, Kiddo, I'm an expert.

ANDY Then who is my Dad?

ANA …That…

ANDY Who is he?

ANA Your Dad is… m– uh– much older than you.

ANDY Who is he?

ANA You don't even know him, Andy, it doesn't make a difference.

ANDY Why can't you just tell me?

ANA Because it doesn't matter. He's not here. He's never going to be here. He's gone.

ANDY But who is he? Where did he go so fast? Why can't I know where I came from?

ANA W– Y– …Why are you asking me this? You've never asked this before,

why are you all of a sudden asking me this?
ANDY W'll... ...because–
ANA I'm asking about your life, now, what you wanted! Why do you need to ask me this?
ANDY Just because!
ANA Oh, just because! Just because is not a good answer, Andy!
ANDY Because you never say anything and I have a right to know!
ANA You don't have any rights until you're eighteen!
ANDY I have a right to know who I came from!
ANA You came from me!
ANDY And a Dad!
ANA ...And a Dad.

> *Silence. ANA puts her hand on her head, fighting off a feeling. ANDY eventually walks up to her. ANA stops him with a hand on his head. Then her hand slips over his eyes.*

ANA I'll make dinner later.

> *ANA leaves the room.*

Scene 9 – We Meet Again

> *ANNIE, with her suitcase, a bit frantic, wanders into a park and sits down for some peace. ANDRE enters and spots her.*

ANDRE Well we meet again, / how are yuh?
ANNIE Oh hi. I'm fine.
ANDRE You're still carting around that suitcase. You're not living here in the park are you? Oh hey, did you get those pictures developed yet?
ANNIE No I, haven't had the chance.
ANDRE Well you need to take the chance.
ANNIE I haven't had the chance.
ANDRE I believe you. Why haven't you unpacked? The trip's over now, come on. No clinging to the past, you gotta move on you know. You bump into things if you're always looking over your shoulder.
ANNIE Thanks. I understand.
ANDRE ...You probably thought– well, you probably *think*– I'm wacko because I was talking to you on the bus. Right?
ANNIE No.

ANDRE Mm-hm. Most people do. Most people don't give me the time of day, so, thank you for being a surprise. You gave me hope in a dark world.

ANNIE You talk to a lot of strangers?

ANDRE I try. *(clandestinely)* It is my Mission.

ANNIE Oh really. Talking to strangers.

ANDRE Yes. It is my Mission. Public transportation is a kind of purgatory between various Hells and Heavens. People go silent and rigid, it's awful. We're all pressed up together in some humid rush hour bus, trying desperately to pretend that we're not. As if that's so terrible, really, I mean come on. Yet we stand there, ready to be annoyed at a moment's notice, desperately feigning isolation. Oh my space, my space! And then we push through the doors and just rush rush rush as quickly as possible away from the bus to wherever it is we're going, more *from* than *to*. …It's a small example of greater things.

ANNIE I guess. But I don't think wanting to keep to yourself on a bus means the end of civilization. I think it's more a sign of a long day at work.

ANDRE What about in the morning?

ANNIE People are tired. Or they're embarrassed because their hair is still wet from the shower.

ANDRE Well who cares? Everyone's hair is still wet from the shower. So? Talk to each other. Talk about your hair. Why pretend like the person next to you doesn't exist? It is the perfect example of how individuality in this country has over the course of History rotted down to fear. Fear. We don't want to be alone in life so that we can be an individual or, free or, some cowboy great Americannn rrrebelll loner. People want to be alone because they're afraid. I mean, naturally, if someone on the bus is talking out loud when everyone else is silent, well then clearly the next thing that person is going to do is pull out a knife and stab everybody. I mean obviously he's a killer. That's why I try to talk to people, and make contact. To prove that all strangers aren't out to kill you. All neighbors don't have dead bodies buried in their backyards. We can help each other with more than small talk.

ANNIE I think you're exaggerating.

ANDRE …Only to make a point.

ANNIE I mean I agree, people are angry, people are afraid, people aren't as happy now as they used to be. Or, you know, that's not even true, we don't know that. We weren't around before we were born so how do we know how things used to be? It's like we confuse our childhood bliss with past decades. I'm sure it's been rough each and every year since the Pilgrims landed. But, people are afraid, yes, people now are afraid. Or anxious, and that makes them afraid–

ANDRE But why are they so anxious?

ANNIE …You have an answer, right?

ANDRE Well, yes I do, but I want to hear yours too.

ANNIE Why, so you can counter with your own?

ANDRE …Where did we go wrong? When we first met I actually thought it went pretty well. Well that is until I– got all excited. That's usually when I lose people. It is quite frowned upon to express conviction in public these days.

ANNIE Well if you shove all your theories down people's throats, they're not going to want to listen to you.

ANDRE I was good, I was asking you questions about yourself.

ANNIE Yeah but I don't know you, you could be anyone.

ANDRE See? A killer! Right?

ANNIE Nooo, not a– well yes, yes you could be a killer. Now I hate to say that because it just gives you proof for your theory about America's collective paranoia but yes in this day and age you could very well be a killer. It is possible.

Silence. ANDRE nods a bit.

ANNIE Sorry. You've caught me in a bold moment. I don't usually talk to strangers.

ANDRE Really? Too bad for you.

ANNIE …My name is Annie.

ANDRE …My name is Andre. "A" names. We've run into each other twice, we both have two-syllable "A" names.

ANNIE I wonder what it means?

ANDRE Greater things. …So, come on, what's with the suitcase now.

ANNIE Actually, I *don't* have a place to live. I'm going to try to find a youth hostel, I think. I hadn't planned on coming back from Scotland.

ANDRE You can't crash at a friend's place? It's cheaper.

ANNIE Cheap would be good. But I don't have any friends. Well, whom I would feel comfortable asking if I could crash at their place. I'm not very social, actually. That's partly what I learned how to do by traveling *alone,* ironically. I *had* to be social in Scotland. It was survival. Otherwise I'd go crazy all by myself. I thought I didn't need people but, I think people do.

ANDRE Come over to my house.

ANNIE I'm sorry?

ANDRE Come over to my house.

ANNIE That's okay. But thank you.

ANDRE I think you should.

ANNIE Why?

ANDRE Two chance meetings, "A" names. –Because you don't have a place to stay!

ANNIE I'll be okay. Thank you.

Pause. ANDRE stands and puts out his hand. Pause. ANNIE shakes it.

ANNIE It was nice to meet you.
ANDRE And perhaps we'll meet again, so, I'll see you next time.
ANNIE We'll see.
ANDRE Now come on you never know.
ANNIE Okay.
ANDRE *(goes, stops)* …Because the coincidences, you know, small examples and all. We can't see the pattern right now but one day we'll know what it all means.
ANNIE You're probably right.
ANDRE …*(right in her face)* Because see when I'm this far away, you can't tell who I am, I'm just blurry. *(backs up a bit)* This far away, now you can see who I am. *(etc.)* If I back up farther, then you get the whole picture. You need the distance to see what's what.
ANNIE …Were you leaving? You were kind of behaving as if you were going to go and then– you didn't.
ANDRE Yeah I do have to go. *(doesn't go.)*
ANNIE …So, see you next time.
ANDRE Oh sure… *(goes, stalls)* Bye Annie… *(goes, stalls again)* You can come to my house if you want, really!
ANNIE I believe you. I'm okay. Thank you.

ANDRE exits.

Scene 10 – Economics

ANDREW and ANNE leap in and stop at the sight of each other. THEY both start their respective speeches at once. THEY stop. When THEY try again, stop again, and realize no one is going to budge, they each plow ahead and deliver the following monologues simultaneously, with each paragraph coinciding with the other. THEY check in with some sort of glance between each paragraph.

As the monologues progress, the following actions develop simultaneously… ANDY and ANDRE watch Washington, D.C., on their respective television sets with no particular interest, changing channels with each new paragraph of ANDREW and ANNE'S; by the fourth set of paragraphs, ANNIE realizes she has lost something of great import and scrambles through her stuff, frantic but trying to stay calm, eventually giving up and staring out intensely; also by the fourth set of paragraphs, and after quite a long wait at a bus stop, ANA decides to walk home but stops when she spots a small purse or envelope containing a significant amount of money. Each event manages to climax simultaneously with the end of ANDREW and ANNE'S monologues and to the swelling noise of what sounds like jet planes, music, cash registers, and other things...

ANNE... / Throughout the tumult of the last presidential election, political commentators were perplexed by a stubborn fact. The economy was performing splendidly, at least according to the standard measurements of the Gross Domestic Product. Productivity and employment were up; inflation was under control. And the World Economic Forum in Switzerland declared that the United States had regained its position as the most competitive economy on earth after years of Japanese dominance. So if the economy was up, why was America down? Voters didn't feel better even though the economists said they should. President Clinton actually sent his economic advisers on the road to persuade Americans that their experience was wrong.

Sounding much like a progressive grammar school guidance counselor, The Clinton Administration said that Americans were simply suffering the anxieties of adjusting to a wondrous new economy. Those silly people. But could it be that the nation's economic experts live in a statistical Potemkin village that hides the economy Americans are actually experiencing? Isn't it time to ask some basic questions about the gauges that inform expert opinion, and the premises on which those gauges are based? Is there a difference between mere monetary transactions and a genuine addition to a nation's wellbeing?

There have been questions regarding the accuracy of the numbers that compose the Gross Domestic Product, and some occasional tinkering at the edges. But politicians and economists have not been eager to see the system changed; that would be a lot of work. The GDP is a set of numbers that tells us next to nothing about what is actually going on. It makes no distinction whatsoever between the desirable and the undesirable.

For example, the crucial economic functions performed in the household, volunteer sectors, and in nature, go entirely unreckoned. Family, community, and the natural habitat have no market price, and so are invisible in our national accounting. Divorce adds several billion dollars a year in lawyer bills, second homes, and counseling for the kids – kids talking to their parents is of no value; they aren't adding to the economy. But watching three hours of television a day trains them to be ardent, GDP-enhancing consumers. Crime has given rise to a burgeoning security industry, adding more than $65 billion a year to the GDP. The car-locking device called The Club adds some $100 million a year itself, and even the Oklahoma City Bombing stirred an interest in Security Systems that added an economic uptick to the nation. Prozac alone adds more than $1.2 billion to the GDP as people try to feel a little better amid all this progress. Isn't something fundamentally wrong?

...AND ANDREW One of the great changes of the last twenty years has been the rise of the world market. We came out of World War II feeling unrealistically invulnerable; all of our major competitors had been bombed. We have had such a powerful national economy for so long that it is difficult for us to adjust to the overwhelming realities of the world market. All current economic textbooks are based on the national economy as though that were still the keystone of an understanding of how the world works. Yet the fact is that the world economy is now an interconnected system. And if we intend to give our children the best job security in the world, then we are going to have to rethink our entire approach to being competitive in the world market.

No nation can lead the world if it cannot economically sustain itself. As we enter the Information Age, there is an enormous opportunity for this country to develop the new products, the new wealth, the new jobs, and the new quality of life that will transform both the lives of Americans and those of others. If we lead the economic and technological transition, then our children will have the highest value-added jobs, with the highest productivity, the highest take-home pay, the greatest job security, and the widest choices in quality of life, offering them a strong and genuine sense of the nation's wellbeing.

There has been a general rule that each generation would live within its means so that our children would not be stuck with the task of paying off our debts. The principle was that we would pay off the mortgage and leave the farm to our children. Only in the last generation has this reversed. Now we are borrowing against the farm to pay today's living expenses and leaving our dept to the children. This is entirely undesirable.

For our future, the crucial task that we must perform is to balance the federal budget. Individuals and families must plan years ahead for retirement; the same thing is true of generations and nations. As I speak, we are paying $250 billion in taxes just to satisfy the national dept. But that's just the beginning. By the next century, the cost of servicing the accumulated dept– rising at $200 billion a year– will skyrocket. By 2005 we will be paying $412 billion in interest on the dept and the cumulative interest will be more than $3.9 trillion. That's an amount almost equal to the current national dept. It is also two and a half times the current national budget. America now owes $5 trillion in national dept. By the end of the decade, the Clinton administration expects us to owe approximately $6.5 trillion. By 2012 that dept will approach $9 trillion. When your national dept is more than doubling in fifteen years, there is something fundamentally wrong!

Pause. ANNIE dashes off upstage while ANDREW and ANNE stalk away to stand off stage left and right respectively, where they eye one another throughout the following scene.

Scene 11 – The Open Road?

ANA I'm home.
ANDY Hello.

ANDY gets up from the television, takes a chair and sits facing a wall. ANA steps forward, still looking at the money in silence, her mind turning and not fully focused on ANDY.

ANDY …Don't you want me to go away and become someone big enough to make our lives run smoothly?

ANA hides the money.

ANA I do. Someday. Andy don't be upset about yesterday; I didn't mean to hurt your feelings. You startled me, that's all.
ANDY Are you going to tell me?
ANA I can't promise that I'll do that right now. I'm sorry. Uhm. Andy come here.
ANDY Why?
ANA Please just do it.
ANDY Why?
ANA Andy that's an annoying question now come here.

ANDY does, remaining at a distance.

ANA You feel okay by yourself when I'm not here. You feel okay with that.
ANDY Is that a question?
ANA Yes.
ANDY I guess.
ANA And you can make dinner for yourself, you have before.
ANDY Yeah, spaghetti, Campbells, fish sticks. Carrots. Why?
ANA If someone–? If you were able to live by yourself–?
ANDY Where are you going?
ANA Nowhere nowhere, I'm not going anywhere. But one day you're going to have to live alone, you're going to grow up and have to live on your own and I'm just, wondering if you've thought about that.

ANDY Well. When I grow up I'll live in a bus and drive all over the country and take pictures of people. Then I'll go to Washington D.C. and show the president all the pictures I took. And then I'll get him to help me find my Dad.

ANA Andy, he's gone. I don't want to hurt you but he's gone. You need to stop worrying about that now. One day the time will be right and you'll know. You just have to be patient and wait.

ANDY Yeah 'til I'm dead.

ANA No, Andy.

ANDY Are you going somewhere?

ANA …No!

ANDY You can go on a trip if you want. I can make my own dinner.

ANA I know. I know you can. I wish I had an Aunt for you, or a Grandmother. Anybody. Of course you're always wondering where you came from, you only know Mom. You and I make one small family… You know in other countries people live with their parents and grandparents all their lives, in the same house. Families are big. And they do everything together. You and I are all American, Kiddo. Things aren't what they used to be, if they ever were… I'm not sure what's right, or what to do.

ANDY Why?

ANA Well if I knew the answer then I wouldn't have to ask.

ANDY I've learned everything from asking. And the dictionary. Except sometimes I disagree with the dictionary. Or people won't tell me.

ANA I heard that. …I know you can't understand now but one day I think you will… You know they say absence makes the heart grow fonder. Sometimes it can be a blessing to be far away. Or to not know the answer. Sometimes that's the best thing. I've never had any money Andy. I can't ever get away. We became a family when Mom was still a kid. We got an early start, and we got stuck starting so we're always trying to start and we never get anywhere. It's going to take us a while to– to figure everything out. And if an opportunity comes along to make something of ourselves then we have to do that even if it's scary or wrong, right? Otherwise we'll never know, right? How do you know unless you ask… Right?

ANDY I'm confused.

ANDY palms his toy bus.

Scene 12 – The Charm

ANNIE frantically boards the bus, filled with the usual passengers, hoping she'll run into ANDRE again. ANDRE is sitting up front. ANNIE is standing in the back with her suitcase in hand. SHE spots him immediately.

ANNIE Andre!
ANDRE Oh my goodness, it's the charm!
ANNIE What?
ANDRE We're meeting for the third time. Third time is the charm.
ANNIE I was hoping to find you again. I've been riding this bus all evening.
ANDRE You have? Well. Here I am stranger.
ANNIE Something terrible has happened.
ANDRE What?
ANNIE I lost my money. All of it. I don't know what happened.
ANDRE It's not in your suitcase?
ANNIE No it's nowhere I looked everywhere, everywhere I've *been*, where I used it *last*. I called the bus people and they said they'd keep an eye out but they're not going to find it.
ANDRE That's terrible. You don't have a bank account?
ANNIE I didn't think I was coming back to America.
ANDRE Well, what are you going to do? Do you know anybody?
ANNIE Just you… I don't even want to ask but…
ANDRE Uh.

ANDRE scratches his head. HE keeps doing that. For too long a time.

ANNIE Are you alright?
ANDRE Yeah I'm fine. Uhm, yeah you can come over.
ANNIE I mean if it's not okay I understand, I know you were just trying to be nice when you offered. But. I don't know what to do. I don't know anyone in San Francisco, I just came here because I didn't want to go back home. I have to find that money. It's a lot of money. Oh! I hate this! Everything costs money, which is just a bunch of paper and numbers we decided meant something and now it means *everything!* …Oh and I lost *all of it! Damn it!*
ANDRE It's okay it's okay, you can come over.
ANNIE No, I'm alright.
ANDRE Oh no don't cry, you can come over I'm just, I mean, you know. This is, sudden, but, obviously it's all meant to be.
ANNIE No: my trip was depressing, I didn't find anything I crossed an entire ocean to find, and if I'm fucking *meant* to have lost all my money *and* my ancestors then that's just fucked! …Sorry.
ANDRE I just meant that we keep running into each other and so that must mean something.
ANNIE And we both have "A" names.

ANNIE has caught ANDRE at his own game. He can't deny it. ANDRE struggles for a moment but quickly manages to distract himself with an increasingly impassioned line of thinking. Over the course of the monologue, everyone else on the bus slowly leaves.

ANDRE We do. And I did offer you my place to crash and– now a reason hasss– accidentally come along for you to– actually– need a place to crash. Accidents aren't always accidents, see? We need to invent a new word that puts accident and pattern together. Oh, well that would be synchronicity! You know, I *put* that come-over-to-my-place idea out there and now by accident it might happen. That means something. But it's not *just* synchronicity that– reveals *meaning* or, one thing causing another thing to happen, like dominoes– which are a series of *planned* accidents. It's more like a whole bunch of things simultaneously working toward similar ends – rocks, plants, people, swarms of bees, light – and the mere fact that – completely independent of one another! – they're all doing essentially the same thing, matching the same general rhythms, *that* fact reveals something about a great pattern to living we're all working away at. That's meaningful.

ANDREW leaves.

ANDRE You know like how a waterfall looks the same as a landslide. Or how a landslide started decades ago when one grain of soil slipped, that's just like water on the stove slowly coming to a boil, or a crowd of people getting more and more restless and then boom,

ANA leaves.

ANDRE mayhem– well, we call it mayhem. I mean, according to new physics theory the world is made up entirely of information; that's what matter and energy *is*. And so even something as intangible as a thought– a thought is information– that hooks up to the pattern as well. So coincidences happen that are really in a way a revelation of the big picture or– or like kids today pick up on computers faster than kids did ten and twenty years ago because now all this computer information is in the air, it's a part of the world now and kids are born into that. Oh Oh!

ANNE leaves.

ANDRE Or there's that monkey thing. The way the story goes, there were these monkeys on an island in Japan who had never seen sweet potatoes before, and these scientists gave them sweet potatoes. But the sand from the beach made the potatoes hard to eat. But this *one* monkey learned that if it swished the potatoes around in the ocean water not only did it clean them off but it also gave them a nice salty taste. And so other monkeys picked up on this and learned it from the first monkey. And soon more and more monkeys knew how to wash potatoes in the ocean. And then eventually so *many* monkeys knew how to do this that it reached a point of critical mass, and suddenly other monkeys on other islands, who had had no contact with the first monkeys, they all just, boom,

ANDY leaves.

ANDRE knew how wash potatoes! It was suddenly a part of the culture! That could explain how wishes come true, or dreams, or how prayer works! People get together and they all pray for some terminally ill person who then ends up living another thirty years! So our thoughts are the angels! And God's not a man floating in the clouds he's just some being that is the sum total of all information of which we are one part! We can't even comprehend this God because of the limited amount of info that goes into making us what we are! And likewise, the rocks can't comprehend us because we are made up of so much more information than they are! We're just more complicated than the rock; that's the essential difference! We need to take a step back. And if we got far enough away from the pattern of the universe and could see all of that information at once, then maybe we'd be able to see God! …That would take some time though!

ANNIE …So can I come over?

ANDRE …Yes. Uhm. Well. My apartment is a mess.

ANNIE My life is a mess, so– It's okay.

ANDRE Are you sure you don't feel strange, I mean, you don't know me, really.

ANNIE Look, if it makes you uncomfortable, it's okay, just say so. …I *liked* the monkey story, it was interesting.

ANDRE Well, it's just a story, I mean, the reality of it is debatable, you know, but…

ANNIE It could be true. I'd believe it. I mean it makes sense. The world is changing. We have to learn how to– to think in new ways. …You're interesting.

ANDRE Thank you. We should go to the beach some time.

ANNIE Okay.

ANDRE *(poorly feigned enthusiasm)* …Well, okay, let's *go* to my place.

ANDRE looks out and his smile fades.

ANNIE Are you sure?
ANDRE Yeah yeah it's okay, I want you to. I want to help. We only have a few more stops actually.
ANNIE I appreciate it... ...We're the only people left on the bus.
ANDRE That's not good for my Mission. I need strangers...

> *ANNIE looks at ANDRE who is looking ahead at the road. SHE takes him in. ANDRE appears to be uneasy with his thoughts.*

Scene 13 – The Sweep of History

> *ANDREW darts onto the stage–*

ANDREW In 19–!

> *–but stops when ANNE does not. HE looks at her. ANNE gestures for him to "be my guest" and then listens carefully, taking notes like a good journalist.*

ANDREW In 1936, President Franklin Delano Roosevelt told the American public, "Our generation has a rendezvous with destiny." That generation met its challenge, and triumphed. Now it is our turn.

We must reassert the original American definition, a civilization that emphasizes personal responsibility as much as individual rights. There has been a calculated effort by cultural elites to discredit this civilization and replace it with a culture of irresponsibility that is incompatible with American freedoms as we have known them. Our first task then is to return to teaching Americans about America.

A sense of anxiety has increased in this nation.

> *ANDRE and ANNIE get off the bus together.*

ANDREW Any reasonable person should feel anxious when twelve year olds are having babies, high school graduates cannot read their diplomas, and good workers suddenly find themselves downsized. Anxiety is a rational response to this world of rapid change.

It has been said that some people are born into greatness, while others have greatness thrust upon them. In America, we have both. But no single person needs to be a hero. Everyone needs to be a little bit heroic. Not heroic in the tradition of Jefferson, Lincoln, or Roosevelt. Quite the opposite. I believe the heroism we need today is the quiet steady work of millions. To reassert the true

American character, we simply have to convince ourselves that our country, our freedom, and our future are worth a little extra effort.

ANDRE and ANNIE enter ANDRE's apartment.

ANDREW   That is the choice that each of us must make, one at a time, day by day. And at no time in the history of our great nation has the choice been clearer.

ANNE   May I ask a question please?

This puts ANDREW in a position resembling a politician at a press conference, with ANNE the reporting press. ANDREW obliges her request with a gesture.

ANNE   What would you say has been the role of propaganda in the process of defining American history?

Isn't it true that those who define history get their information from the Associated Press?

And doesn't the Associated Press get its information from the *New York Times*?

How does the *New York Times* arrive at our doorstep?

And in the end, who writes this "History?" A, those who live it. B, those who read it. Or C, those who purchase ad space to pay for it?

Does contradiction exist?

Are details important?

Is authority subject to change?

Which of the following is an example of a black and white issue? A, freedom of speech. B, free speech. Or C, the freedom to speak.

If you *believe* in freedom of speech then you do believe in freedom of speech precisely for the views you don't like; is that true or false?

I do admit that when the voice of the people can be heard, you have this problem, they become curious and arrogant and then things happen like the American Revolution or the Nineteen Sixties, for example. Considering that, what do you feel we can create to help avoid such events? A, propaganda. B, necessary illusions. Or C, apathy?

And finally, in reference to your comment on greatness, if some people are born into greatness while others have it thrust upon them, is there any room in that equation for a person to *choose* to be great? Or is greatness simply an accident?

And now THEY revert to wrestling.

ANDREW If my inquisitive friend will allow, I shall recapitulate the primary facts of my thesis so that she and her kind might perhaps comprehend the state of the nation.

ANNE If the public wants to hear the facts, then we must ask first: the facts according to whom?

ANDREW I would be much obliged if someone would please point out to the young lady that although she is brimming with a great many provocative questions, she herself has never provided any answers.

ANNE Could someone please ask the gentleman why he does not *ask* if answers are what he seeks?

> *ANDREW spouts. ANNE takes her place beside him and simultaneously does the same.*

ANDREW... / We risk, by our own hand, not being able to understand the world we have invented. It is time to decide. It is time for conviction. It is time to remember our History. I am not talking about America. I am talking about you, each of you, each of us, reclaiming our Definition of who we are!

...AND ANNE When you were young did you resist the temptation to cry? When do you feel most free? Alone? Or *with others?* When did you discover that you could be the cause of an effect? Why do I have to blow the room up to get your attention? What is it you plan to do with your one, wild and precious life?!

> *A brief and awkward pause.*

ANNE Could someone please ask this gentlemen, if he would agree that we have been– perhaps– ...running in circles?

ANDREW I would appreciate someone informing my– companion– that I do recognize a certain– ...motif.

ANNE And could you please ask him: where exactly is he– are, we– ...getting to?

ANDREW And would you please tell her... uhm...

Scene 14 – Home/Home

> *ANDRE plucks out "Worried Man" on his guitar. ANNIE unpacks her suitcase and sets her clothes in piles. ANA comes home only to find ANDY.*

ANA Andy! What are you doing home?

ANDY School was cancelled. What are you doing home?
ANA I uh, I took a long lunch, so I came by to– get some things I forgot, for work. What are you reading?
ANDY My history book.
ANA Oh. Is that homework?
ANDY No I'm just reading it.
ANA Well, I won't disturb you. Why did school get cancelled?
ANDY Bomb threat.
ANA Bomb threat? That's crazy. …Okay. Well. I'll just go get my things and go, so, be good.
ANDY Okay.
ANA And be careful.
ANDY About what?
ANA I don't know, people are making bomb threats.

ANNIE enters ANDRE's front room. ANA exits and hurriedly packs her suitcase with clothes, including The Money. When she is done, she stays near the suitcase contemplatively.

ANNIE Good morning.
ANDRE *(stops playing guitar)* Hey there.
ANNIE You have a pretty clean place for a boy.
ANDRE Thank you.
ANNIE You play the guitar?
ANDRE I play the guitar. *(with a fancy trill, he stops)* Did you sleep okay? I'm not exactly set up for guests.
ANNIE Oh I was fine. It's nice.

ANDRE starts playing again.

ANNIE You don't have a lot of things here.
ANDRE I try to gather only what I need. Waste not, want not, you know.
ANNIE A good philosophy.
ANDRE Good economics, really.
ANNIE Yes. …I, I unpacked my clothes, I hope it's okay. I was thinking I should probably get to a Laundromat pretty soon.
ANDRE *(stops playing)* There's laundry in the basement downstairs. I guess I should make us something to eat, too. Are you hungry?
ANNIE Oh no, don't go to any trouble.

ANDRE Annie, you don't have any money. What are you going to eat?
ANNIE Thank you...

ANDRE starts playing again.

ANNIE Look, you're still uncomfortable with this, I can tell.

ANDRE stops playing.

ANNIE I'll just go. I can figure something out.
ANDRE No, come on now, how many times do I have to say it's okay?
ANNIE Well, you look awkward.
ANDRE Well I've got a stranger in my house.
ANNIE Then I should go.
ANDRE No, it's just, you know, I never have guests, so– *you* said you aren't very social and neither am I; I'll get over it. Go get your laundry. *(starts playing)*
ANNIE ...I don't have any quarters.
ANDRE *(stops playing)* ...I've got quarters.
ANNIE Thanks.

ANDRE starts playing again.

ANNIE Don't you have to go to work?
ANDRE Not today.
ANNIE Where *do* you work?
ANDRE The Main Library. *(stops playing)*
ANNIE Oh. Of course.
ANDRE *(a book)* What, this?
ANNIE And those. You have quite a library of your own.
ANDRE I try to keep up. Survival of the fittest, you know. *(a short loud riff, then puts the guitar away)* You know going back to this whole pattern thing, we always say that history repeats itself, which is really just a folksy way of acknowledging fractal pattern. And I'd say our short history together is a tiny example of that, having met each other three well-placed times? But the wrench is always the details. That's the chaos. I've met all kinds of people, like that old guy I told you about before. But he's never seen my place. You're the first, really.
ANNIE You never invite friends over?
ANDRE ...No it's too small here. So tell me more about Scotland and your family.
ANNIE I don't really want to. It wasn't the best experience.

ANDRE Fair enough.

ANNIE I went to Scotland to find out who I am but found nothing. I have no family in America, I have no family across the sea, I have no home anywhere. That's my story to date.

ANDRE Fair enough.

ANNIE What about you? Why do you keep to yourself here if meeting strangers is your mission?

ANDRE I meet strangers on the bus. The problem is obvious there so that's the best place to do it. I just want to meet them, I don't bring them home.

ANNIE Well that makes me feel swell.

ANDRE AH! Okay. What are we doing here?

ANNIE Please, go ahead and tell me! I don't have a home, okay? I lost all my money. So I'm a little anxious right now. I'm sorry but *this* is new for *me*!

ANDRE What *about* your folks, why don't you call them?

ANNIE If I knew where they were, I would. I know *who* they were, after much prying and many phone calls, but I've never met them, my real parents.

ANDRE So the stork brought you.

> *Over the course of the following, ANA stands with her suitcase, resolved, takes a long look at ANDY, and tiptoes out the door. ANNIE feels what she says deeply, but we get the sense the cork has not fully popped though it is clearly straining.*

ANNIE That's one way to put it. No. I was a case of bad timing. And I hate to sound ungrateful but my *adoptive* folks were a bit over eager when they took me on. They ran out of steam. And so I was bad timing twice. I haven't seen them much since I left home and that was years ago. I don't know. I just needed to know who I was. I felt like I couldn't settle down until I knew that. And then several things happened at once: I found out my real Dad was of Scottish descent. *And* I wanted to travel. And maybe leave this fat country for good to live someplace less, I don't know, adolescent. Americans all come from somewhere else. How can a person feel rooted in a country that's not The Mother Country? America is the kid that left home. …So I left America.

ANDRE Well. You can't just *abandon* America. Well you *can;* you can do anything you want. I mean, *you* said: people have it rough over in Scotland. People have it rough *all* over. People have it rough here. You can't escape *that.* You're American because here you are, and if you leave then you're just an American abroad. It seems more practical to deal with what you've got. So we don't get to have deep roots in America, too bad. But we do get to live comparatively well considering the rest of the world.

ANNIE So, what, I shouldn't complain? *I know* it's rough all over. And everywhere that it's rough people still laugh. So? Do we just sit around and be grateful that at least we laugh now and then and pretend that there aren't other things happening that insult us, or hurt us–?

ANDRE –No–

ANNIE –I mean what you're saying sounds like some kind of apathy.

ANDRE Oh no no no!

ANNIE Then what are you saying? I mean you spit out all these theories at me but really, what are you talking about? Landslides? Monkeys? Where does all this stuff get you? You're out there trying to save the nation by bringing strangers together but you've *never had anyone over to your apartment?* What are you saying?

ANDRE I– …I– …I'm saying– …that you are in a crappy mood– which I understand– and that I should go get us something to eat while you do your laundry.

ANNIE Sorry.

ANDRE Don't be sorry. I'll catch a bus to the grocery store and get us something to eat.

ANNIE Don't buy anything for me. I'm only going to stay long enough to get my laundry done, and then I'll– figure something out.

ANDRE Whatever. …So, I'll be back.

ANNIE I'll be here.

> *ANDRE waves, leaves, and stands troubled by his thoughts. ANNIE stands troubled by her own. ANA does the same. ANDY, who has been thinking, sits up suddenly.*

ANDY Mom? Mom?

> *ANDRE makes his way to a bus while ANDY pulls a folded piece of paper from his book and reads it.*

ANDY Questions to ask Mom. One. Why are you mad when I ask you who is my Dad? Two. Why are you my only family? My friends have grandparents. Three. *(writes)* What is my history? *(reads)* Questions to ask Dad, when found. One. How are you? Two. Where have you been? Three. Mom said I was born when she was a kid but grownups have kids so when are we grownups? *(writes)* What does it mean?

Scene 15 – Last Bus

> *ANDY pulls out his toy bus and holds it in his lap as he thinks. ANA*

is on the bus already when ANDRE gets on and sits across from her. ANDREW and ANNE stand to either side, justifying.

ANDREW America is the leading country on the planet, providing the opportunity to pursue happiness to more different kinds of people from more backgrounds than any society in history.

ANNE Will historians record America as the meteor that emerged as a world power in the twentieth century, only to find itself unable to solve it's own internal problems?

ANDRE Business trip or pleasure?

ANA ...Business.

ANDRE *(distractedly)* ...What is it that you, uh... What uh...

ANA ...I'm sorry?

ANDRE *(smiles disapprovingly at himself)* Uh, nothing. Sorry. Enjoy your trip.

ANNE Is it even possible for us to know whether our great strengths or our great weaknesses will prevail?

ANDREW For the past thirty years we have been influenced to abandon our culture and seem to have lost faith in the core values, traditions and hopes of our civilization.

ANA Can I talk to you about something?

ANDRE ...Sure.

ANA I'm sorry, I know we don't know each other. I'm not crazy; I don't just go around talking to strangers. But, can I talk to you for a second?

ANDRE Yeah.

ANDREW Americans need to tell themselves to wake up and remember what brought us here.

ANNE Or, rather, to ask why we chose to fall asleep in the first place?

ANA I'm on my way to the airport. I went to work this morning to quit, and I did. Now I don't have a job. I did this because yesterday I f– well, I came into some money. So I quit my job and I'm going to go to the airport and point to a map of the world and buy a ticket to wherever my finger lands and that's where I'm going to go. This is my plan. I'm doing this because: with the money I now can, I've always wanted to, and when I was seventeen I had a baby I did not want to have, the father of which– ...the father of which I did not choose, not when I came into this world, and not when I was seventeen. And because of that I have had a life I did not choose, with a little boy who every time I look at him I remember that he was forced upon me and that we live in a world where even the people we are supposed to love are capable of changing us forever in ways we would never– huh! –no one would *ever* choose themselves. And if we would all quietly go about taking control of our lives back from the people who hurt us, even if that means someone else gets hurt in the process that's *still* the best thing to do. We have to be responsible for ourselves. It's my life that I live! We don't live other people's lives, they do! And if we each take care of ourselves then eventually one day nobody will be hurting anyone, and any pain getting to that day will have been worth it because everybody will be individually responsible!

ANDREW Where else can we glimpse our future better than in the pages of our nation's history?

ANNE Society tends to believe what it hears *repeatedly*. Repetition is persuasion's tool. Whose history is our nation's history? Mine?

ANA But I'm getting off the subject. Other people can do whatever they want. The important thing is that I take control of my life, right? We can't get through life without hurting someone once in a while. The odds are it is going to happen! But: we are separate individuals, and sometimes that means we do things that other people say are wrong. But it could be that they've just never walked in our shoes. You don't know anyone until you've walked in their shoes, isn't that how the saying goes? We could argue about these things forever, there are as many points of view as there are people and nobody has the right to say which ideas are correct for everyone; *That's* up to the individual. So I don't have to justify the choices I make in my life to everyone else because the important thing is that I am making the choice! I am making the choice! I am taking control of where my life is going after *ten years, a decade,* of being a slave to a life someone *else* chose for me! And after that many years the only thing I *can* do is to cut it off completely and just start again! I have to cut myself off!

ANDRE You can't do that.

ANA Why? According to who? *You?!*

ANDRE No it's not that it just– it can't be done.

ANA What?

ANDRE Cutting yourself off. *(beat, epiphany, gets up in a rush)* ...I'm sorry, I hope things work out for you. And they will, because– well that's just what things do. *(to bus driver:)* Back door! *(to ANA:)* Thank you!

ANDRE gets off the bus.

Scene 16 – Critical Mass

ANDRE runs back home. ANDY goes to the bathroom, washes his face and looks in the mirror. ANA remains on the bus. ANNIE writes a note on a piece of paper, leaves it to be found and goes to collect her clothes. ANDREW and ANNE continue as before.

ANDREW When I was ten years old I marched down to City Hall in my hometown to lobby for a zoo. It was a slow news day and a ten-year-old making an appeal for a municipal zoo made a nice story. When it appeared in the paper the next day, I was impressed with the idea that you could make an impact, and I was hooked.

ANNE When I was ten years old I saw the film clip of that Buddhist monk lighting himself on fire in Vietnam. All the other monks just sat there, absolutely still, and so did he until he fell over. I cried for the rest of the night, and when I finally stopped it was because I knew what I wanted to do.

ANDREW Ha!

ANNE I was ten years old.

ANDY Hello Mister President. *(mimes handshake)* My name is Andy. I came to give you some pictures I've taken of people all over the country since I know you and your friends don't really have a chance to meet much of anyone. You're welcome. No *(take two:)* Oh you're welcome. And I was wondering if I could ask you a favor. I want you to find my dad.

ANNE I *realized* / that some people had to be willing to dedicate their lives to protecting our way of life, our freedom–

ANDREW *I* realized that some people had to be willing to dedicate their lives to protecting our way of life, our freedom, and our people.

ANNE *(looking at ANDREW)* …and our people.

ANDY Mom won't tell me. So I left. I can live by myself. I can make my own dinner and read my own books. And I know everything about history. I don't look like her and I don't need her. I'm my own– uh– I'm my own self by myself! …She's gonna to leave *me* one day anyhow.

ANDRE has entered his apartment and found ANNIE's note.

ANDRE Damn it! Damn damn damn!

ANDRE stutters in space for a moment then makes for the door. ANNIE has heard him and comes out from the other room.

ANNIE That was quick.

ANDRE I didn't go to the store, there's food in the fridge!

ANNIE Then why'd you leave?

ANDRE I just– I I needed to go! But that's not important now! What is this? Were you just going to leave?!

ANNIE I think that would be best.

ANDRE But you can't do that!

ANNIE Yes I can.

ANDRE No you can't. You don't have any money.

ANNIE Why do you care so much? If anything I should be freaked out *because* you care so much. I don't know you.

ANDRE You're the first person I've ever gotten more than three meaningful words out of on a bus and I can't just ignore that!

ANNIE Andre what are you talking about?

ANDRE Why would I run into you over and over again in such a big city?

ANNIE It's an accident!

ANDRE Exactly! It means we're touching the pattern. And it all happened so fast, see? The world is speeding up and we are just rush rush rushing toward the year 2012 and all these theological and mathematical predictions that some great change is coming! We are going to be unrecognizable to ourselves! It would be idiotic to ignore any hint of what this world we've made means. We have to act on things like *this!*

ANNIE Andre, I act on things. I up and moved across the Atlantic ocean. A whole damn ocean! I can make it by myself in San Francisco.

ANDRE But *why* by yourself? It doesn't have to be that way; I can help you!

ANNIE That's very nice but I can't accept that. Beside the fact that I don't know you– *I don't know* you– you have to understand I want to figure things out by myself.

ANDRE Well, okay, now let's talk about that for a second. What are you figuring out? Where you *came* from? You *know* that! You said you know who your real parents are; so why did you run off to *Scotland* instead of straight to them? It makes no sense!

ANNIE I wanted to travel!

ANDRE You left home. You left America. You left Scotland. Now you want to leave here. You don't want to travel you want to give up.

ANNIE *That* is not true! That is *not* true! I went to Scotland to start over and have a life! I couldn't do that here! I had to get away!

ANDRE Ah ha ha, "get away, get away," that's it! You said it!

ANNIE Oh god you are crazy! Don't you analyze me!

> *ANNIE runs in the back room to pack her suitcase. At the airport, ANA, ticket in hand, has set her suitcase down and dialed up ANDY from a pay phone. The phone rings at home.*

ANDRE Where are you going?

ANNIE To pack my things! Don't come in here I'm naked!

ANDY Hello?

ANA Hey, kiddo, it's mom.

ANDRE You're not naked; how did you get naked so fast?

ANDY Hi. Where are you?

ANNIE I'm changing my clothes, I'm packing and I'm leaving.
ANA I-I'm at work. I just wanted to call and say hello.
ANDY Why?

ANDRE sits down to wait by the door.

ANDRE *(to himself, triumphant)* You're running away again.
ANA Well, I– I'm going to be staying late at the office tonight, so, just make yourself some dinner and put yourself to bed okay?
ANNE Why is it that we live in a pluralistic culture with contradictory paradigms?
ANDY What's all that noise in the background?
ANA That's traffic outside the office.
ANDREW A Democracy may be a far less orderly society, but it is a vastly superior one!
ANA So, Andy, I won't be home until really late, okay, so put yourself to bed. I don't want to find you up when I get home. Okay?
ANDY What's the matter with your voice?
ANA Nothing I'm just tired.
ANDY Are you going to wake me up in the morning?
ANDREW And we need conviction, something to believe in, if we hope to succeed!
ANA Well, you know how to do that. You're a big boy, you can take care of yourself. Mommy's gonna sleep in late, okay, so just get up and go.
ANNE By a show of hands: Who is willing to believe without ever asking why?
ANDY Okay.

ANNIE emerges with her suitcase.

ANNIE I'm leaving.
ANDRE You'll have to kill me first.
ANNIE I'm not kidding. Get out of the way.
ANA Alright, well, sleep tight tonight then.
ANDY Okay.
ANA ...Okay–
ANNIE –Andre! Get out of the way!
ANDRE Please stay! Please! Just don't go! Please!
ANNIE Why is it so important to you?
ANDY Mom?

ANA Yes honey?
ANDRE Because you need to!
ANDY Should we hang up now?
ANNIE What?
ANA …Okay.
ANNE Every belief, every answer, needs to be questioned.
ANNIE Andre, you make no sense whatsoever!
ANDY Are you really coming home?
ANDREW We do hold *some* truths to be self evident!
ANA Of course I'm coming home; you have enough books to read, right?
ANNIE You keep saying you want me to stay but you haven't acted like you really want that.
ANDRE Well, I know, I I was confused. But I'm not confused anymore; and if you leave now you won't know what it's like to stay.
ANNIE Stop it!
ANDY When are you coming home?
ANNE Is truth, then, simply a matter of enough repetition?
ANA I'm– okay, Andy, the truth is– …I'm going on a business trip! There! I was *going* to surprise you with a postcard!
ANDY When are you coming back?
ANDRE Okay look, *I* need you to stay! Okay?
ANNIE What for?
ANDREW Self. Evident.
ANDRE Because you're the first person to respond to me!
ANNIE I'm not a guinea pig!
ANDY Mom?
ANDRE I know!
ANNIE I didn't pop into your life to be a test for your theories!
ANA It's a business trip!
ANDRE I know!
ANNIE I need to take care of myself! That's what I need!
ANDRE You should! With me!
ANNIE AAAH!
ANDY Okay.
ANA Look, I have to get off the phone Andy.
ANDRE You don't have anywhere to go and I don't have anyone to go anywhere with. I'm making an offer here! I want you to stay!
ANNIE Stop saying that! You don't know *what* you want Andre!
ANDRE Yes I do! *Yes I do!* I want us to need each other! Because *I need that!*

And you need that!
ANA *(long, silent pause)* Okay. So. Goodbye.
ANNE Where are you?
ANDREW It is time to decide.
ANDY Goodbye. Mom?
ANNIE We don't need each other.
ANDRE We could.
ANNE Where did you come from?
ANNIE You don't know me.
ANA What honey?
ANDRE Well–
ANDREW I am not *talking* about America!
ANDRE I will know you, but it takes a while!
ANDY Mom, I–
ANDRE And besides, if you leave then all of this will have meant nothing!
ANA What!
ANNIE I– I'm–
ANDY Uhm, I–
ANA Goodbye Andy.
ANNIE No, look, you're wrong, I'm going!
ANDY No, wait!
ANA Andy!
ANDRE Annie–
ANNIE Andre–!
ANNE And where are you going?
ANNIE Goodbye.
ANDREW Do you ever answer these questions yourself?
ANDRE Look!
ANNE You're hiding behind your desperate certainty!
ANDRE Just try it once in your life, please!
ANA Okay goodbye now.
ANDREW You don't know what certainty is!
ANNIE I don't need you Andre!
ANDY I don't want you to go!
ANA I can't miss my flight, Andy!
ANDRE I need something more than strangers!
ANNE Your entire life is built on lies!
ANNIE Well good for you but I don't!

ANDREW What did you say?! *(goes after her)*
ANNIE Goodbye!
ANA / Goodbye!
ANDRE You're making / a mistake!
ANDY Mom / don't leave!
ANNIE & ANA / Goodbye!
ANDREW / You are so worthless! All you want to do is destroy for the sole sake of destruction and you have *no* answers to replace what you tear apart! You have done nothing but harass me since I got up here you lousy liberal fucking shit now stop it! stop it! stop it!
ANNE You don't have the guts to question a thing you believe in! You're so desperate to protect what you have that you've gone blind! And you haven't answered a single question I've asked all evening you stupid fucking rightwing shit now answer me! answer me! answer me!

ANA, ANDY, ANDRE and ANNIE are each staring at ANDREW and ANNE. There is a stunning moment of silence. EVERYONE looks at EVERYONE for the first time. THEY look at the audience as well. Finally, ANDREW breaks the silence and addresses the audience awkwardly.

ANDREW Uh. Uh, huh, excuse me, uh, ladies and gentlemen. I apologize on behalf of both myself and my uh– uhm, opponent, for this outburst. It was a very unprofessional act on our part, and I am sure she would agree– that– we both apologize and would like to proceed. For there are issues which must be addressed and I am afraid that with all the– hoopla, if you will, we have lost sight of the central matter at hand.

We hear "This Land Is Your Land" over the loudspeakers. ANDREW is startled momentarily but continues.

ANDREW Uh. Uh, we must, as a nation, ask ourselves– Uh, I I I mean remind ourselves– that we started with nothing but hope in 1607, and have managed to arrive where we are today. And if we simply continue operating– as we once did before the advent of the Nineteen Sixties and all that that era entailed– under the clear definition of the American Civilization which our founding fathers gave to us, we will continue as a nation to succeed. I mean it's worked pretty well so far now am I right, or am I right?

ANDREW turns to the rest of the cast and looks at them. THEY look at him, then at each other. The song continues. ANDREW steps forward and attempts to secure the room's attention. Under his increasingly desperate speech, the other characters peel off one by one, almost beyond their own will, moving around with increasing speed like atoms in an attempt to either avoid, deny, escape, review, summarize, or find their way back to certainty, each according to character. Only ANNE remains still, watching the whole thing unfold around her.

ANDREW Mm-m-m-m-m! No no no no no. If I could just return our attention please to the matter at hand, the matter of definition. If you would all– Uh. What–? Ah! We are a group of people in a particular country at a particular time, all squinting into the distance to witness that Millennium as it rolls over the horizon into the twenty-first century – our Eden or our Armageddon, depending on who you talk to!

Uh. But *we* approach the Millennium and we are interested in angels, in UFOs, horrifying natural disasters and near-death experiences caught on tape. We have more faith in these things than we do in the Social Security System. We are afraid of what might lurk ahead. And the more we give up our power to the unknown, the more we *will be* afraid. There is ignorance in letting go of one's certainty! *That* is something to fear!

We in America have reason to be certain, not to fear. For we have our American History. We *have* our definition! Not because we have sat about fingering our chins and pondering the possibilities. But because we have gone West. We have set out to discover. We have built. We have invented. We have stood and we have taken action. We have dared to do what no nation has done before: we have created a country where every man and woman of every race and religion is welcome to be born with equal rights to life, liberty, and the pursuit of happiness!

We have split atoms! We have touched the moon! We *used* to have friends and neighbors to tell us who we are, now we have is– uh, what do we have? –Doubt!

There is something fundamentally wrong! We risk, by our own hand, not being able to understand the world we have invented!

It is time to decide! It is time for conviction! It is time to remember our History. I am not talking about America. I am talking about you, each of you, each of us, reclaiming our Definition of who we are!

ALL stop. ANDREW is saluting his country.

ANDY walks to ANA and places his hand on her head. SHE cries but does not look at him.

ANDRE walks to ANNIE, takes her suitcase out of her hand and sets it down. SHE does not look at him.

ANNE walks to ANDREW and pulls his saluting hand down, which he resists at first. ANDREW looks at ANNE.

Black out, with music continuing through bows.

The end.

The Death of Meyerhold

a tragedy with a smile on the lips

The Death of Meyerhold

The world premiere of *The Death of Meyerhold* was presented by Shotgun Players at the Live Oak Theatre, Berkeley, CA, on December 6, 2003. The production was transferred to the Julie Morgan Center for the Arts, Berkeley, CA, reopening there on January 8, 2004. The production was directed by the author, with the following cast and staff:

W1	Beth Wilmurt
W2	Isabelle Ortega
G1	Natalie Grant-Villegas
M1	Cassidy Brown
M2	Richard James
M3	Reid Davis
M4	Clive Worsley
M5	Benjamin Privitt
M6	Patrick Dooley
M7	Andy Alabran
M8	Kevin Clarke
M9	Dave Maier
Set	Mark Jackson
Costumes	Valera Coble
Lights	Rob Anderson
Sound	Jake Rodriguez
Stage Manager	Marilyn Stanley

The Death of Meyerhold was subsequently produced by The Studio Theatre, Washington, D.C., opening January 23, 2005. The production was directed by Rick Simas, with the following cast and staff:

W1	Becky Peters
W2	Katya Falikova
G1	Ann Coventry
M1	Joel Reuben Ganz
M2	Richard Henrich
M3	Cecil E. Baldwin
M4	Gregory Stuart
M5	Jon Townson
M6	Peter Klaus
M7	Jason Lott

M8	Scott Kerns
M9	Andy Greenleaf
Choreography	Beth Wilmurt
Costumes	Robyn Shrater Seemann
Lights	Colin Bills
Sound	Jake Rodriguez
Stage Manager	Kristen J. Bishel

Cast of Characters

Two women, one girl, and nine men play the various roles according to the following breakdown:

W1 – Actress, Old Woman, Wife, Imperial Bourgeoisie, Maria Babanova, Stella Adler, Dresser.
W2 – Razonova, Woman, Imperial Bourgeoisie, Zinaida Raikh, Phoebe Brand.

G1 – American Girl, Granddaughter, Imperial Bourgeoisie, Muscovite, Paperboy.

M1 – Meyerhold, Lee Strasberg.
M2 – Stanislavsky, First Secret Police Man, Lunacharsky, Muscovite, Critic #4.
M3 – Chekhov, Second Secret Police Man, White Guard Sniper, Kugel, Mother, Muscovite, Critic #1, NKVD 1.
M4 – Danchenko, Husband, Third White Guard, Mayakovsky, Waiter, Baker, Critic #5, NKVD 4.
M5 – Jackson, First Secretive Man, Bolshevik Soldier, First White Guard, Garin, Clifford Odets, Critic #2, Yury.
M6 – Artistic Director, Second Secretive Man, Bolshevik Soldier, Second White Guard, Ilinsky, Harold Clurman, Critic #3, NKVD 3.
M7 – Kosheverov, Actor, Third Man, Imperial Bourgeoisie, Second Prisoner, a student, Sanford Meisner, Gladkov.
M8 – Counter Revolutionary, Actor Playing Sorin, Suspicious Man, Imperial Bourgeoisie, Abrosimov, Tereshkovich, Shostakovich, Malcontent.
M9 – Yakov, Train Conductor, Shady Man, Bolshevik Soldier, First Prisoner, Bebutin, Samoilov, Elia Kazan, NKVD 2.

Other characters played by the company.

Notes

All TITLES are to be projected on a screen above the set.

A slash in the dialogue (/) indicates that the next actor should start their line, creating overlapping speech.

Regarding the Prologue, the ARTISTIC DIRECTOR'S lines may be adjusted to accurately reflect the speech pattern of the Artistic Director of the producing organization. This character could also be the Dramaturg or some other representative of the theatre.

Preshow

TITLE: "The Death of Meyerhold"

Joyful, catchy, and heroic Soviet era music plays over the loudspeakers.

Prologue

TITLE: "The Death of Meyerhold"

The immediate present. Two chairs in a spotlight DSC of the set, itself a useful construction of stairs, platforms, and curtains. Prop tables, furniture, and racks of costumes off SL and SR – visible, but unobtrusive. The ARTISTIC DIRECTOR of the producing organization and MARK JACKSON enter and sit as the preshow music concludes. Over the course of their dialogue we gradually become aware of the presence of a ten-year-old AMERICAN GIRL upstage, who sits watching television in 1953. Eventually the presence of numerous other less discernable people can also be felt, listening from the shadows of the space.

ARTISTIC DIRECTOR So. Evening everybody. Thanks for coming. I assume you know who we are since you're *here*. But just in case, so you know who's who, I'm _____ , Artistic Director of _____ , and this is Mark Jackson, writer and director of *The Death of Meyerhold*. Which, for anyone who *might* have wandered in off the street: plays through _____ on this very stage.

JACKSON Yes.

ARTISTIC DIRECTOR So why don't we start with the big picture and narrow it down from there.

JACKSON Okay.

ARTISTIC DIRECTOR So who is this Meyerhold guy?

JACKSON Well, this Meyerhold guy was a Russian theatre actor and then director during the first forty years of the twentieth century, which was of course a very interesting time to live in Russia.

ARTISTIC DIRECTOR How so?

JACKSON *(laughs)* Well, by 1900, sentiments against life under the Tsar had already been smoldering for decades; major strikes and protests by workers were *all* ending in bloodshed. A revolutionary group made up of two factions, Mensheviks and Bolsheviks, was illegally established under the umbrella name of the Social Democratic Party. And in February 1917 the Tsar finally abdicated and the Social Democratic Party took over. Then: power struggles within the Party ended with the Bolshevik faction, led by Vladimir Lenin, seizing control in October 1917 – and so a Civil War broke out, World War One was winding down, and then when Lenin died in 1924 Stalin took over and kept the ball rolling in his way.

ARTISTIC DIRECTOR Yowza.

JACKSON Right. So, rewind, back to the turn of the century, when the Tsar was still in power: Meyerhold was a young student and then actor in Stanislavsky's company, the Moscow Art Theatre.

ARTISTIC DIRECTOR And for anyone who didn't study theatre in college, Stanislavsky is the grandaddy of what we think of as modern, psychologically realistic, emotionally truthful: Acting.

JACKSON Yes. And Meyerhold felt there was more to theatre than just that. So he broke off and started doing his own thing, which was much more physically and musically based, much more theatrical. And the two of them in their separate theatres in Russia basically created what we think of as the modern theatre. In fact you could say that Stanislavsky brought theatre out of the 19th century, and Meyerhold carried it into the 20th. And that everything *since* then is really just a repackaged variation of what they essentially came up / with.

ARTISTIC DIRECTOR Right. ...Now, you're a director and writer who's often going back to the classics, but adapting them to a more contemporary American context. Why? What's up with that?

JACKSON It's called stealing, actually. All my ideas are stolen. It's easier than comin' up with your own ideas. And of course I only steal from the best.

ARTISTIC DIRECTOR Of course.

JACKSON But, really, you know, Shakespeare, for example, is the most produced playwright in America, so clearly there's something there that Americans respond to very deeply. And all the classic plays I've been drawn to deal with subjects that are meaningful in America now, which is why they still catch our attention I think. Somebody said – a *buto* artist – he said that "cultural exchange begins with misunderstanding." I think that's very interesting. That impulse we have, that *need*, really, to understand. That we can see ourselves and our country in a play written a hundred or four hundred and fifty years ago is very interesting, or in somebody's life who lived long ago in a very different time / and place.

ARTISTIC DIRECTOR Right, right. …So, most people are probably more familiar with the name Stanislavsky than with Meyerhold. But those who do know of both usually pit them against one another – Stanislavsky is the wise benevolent sage and Meyerhold is the brilliant manipulative dictator. What's your handle on that?

JACKSON Well, there's a lot more to Stanislavsky than we've been shown, certainly in America. His portrait has actually been airbrushed quite a bit. But he and Meyerhold were essentially approaching the same thing, experimenting from *very* different angles, but heading in the same direction. We conveniently forget that, or just don't pay attention to it, because to actually deal with it would mean rethinking what we've all spent a lot of time and money learning, and, you know, who wants to do that! But the coming together of the two men toward the end of their lives is very telling, I think – that moment when two *very different* people could actually have a conversation with one another. How often does *that* happen in the world, on any level? We like to approach the world in such an Either-Or way: mind or body, Stanislavsky or Meyerhold, Democrat / or Republican.

ARTISTIC DIRECTOR Or Republican, right.

JACKSON Everything must be very black or white even though we all know the grey area is mmmuch more interesting. More *difficult*. And more interesting. Which is not a coincidence!

ARTISTIC DIRECTOR That something difficult is more interesting than something that's more immediately comprehensible.

JACKSON Exactly. Again it's that need to understand; it makes us feel more comfortable, but ironically we don't actually like taking the time to understand. It's too exhausting. So we make these plays and TV programs and we shape the news such that it's Easy to Understand, and so it actually becomes less true. Because the world is complicated. It's grotesque. And Meyerhold knew that.

ARTISTIC DIRECTOR Yeah it's always interesting how people with different agendas construct different versions of history. How does that sort of thing play out with Meyerhold?

JACKSON Oh, well, when the Soviet Union collapsed everything got thrown in the air. Now we're trying to figure out: what *is* Russia exactly? What is "Russian," meaning what can we keep from our view of the Communist period, and what do we have to redefine? …Most people probably aren't thinking about this actually. I think the Berlin Wall came down and, you know, "good, there, that's over. What's next? Oh Saddam, oh okay," and we moved on. But, in regard to Meyerhold, basically there are two camps. One says he didn't hold any political opinions and was just an opportunist. The other claims that he was actually very political and in fact had the same totalitarian impulse as Stalin. And the academics muse over the "rich complexity" of his art, and write articles about it, and the directors and actors read the articles and go off to some room and try to work out his techniques. But whatever the angle, there's still an overall tendency to want to figure out whether or not Meyerhold was, really, deep down, a Communist.

ARTISTIC DIRECTOR Was he at heart a kind of theatrical Stalinist, or was he just an independent artist in political times making the best of the / situation.

JACKSON Yeah. Exactly. And either way, I think the important thing ultimately is Asking The Question, which is what made Meyerhold so irritating to Stalin. You see, something we really can't identify with today, particularly in America, is just how important artists were to Russia back then. Art was really seen as a functioning arm of society. And everyone knew Meyerhold's name. Everyone. He was a big celebrity. You could go to kiosks on the street and buy souvenir combs with Meyerhold's name written on them. So anything he did was extremely influential and the government watched him very closely. Meyerhold was making art that invited the audience to participate in the shaping of their life experience – economically, politically, their relationship to family, to co-workers, to the government. Not an artist you want around when you're trying to shape a nation's mindset. Now, the tragedy in *America* today is how we've so willingly traded our civil rights for good PR. It's this trend of not discussing serious issues without cutting to a joke, or, artificially imposing happy endings. We don't really want to educate people about how the system works. And we don't really want people to question it. So instead we celebrate Individuals. And that way you can say that some people are simply lucky and some people aren't, when the fact that 12% of the people own 78% of the country is really a question of design not luck. Meyerhold was using theatre to ask his audience to think. So, you know, President Bush, for example, probably wouldn't like him anymore than Stalin did. ...I stole all these ideas from Mel Gordon and Peter Sellars, by the way.

ARTISTIC DIRECTOR I knew it. You cheap bastard.

JACKSON Or "adapted" them, rather.

ARTISTIC DIRECTOR *That's* right. So, in the end, if he didn't like him very much, what did Stalin do with Meyerhold?

JACKSON ...He shot him.

Sound of a gunshot! Blackout.

TITLE: "Berlin. November 1989"

Followed by Ronald Reagan delivering his famous line, "Mister Gorbachev, tear down this wall." Then cheering that quickly smears into

1950's alien-invasion and Red-Scare movie soundtracks mixed with gunshots and McCarthy's voice asking "Are you now, or have you ever been, a member of the Communist Party?" followed by the answer "No sir I have not" as various PEOPLE escape from one place to another. The noise cuts into the short intro theme of a 1953 news program. The RUSSIAN PEOPLE all stop to listen.

TITLE: "Salinas, California, March 5, 1953. Eleven-year-old Joanie Caswell watches television at home."

ANCHOR MAN (VOICE OVER) Joseph Stalin, Soviet Communist Party leader of the USSR since 1924, died of a stroke today in Moscow. The Stalinist era in Russia has come to an end.

The AMERICAN GIRL jumps up and down with joy and cartwheels off the stage to extremely grand tragic Russian music.

TITLE: "Moscow"

The RUSSIAN PEOPLE wipe tears of shock and sorrow. A COUNTER REVOLUTIONARY leaps forward triumphantly and runs up on the raised platform.

COUNTER REVOLUTIONARY The murderer is dead! The murderer is dead! Let Russia live again! The murderer is dead!

The COUNTER REVOLUTIONARY is shot dead by an unknown source and falls into the PEOPLE. They catch him, continue to mourn for Stalin self-consciously, and drag him away. All of this as the scene changes to…

Act One, 1898–1917

Episode One – The Seagull

During the following, rehearsal furniture and whatnot are set for Act One of The Seagull. *MEYERHOLD is up on the edge of a platform, perched like a young wolf, clocking CHEKHOV who is speaking with ROZANOVA, the young actress who plays Nina. OTHERS, including NEMIROVICH-DANCHENKO, are bustling about during what appears to be a break.*

CHEKHOV I can hear the audience now.

TITLE: "Rehearsal for The Seagull *at the Moscow Art Theatre. September 1898."*

CHEKHOV "Did you notice darling how the vase of flowers fell over? And how the clock ticked? And the crickets? And the thunder? And the rain? And how the harness bells tinkled?" And not one word about my play!

ROZANOVA But it's realistic.

CHEKHOV Realistic! The stage is art, my dear Rozanova. What would happen if you took a Kramskoy painting, cut the nose out of one of the faces and substituted a real one? The nose would be "realistic," and the painting would be *ruined.* Stanislavsky has ruined my play!

ROZANOVA Careful. He'll hear you.

CHEKHOV I will write a new play, and the stage directions will begin like this: "How wonderful, how quiet! No birds, no dogs, no cuckoos, no nightingale, no clock, no jingle of bells, no exploding corn cakes, not one damn *cricket* can be heard!"

ROZANOVA Anton Pavlovich, you know he plans to bring on the entire household, including a woman with a crying child, at the end of the third act.

CHEKHOV What? My god, why? It will be like playing pianissimo on the piano and having the lid come crashing down.

ROZANOVA But in life it often happens that the pianissimo is interrupted by the forte.

CHEKHOV This is not life. It's a play. As an actress you should make yourself aware of this lest you be carted off in a straightjacket.

MEYERHOLD Anton Pavlovich! If I may speak.

CHEKHOV Please. Give me some hope.

MEYERHOLD I think... I feel... Your play–

STANISLAVSKY enters and suddenly EVERYBODY moves into place.

STANISLAVSKY Forgive me, everyone.

DANCHENKO Alright then, if we could return to the scene.

STANISLAVSKY Yes, if we could take it from Treplev and his daisy. Sorin, as you were. Aaand Vsevolod. ...Vsevolod Emelievich.

MEYERHOLD Oh. Yes. Sorry. From?

DANCHENKO Your daisy.

MEYERHOLD Daisy...

STANISLAVSKY ...Something you'd like to say?

MEYERHOLD Me?

DANCHENKO No, Meyerhold: the scene. Begin the scene.

MEYERHOLD Right. *(looks to ACTOR PLAYING SORIN)*
ACTOR PLAYING SORIN It's your line.
MEYERHOLD *(annoyed smile)* Thank you.
STANISLAVSKY Aaaaand commence!

> *MEYERHOLD begins his monologue, punctuated by the sounds of coughing and hammering made from YAKOV behind a curtain.*

MEYERHOLD "She loves me, she loves me not. She loves me, she loves me not. She loves me, she loves me not. You see? My own mother does not love me. Well, why should she? She wants to lead a glamorous life, dress like an eighteen-year-old girl, make love to that man. And then there's me, her son, that constant reminder she's no longer young. When I'm not here, she's thirty-two. When I am here, she's forty-five. This is why she hates me. Besides, I can't stand her kind of theatre. She adores the *Theátuh*, thinks she's serving the cause of humanity. But if you ask me her kind of theatre is tired, useless, it's all worn out. The curtain goes up, the lights come on, you're in a room with three walls, and there they stand: those servants of Art, showing us how people eat, drink, sit, walk, wear clothes! And then: they try to wring some nice easy little moral out of it, some little thing you wouldn't mind having around the house! You go, you sit down, and they give you the same shit/

DANCHENCKO / Stuff, stuff, the line is "stuff!"
STANISLAVSKY / Vsevolod Emelievich!
MEYERHOLD over and over and over! And it makes me utterly sick! I want to run screaming from it all and never look back!"
ACTOR PLAYING SORIN "But we need the theatre! How could we do without it!"
MEYERHOLD "We *need:* New Forms! And if we can't have them then we're better off with no theatre at all!"
STANISLAVSKY Stop!
MEYERHOLD "Stuff." My apologies Anton Pavlovich.
CHEKHOV I like your word better. It's much more to the point.
DANCHENKO It can't be said on the stage.
STANISLAVSKY He knows this, Vladimir. You must live the role, Vsevolod, not rewrite it. This text is poetry. You mustn't alter it to your taste.
MEYERHOLD I know this. It was a mistake.
STANISLAVSKY Yes, very well. Well done. I believe you when you speak these words. They leap from deep within you.
MEYERHOLD Yes.
CHEKHOV Konstantin Sergievich! May I ask a question?
STANISLAVSKY Of course.

CHEKHOV Why is Yakov still coughing and hammering while poor Vsevolod is trying to speak?

STANISLAVSKY Why it's your stage direction, Anton. "Sounds of coughing and hammering."

CHEKHOV But not through the entire act! Just at the beginning, that's all it needs.

STANISLAVSKY I'm sorry, Anton, I didn't understand. Perhaps you could find a reason for Yakov to exit a few pages earlier.

CHEKHOV Or perhaps he could shut up! I told you Vladimir: my play will be hissed off the stage – *again!* You've lured me back into hell!

DANCHENKO Anton, I promise you, the Alexandrinsky held only eight rehearsals, their actors didn't understand you, their audience came expecting light comedy – how could it succeed? We love your play, we are devoted to it, we understand what you have written for us, don't we Konstantin?

STANISLAVSKY Wwwell–

DANCHENKO Yes, we do!

STANISLAVSKY Yes, we do. Anton, perhaps the play will not provoke storms of applause, but, after seeing your play, society women across Russia will be wearing dresses and hairdos just like Arkadina's.

CHEKHOV Do you hear this? Dresses and hairdos just like Arkadina's. Have I written a fashion catalogue?!

DANCHENKO What Konstantin means is that a genuine production, properly prepared, with exquisite details and fresh qualities, liberated from routine, will be a triumph of art – I guarantee it!

CHEKHOV How can it be a triumph of art if the actors can't be heard beneath his *constant racket?* Stanislavsky is ruining my play!

STANISLAVSKY Anton, your characters are real people. They must live in a real world.

CHEKHOV They are not real people! They're characters! And the audience must be able to hear them! Coughing and hammering and crickets and thunder, these are not realistic! They're noise! Everything must be simple, do you understand? Like in life. Not life! *Like* in life. It's theatre for god's sake!!!

MEYERHOLD I understand you, Anton Pavlovich!

DANCHENKO Be quiet Meyerhold.

MEYERHOLD Why? Why? Are we actors to do nothing but act?

STANISLAVSKY Vsevolod.

CHEKHOV shortly begins to cough.

MEYERHOLD We want to be able to *think* while we act! We want to know *why* we are doing what we are doing! Why does this play matter? Why must

the audience see it? What is happening in Russia? We must know these things! Only then can we convey his ideas! Only then will the audience understand what Anton Chekhov has written! With all due respect, Konstantin Sergievich, these realistic techniques you worked out years ago which you still employ regardless of whether a play is a mood play or a period piece – well I have no need to explain why this is simply wrong!
DANCHENKO Meyerhold!

> *CHEKHOV's coughing has escalated. DANCHENKO goes to him. Everyone else stands frozen with fear while CHEKHOV coughs violently. Once the attack subsides...*

DANCHENKO Are you pleased?
ROZANOVA Vsevolod, how could you?
DANCHENKO You could have killed him.
MEYERHOLD I'm sorry, I only wished to–
DANCHENKO Be quiet. This isn't the Academy, you*ng* man. This is the Moscow Art Theatre.

> *DANCHENKO helps CHEKHOV stand and they exit.*

MEYERHOLD Forgive me.
STANISLAVSKY For a moment I thought you were acting Treplev again.
MEYERHOLD We do need new forms.
STANISLAVSKY And patience. Am I right?
MEYERHOLD Most likely. ...Shall we take the scene again?
STANISLAVSKY No I don't think so. I've heard enough for today. And you are correct: actors should think.
MEYERHOLD Konstantin Sergiev–

> *But the look in STANISLAVSKY'S eye stops MEYERHOLD. A tense pause. The OTHERS in the room all take a collective step back. STANISLAVSKY walks out after DANCHENKO and CHEKHOV. Pause. MEYERHOLD throws down his text.*

Episode Two – In The Provinces

> *TITLE: "February 1902. Meyerhold quits the Moscow Art Theatre and sets out on his own to make theatre in the provinces of Russia."*

> *Piano music of great momentum plays under the following onslaught of*

changing locations.

MEYERHOLD "Anton Pavlovich. Our season opened today with your *Three Sisters*. Huge Success! Beloved author of melancholy moods! You alone give true delight!"

CHEKHOV "Konstantin Sergievich. The Art Theatre was wrong not to make Meyerhold a shareholder in the company. Perhaps he has written you something of his success in the provinces. I am glad for him, for a life in art is not likely to continue so easily in Kherson. There's no public for plays there; all they want is the next touring show. After all, Kherson is barely Russia, or even Europe!"

MEYERHOLD "And soon we shall add *Ivanov*, *Uncle Vanya*, and *The Seagull* to our repertoire."

ALEXANDER KOSHEVEROV And then what?

MEYERHOLD Alexander, don't worry.

KOSHEVEROV Kherson will think we are The Chekhov Theatre. Who is our next author?

MEYERHOLD Ibsen.

KOSHEVEROV Ibsen. Ibsen! Ibsen, everyone, let's go, Ibsen Ibsen!

As MEYERHOLD calls out titles, the ACTORS reconfigure to various Ibsen-esque stage pictures.

MEYERHOLD Annnd *Enemy of the People!* Good! Annnd *A Doll's House!* Good! Annnd *Hedda Gabler!* No. No. No. Good! Annnd curtain up!

The ACTORS cycle through all three plays, then bow to applause.

KOSHEVEROV Okay! What's next?

MEYERHOLD Gorky.

KOSHEVEROV Gorky! Which?

MEYERHOLD *The Petty Bourgeois*.

KOSHEVEROV *The Petty Bourgeois!*

The ACTORS arrange themselves accordingly.

MEYERHOLD No. More petty. More. Still more. I don't believe you!

ACTRESS Sorry Stanislavsky.

MEYERHOLD That's not funny. Annnd curtain up!

Applause. Bows.

MEYERHOLD Well done. I wonder if anybody noticed.
KOSHEVEROV *Whew!* What's next?
MEYERHOLD Tolstoy.
KOSHEVEROV Tolstoy! Title?
MEYERHOLD *The Death of Ivan the Terrible.*
KOSHEVEROV *The Death of Ivan the Terrible!*

The ACTORS arrange themselves accordingly, leaving a conspicuous hole in the stage picture.

MEYERHOLD Something's wrong.
KOSHEVEROV *(pointing to the conspicuous hole)* You.
MEYERHOLD No. *(Changes someone's head)* That's right. *(Enters the picture as Ivan)* Annnd curtain up!

Applause. Bows. The ACTORS exhibit signs of fatigue.

MEYERHOLD Don't be tired. Smile. You're actors.

The ACTORS groan; they've heard that line before.

MEYERHOLD And curtain up!

The ACTORS snap into place and then cycle through all their plays in slow motion under the following.

MEYERHOLD "Anton Pavlovich. You are right: there is no audience for plays in Kherson. The critics are very complimentary but the number of avid theatregoers in this backwards nowhere fills one house at best. To keep food on our plates we must offer them something new each night. It is a furious pace, but: we Must Burn at Both Ends if we hope to succeed. For myself, I've accomplished little as director but to recycle the work of Stanislavsky. At least I'm stealing from the best. And now Kherson's local color will suffer no surprises should they ever make a cultural expedition to Moscow. But as they don't seem to *like* surprises much: I trust they'll be grateful."
STANISLAVSKY "Anton Pavlovich. I *have* read of Meyerhold's success in Kherson. Hopefully he is content. I, meanwhile, am not. Give us a new play, Anton Pavlovich! Save us from my boredom."
DANCHENKO "Konstantin Sergievich. Regarding your request to Chekhov: I

recognize your boredom in my own, but I am afraid it is not Chekhov who can help us in the end. Without bright, truly poetic images our theatre is doomed to death. Chekhov's sweet lyrical people are no longer alive. We must look elsewhere. Have you considered Symbolism?"

Applause. The ACTORS in Kherson collapse after their final bow.

TITLE: "September 1903"

MEYERHOLD   "Anton Pavlovich. We begin our new season with a new name: The New Drama Association. We desperately need new forms. *(the ACTORS concur)* To that end, I will experiment with Symbolism – whether Kherson is interested or not."

Gunshot!

TITLE: "The illegally organized Russian Social Democratic Party splits into Mensheviks and Bolsheviks. The smaller Bolshevik faction is led by Vladimir Lenin."

The music is silent. The ACTORS all look off in the same direction. Gunshots continue in the distance. STANISLAVSKY closes his window. Silence.

MEYERHOLD   "I feel our nation's plot thickening. Or perhaps it's just our patrons' skulls. I am disturbed by my comrades who don't want to rise above their narrow interests. I wish all those who give their lives to *theatre* would become aware of their great mission; Russia has a fever and we must look to it. True, the new century has only just begun, but I do not see our reality, I do not know this century. I long to burn with the spirit of my time. Give me life or death, only not sleep."
TRAIN CONDUCTOR   All aboard!

TITLE: "February 1904"

Music again. The ACTORS now perform their repertoire in extreme slow motion, offering their first play in the symbolist vein before returning to their customary style.

MEYERHOLD   *(an abrupt shift of tone)* "Meanwhile, our tour to the neighboring provinces reveals that a lack of taste and curiosity is not limited to Kherson. Symbolism seems to escape the provincial senses. I am growing weary of the potboilers and Art Theatre knock-offs we must churn out to satisfy the unimaginative local appetite. Your new play sounds brilliant, by the way. Does it have a title yet?"

CHEKHOV "Konstantin Sergievich. Enclosed you will find the completed manuscript of my latest endeavor. I hope you enjoy it. And please, not so much noise this time; my fate is in your hands. You should know I have also sent a copy to Meyerhold. He is a bright young man. Do not mistake my gesture to him as a slight against you. Take it as either vanity or desperation that I hope quantity may improve my odds for success. Ever yours, Anton Pavlovich Chekhov."

CHEKHOV soon begins to cough again.

STANISLAVSKY "My dear Vladimir, *The Cherry Orchard* is Chekhov's finest achievement to date. And I am sorry to say that Moscow couldn't agree less. Apparently it has also gone poorly for Meyerhold out in the provinces. I must admit that, like you, I too feel heartily tired of the realistic crowd. Our upcoming trio of Maeterlinck plays might prove the antidote! Maeterlinck strikes a new note in literature! Though I admit I am having trouble making his literature into theatre. And I am growing desperate for hope. Yours in despair, Konstantin Sergievich Stanislavsky."

DANCHENKO "Konstantin Sergievich. I read your recent note with sympathy, and encourage you to press forward in your struggle with Maeterlinck's symbolism. The fate of Chekhov's *Cherry Orchard* reaffirms my feeling as to the direction of theatre in this new century. And so perhaps Chekhov has completed his contribution to the Moscow Art Theatre repertory. The future belongs to poets, not to Chekhov. Yours in certainty, Vladimir Nemirovich-Danchenko."

CHEKHOV's coughing reaches a terrible intensity. Everyone looks at him and is still. The coughing ends.

TITLE: "July 1904. Anton Pavlovich Chekhov dies from tuberculosis."

No music under MEYERHOLD's final letter.

MEYERHOLD "Konstantin Sergievich. In two seasons I have presented over 140 plays. I have personally played 44 major roles. I have alternately succeeded and failed, but always struggled, in the provinces of Russia. It is clear to me that there is no future for Art here, or for me, and so it is with great anticipation that I – accept – your invitation to meet in Moscow… The death of Anton Pavlovich saddens me more than I can say… Yours, Vsevolod Emelievich Meyerhold."

Episode Three – The Moscow Art *Studio* Theatre

TITLE: *"Moscow. October 1905."*

Moscow music – cut off by a volley of gunshots. The distant sound of rioting masses fades with them.

TITLE: *"Stanislavsky plans to liquidate the recently formed Studio Theatre, an experimental wing of the Moscow Art Theatre under Meyerhold's direction."*

STANISLAVSKY's office, where DANCHENKO speaks rather agitatedly at STANISLAVSKY, pausing periodically as if engaged in a dialogue rather than a monologue. He begins in pause before the first cork pops...

DANCHENKO ...And if you had shown me what I saw yesterday before seeking my advice on what to do, I would have told you at once: the sooner you put an end to this, the worst mistake of your life, the better it will be – for the Art Theatre, for you, and for your reputation as an artist. ...Meyerhold has done *nothing* but to confirm that his idea of Symbolism and the New Theatre does not work. We must rid ourselves of the entire endeavor. The studio must be closed. ...Exactly my point! It hasn't done *any* good. Meyerhold is a rifle with not a care in the world for aim. He just blasts away. And yesterday is what we get for it. What were those actors doing exactly? Was that Maeterlinck's play? No, it was Meyerhold: *playing!* Yes yes yes he came running from the Provinces and severed the chains of creative despair from your soul; you were *renewed* by his passion yes I remember it clearly: "Meyerhold! Meyerhold!" *(to himself)* One hundred and forty plays in two seasons. My god. It's a wonder he was able to drag his bones back to Moscow at all. Chekhov did give him *The Cherry Orchard (to STANISLAVSKY, vehemently)* only minutes after delivering it to us. *(to himself again)* Meyerhold must have been doing something right. *(back to STANISLAVSKY)* Flattery earns the favors of any playwright, you know that as well as I; Chekhov was throwing Meyerhold a bone. ...What is the point in arguing with me? Regardless of what Chekhov, or you, or even I might have once thought of Meyerhold's potential to help usher the Art Theatre into the future, his work has proven otherwise and for reasons I need not go on about. ...And it *has* to come from you for the simple reason that he doesn't like me and never has. God knows *what* he would do.

MEYERHOLD enters.

DANCHENKO He's always been a brazen, burning thorn. *(admitting)* Talented, passionate. *(bitterly)* Brilliant. *(180°)* Belligerent suspicious hateful and angry! Meyerhold–! *(notices MEYERHOLD standing there)* We were just talking about you.

STANISLAVSKY Vsevolod Emelievich, please, sit down.

MEYERHOLD Thank you but I prefer standing. Besides, I hope to get back to rehearsal as soon as possible.

STANISLAVSKY Thank you for taking a break for us. But please, do sit.

MEYERHOLD I'm better on my feet, that's all. Don't be offended.

DANCHENKO Tsch!

STANISLAVSKY Very well. You must sense why I have asked you here today.

MEYERHOLD For very different reasons than you asked me here eight months ago, I think.

STANISLAVSKY Yes.

MEYERHOLD Well let me say that I am neither Konstantin Stanislavsky nor Vladimir Nemirovich-Danchenko. You asked *me* to run your Studio. If you wanted it done your way you should have run it yourselves. You asked for a New Theatre and I have done my best to carve this New Theatre out of nothing, do you understand? A void. The materials I have to work with are old – an irony given their youth. Those kids you hand me are schooled in worn out methods and these are new ideas what model what ideal could you possibly be holding me to?

DANCHENKO Meyerhold, please, we aren't the Tsar's secret police; you are not under interrogation.

STANISLAVSKY Allow me to explain my intentions.

MEYERHOLD I think I have *never* understood your intentions toward me!

STANISLAVSKY Then allow me to explain them… Obviously the Art Theatre does not represent the last word and has no intention of remaining frozen to the spot. The young Studio Theatre, under the roof of its parent, should continue the artistic process and move forward.

MEYERHOLD Oh so am I the nanny, then, hired to entertain student actors whilst Father is busy doing the real work? You cannot expect an experiment to succeed with every trial. Isn't failure in fact the nature of it? Don't we fail and fail and fail so that one day we might succeed?

DANCHENKO Not a very practical plan of action.

MEYERHOLD suddenly moves to attack DANCHENKO, but…

STANISLAVSKY Let me be quite plain! …It is the actor I am interested in, not the director. I asked you to run an actor's studio. Quite promptly you instigated a director's studio. Your studio. And during uncertain times such as these, I cannot afford to provide you, Vsevolod Emelievich, with a playground for your own betterment.

MEYERHOLD A playground?!

DANCHENKO / Yes! A playground!

STANISLAVSKY Please Vsevolod–

MEYERHOLD I'm sorry, I have to break the fourth wall for a moment. I'm terribly sorry ladies and gentlemen. You may not know this but Russia happens to be in the grip of a general strike at the moment.

DANCHENKO What are you doing?

MEYERHOLD The year 1905 kicked off with Bloody Sunday and there have been riots and civil disorder ever since.

DANCHENKO What's he doing?

MEYERHOLD The Grand Duke Sergei, Governor of Moscow, was assassinated.

DANCHENKO Meyerhold!

MEYERHOLD The battleship Potempkin mutinied in June. Other fleets were sunk in a stupid war with Japan.

DANCHENKO Stop that!

MEYERHOLD And the Russian Army was defeated by the Japanese at Mukden.

DANCHENKO Konstantin!

MEYERHOLD The Art Theatre has periodically been shut down and used as a casualty station – how *fitting*, now that I think about it – with our actresses playing the role of auxiliary nurses.

> *DANCHENKO charges MEYERHOLD, stops abruptly when he realizes the audience would see anything he might do, shields his face and tiptoes back as inconspicuously as possible. MEYERHOLD doesn't bat an eye.*

MEYERHOLD We've only recently reopened after an Imperial manifesto proclaimed a new cons*titut*ional monarchy, though we're all wondering what exactly that means. So a lot's been going on. Meanwhile, the famed Moscow Art Theatre has been outrun by the people who populate her balcony, preferring instead to lag behind in the 19th century with those who clog up the orchestra. The nation moves forward, and the bastions of Art stand still with their backs to the dawn, clinging to their dreams of an old and rotten Russia! *(lets out a huge sigh of release)* Wooo! My god that felt good. I hate pretending you're not there. *(mocking a blinder w/ one hand)* "Blah, blah blah blah, blah blah…"

DANCHENKO This childish romantic mockery is unbearable.

STANISLAVSKY Vsevolod Emelievich, if I may interrupt your soliloquy. The Moscow Art Theatre stands for Truth in Art, nothing less.

MEYERHOLD Are *they* less true than your Art?

DANCHENKO Speaking to the audience is neither truth nor Art. It's conversation! And usually one-sided.

MEYERHOLD Why don't you just rehearse forever then? Why bother with an audience at all if you're not going to speak to them? Why are they here?

STANISLAVSKY To see a play.

MEYERHOLD When they're stepping through blood and dodging bullets in the streets–

STANISLAVSKY Vsevolod Emelievich, I know I need not explain to you the difference between the stage and the street.

MEYERHOLD Russia is changing.

STANISLAVSKY And it is precisely for this reason that I must close the experimental studio. 1905 is not the time and Moscow is not the place. Not right now. Not while we're stepping through blood and dodging bullets in the streets. Not when we could be shut down at any moment to house wounded imperial soldiers. Not before we know *who's won*. Do you understand what I am saying?

MEYERHOLD You're standing backwards.

STANISLAVSKY I do not deny reality. On the contrary. It has been my life's work to seek out reality in every moment. But if you wish to fight the army's battles, join the army. If you want to change government policy, don't direct a play. An artist makes art. That is all. And that is quite a great deal. Art feeds the soul. Not the stomach. The audience understands this. They don't come here expecting bread. Understand your purpose: we are artists, Vsevolod Emelievich, do not forget. The Mensheviks, the Bolsheviks, or the Tsar will not forget. …Your studio is closed. Good day.

> *As STANISLAVSKY turns away he stops and glances over the audience, smiles. But DANCHENKO urges him on his way with an abrupt shove of disapproval and he exits. DANCHENKO follows, after a smirk to MEYERHOLD.*
>
> *MEYERHOLD turns and stands DSC thinking. Upstage of him, an ACTOR runs on SL and off SR in the classic Biomechanical run. After he's gone, MEYERHOLD turns to look, then sits on the edge of the stage DSC.*
>
> *Snow begins to fall. The stage grows dark and it is night on the streets of Moscow. Music – a violin. There is a dreamlike feel to what unfolds.*
>
> *A SHADY MAN in a long coat stands beneath a street lamp. He is approached by a SUSPICIOUS MAN who passes him a package. Currency is exchanged. The latter exits quickly and the former stands back to lurk in the shadows.*

A poor OLD WOMAN and her GRANDDAUGHTER pass by.

TWO SECRETIVE MEN meet and whisper. They move to the side when they spot a THIRD MAN whose rhythm and gate makes them uneasy. The THIRD MAN meets eyes with the SHADY MAN and each feigns a casual air.

A WOMAN with a "baby" moves past but drops her bundle. Oranges spill out. She gathers them quickly, as do the TWO SECRETIVE MEN.

The THIRD MAN whistles. Two SECRET POLICE men converge upon the scene and the SHADY MAN grabs the WOMAN as hostage. Both are shot from an unknown source. The SECRET POLICE men draw their guns. Another gunshot and the THIRD MAN is killed. The SECRET POLICE run to him. Gunshot. The first SECRET POLICE man falls. A HUSBAND and WIFE hurry past. The two SECRETIVE MEN surprise the second SECRET POLICE man and knife him. They take some of his belongings and search the other bodies as well. The FIRST SECRETIVE MAN whistles and they exit.

MEYERHOLD has remained seated and lost in thought. Now he stands, having reached an epiphany.

MEYERHOLD   Thank you Stanislavsky!

TITLE: "1905–1917. Meyerhold's theatrical career takes off and the Bolsheviks climb to power."

Soviet music. All of this, from staging to costumes, is orchestrated with panache by MEYERHOLD, the director.

A line of IMPERIAL BOURGEOISIE arranged just so.

A WHITE GUARD SNIPER positions himself atop a platform. BOLSHEVIK SOLDIERS enter, take position, and execute the IMPERIAL BOURGEOISIE. It is not to MEYERHOLD's liking. He restages the execution two more times. On the third, one of the IMPERIAL BOURGEOISIE says:

IMPERIAL BOURGEOISIE   God save Russia from these bandits!

The BOLSHEVIK SOLDIERS' guns go off and a massive red flag unfurls from above, falling over the dead IMPERIAL BOURGEOISIE. The WHITE GUARD SNIPER atop the platform is also shot by the BOLSHEVIK SOLDIERS before they exit. MEYERHOLD exits as well.

STANISLAVSKY and DANCHENKO cross by, shielding their eyes so as not to witness the carnage. They are met by the BOLSHEVIK SOLDIERS who re-enter marching with red flags on poles. STANISLAVSKY and DANCHENKO change course, stepping through the dead bodies and exiting upstage. The BOLSHEVIK SOLDIERS end standing amongst the dead bodies in a poster-perfect tableau of Bolshevik victory. MEYERHOLD enters, now with a red band around his left arm, tidies up the tableau, and greets LUNACHARSKY who also sports a red armband and is evidently quite pleased with how everything looks. MEYERHOLD and LUNACHARSKY shake hands in a splendid photo opportunity.

End of Act One.

TITLE: "Intermission!"

Act Two, 1919–1928

Episode Four – White you're right, Red you're dead.

Music. MEYERHOLD and two other PRISONERS are brought in by three WHITE GUARDS and locked in their cells. A round of gunshots outside the prison punctuates the end of the music. MEYERHOLD and the PRISONERS turn and look.

TITLE: "The Bolshevik victory in October of the 1917 Revolution is followed by Civil War."
TITLE: "In September 1919, at a White Army prison in the coastal town of Novorossisk, three Red prisoners await execution."
TITLE: "One of them is Meyerhold."

FIRST PRISONER So where was I?
SECOND PRISONER Lenin.
FIRST PRISONER Lenin! Right. So *then* he says, "If we aren't ready to shoot a saboteur, what sort of Revolution is that?"
SECOND PRISONER Yes but what's the point then? I mean in the end what does it matter if you get shot by a Bourgeois or a Bolshevik? Either way you're dead. So why make a fuss in the first place?
FIRST PRISONER A fuss? You're calling the Revolution a fuss?

SECOND SOLDIER A dead man builds no road. A dead man bakes no bread. That's all I'm saying.

FIRST PRISONER Can't eat that bread walking down that road with White Army snipers at your back, now can yuh? Where's your brain? You've got to take the bad with the good; we shoot now so we don't have to later. Besides, *you* don't have to worry about being shot by a Bolshevik. You *are* a Bolshevik.

SECOND PRISONER What I'm saying is: what does it matter if I'm a Bolshevik or a Menshevik or a Tsarist or whoever if I'm still getting bullied and shot at? Isn't a new way of life the whole point?

FIRST PRISONER Exactly.

SECOND PRISONER Okay well bullets and being told what to do are nothing new on my street.

FIRST PRISONER You know what you're problem is? You lack scope. You've got to start thinking beyond the material world.

SECOND PRISONER No. I'm specifically not to do that. *That's* not realistic. *That's* bourgeois decadence.

FIRST PRISONER Listen, I'm talking about Vision. I'm talking about the new Utopia. We're building a proletariat nation. It's unprecedented. You can't expect Lenin to have it *all* figured out in advance. We gotta start somewhere. The Revolution is Russia's second birth.

SECOND PRISONER And I suppose prison is a labor pain.

FIRST PRISONER Very funny. Try being a little more optimistic. ...What's your take, Meyergold?

MEYERHOLD Meyer*hold*.

FIRST PRISONER (*a joke*) Your lips say Meyer*hold*, but your nose says Meyer*gold*. ...Oh come on, I'm joking. I thought a theatre man like you would have a sense of humor.

MEYERHOLD What would you know about a theatre man like me?

FIRST PRISONER Hey. Before I was behind the lines I was in the audience. I've seen plays.

MEYERHOLD Have you.

FIRST PRISONER Yep.

MEYERHOLD And what plays have you seen?

SECOND PRISONER Hey I've seen plays too.

FIRST PRISONER Be quiet. Yours.

MEYERHOLD Mine?

FIRST PRISONER *Don Juan* at the Alexandrinsky, 1910. *The Fairground Booth*, Tenishevsky Hall, 1914. *Masquerade*, the Alexandrinsky, 1917.

MEYERHOLD You saw *The Fairground Booth*?

FIRST PRISONER Yes I did. I thought it exhibited a stunning use of space.

Rather unique in my view. A striking juxtaposition of comedy and tragedy one *might* describe as Grotesque. And furthermore: I found the balance of content and form to be quite extraordinary.

MEYERHOLD ...Who are you?

FIRST PRISONER I'm a Red Army soldier in a White Army prison. And I like the theatre.

SECOND PRISONER I like theatre.

FIRST PRISONER Don't listen to him. He's from Poltava.

MEYERHOLD Where?

FIRST PRISONER Exactly. He spots a pair of young lovers on a pretty set and happily falls asleep.

SECOND PRISONER I think *Romeo and Juliet* is well written.

FIRST PRISONER See what I mean.

SECOND PRISONER It's got everything you need in a good play. Action. Romance. Jokes.

FIRST PRISONER "He's for a jig or a tale of bawdry, else he sleeps."

MEYERHOLD *Hamlet*, act two scene two.

FIRST PRISONER Very good.

SECOND PRISONER I knew that too.

FIRST PRISONER No you didn't. So Meyerhold, what *are* you doing down here anyway? Shouldn't you be up in Moscow makin' art?

MEYERHOLD I came here for my health.

FIRST PRISONER What's the matter with you?

MEYERHOLD Tuberculosis.

FIRST PRISONER Well that's not very original. I thought you were avant-garde.

MEYERHOLD In matters of health I remain embarrassingly passé. Also, I'm told I work too much.

FIRST PRISONER Not quite the resort you had in mind, is it?

MEYERHOLD I won't be staying long.

FIRST PRISONER How's that?

MEYERHOLD The Moscow Art Theatre stops in Novorossisk on tour. They should have arrived yesterday, actually.

FIRST PRISONER Oh. I *see*. Old man Stanislavsky gonna bail you out himself? Where's my helping hand?

MEYERHOLD I'm sure you know somebody.

FIRST PRISONER I'm the audience, not the *artiste*. And I came south to fight, not to relax. We're different men, you and I.

MEYERHOLD We have different jobs. We play different roles. But at the end of the day we're both Communists, are we not?

FIRST PRISONER Maybe.
SECOND PRISONER …Mimi dies of tuberculosis in *La Boheme*, and still manages to get an aria out before she goes.
FIRST PRISONER It's the aria that kills her.
MEYERHOLD It's the entire last act. She dies of boredom.
SECOND PRISONER Depends on the production! …*Tosca* isn't bad. Suicide is always a more satisfying way to go. At least you have a say in the matter… Hey Meyerhold. You ever directed Puccini?
FIRST PRISONER Puccini! Huh! What a waste!
SECOND PRISONER Puccini's nice. I like his songs.
FIRST PRISONER You would. Can't get that provincial mud off your boots, can yuh?
SECOND PRISONER Hey there's plenty of mud under the streets of Petrograd. You can pave over and over it all you like, my metropolitan friend, but deep down you'll still have Russian mud underfoot.
FIRST PRISONER Don't wag your finger at me. I'm no socialite. I signed up just like you. Did nobody tell you, or weren't you listening: We're paving over *all* of Russia. And we'll mix the mortar with blood if need be. We're building a new world over the old with our arms and our brains, where workers get what they work for and fat men with monocles and diamond studded wives don't clog up the doors to life. Where you can speak your mind in restaurants without the waiter sending a transcript to the Tsar. Where your neighbors don't disappear overnight. Where everyone goes to school. Everyone eats. Everyone thinks. Everyone works. And the French and the Germans read *our* books! Where we drink vodka and dance and laugh because we're happy, not because we desperately wish we were happy! I'm on the wrong side of these bars and in a minute or a day I might be dead! But I'm not sorry! Because my kids will know why they love their country! For the first time in history they'll know what it means to be Russian, and free!

Two WHITE GUARDS have entered.

FIRST WHITE GUARD Borovsky.
SECOND PRISONER Yes.

The WHITE GUARDS open the SECOND PRISONER'S cell and lead him out. There follows a very long pause.

FIRST PRISONER *(Derisively)* …Puccini.

Another long pause. Gunshot outside. Another long pause.

FIRST PRISONER Is he dead yet?

MEYERHOLD looks at him.

FIRST PRISONER Puccini.
MEYERHOLD No.

Another pause. MEYERHOLD checks his watch. Then in the far distance we can hear "O, Soave Fanciulla" from La Boheme. *MEYERHOLD and FIRST PRISONER listen to the opening strains before the music takes over and the scene transitions to...*

Episode Five – October in the Theatre!

TITLE: "Moscow. February 1921."

A busy theatre. Young actors warming up. ILINSKY, already a student of Meyerhold's, is present to assist. The room is electric with a sense of anticipation. Alexander KUGEL, a mature arts critic, chats condescendingly with ILINSKY.

KUGEL It was February, 1917.

TITLE: "Auditions at the State Theatre No. 1 for Meyerhold's Free Actors Workshop – or, depending on who you talk to, for his revival production of Mayakovsky's revolutionary play Mystery-Bouffe."

KUGEL The streets empty, dimly lit, scarce cabbies asking incredible fees. But at the entrance to the Alexandrinsky Theatre there stood tight black lines of automobiles. All the rich, all the aristocratic, all the prosperous Petrograd pluto-, beuro-, and homefronto-crats were out in force. And when that Babylon of obscene extravagance otherwise known as Lermontov's play, *Masquerade*, was unveiled before us I was horrified. I knew – everybody knew – that two or three miles away crowds of people were crying "bread" and the Tsar's policemen were getting seventy roubles a day to spray those people with bullets. Where were we – Rome after the Caesars? And after the show go feed on swallows tongues while the poor starving wretches go on shouting for bread and freedom?
ILINSKY You've got it all wrong. Meyerhold knew what he was doing. That production was a requiem for the empire, funeral rites for the Tsar and his kids.
KUGEL Of course he says that but of course he has to say that. He may be a petty decadent under that leather coat but he's no idiot.

ILINSKY Hot words for an unexpected guest.
KUGEL Just talking.
ILINSKY Didn't know there was such a thing.
KUGEL Well now you know.
ILINSKY Tell me something: you ever directed a play?
KUGEL Nope.
ILINSKY But you write your opinion about *other* people directing plays.
KUGEL Yep.
ILINSKY Well alright then. Now I know who I'm dealing with. And you can quote me on that.

> Enter MEYERHOLD and MAYAKOVSKY, down the aisle of the theatre, already talking. MEYERHOLD wears the requisite Bolshevik attire: leather coat, boots, cap, dark red wool scarf.

MAYAKOVSKY But you'll never guess what happened on my way to the Theatre.
MEYERHOLD Tell me.
MAYAKOVSKY A nudist leapt onto the tram naked from head to toe. "A revolutionary act of ideological affirmation" he said.
MEYERHOLD *(laughs)*
MAYAKOVSKY A dapper fellow to my right complained about indecency. Old brains still having trouble wrapping around the new times. *I* thought it was funny. A naked guy on a crowded tram: the comedy writes itself.
KUGEL Comrade Meyerhold, Comrade Mayakovsky.
MEYERHOLD Who are you?
KUGEL Alexander Kugel, *Theatre and Art*. We've met before.
MEYERHOLD You write terribly ignorant articles about my productions and therefore I try my best to forget our having met. What can I do for you? I'm very busy, as you can see.
KUGEL Yes, auditions, I understand. That's actually why I'm here. Thought I might get an inside look at preparations for the revival production of Comrade Mayakovsky's *Mystery-Bouffe*. *(claps MAYAKOVSKY on the shoulder in congratulations)*
MEYERHOLD Visitors are not allowed at auditions. Good day.
KUGEL I think my readers would be interested.
MEYERHOLD Tell your readers we're not holding auditions for *Mystery-Bouffe*. We're auditioning students for the Free Actors Workshop.
KUGEL Really? Will Comrade Mayakovsky be auditioning for the workshop then?

MAYAKOVSKY Perhaps I should. I might learn a thing or two.

KUGEL I recall reading something about auditions for the original production of *Mystery-Bouffe* not going so well. Actors were a bit hesitant to work for the one director and playwright to answer Lenin's call, and at the last minute *you* made your stage debut by necessity it seems.

MAYAKOVSKY You know Alexander Blok was at that conference too.

KUGEL Okay, two playwrights.

MEYERHOLD And it was Anatoly Lunacharsky who called. I've never actually had the pleasure of speaking with Comrade Lenin.

KUGEL At any rate: I suppose you can't blame people for being leery of a brand new government. Takes a while to get settled in. A degree of apprehension is natural I suppose.

MAYAKOVSKY Depends on your position.

KUGEL Yes.

MAYAKOVSKY And how *are* you feeling about Bolshevism these days Comrade Kugel?

KUGEL *(to the point)* Will today's new crop of "students" as you call them form the cast of *Mystery-Bouffe*?

MEYERHOLD If they're lucky perhaps one day they will. But now if you will excuse me I've got work to do.

KUGEL Likewise. Good day. Comrade Mayakovsky.

MAYAKOVSKY See yuh in the cartoons.

KUGEL exits, glancing about him as he goes.

MEYERHOLD My canary looks forward to each of his articles with great anticipation. Ilinsky! Shall we commence!

ILINSKY Yes. Ladies and gentlemen, please gather here. You will be called by the Director one at a time.

GARIN I'm nervous, Ilinsky.

ILINSKY You should be.

GARIN Is it true he was arrested by the Whites?

ILINSKY And almost executed. The Red Army saved his neck at the last minute. But you should be thinking about your audition, Garin.

MEYERHOLD First candidate!

ILINSKY See.

MEYERHOLD Ilinsky!

ILINSKY Yes. First candidate. Abrosimov!

ABROSIMOV steps forward timidly.

MEYERHOLD Your name.
ABROSIMOV Abrosimov.
MEYERHOLD Louder!
ABROSIMOV Abrosimov.
MEYERHOLD Louder!
ABROSIMOV Abrosimov.
MEYERHOLD Dismissed! Next!
ILINSKY Bebutin!

BEBUTIN steps forward timidly.

MEYERHOLD Your name.
BEBUTIN Bebutin!!!
MAYAKOVSKY You are a quick study, Bebutin.
BEBUTIN Thank you Comrade Mayakovsky! I respect your poems immensely!
MAYAKOVSKY Give him the part.
BEBUTIN *(smiles)*
MEYERHOLD What have you prepared?
BEBUTIN Uh– Hamlet, Sir!!!
MEYERHOLD Proceed.
BEBUTIN …To be–
MEYERHOLD Thank you. Would you please recite a fable.
BEBUTIN But I haven't prepared a fable.
MEYERHOLD Dismissed. Next!
ILINSKY Babanova!

Maria BABANOVA steps forward, nervous but present.

MEYERHOLD Your name.
BABANOVA Maria Babanova!
MEYERHOLD …What have you prepared?
BABANOVA *(a bit worried)* …Hamlet.
MEYERHOLD You mean Ophelia.
BABANOVA No. *Hamlet.*
MEYERHOLD …Proceed.

Without speaking a word, BABANOVA *enacts* Hamlet *in its entirety in about a minute. It is rather impressive. LUNACHARSKY has entered unobtrusively and watches from the side, near ILINSKY. When BABANOVA is done, LUNACHRASKY whispers to ILINSKY.*

MEYERHOLD Your name again.
BABANOVA Maria Babanova.
MEYERHOLD ...Very well. Ilinsky.
ILINSKY Uh, Garin.
GARIN Garin!! I mean, yes, hello.
MEYERHOLD You must be Garin.
GARIN Yes.
MEYERHOLD Just Garin?
GARIN Erast Garin.
MEYERHOLD What have you prepared?
GARIN An original monologue.
MEYERHOLD Proceed.

GARIN takes a breath and suddenly a voice storms down the aisle.

MOTHER Where is this Meyerhold! Where is Vsevolod Emelievich Meyerhold!
MEYERHOLD What is that noise?
MOTHER There you are. I see you. I recognize that Jewish mug.
MEYERHOLD Who let this woman in the theatre?
MOTHER Ah! You speak Russian. I thought I'd have to learn German to be understood by you, Herr Meyerhold.
MEYERHOLD And who are you?
MOTHER I am Vera Vapidkovska Maximovna! My son auditioned for you yesterday and was summarily dismissed! I have come to inform you of your great error! You are a fool not to welcome my son onto your stage! I see everything produced in Moscow, and I say he is an extraordinary talent. He is perhaps the most talented young actor in all of Russia! You should have begged him to join your theatre!
MEYERHOLD Madam! How dare you interrupt my work with your petty pro-offspring propaganda! Who I do or do not accept into my theatre is no business of yours. And if you do not leave immediately on your own legs I will have you thrown out on your ass.
MOTHER Oh! ...Did you know that my son is a Communist?
MAYAKOVSKY *(laughs)* Ha!
MEYERHOLD I am a Communist. What of it?

MOTHER Ha! If you must ask than you are not a Communist.
MEYERHOLD That I *am* a Communist pops a little hole in that theory, doesn't it?
MOTHER Then you are not a very good Communist.
MEYERHOLD Good? What has good to do with it? I am a Communist because it is the truth – that is all. And if you think your child's Party Card makes him good, or an actor, then you are sorely mistaken. Now remove yourself before I have you removed!
MOTHER Well! I assure you I will not be attending your misguided theatre in the future.
MEYERHOLD On that we agree. Good day.
MOTHER Guten Tag to you, too, Herr Meyerrrhold!
MEYERHOLD I said Good Day!
MOTHER Jewish fraud!

And the MOTHER is gone.

MEYERHOLD What was that?
MAYAKOVSKY I think that mother was a man.
MEYERHOLD Who let that woman in the theatre? Ilinsky!
ILINSKY Yes.
MEYERHOLD Look up my audition notes on this Maximov. Find out why I didn't hire him. If he has half the personality of his mother I've made a terrible mistake.
ILINSKY I will do it. And, I beg your pardon / but–
MEYERHOLD / Comrade Lunacharsky!
ILINSKY Comrade Lunacharsky / is here to see you.
LUNACHARSKY Meyerhold, *and* Mayakovsky. What are you boys up to this time?
MEYERHOLD Auditions for the Free Actors *Workshop*. Comrade Mayakovsky was curious how they're done.
LUNACHARSKY Not contemplating a return to the boards, are you?
MAYAKOVSKY Not if I can help it. Have you ever had to act in one of this man's plays? They're murder.
LUNACHARSKY Not having trouble finding actors again, are you?
MEYERHOLD Come now, that was 1918. Everyone has realized by now the Revolution is here to stay, and if they haven't: god help them. Or, whomever. *(laughs briefly; then, moving on)* So, what brings you to *us* today?
LUNACHARSKY I was just in the neighborhood and thought I'd stop in. I know you're very busy, but, I was in the neighborhood.

MEYERHOLD Yes. One moment. Ilinsky!
ILINSKY Yes.
MEYERHOLD Run them through the exercise again while I speak with Comrade Lunacharsky.
ILINSKY But I hardly know it myself.
MEYERHOLD Well don't let them know that. Go. *(aside to Mayakovsky)* If you spot anyone you like, make a note. *(back to Lunacharsky)* So: what can I do for you?

> ILINSKY *proceeds to coach the students in the etude "Stab With A Dagger," which it seems they've recently learned something of.*

LUNACHARSKY Your auditions must be very interesting for Comrade Mayakovsky to take time out to watch them.
MEYERHOLD Yes.
LUNACHARSKY Has he finished his revisions of *Mystery-Bouffe*?
MEYERHOLD He has.
LUNACHARSKY And you're sure you're not having trouble finding decent actors?
MEYERHOLD Are you here as Lunacharsky the critic or Lunacharsky the head of the Soviet Commissariat of Enlightenment?
LUNACHARSKY Why have you resigned as head of the Theatre Section? It's hardly been a year even.
MEYERHOLD You know very well why: it's a useless appointment for me.
LUNACHARSKY Useless? I can't think of a more *useful* appointment for you. You oversee nearly every theatre in Russia.
MEYERHOLD Yes, *nearly*. What can I do, how can a theatrical revolution succeed, when you've roped off in your little museum the Moscow Art Theatre, The Alexandrinsky, the Bolshoi, the Kamerny–
LUNACHARSKY Oh, they don't need your brand of help. And to be honest I'm protecting them from your petty revenge.
MEYERHOLD *Petty* revenge? I nearly lost my life in that White Army prison and no one from the Art Theatre lifted a finger to help me. While they were delivering that tired noise they call opera I was down the street listening to bullets crack heads against the wall outside my cell.
LUNACHARSKY Vsevolod Emelievich we are talking about theatre not the Civil War. And they were scared. You would be too. It was war.
MEYERHOLD And the Alexandrinsky remains as bloated today as it ever was. I hated the patrons there: stubbornly resisting all my efforts to disturb them. The old theatres do nothing for the new men and women of the Revolution, *Comrade* Lunacharsky. They ride on our backs while *we work*.

LUNACHARSKY Says you. They are doing something you're not. They are providing a realistic foundation on which we are building the culture of Soviet Russia. You should be grateful. I am fully prepared to entrust you with the destruction of what is old and bad, but not with the preservation of what is old and good, as you seem willfully unable to understand the difference. The people understand Realism. *Lenin* understands Realism. It's practical.

MEYERHOLD It's boring. It's out of date. It's backwards.

LUNACHARSKY It makes sense. You can follow it. You know what's going on. Half the time I haven't a clue what your productions are up to. Theatrical fits and starts. And yet I believe you are striving to build something new, something born of the Revolution. And we need that now. So build, build. Cast *Mystery-Bouffe*. Do more Soviet plays.

MEYERHOLD I won't do bad plays. We need more Mayakovskies.

LUNACHARSKY Find them. And stop using these student actors. You need real actors.

MEYERHOLD If I knew of any I'd hire them. I don't have much use for the old actors. I have to build them from scratch, you see.

LUNACHARSKY The young boys and girls willing to play your games don't always make the best impression. *Talent* deserves a role on the proletariat stage.

MEYERHOLD You mean *tradition*.

LUNACHARSKY Expertise. Everything prior to 1917 wasn't backwards.

MEYERHOLD Mm-hm.

LUNACHARSKY Vsevolod Emelievich. Let me be frank. When illiteracy is at 80%, and the church is no longer viable, theatre becomes a very important means of making a culture. Art is our machine. We are building a new world. Yes, let's face forward and get to work. But let's not forget how we got here. There is some good to be found in the past. Some foundation for reality. It's our history too after all.

MEYERHOLD …You know I was chased out of the Kommissarzhevskaya for daring to breathe life into that place – at Vera's own invitation, by the way. She begged me, wooed me. She just couldn't stand that I got all the attention and not her!

LUNACHARSKY Yes yes, and now it's 1921. Please reconsider your resignation, that's all I ask. You are the first Communist director. Actions speak. I know that you agree. And I don't make many personal visits.

LUNACHARSKY offers his hand; MEYERHOLD shakes it.

LUNACHARSKY …I hope you find some promising "students."

LUNACHARSKY exits. MEYERHOLD wanders back to MAYAKOVSKY

as the STUDENTS and ILINSKY continue.

MEYERHOLD Well? Anybody good?

MAYAKOVSKY Babanova. Garin. I still say Ilinsky would play a decent Menshevik.

MEYERHOLD He's young.

MAYAKOVSKY *(shrugs)* So he is.

MEYERHOLD So he is.

MAYAKOVSKY Don't worry. You never know who you might find. When you least expect it.

MEYERHOLD Yes.

A waltz begins to play as the STUDENTS continue to work on the etude. MEYERHOLD strolls distractedly among them, correcting an arm or leg here and there.

Zinaida RAIKH enters. She is striking and confident until she realizes that she is late. She sees that the actors are at work and frantically removes her coat and hat and prepares to join them.

MEYERHOLD and RAIKH see one another from across the crowded room and are stopped for a long time. The STUDENTS continue their work. MEYERHOLD and RAIKH eventually approach one another, meeting center stage.

MEYERHOLD Your name.

RAIKH Zinaida Raikh. I am working class in origin. My father was a railway worker who joined the Social Democratic Party in 1897. I was married to the poet Sergei Yesenin but ours was a stormy relationship. Also he was a bisexual, and though I actually rather liked that, he left me. Now I work for the Soviet Commissariat of Enlightenment and am a member of the Bolshevik Party, having previously been a member of the Socialist Revolutionaries from the age of nineteen.

MEYERHOLD Nice to meet you. I am Vsevolod Emelievich Meyerhold. Theatre director.

RAIKH Yes.

MEYERHOLD Are you still married to your poet, Zinaida Raikh?

RAIKHE No. Are *you* married?

MEYERHOLD Yes.

TITLE: "Oh, yeah, sorry. Meyerhold had been married to Olga Munt since 1896, but the relationship was marked by long separations and breakdowns in communication."

MEYERHOLD I am. But I'll get a divorce.
RAIKH Am I too late to audition?
MEYERHOLD What have you prepared?
RAIKH Ophelia's mad scene.
MEYERHOLD Proceed.

> *RAIKH kisses MEYERHOLD full on the lips. They embrace and the kiss continues as the STUDENTS burst into a waltz around them. It all ends spectacularly well, with RAIKH dipping MEYERHOLD and the students severing the end of their waltz with the stab.*

Episode Six – *Magnanimous Cuckold* **rehearsal**

MEYERHOLD Stop!

> *BABANOVA and TERESHKOVICH stop in the middle of a scene and look to MEYERHOLD. RAIKH is present, as well as GARIN, who jots down notes on what MEYERHOLD says. ILINSKY sits off to the side, apparently agitated. They all remain suspended while the following titles click past...*
>
> *TITLE: "February 1922. Rehearsal for* The Magnanimous Cuckold *at Meyerhold's Actors Theatre, newly formed, with students of the Free Actors Workshop."*
> *TITLE: "Meyerhold and Zinaida Raikh are now married."*
> *TITLE: "Oh, and the revival of* Mystery-Bouffe *went off very well back in May 1921, by the way – though Soviet critics were divided as to the play's political "suitability." The State Theatre No. 1 was dissolved a few months later, at any rate…"*
>
> *And now the action proceeds. BABANOVA punctuates MEYERHOLD's speech with staccato "yes" and "right" and that sort of thing.*

MEYERHOLD Babanova, it must look easy. The work should always be joyful! An actor playing the dying Hamlet trembles with joy! Do you know that in America a lot of research by a man named Taylor is being devoted to the possible means of incorporating rest into the work process rather than regarding it as separate. Why? It's more efficient. If we observe a skilled worker we notice in his actions: rhythm, stability, good balance, an absence of superfluous movement. The worker moves like a dancer. Work approaches art. And the spectacle of an efficient worker gives us pleasure. It is the same with the actor. The actor's constant joy and concern is the efficient use of his material – his body. The actor: is both the artist and the object of his art. The entire creative act is a conscious process. Very scientific. As precise as a clock. With those old acting methods, the, "inspirational" method or, the method of "authentic emotions," the actor is always so overwhelmed by his emotions that he's entirely unable to coordinate *around* them his body *or* his voice. He has no control. Consider Pushkin, who wrote that "inspiration is as necessary to geometry as it is to poetry, but: blind ecstasy is necessary to neither." That notorious "inner experience," that: "authentic emotion." It is the system of my teacher, Konstantin Stanislavsky – who by the way will probably abandon it any day now. A theatre built on psychological foundations is as sure to collapse as a house built on sand. But: a theatre that relies on efficient physical work is at very least assured of clarity. Joy! Work! Ease! There you have it.

BABANOVA So: …how should I do the scene?

MEYERHOLD What have I just explained to you?

BABANOVA Something very interesting, but, not the scene.

MEYERHOLD Try it again. From "Stella Stella." And!

TERESHKOVICH "Stella! Stella! Adorable girl."

BABANOVA "You werewolf! Go to the forest, go there every morning until–

MEYERHOLD Stop! No. Why do we do the exercises all morning? Why? To set them aside and then rehearse? No. It is the same. Rhythm. Try it again… Joy, Babanova, joy. More theatre. More precise. Try it again… It must be clear. It must be extremely Stella. Not a little bit Stella. *Very* Stella. Try it… Go ahead…

> SHE does. It is better right away. MEYERHOLD punctuates the scene with cries of "Good!" as it progresses.

TERESHKOVICH "Stella! Stella! Adorable girl."

BABANOVA "You werewolf! Go to the forest, go there every morning until Bruno catches you in a trap like a nasty beast. The cowhand was dirty but I prefer him to you. Your soul is as dark as soot."

TERESHKOVICH "Don't be angry with me. If only I had married you instead of Bruno."

BABANOVA "Go away you terrible man!"

TERESHKOVICH "Well. Goodbye then, dear child. My horse is waiting."

BABANOVA "May it throw you on your ass, you Jackal! Owl! Fox!" *(spits)* "Thu! Thu!" *(pause… then again)* "Thu! Thu!"

MEYERHOLD Ilinsky!

ILINSKY This is what I am talking about! It doesn't work without the backdrop and side curtains!

MEYERHOLD Make your entrance!

ILINSKY I'm too far away!

MEYERHOLD So run!

ILINSKY From all the way off stage?

MEYERHOLD No, from right there.

ILINSKY The audience can see me there!

MEYERHOLD Yes. But barely. They'll be looking at Babanova where the lights are brightest. They'll see you there but barely.

ILINKSY But if they can see me then they can see anyone else, the other actors, the stagehands crossing back and forth.

MEYERHOLD Yes. It'll be interesting. The actors will be acting downstage and upstage in the half-dark people will move about freely.

ILINSKY Walking and talking? And drinking tea between scenes! The audience will be distracted.

MEYERHOLD That's fine. Let them drink tea. It'll be interesting.

ILINSKY That's impossible! It will destroy everything you've been building with us. All the details and nuance will be lost. We'll have to act like street players!

MEYERHOLD Listen to him! If you want aesthetic finery go to the Alexandrinsky! What do you want me to do, hang up plush embroidered curtains and backdrops like an exhibit in some art museum?

ILINSKY I want you to *do* something! Hang *something* behind the set, your mother's old petticoats, I don't care! I don't want some stupid stagehand interfering with my acting!

MEYERHOLD How dare you talk like that about one of my workers! Get out!

ILINSKY storms off to the side.

RAIKH Vsevolod, let me talk to him.

MEYERHOLD Don't waste your time on that aesthete, that *(shouts)* childish saboteur!

RAIKH Vsevolod, please.

MEYERHOLD Babanova!

MEYERHOLD talks to BABANOVA and TERESHKOVICH up close on some of their moves.

RAIKH Igor, come back to the stage.

ILINSKY No Zinaida, I won't.

RAIKH Don't be upset, Igor.

ILINKSY Vsevolod Emelievich should apologize to me himself, not send his wife as ambassador.

RAIKH He didn't want me to talk to you, you heard him. Don't be angry, Ilinsky. It will all work itself out and it won't be bad. Vsevolod Emelievich will back down if it doesn't work. Of course he doesn't want to ruin things for you or for himself. Trust him. You see he's working with you and he loves you.

ILINSKY Loves me? He called me childish. And a saboteur. I heard him.

RAIKH You know he doesn't mean it.

ILINSKY Meanwhile he works poor Babanova like a dog.

RAIKH He wants her to do well.

ILINSKY Well I need a backdrop to do well.

RAIKH Ilinsky, maybe there is no money for a backdrop. Have you thought of this?

ILINKSY Please, a backdrop, it's basic, we can afford a backdrop.

RAIKH Oh really. And what did *you* have for breakfast today? We can't even keep the theatre heated. Do you understand me? Vsevolod Emelievich is doing the best he can with what we have.

MEYERHOLD Ilinsky!

RAIKH Do the scene. You can make it work.

MEYERHOLD Ilinksy! We are ready for you!

ILINSKY stands and walks off to make his entrance.

MEYERHOLD And what did he say about me?

RAIKH Nothing. I was complaining to him about playing only secondary roles.

MEYERHOLD Zinochka, please.

RAIKH "Please, please." At least he listens to me. You give the best roles to Babanova.

MEYERHOLD She is doing well.

RAIKH I would like to do well. Am I not doing well in the training?

MEYERHOLD Yes, you are improving.

RAIKH Improving.

MEYERHOLD Don't worry, Zinochka.

ILINSKY Are you ready for me or not?

MEYERHOLD I am not only ready but waiting.

ILINKSY You were talking.

MEYERHOLD Ilinsky, before I die of old age, entertain me, please!

> *ILINSKY hits the scene, enacting with BABANOVA the most grotesquely proportioned, extremely physical reunion of two lovers ever seen – bright with youthful energy.*

ILINSKY "Ooooooh-ho-ho-ho-ho-ho! Stellums!"
BABANOVA "Oh! My man! My man has come back to me!"
ILINKSY "Stellakins!"
BABANOVA "My manekins! Oh my snookykins!"
ILINKSY "How sad I have been without you my Stradivaria!"
BABANOVA "More, more kisses, long ones, better ones, and I-love-youses and I-adore-youses!"
ILINSKY "Oh Columbia, three times America. The newly founded! Let my heart overflow. Enchanted enchantress! I will drink your freshness infinitely and be grateful and cry yum yum as I would for sweet mountain springs on burning days!"
BABANOVA "Oh my Bruno! My darling husband, my dearest treasure!"
ILINKSY "Let your clouds descend upon me, you heaven full of Stellas, bright with stars!"
BABANOVA "They shine for you Bruno! All for you!"

> *Spotlights and a roar of applause. ILINSKY and BABANOVA join hands and take a bow. ILINKSY steps forward and takes a bow. Then BABANOVA steps forward and there is a major whoop and stamping of feet throughout the theatre. BABANOVA and ILINSKY exit and the applause continues.*

Episode Seven – *The Inspector*

> TITLE: "Four years later, December 1926. Meyerhold's landmark production of *The Inspector* opens at the Meyerhold State Theatre to great acclaim and controversy."

> *The cast is now that of* The Inspector *taking their bows, with GARIN singled out.*

> TITLE: "Meyerhold gives Babanova the secondary role of Maria Andreevna."

> *BABANOVA enters and gets wild applause for her bow.*

> TITLE: "Zinaida Raikh is given the leading role of Ana Andreevna."

RAIKH enters and takes a bow and the applause turns to crickets. RAIKH is visibly displeased. The applause returns when she is done. The cast all bow once more and exit the stage as music takes over the applause.

And now we're at a post-performance party already in full swing. Jazz is playing on an old record.

TITLE: "At a party onstage after the show..."

SAMOILOV I read in *Theatre & Art* today that Meyerhold says he doesn't need actors.

MAYAKOVSKY No, he would not have said it. Who wrote that, Kugel?

SAMOILOV All he needs is a number of men and women with this and that characteristic and he could train them for any role, from Hamlet to peasant number three, like dogs trained for the hunt.

MAYAKOVSKY No, Vsevolod Emelievich loves actors. Good actors.

SAMOILOV Ha! With all due respect, Comrade Mayakovsky, whether a person is good or not is irrelevant. This is Soviet Russia, you know. To distinguish between good, bad, fair, poor, well that would be an act of discrimination, and what good Communist would advocate such a bourgeois and reactionary idea as discrimination? Or talent? Everyone is equal. It's just that some people are a little more equal than others.

GARIN Quiet Samoilov. Have another drink.

SAMOILOV "Every actor will be given a role as deemed appropriate." Ha! Appropriate to what? Why his talent, of course. But who decides this? The man in the theatre who is more equal than anyone else: the director. And if you're friendly with the director, or screwing him in the dressing room / after the show, you can play the lead.

GARIN *(laughing)* Shhhhhhhh.

MAYAKOVSKY Quiet Samoilov. ...You know it is just this "bourgeois reactionary discrimination" you talk about that keeps Meyerhold's theatre from degenerating to that mediocrity achieved by those proud Proletarian theatres, with their good Communist casting policies. Their shows are crap. All you need is a party card or peasant grandfather and you're an actor.

GARIN Mayakovsky is right. If you want better roles, Samoilov, you should tell him so.

SAMOILOV Tell him? Do you think Maria Babanova needs to tell him? No! Anyone walking down the street will tell you Maria Babanova can act circles around Zinaida Raikh. But who gets the lead roles? The wife, not the actress.

GARIN You should lower your voice, Samoilov.

SAMOILOV Why? I'm not talking about the distribution of bread. I'm talking about theatre. Comrade Stalin doesn't care what some actor who's played the same little role in the same play for two years has to say anymore than Lenin did.

> TITLE: "Lenin died of a stroke in January 1924. He was succeeded by General Secretary Joseph Stalin."

SAMOILOV Stalin's got other things to worry about right now, like holding on to his seat.

> *One of the actors nearby moves away.*

SAMOILOV If you ask me the theatre doesn't need a director any more than Russia needed the Tsar. The director is an old fashioned Imperialist idea. We don't even need Stalin. What do we need Stalin for? We're Bolsheviks you know. A dictatorship of the people, isn't that right? Let the people decide. They want Babanova, give them Babanova! They want Samoilov, give them Samoilov!

> *MAYAKOVSKY and GARIN move away, GARIN laughing and clapping SAMOILOV on the shoulder as he goes.*

SAMOILOV Go ahead and laugh. What is the matter with you? You are all afraid. I am *not* afraid. I will tell him… *(drinks)*
GARIN Maria, congratulations, / you were great tonight.
BABANOVA Oh. Thank you Erast.
GARIN I was just talking with Samoilov. I think he is crazy, you know, but I do agree with him: you should be playing the leads.
BABANOVA Oh.
GARIN You heard the audience tonight. Meyerhold is not doing right by you.
BABANOVA Can I tell you something Erast? Will you keep it a secret?
GARIN Of course.
BABANOVA I'm thinking about leaving Meyerhold's theatre.
GARIN Don't we all think about it? But we stay. He is terrible, but he is the best.
BABANOVA Ilinksy left. And he is doing very well.
GARIN Yes but Ilinsky left because he is too proud. Oedipus was proud and look what happened to him.
BABANOVA You think I am being too proud?
GARIN No. I think you are right. It isn't fair.
BABANOVA Do you think I am right to leave?

GARIN I think you have to decide.

BABANOVA But I can't decide. I love Meyerhold. I am grateful. But I hate him. *I* could play Ana Adreevna just as well as Zinaida Raikh. She gets all the leads now, ever since he gave her Aksyusha in *The Forest*. And Alexei Faiko wrote Stefka specifically for me, he even told me so, but *she* played it. Is that what I have to look forward to? I am a good actress. I know what I am doing. I can feel that now. For so long I thought it was all because of Meyerhold, that as long as I did what he told me to do I could fool everybody. But now I think I actually know what I am doing. Don't laugh. Oh! How can I tell him? He would never hear it. He loves Zinaida too much, I think, to listen to me. I don't have the courage anyway.

GARIN Why don't you get drunk like Samoilov? Vodka makes everything easier.

BABANOVA I'm not joking, Erast.

GARIN Neither am I. To the best actress in Russia.

BABANOVA And the best actor. They will write about you in history books after tonight.

GARIN Maybe. But it will be your picture they clip from the magazines.

They clink glasses and drink. MEYERHOLD and RAIKH enter arm in arm and there is a whoop of applause and chatter from the ACTORS. SAMOILOV becomes very attentive.

MAYAKOVSKY Meyerhold!

MEYERHOLD Mayakovsky!

MAYAKOVSKY You have started a long debate tonight, I guarantee it.

MEYERHOLD I expect you to defend me, Vladimir.

MAYAKOVSKY Entire books will be written about this production. That's defense enough.

MEYERHOLD It pleases me that you are pleased.

MAYAKOVSKY And you were superb.

RAIKH Thank you, Vladimir.

MEYERHOLD Where is the vodka!

GARIN Here, Vsevolod Emelievich, here!

BABANOVA It went well tonight.

RAIKH Yes.

MEYERHOLD Zinaida, come, have a drink. Does everybody have a drink?

ALL (except SAMOILOV) Yes! Yes Director! Yes Meyerhold! Etc.

MEYERHOLD To Gogol, our master playwright, who despite what the critics might say tomorrow would be damn pleased had he lived so long to join us

tonight! To Erast Garin! To Zinaida Raikh! To our theatre! To the Revolution! …And to Samoilov, quickly, before he falls down!
ALL *(laughing)* Hey! To Samoilov! Etc.
MEYERHOLD Good! Good! As you were!

> *Different people clap MEYERHOLD and one another on the shoulders and continue as they were. MAYAKOVSKY occupies RAIKH in conversation. SAMOILOV still stands rather close. GARIN and BABANOVA stand nearby a few steps. MEYERHOLD's tone during the following is an unnervingly pleasant one.*

MEYERHOLD Yes Samoilov. …?
SAMOILOV I…
MEYERHOLD What did you think of the show tonight? Was it good?
SAMOILOV Yes, of course.
MEYERHOLD Good. And how about Zinaida Raikh?
SAMOILOV She was… very good.
MEYERHOLD You think so?
SAMOILOV Yes.
MEYERHOLD Yes, she is very good. How do you explain the audience then?
SAMOILOV …I–
MEYERHOLD Somebody must have orchestrated such a thing, of course, how else can one explain it?
SAMOILOV Orchestrate it? Who would orchestrate it?
MEYERHOLD *(pretends to notice for the first time)* Babanova.
BABANOVA Oh. Congratulations, Vsevolod Emelievich.
MEYERHOLD Congratulations to you. If they were still here I believe the audience would say the same.
BABANOVA …Oh.
MEYERHOLD Interesting, don't you think?
BABANOVA What? The audience? Yes. They're always a mystery.
MEYERHOLD I think they were very clear about themselves tonight, wouldn't you say?
RAIKH *(joining)* I am tired Vsevolod. And drunk already. Are we staying here tonight or going home?
GARIN We may have no choice at this point. The streetcars have already gone home, I think.
RAIKH I don't want to stay here. Hello Maria.
BABANOVA Hello.
MEYERHOLD …Is there anything else you wish to say Babanova?

BABANOVA Say? No. ...?

> *SAMOILOV grabs MEYEHOLD by the head, stopping the party dead in its tracks.*

SAMOILOV Well I have something to say! I want to act! Do you understand me? I want to act! I want to act! I want to act!

> *MEYERHOLD breaks free after some spectacular difficulty. There is a tense pause before:*

MEYERHOLD Now that's what I call an audition.

> *General laughter.*

MEYERHOLD Who knew you had such passion in you, Quiet Samoilov.
SAMOILOV I am sorry, Vsevolod Emelievich, I, I don't know what I–
MEYERHOLD Have another drink, Samoilov.
SAMOILOV I did that already.
MEYERHOLD Yes. So tomorrow at rehearsal do that without the drink and you will be an artist.
SAMOILOV Thank you, Comrade Director. I– thank you.

> *SAMOILOV walks away. MEYERHOLD turns to BABANOVA.*

MEYERHOLD Well.

> *After an uncertain moment, BABANOVA exits. The music on the old record player grows louder as the party breaks up and the scene shifts to...*

Episode Eight – Beginning of the end...

> TITLE: "January 1928. Late at night in Meyerhold's office above the Meyerhold State Theatre."

> *MEYERHOLD at his desk. LUNACHARSKY has just arrived. MAYAKOVSKY and SHOSTAKOVICH are already present.*

LUNACHARSKY I hope I'm not interrupting anything. I was just in the neighborhood and thought I'd stop in and see what the midnight oil is burning for these days.

MEYERHOLD Comrade Shostakovich will be writing music for Vladimir's new play if I can convince Valdimir to write his new play.

LUNACHASRKY Ah, what is the play?

MAYAKOVSKY …Don't look at me, I haven't written it. Whatever it is I'm sure Comrade Shostakovich will write something quite appropriate.

SHOSTAKOVICH I will try.

LUNACHARSKY It's good to know you will be producing something new.

MEYERHOLD Everything we do is new. We are constantly new.

LUNACHARSKY You know what I mean.

MEYERHOLD The classics are always new. That's why they are called the classics.

MAYAKOVSKY The classics are old. *That's* why they're called the classics.

MEYERHOLD Not when I do them. As a matter of fact I've just written Picasso again about his designing *Hamlet* for me. *That* will be something new.

LUNACHARSKY I've touched a nerve.

MAYAKOVSKY Easily done.

MEYERHOLD Nikolai Erdman has been putting "finishing touches" on *The Suicide* for two years. I've been begging Vladimir here to give us a new play for ten. The theatre is dying, I tell him, there are no plays. Finally he agrees.

LUNACHARSKY Good. Your repertoire needs more red blood.

MAYAKOVSKY Soviet blood, why not just say it directly?

LUNACHARSKY *(shrugs)* My humble attempt at speaking poetically.

MAYAKOVSKY You don't need to speak "poetically" with us, Anatoly, we've known each other long enough. Why choose your words so carefully – you're *here*, after all. Head of the Soviet Commissariat of Enlightenment having a late night chat at the office of Vsevolod Meyerhold? The potential for rumor is spectacular. Did you hear? Mayakovsky was there. And Shostakovich. Who knows what sort of deviance those boys were up to.

SHOSTAKOVICH laughs nervously.

LUNACHARSKY Your candor is unparalleled, Comrade Mayakovsky.

MAYAKOVSKY Candor is oxygen. Silence is unbearable.

Silence.

SHOSTAKOVICH …Well, gentlemen- er uh, Comrades. I think I will go. Thank you. I'm glad to be writing music for you.

MEYERHOLD We are glad to have you. You will find your way out?

SHOSTAKOVICH Yes. Goodbye. Goodbye Comrade Lunacharsky. Goodbye.

SHOSTAKOVICH *leaves.*

LUNACHARSKY Tense one, isn't he?
MAYAKOVSKY I think I unnerved him with my unparalleled candor.
LUNACHARSKY What sort of man is he?
MEYERHOLD Very talented.
LUNACHARSKY I mean does he wave the red or the lavender flag?
MAYAKOVSKY If the man stirs his red with a little blue, what of it? He writes good music.
MEYERHOLD *(changing the subject)* So, how was which theatre tonight?
LUNACHARSKY The Moscow Art Theatre.
MEYERHOLD Ah yes. And how *is* Uncle Vanya doing?
LUNACHARSKY Fine. No surprises.
MEYERHOLD Naturally. But I can't imagine you've dropped by to talk about Uncle Vanya.
LUNACHARSKY What do you think about Trotsky?
MAYAKOVSKY *I* think Comrade Stalin doesn't like Jews.
MEYERHOLD What do *you* think about Trotsky?
LUNACHARSKY If he was a danger to Soviet unity, then Stalin is probably right to let him go.
MAYAKOVSKY "Let him go." Listen to you. Your poetics get worse and worse.
MEYERHOLD You came here to talk about Trotsky?
LUNACHARSKY *(smiles)* No. …I read Maria Babanova's letter to the press today.
MEYERHOLD Ah.
LUNACHARSKY She will be missed.
MEYERHOLD She will be replaced. I've already scheduled rehearsals for Zinaida Raikh to take over the role of Stella in *Cuckhold*.
LUNACHARSKY Zinaida Raikh?
MEYERHOLD Zinaida will bring out the tragic essence of the play that Babanova could not.
LUNACHARSKY That *will* be tragic.
MEYERHOLD The company no longer needs Maria Babanova. We haven't needed her for some time now. Her resignation saved me the trouble of having to let her go. …Still she might have spoken to me directly rather than going to the *pressss*. …At any rate, life marches on.
LUNACHARSKY Yes. …I've considered handing in my own resignation.

MEYERHOLD Have you. Why is that?

LUNACHARSKY The other day I was asked – quite casually, it seemed – what I thought about the idea of an appointment as Ambassador to Spain.

MEYERHOLD Ambassador to Spain. Would you take it?

LUNACHARSKY It hasn't been offered. And if I resign first, I think it *won't* be offered. That's my point. There have been a few "Ambassadors to Spain" already, none of whom anyone has heard from again.

MEYERHOLD I see.

LUNACHARSKY Yes. There are people who think I have been too soft, that I lack a proper Communist vigilance and don't understand the significance of class war on the cultural front. These past ten years we have basked in the sunlight of the Revolution. Back in 1921, Lenin's New Economic Policy did sound a bit odd. That it would take a dash of Capitalism to get Communism on its feet was an irony lost on nobody. But: now the Revolution *is* on its feet. Industry is on the move. And a sharp cold wind is felt all the time… I have not always agreed with you, Vsevolod Emelievich, but I have always defended what you are trying to do. Your theatre is very interesting. It makes one stop and think. Be careful with it.

MEYERHOLD Careful? Of what? The truth? Russia is riddled with saboteurs bent on wrecking the Revolution from the inside out. The old bourgeois bureaucrats and hypocrites have been replaced by Communist bureaucrats and hypocrites. Everyone knows, it's no secret.

LUNACHARSKY It's one thing to say so here in this room, and quite another to say it on stage.

MEYERHOLD Yes, on stage it's art. Here it's conversation.

LUNACHARSKY Vsevolod Emelievich, let me speak with as little poetry as possible: if I resign, I will no longer be around to defend you. That is what I am saying.

MEYERHOLD Thank you for saying so.

LUNACHARSKY …Well. *(standing)* If I were you, and I am not, I would beg Maria Babanova to stay.

MEYERHOLD Maria who?

LUNACHARSKY …Good luck, Comrade.

MEYERHOLD *(stands)* Good luck to you.

LUNACHARSKY exits. MEYERHOLD sits down again.

MAYAKOVSKY It's late. I'd have gone with him just now only it sounds like it might be better to leave some distance between us.

MEYERHOLD Oh, I am disappointed with you.

MAYAKOVSKY My apologies. It's just that I'd rather not end up Ambassador to Spain.

MEYERHOLD That's nonsense and paranoia.

MAYAKOVSKY He is right, Vsevolod Emelievich. The wind *is* cold. And sometimes our Great Red Flag seems to me a small white handkerchief trampled to a bloody rag. …When even Utopia is stained, where do we find our hope?

> *MAYAKOVSKY exits. MEYERHOLD collects himself and turns out the light, then descends the stairs from his office. The stage is dark, but for the ghost light. BABANOVA enters and crosses the stage.*

MEYERHOLD Who is there?

BABANOVA Oh! Hello.

MEYERHOLD What are you doing here?

BABANOVA I–I was just collecting some things from my dressing room. …I want you to know–

MEYERHOLD –Yes?

BABANOVA …You are a great teacher. And I'm grateful.

MEYERHOLD Grateful.

BABANOVA Yes. It's just time for me to move on. Thank you for all you've done for me.

> *BABANOVA puts out her hand. MEYERHOLD does not move.*

BABANOVA …It wasn't an easy decision to make. …I feel like I grew up here. You've been a father to me, and– despite everything– …well– …I just thought– …I thought the best thing– … …I never organized anything against Zinaida. It's the truth. …

> *…No response from MEYERHOLD. BABANOVA exits. After a moment, MEYERHOLD starts to go himself. The ghost light flickers momentarily with a sputtering electrical buzz. MEYERHOLD stops and crosses closer to look at it. The ghost light goes out.*

End of Act Two.

TITLE: "Intermission"

Act Three, 1930–1940

Episode Nine – The Death of Mayakovsky

TITLE: "April 1930"

Sound of a small clock ticking. MAYAKOVSKY enters and ascends some stairs to a platform where there is a chair and a small table. He takes a seat, then unfolds a letter and looks at it.

TITLE: "To all. Do not blame anyone for my death and please do not gossip. The deceased terribly disliked this sort of thing. Mama, sisters, and comrades, forgive me – this is not a way out. I do not recommend it to others. But I have none other. Do not think me weak-spirited. There was nothing else I could do. Vladimir Mayakovsky."

MAYAKOVSKY sets the note on the table. He puts one bullet in a revolver, spins and closes the chamber. He puts the gun to his head and pulls the trigger. There is a loud bang and MAYAKOVSKY falls off his chair, dead.

Episode Ten – New York/Moscow

TITLE: "New York. June 1935."
TITLE: "Actors from the Group Theatre gather at a restaurant after performances of Awake and Sing *and* Waiting For Lefty."
TITLE: "In Moscow, people gather outside State Bakery No. 10 waiting to buy bread."

In Moscow, a line of MUSCOVITES waiting to buy bread.

In New York at a sidewalk restaurant, the Group Theatre crowd has crammed around a table with wine and glasses. Nearby sits Lee STRASBERG shielded by a newspaper. Harold CLURMAN is just arriving with Stella ADLER. (Shortly into the scene a WAITER arrives to replace an empty bottle with a new one.)

ADLER Ladies and gents, Mister Harold Clurman.
ALL / Hey Harry! Clurman! Welcome back old boy! Etc…
CLURMAN Hello Sanford! Phoebe! Hello Cliff! I was just tellin' Stella: I slipped in at Act Two: great show tonight. Not too shabby at the box office, either. Hey Kazan, how was *Lefty* over at the Longacre?
KAZAN Crowd sure is polite on the Broad Way. Yuh ask me I miss 14th Street.

But: they're payin', so who's askin'.
CLURMAN You said it. Hey Lee! Strasberg!
BRAND Leave him alone. He likes it that way.
CLURMAN Still, huh?
ADLER You'll need to go farther than Russia and back to notate any evolution on that ape.
KAZAN So? How was it?
BRAND Yeah, give us the dish.
ODETS Say, where's your fur cap?
CLURMAN Aw thanks ever so much for the ticket Cliff.
ODETS Well I owed yuh one. Two even!
CLURMAN Well it sure was swell o' yuh. Russia is a fine place to be, ladies and gentleman. Music. Art. *Theatre!* My god. Over three hundred theatres in Moscow alone. And *everybody* goes. Three or four times a *week* they go. Cheering for their favorite directors like we cheer for baseball teams.
KAZAN *(laughing)* Now that's un-American.
BRAND Sad but true.
MEISNER You can say that twice.
CLURMAN But get this, even with those figures, Meyerhold still complains about the lemon-lipped expectations of his audience. From Broadway to Gorky Street, it's all the same.
KAZAN Which one's Meyerhold again?
ADLER He's the one who trains acrobats instead of actors.
CLURMAN Stella. I'll tell you the truth, though: I'd watch Meyerhold's acrobats over most New York actors any day.
BRAND Hey!
CLURMAN Present company excepted of course.
BRAND Of course.
CLURMAN No sir, the Group Theatre's got no cause to blush in the acting department. But I tell yuh this: we got more than Communism to learn from the Reds. The Moscow Art Theatre alone employs two hundred and forty actors.
MEISNER Two-hundred and forty actors?
CLURMAN Two hundred and forty actors.
MEISNER Two hundred and forty actors.
KAZAN Now that takes a wad o' jack.
CLURMAN State money, that's how they do it. It's the only way.
BRAND Can you imagine if the Group Theatre had two hundred and forty actors?

MEISNER Two hundred and forty actors.
KAZAN Meisner please.
MEISNER "Meisner please."
KAZAN I *said* please.
MEISNER Please yourself, I'm in shock. Can't a fellow go electric when he hears there's a place on earth where one theatre gives work for two hundred and forty actors? And multiply that by three hundred theatres? Utopia. It bares repeating.
CLURMAN They're not *all* that big. That's the Moscow Art Theatre. And Meyerhold's Theatre too. Some of them aren't much bigger than the cellars we got off the beaten track here. But large small or in between they all get money from the State. And get this: it's normal. The people expect it.
ADLER I should live so long.
MEISNER That's a lot of men and women collecting a regular paycheck. Here we finally got two hits goin' simultaneous and we're *still* just gettin' by.
ODETS That's the Depression for you, brother: depressing.
ADLER You should howl Mister Big Shot Playwright. Is that a *new* hat you're wearing?
CLURMAN Stella.
ADLER Who'd you have dinner with *last* night, Greta Garbo? Good dialogue I bet.
ODETS What are you so hot for? You're makin' *rent* on my dialogue aren't yuh?
BRAND *(changing the subject)* Eh-ehm! Say Harold I hear those Russian actors get vacation time.
CLURMAN Oh yeah, four weeks paid.
MEISNER Four weeks paid?
CLURMAN Four weeks paid.
MEISNER Four weeks paid.
BRAND Gee, can you imagine? I don't know what I'd do with four weeks paid.
MEISNER Four weeks paid.
KAZAN I know what I'd do.
CLURMAN Go back to Moscow in a snap. The Russians know how to treat an artist, what art can *do* for a country. And talk about pullin' up your bootstraps. Cranes everywhere, building building and building. It's incredible the energy. I bought a ticket to the new Metro, just opened. And everybody crowding in like a Coney Island roller coaster. To see the workers who built this subway, with their rough clothes and earthy untutored ways, crowding into these grand, modernistic halls *they built!* It hits yuh between the eyes the inspiring contradiction, the glorious and unparalleled paradox of the Soviet Union. A

real modern nation of the people.
BRAND That's right. American Comrades don't know what Communism is. Here the Party's just that: a party. A social club for artists invited in for good advertising but they don't know red from yellow.
ODETS Hey!
BRAND *(without apology)* Sorry Cliff.
CLURMAN Oh, Cliff, by the way, Stanislavsky said to tell you.
ODETS *(smiling)* Oh yeah?, wha'd he say?
CLURMAN I was tellin' him about our success with *Lefty* and *Awake and Sing* and *he* said: "Tell Mr. Odets not to give up acting."

Everyone laughs. CLURMAN clarifies:

CLURMAN Because: "It'll help his writing. And when he needs time off to write a play, give him time off."
ODETS Thanks, I'll take four weeks. Paid.
CLURMAN "But let him keep acting."
KAZAN You keep writin', Odets. We need yuh behind the pen.
ODETS Yeah, don't I know it.
ADLER Listen to him. Aren't we doin' your plays, Cliff? What you always wanted?
CLURMAN Stella.
ODETS Sure, after *Lefty* took off like a shot. Until then my mouth was full of nothin' but please.
ADLER You eat off us as much as we eat off you. Without actors your words wouldn't even be plays.
CLURMAN Stella.
ADLER Stella, Stella. Stop repeating yourself. You sound like Meisner. Like a hotshot he's been ever since the front pages fell in love with him. Hollywood callin' regular. They're callin' us too, yuh know. You're not the only one hangin' up on the Warner Brothers lately. We're all holding tight to the Group. You're no martyr.
ODETS Who said I was?
ADLER Your ungrateful smirk, that's who.
ODETS You're tellin' *me* ungrateful? Well catch this, Lady Adler: I ain't no show-shop. I don't crank plays off a conveyor belt like some Henry Ford. It's hard work writin' plays.
CLURMAN We know it, Cliff, we know it.
ODETS Sure I got some dough now, why shouldn't I? *Lefty's* playin' in every work hall across the country, raisin' more dust than the wind in Kansas. Why

an actor out in Hollywood got beat up by some "friends of the New Germany" for doin' *Lefty* just last week.

ADLER What's that got to do with anything? So some Hollywood Germans don't like actors with a mouthful o' Red. That make you special? What are you *happy* that boy got himself in the hospital over your play?

ODETS That's not what I'm sayin'.

ADLER What *are* yuh sayin' huh? Not much.

ODETS I'm sayin' I might not be gettin' my head cracked open in Frisco or Tennessee like a model Comrade, but I'm doin' *somethin'*. Everyday you walk down Wall Street it's rainin' business men. A new set of brains hits the road everyday, they gotta scrape'm together like broken pancake batter. America's black and blue all over. Kids like ghosts on every corner sellin' apples. And people need more than a New Deal on Uncle Sam's lips to put a little red in their cheeks. Hope. Vision. Artists to paint the possibilities. Poets spelling it out. Sounds like from what Harold here says in Moscow I wouldn't have to explain that to a fine lady of the stage such as yourself.

ADLER So don't waste your breath. I've read Marx.

ODETS You've read Marx. We've all "read Marx." Why don't yuh shut your books and volunteer to work the bread line on Sundays like Phoebe and Kazan over here?

ADLER Why don't you? Ha! Don't have an answer for *that* under your new hat, do yuh?

BRAND Welcome back, Harold. Welcome back.

CLURMAN Now if only I could get Strasberg to blow up, everything'd be in order. Strasberg, you talkin' yet?

ADLER Don't bother. He's kept his cork on tight ever since Cliff's plays went off well without his help. Got enough steam bottled up inside to power a freight train.

KAZAN Who's the pot and who's the kettle in this scenario?

ADLER Can it Kazan.

MEISNER Hell of a way to spend an evening with friends.

CLURMAN Could be worse.

BRAND How's that?

MEISNER Yeah, how's that?

CLURMAN Could be joining the breadline on Sunday instead of workin' it.

A sobering thought… In Moscow…

BAKER *(enters)* I am sorry. Nothing today. *(exits)*

MALCONTENT Comrade Stalin is a thief. *(spits)*

The MALCONTENT's fellow MUSCOVITES step away from him.

Episode Eleven – Meyerholditis

TITLE: "Moscow. 1936."

Music. A fast-paced montage of theatrical and critical Moscow, 1936. Two spotlights help us follow the action.

PAPERBOY
Pravda, Pravda! Pravda, Pravda! Thank you, sir.
MEYERHOLD
And what does *Pravda* tell us today?
PAPERBOY
From an editorial in *Pravda,* January, 1936:

Sound of applause under the following as RAIKH steps forward costumed as Marguerite in Camille. *She takes a gracious bow and exits to her dressing room, where a DRESSER helps her to change and then exits.*

CRITIC #1 The glorious Zinaida Raikh has yet to fade in her triumphant portrayal of Marguerite in Alexandre Dumas fils' *Camille.* Since she first astounded Moscow with the unexpected brilliance of her performance at the 1934 premiere, Raikh's grace, beauty, and luminous stage presence have given Meyerhold's otherwise useless production a reason to remain in the repertoire.
MEYERHOLD Useless eh?
CRITIC #1 For what does he offer his fellow citizens but a decorative, pearl-studded antique depicting all the petty concerns of bourgeois women?
MEYERHOLD It's about the abuse of women, you idiot!
CRITIC #1 Like some European Capitalist of the West, Meyerhold lures his audience with sparkle, velvet, and shiny things. Once Raikh has left the stage the spectators are left with nothing to applaud but her husband's decadent nonsense!
MEYERHOLD They love you, Zinochka, but they are very tired of me.
RAIKH They don't understand you, Darling. It's their fault, not yours.
MEYERHOLD *I* know that. But do they?
RAIKH Did you find a new play today?
MEYERHOLD A new play or a good play?
RAIKH Something great to open our new theatre.
MEYERHOLD If they ever finish building the new theatre.

RAIKH We'll do *Hamlet*, like you've always wanted to! Picasso will still be willing, I'm sure.

MEYERHOLD Yes. And you will make a beautiful Hamlet.

RAIKH Oh, yes, what a success we'll have!

MEYERHOLD We could use it now. Too many empty seats these days.

RAIKH Don't worry. You'll find a new play eventually, and the repertoire will be as fresh as it ever was.

PAPERBOY From an anonymous letter in *Pravda*, February, 1936:

CRITIC #2 One can smell the curdling of the Meyerhold Theatre repertoire from here to Siberia. Meyerhold offers nothing to champion the new men and women of Soviet Russia, only pessimistic jabs at old targets demolished long ago. *Camille* retreats to the bourgeois melodrama of yesteryear. *The Inspector* skewers the long-since-irrelevant bureaucracy of the Tsar. And who knows why *The Magnanimous Cuckhold,* that fossil of frivolity, is performed at all these days but to satisfy the vanity of Zinaida Raikh, who fancies herself the ingénue Maria Babanova was fourteen years ago. Comrade Meyerhold's aging repertoire leaves us somewhat apprehensive about his future. He has become, in a word: unnecessary.

In the halls of the Meyerhold Theatre...

MEYERHOLD Gladkov!

GLADKOV Yes, sir!

MEYERHOLD A letter to the editors of *Pravda*.

GLADKOV Yes, sir.

MEYERHOLD "Kind sirs, *(blows a raspberry)*. Very truly yours, Vsevolod Emelievich Meyerhold." Well? What do you think?

GLADKOV I think you're joking.

MEYERHOLD Good. Send it. Let's see if we get a laugh.

PAPERBOY From an anonymous editorial in *Pravda*, February, 1936:

CRITIC #3 It seems Comrade Meyerhold no longer fully appreciates his role in Comrade Stalin's great plan. He stubbornly avoids the comprehensible simplicity of Reality as upheld by Stanislavsky at the Moscow Art Theatre. And not since the late Mayakovsky has Meyerhold offered the people a Soviet playwright worthy of the Revolution. Even Mayakovsky was burdened by Meyerhold with the light pretensions of Shostakovich, that most questionable of Soviet composers.

Morning in the bedroom of the MEYERHOLD's flat. SHOSTAKOVICH is getting dressed. RAIKH is still in her robe. It has evidently been a night of questionable virtue for all three.

MEYERHOLD Shostakovich! Did you read in *Pravda* today?

SHOSTAKOVICH Yes, I did. I don't know what to think.

MEYERHOLD Don't let it worry you. They've been taking shots at me for years. The trick is to keep moving.

SHOSTAKOVICH Doesn't it make you nervous?

RAIKH Ignorance should make you angry, Dmitri, not nervous. *(kisses SHOSTAKOVICH on the cheek, then MEYERHOLD.)*

SHOSTAKOVICH They want something new – I try something new, but no. You think to yourself, "well, if I play by the rules," but what are the rules?

MEYERHOLD Wasn't it Beethoven who once wrote: "there is no rule that cannot be broken for the sake of the beautiful." By the way, how's that new production of your opera?

SHOSTAKOVICH *(dismayed)* Beautiful, I'm afraid.

PAPERBOY From an anonymous review in *Pravda*, March 1936, of Shostakovich's opera:

CRITIC #4 Shostakovich's opera is a mess! From the first moment, opening-night listeners, among them Comrades Stalin and Molotov, were flabbergasted by the intentionally dissonant, deviant, unnatural squeals of the orchestra! This avant-garde monstrosity is entirely alien to genuine Soviet art, and bears the most negative traits of Meyerholditis, a disease afflicting far too many impressionable young artists these days! We recommend that Comrade Shostakovich reflect more seriously on questions of Soviet musical culture, and that he would do well to decline any further influence from the school of Meyerhold! The Soviet people have no need for such vulgar perversity!

> *SHOSTAKOVICH collapses on a staircase, face in his hands, wracked with nerves.*

PAPERBOY At the All-Union Conference of Theatre Workers, March 1936.

> *MEYERHOLD steps up to a podium to a mix of boos from deterrents and his name chanted by supporters (the irony of which he appears to enjoy) all gathered below. RAIKH stands nearby him. GLADKOV writes everything down. The CROWD periodically makes its opinion known.*

MEYERHOLD Comrades, fellow workers in art, and kind Critics. No doubt I am expected to devote this speech to an unsparing criticism of myself, and a plea that I be forgiven for my work and allowed to move on. I would point out that my entire career has consisted of nothing but constant self-criticism, and that in my work I have always moved on. The artist today indeed does *not* divorce himself from Reality, but rather knows he is here to help build the Communist path brick by brick. Should I renounce my 1922 production of

The Magnanimous Cuckhold, a production that helped to bring Revolutionary zeal off the street and into the theatre? Without the unrestrained, youthful energy of *Cuckhold* in 1922, there would have been no sober critique of counter-revolutionary bureaucracy in *The Inspector* in 1926. Without *The Inspector*, there would not have been the precise balance of art and ideology in *Cammille* in 1934. One brick follows another, and slowly the path is built.
...And as for "Meyerholditis," I cannot take credit for the many ignorant and clumsy imitations of my work by others. Neither can I denounce the masterful adaptations of it by the likes of my former teacher, Stanislavsky, nor the application of it by my former student, Sergei Eisenstein, to his great cinematic works. ...Recently, anonymous pens have condemned Comrade Shostakovich as vulgar and perverted...

> *The spotlight picks out SHOSTAKOVICH for a moment and he laughs nervously. The spotlight returns to MEYERHOLD.*

MEYERHOLD ...blaming me for the corruption of this fresh young musical talent. I say Shostakovich is a brilliant artist, and whether certain critics comprehend this today matters little to the fame he will no doubt be awarded tomorrow when reflection sees fit to honor his great contribution to Soviet life. As Comrade Lenin once told us, "Art belongs to the people, and must be loved and understood by them." What is important today is that my intentions be understood by those who would reduce my art to some flamboyant disease. The Party, led by our great Comrade Stalin, has made a stirring demand for artists to pursue the simplest and most direct path to Reality. But in this search for simplicity, one cannot deny one's own identity. I am a Communist. I am an Artist. I am Vsevolod Emelievich Meyerhold. Comrades: do not mistake me for anyone else. Thank you.

> *The gathered crowd turns in silence and faces out to listen to CRITIC #5, a particularly humorless figure whose calm is unnerving. MEYERHOLD and RAIKH slowly descend the stairs together.*

CRITIC #5 It has become quite clear that Meyerhold cannot and apparently will not comprehend Soviet Reality. His entire career has amounted to a struggle against the realistic theatre on behalf of a stylized theatre. His rendition of *The Inspector* was decidedly unsettling and unnatural. In 1932 he stubbornly tried to stage the play *The Suicide*, a hostile slur on Soviet ideals by that enemy of the people, Nikolai Erdman. And despite her success in *Camille*, he has favored his wife beyond her abilities and to the artistic detriment of countless productions. Systematic deviation from Soviet reality, distortion of that reality, and hostile slanders against our way of life have brought his theatre to total ideological and artistic ruin, as well as shameful bankruptcy. I ask you:

does the Soviet public really need such a theatre?

MEYERHOLD and RAIKH now walk past the line and each person either turns away, looks away, or steps away, and disperses.

Episode Twelve – After dinner at the Meyerholds'...

GLADKOV, GARIN, and RAIKH in the sitting room of the Meyerholds' flat. Though they have been drinking they appear to be holding their liquor fairly well.

Four NKVD men lurk in the shadows outside the space of the Meyerholds' sitting room.

GLADKOV Well, it is late.

TITLE: "March 1936. At the Meyerholds' flat on Brusov Street."

GLADKOV I had better go.
GARIN / No, Gladkov. One more drink.
RAIKH Aleksandr, no, have another drink with us.
GLADKOV You are very generous, but I think if I have any more cognac I'll forget I exist.
RAIKH It's bad enough the others left after dinner, Aleksandr, please stay. Garin is staying, aren't you Garin?
GARIN Of course.
RAIKH And Vsevolod is fixing coffee.
GARIN Have you ever had coffee by Vsevolod Emelievich?
GLADKOV No I haven't.
GARIN One cup and you'll be saying "cognac? What cognac?"
GLADKOV I really shouldn't.

MEYERHOLD enters with a tray of coffee cups. He is performing.

MEYERHOLD Madam et Messieurs, le café est servie!
RAIKH Ha ha, too late.
MEYERHOLD Votre café, Madame.
RAIKH Merci Monsieur.
GARIN We are in Paris now.
MEYERHOLD Oui, où autrement?

GARIN It's just that it's a long way to travel for coffee. At dinner our waiter was German.
MEYERHOLD *(quick sound of airplane as he spins in place)* Mein Herr, unsere ist eine Gaststätte der Welt. Kaffee für Sie?
GARIN Vielen Dank.
MEYERHOLD *(quick sound of airplane as he turns to GLADKOV)* Et Monsieur. ...Pourquoi hésitez-vous? Prenez-le!
GLADKOV Thank you. *(sits)*
MEYERHOLD Mon plaisir. Madame, Messieurs: Bon appétit!

MEYERHOLD exits in character with his tray.

GARIN You see? If you leave early you'll miss something for your book.
GLADKOV Not a book. I just keep notes.
RAIKH What is your title now? Do we have a title for you? What *are* you?
GLADKOV Today? I don't know. Research Assistant? Literary Manager? Assistant Director?

MEYERHOLD enters.

MEYERHOLD Right Hand Man. Gladkov will write my memoirs for me because I am too lazy.
GLADKOV No, no.
MEYERHOLD Well? How is the coffee? Is it good?
ALL Very good. Excellent. Good, thank you. Etc.
MEYERHOLD Good. So, Zinaida, tell our friends about the guest you received in your dressing room after *Cammille* the other night. ...Go ahead. They're our good friends.
GARIN Who was it?
RAIKH ...A personal assistant of Comrade Stalin's.
GLADKOV / Really!
GARIN Stalin came to the theatre?
MEYERHOLD No.
RAIKH No. He has never come. That was the point. We have no official box for him and therefore he does not come. This is what the assistant told me. Otherwise he was certain that Stalin would without question love *Camille* and that it could have major consequences for the Meyerhold Theatre and for Vsevolod himself.
MEYERHOLD He said there might be a possibility of Stalin receiving me so that I might express to him my needs. He said he could try to arrange it.

RAIKH He couldn't promise anything in advance, of course.

MEYERHOLD Well I think an autographed photo of *you* might have taken care of that. He was a rather star-struck Personal Assistant of Comrade Stalin's.

RAIKH Perhaps the most star-struck Personal Assistant of Comrade Stalin's one has ever seen.

GARIN Would you want a meeting with Stalin?

MEYERHOLD …I am sharing this with you both as friends, of course, whom I trust completely.

GARIN / Yes, yes, of course.

GLADKOV Of course, Vsevolod Emelievich.

MEYERHOLD And I trust, Gladkov, none of this will go down in any of those little notebooks you have tucked away in your pockets.

GLADKOV Of course.

MEYERHOLD …Yes, I would consider it. I would consider it. You see, ever since I defended Shostakovich at that conference–

RAIKH Ever since you stepped foot on the Russian stage, Vsevolod. People have been clawing at Vsevolod all his life. Stupid and ignorant people who know nothing about the theatre.

MEYERHOLD Zinochka, please.

RAIKH I should have told that man to arrange a meeting with Stalin right away. You *should* meet with Stalin.

MEYERHOLD It can still be arranged.

GARIN What would you say?

MEYERHOLD That is my question. I am hoping for some good advice from the both of you. When faced with Stalin, what does one say exactly? …Gladkov?

GLADKOV Oh. Shit. Well? Uh. First of all I, I think you certainly must meet with him. And, that you should tell him about the problems with your theatre, how inadequate and cramped it is, and maybe ask him to step up the construction of the new theatre. And you should explain to him your own point of view so that he understands it correctly rather than how *Pravda* puts it. And also the misconceptions of art in general! It would be an opportunity to go straight to the top! And who else if not you, a Communist and a leading director of our time, can tell the entire truth to Stalin about how his incompetent assistants are compromising the true meaning of Party policies in art! …That's what I think.

RAIKH I think Aleksandr is right. Only I think you absolutely should not talk on behalf of other people like you did for Shostakovich. Only time and his own work can help him. You should defend *yourself* and your own theatre.

GARIN I don't agree with either of you. I think you absolutely should *not* meet with Stalin because nothing good will come of it anyway. Did Boris

Pasternack not tell you how he telephoned Stalin after the poet Mandelshtam had been arrested, and Stalin simply hung up on him mid-sentence? It is unworthy of you to talk to Stalin, you, Vsevolod Emelievich Meyerhold, to go to Stalin like some petitioner, which is all it would be. A Stalin and a Meyerhold should speak to one another as equals or not at all. An artist is not a beggar. The Revolution needs the theatre to uplift the masses. To teach and to guide them. There is no church anymore. Art is the church of the Revolution. Stalin should thank you and we know that if you meet him now he will not. Therefore I say do not beg to an ungrateful, ignorant man!

MEYERHOLD …You are right. Now is not the time.

RAIKH Vsevolod, wait, think about it a few more days.

MEYERHOLD No. He is right. And we should all forget about what has been said tonight.

RAIKH But think what it could mean if–

MEYERHOLD Zinochka, it will all work itself out. Let's forget about it. Who needs more coffee?

> *Suddenly there is a loud pounding at the door. Everyone, including the NKVD, turns and looks. Pause. The knocking pounds again. MEYERHOLD, RAIKH, GARIN, and GLADKOV look at one another.*

RAIKH What time is it?

MEYERHOLD Maybe it's Shostakovich. I told him to come by after his rehearsal if he was feeling up to it.

> *Pounding again, and MEYERHOLD stands. Pause. MEYERHOLD exits to answer the door. A very tense pause. RAIKH stands, nervous, looking after MEYERHOLD. Pause. Suddenly SHOSTAKOVICH bursts in, followed by MEYERHOLD, in a very anxious and distracted state.*

SHOSTAKOVICH I have to sit down! I have to clear my head! I don't know if I can– Oh! Hello. I'm very sorry. I don't mean to interrupt your party, please, keep talking. Drink, drink. Talk.

RAIKH Dmitri, what is the matter?

SHOSTAKOVICH I'll write another symphony. I'll write a different one.

MEYERHOLD *(touching him)* Dmitri–

SHOSTAKOVICH *(startled)* AAH! …I shouldn't be seen with you.

MEYERHOLD By whom? Zinaida Garin and Gladkov?

SHOSTAKOVICH I should not have come here.

MEYERHOLD Please, sit down.

SHOSTAKOVICH No, I'm sorry, I should have gone straight home. Wait:

now if I leave I will be seen leaving. I'm trapped. No, I just want to be left alone, to the peace of my music and this destiny to which I must *resign myself.*

RAIKH   Dmitri you are scaring us, please!

MEYERHOLD   What has happened?

SHOSTAKOVICH   I just came from rehearsal at the Philharmonic.

MEYERHOLD   *(brightly)* Oh, how'd it go?

RAIKH   Vsevolod!

MEYERHOLD   *(sotto voce)* I didn't mean / it like that.

SHOSTAKOVICH   Apparently there is a rumor going around that my Fourth Symphony is "diabolically clever," and "riddled with decadence." The orchestra has been practicing with nervous fingers all week.

RAIKH   Who is saying this?

SHOSTAKOVICH   A man from the Composers Union and another man from Party Headquarters came to the Philharmonic today. They spoke with Renzin the director and Fritz Stiedry the conductor for over an hour. After they left Fritz told the orchestra to go home, and when I arrived Renzin told me that my symphony will not be performed.

GARIN   That's ridiculous. Based on rumor?

SHOSTAKOVICH   Where did I put it? Where's that piece of paper? I am supposed to see a man named Zakrevsky or Zanchevsky or Zakovsky. Something. I am supposed to report to the NKVD office tomorrow and meet him. He wants to ask me about Tukhachevsky.

GARIN   Who is Tukhachevsky?

> *SHOSTAKOVICH becomes increasingly more excited, eventually scrambling all over the set looking for safety. The NKVD watch him attentively and openly, unseen by the others. MEYERHOLD slowly and soberly sits down, and as SHOSTAKOVICH climbs the heights of his horror, MEYERHOLD closes his eyes and turns his head away. Intense music builds throughout the speech.*

SHOSTAKOVICH   He is my protector in– UH UH my *friend* in the military who was arrested and *shot* I think! Elena Konstantinovskaya and Galina Serebryakova have also been arrested. This Zanchevsky or Zakovsky or whomever will ask me about them too no doubt. The last time I saw Tukhachevsky was at dinner back in, I don't know, I need to remember, what did we say what did we say? We talked about music! What else would we talk about? The Revolution? Stalin? The second Five-Year plan? The glory of Communism? I am going to be arrested, don't you see? If I meet with this man I am going to be shot! That is what happens! Names are dropping like flies! My god! Why does one person get killed and another only exiled? What are the rules? Why is *this* note bad and *that* one good? Who decides these things? Someone in a leather coat likes your apartment and a few days later you are arrested and that leather coat is hanging in your closet by nightfall! This is what happens! Who is running this country? Who is in the audience? Who are the people on the streets? Who are the critics who write in *Pravda* and show up at public debates to scream about the use of this or that major or minor key? What has this Party of yours become? Nothing but a herd of sheep! Is that Russia? Is that what you fought for? They intend to create on the bones of millions something impossible to create! My god! How sad is our country! How sad is our Russia! I only wish to make music and to live!!

> *And tremendous music has indeed filled the air to capacity. MEYERHOLD stands, turns, and walks slowly toward a very old STANISLAVSKY. They meet center stage to greet one another and when their hands finally connect –*

Episode Thirteen – The Death of Stanislavsky

> *– the scene has suddenly changed to the home of STANISLAVSKY. The NKVD men remain lurking attentively in the shadows.*

STANISLAVSKY You must sense why I have asked you here today.

> TITLE: "January 1938. At Stanislavsky's home on Leontevsky Lane."

MEYERHOLD For very different reasons than you asked to see me thirty years ago, I think.
STANISLAVSKY Thirty-three. But who is counting? Please, sit down. Or do you still prefer to stand?
MEYERHOLD Thank you.
STANISLAVSKY I am very sorry that your theatre has been closed.
MEYERHOLD Zinaida has been very distressed. She fainted after the final performance of *Camille*. The theatre was packed!
STANISLAVSKY Well, Kerzhentsev was very wrong to do it.
MEYERHOLD Kerzhentsev is a very determined man, I fear. To be honest, I miss Lunacharsky.
STANISLAVSKY I think many people miss Lunacharsky. Many people miss a lot of things. Most people miss the point of much of what happens in life. It's not just actors who need to learn how to observe Reality, because it's not just actors who have learned to create Reality. But, who has the patience today? I look at young people, people who grew up after the Revolution, and they seem to me entirely New People. It takes time to understand the truth about

anything. ...Do you know why I work from home so much these days?

MEYERHOLD Your health.

STANISLAVSKY Yes. My health. Comrade Stalin has been very gracious to me. He attends all my productions. He is very supportive. And he has seen to it that I get the doctors I need. I am very well preserved. ...I have never pretended to be a political man. I see the world as an artist. They think I don't know that I have been made the featured exhibit in this Museum I call home. Look what fine props and set pieces. Look at my costume. How authentic. How real. Don't I look just like Stanislavsky. And if you are an internationally reputable Soviet such as yourself, or from America or Europe, the doors are open. Otherwise I am afraid I am too ill to see you today.

MEYERHOLD You must have some control.

STANISLAVSKY Yes, yes, of course. And I *am* old. It's true. They will keep me alive as long as they can. And I thank them, because I still have so much I want to do. One thing I have learned: Truth and Reality are two different things. The truth is already there, immovable, as obvious as it is buried. One can build Reality. We need something more than Reality in order to get to the Truth. I know you understand this.

MEYERHOLD Yes.

STANISLAVSKY They have closed your theatre. It is a terrible thing. Perhaps more terrible than anybody realizes. So. I am asking you to come work for me. The Moscow Art Theatre needs you, Vsevolod Emelievich. I need you. Nobody else understands what I am trying to do. I have spent my *life* in search of the truth and so have you.

MEYERHOLD You are offering me a job?

STANISLAVSKY Tell me that you will accept it.

MEYERHOLD Are you... Are you not– concerned–?

STANISLAVSKY –About the truth, yes I am. That the Moscow Art Theatre has been robbed of its vitality in exchange for certain privileges, yes. That I have agreed to allow my books to be edited and translated abroad in the most haphazard manner because I've needed the money, yes. That my name is no longer mine but rather a nation's official acting technique, one I do not even fully believe in, yes, I am very concerned. They don't like it that I practice yoga. They don't like it when I talk about the spirit or the soul. The soul, it seems, is too mystical for the new Reality. I have been packaged up in red ribbons and locked away. And my life's work will soon be buried beneath History's books. Help me to tell the truth. Help me to keep my theatre alive. Tell me that you will do this.

MEYERHOLD ...I will.

STANISLAVSKY Good. I will have it announced right away. How surprised they will be. The world would love for Meyerhold and Stanislavsky to be enemies. What fun we'll have confounding them all.

MEYERHOLD *(Laughs hard; then...)* ...I don't know what to say... *(laughter still, through tears:)* Do you know: people cross the street now to avoid being seen walking past my home. I don't know why I'm laughing. It's terrible.

MEYERHOLD'S laughter subsides with some heavy, short breaths.

STANISLAVSKY ...We will astonish all of Moscow.
MEYERHOLD I should hope so.

YURY enters.

YURY Comrade Stanislavsky. It is time for your tea.
STANISLAVSKY Thank you, Yury.

YURY exits.

STANISLAVSKY Yury is a fine dramaturg. He works with me here at the house. You will like him. *(stands)* ...So. We will talk more. I am working out *Rigoletto* and I need your advice. I will call you and we can talk about it.
MEYERHOLD I look forward to it.

STANISLAVSKY sits and leans back in his chair. GLADKOV enters, and now we are on the empty stage of the Meyerhold Theatre. GLADKOV and MEYERHOLD are alone.

GLADKOV And have you talked about it yet?

TITLE: "A few days later. On the stage of the former Meyerhold Theatre, now empty..."

MEYERHOLD What? Oh. Yes. It will be a very exciting production, I have no doubt.

YURY enters with STANISLAVSKY'S tea, sees the old man is sleeping, exits and hands off the tea to an NKVD man. After a short exchange we cannot hear, YURY returns to take MEYERHOLD'S chair.

STANISLAVSKY Yury.
YURY Yes sir?
STANISLAVSKY We must take care of Meyerhold. He is my sole heir in the theatre.

YURY ...Yes sir.

STANISLAVSKY closes his eyes. After a moment, YURY leaves with the chair.

GLADKOV ...They're probably finished by now.
MEYERHOLD What?
GLADKOV I said they're probably finished. Assigning the actors to new theatres. I would think you'd want to take part in that.
MEYERHOLD Oh, let them go where they like. ...Oddly enough, I will miss this drafty auditorium, the broken seats. It always felt very authentic.
GLADKOV Yes. Did you read Danchenko's comment about the closing of the theatre?
MEYERHOLD *(smiles)* What did Danchenko say?
GLADKOV A journalist asked him what he thought. He said that to ask him about Meyerhold is the same as to ask the Grand Duke Nikolas Nikolaevich about the Revolution. ...

A long pause.

MEYERHOLD What is today?
GLADKOV January something. The twenty-eighth. *(surprised)* Almost February.
MEYERHOLD *(smiles)* Did you know: February is my fatal month.
GLADKOV Your fatal month.
MEYERHOLD I was born in February. My father died in February, the same February in fact that I made my stage debut. In February 1902, I left the Moscow Art Theatre. February 1917, my production of *Masquerade* coincided with the February Revolution. Zinaida Raikh and I were married in February, 1922. Mayakovsky's play *The Bedbug*, with music by Shostakovich, opened in February 1929. ...This time I didn't last 'til February. Either that or Fortune in her old age has become careless.
GLADKOV Then again, now you will be working with Stanislavsky.
MEYERHOLD True... Gladkov, let me see your notebook.
GLADKOV You want to see my notebook?
MEYERHOLD What did I just say?
GLADKOV I don't think you will be able to read my writing.

GLADKOV hands over his notebook, which he has in fact been jotting notes in as MEYERHOLD has been speaking. MEYERHOLD leafs through a few pages. He finds something that he reads carefully. He closes the notebook and hands it back to GLADKOV, looking at him quite directly. GLADKOV is struck by all of this, and by what MEYERHOLD says:

MEYERHOLD Thank you. …I suppose I should show my face at that meeting before I go.

GLADKOV Shall I see if it's still going on? …I'll go see.

GLADKOV exits. MEYERHOLD is alone in his theatre. STANISLAVSKY is very still. The NKVD men creep up to STANISLAVSKY and lean in very close. STANISLAVSKY'S hand falls from the armrest.

TITLE: "August 1938. Konstantin Stanislavsky dies at the age of seventy-five."

The NKVD look up and read the title, then immediately go into action.

Episode Fourteen – Terror

The NKVD men converge on MEYERHOLD, three of them aiming rifles.

NKVD 1 Comrade Meyerhold.

TITLE: "June 1939. At the Meyerhold's flat on Brusov Street."

MEYERHOLD looks at NKVD 1, then up at the title.

MEYERHOLD Yes.
NKVD 1 You will please come with us to Party Headquarters.
MEYERHOLD May I ask why?
NKVD 1 You are under arrest for crimes committed against the Soviet people.
RAIKH *(entering)* Vsevolod, what is going on?
MEYERHOLD These men want to ask me some questions, Zinochka, it is alright.
NKVD 1 Please come with us.
RAIKH Where are you taking him?

NKVD 1 and 4 take MEYERHOLD by the arms, while NKVD 2 and 3 push past RAIKH to search the house.

RAIKH No. What are you doing? You have no right to come in here like this!

NKVD 2 We must make a search of the premises. It's procedure.

RAIKH Get out of our house! You haven't any right! Stop! Where are you taking him! Vsevolod!

MEYERHOLD Zinochka, please. Write a letter to Stalin. Tell him what is happening. Somebody has got to tell him what is happening.

RAIKH No! Please! You can't take him! He hasn't done anything!

MEYERHOLD Write to Stalin, Zinochka! Tell him! He will help us!

RAIKH Vsevolod!

MEYERHOLD Do as I say! Everything will be alright!

MEYERHOLD and the NKVD men are gone. RAIKH turns and faces the audience and dictates her letter.

RAIKH "Comrade Stalin. I am writing with great urgency to tell you that Vsevolod Emelievich Meyerhold has been arrested without cause or reason. The police broke into our home and took him without warning. My husband is not the first to fall victim to these saboteurs who would wreck Soviet Russia and pull our country up by the roots. I beg you to return him to the theatre where he has devoted his life to the Revolution, and still has so much to give. …Why, when actors don't interfere in politics about which they know nothing, do politicians interfere in theatre about which *they* no nothing! It must stop! You are the only one who can do it! I beg you to help him! Only you can save him. …I await your answer. Zinaida Raikh."

TITLE: "Lubyanka Prison. Moscow."

RAIKH exits. MEYERHOLD is ushered in by the NKVD men and roughly placed into a chair at a table.

NKVD 1 In a confession given by Yoshido Yoshimasu, a Japanese actor who was captured crossing the Soviet border, you are accused of working on behalf of Japanese Intelligence in a plot to assassinate Comrade Stalin when he visited your theatre.

MEYERHOLD Comrade Stalin never came to my theatre.

NKVD 1 So your plot failed.

MEYERHOLD There was no plot. I don't even know that / actor.

NKVD 1 In a confession given by the journalist Mikhail Koltsov you are accused of having relations with French Intelligence as well as the British journalist Fred Grey who was expelled from Russia for espionage in 1935 and subsequently wrote numerous articles in favor of several enemies of the Soviet

people. Is this true?
MEYERHOLD I knew Fred Grey as a journalist / but-
NKVD 1 And you supplied him with information for his articles?
MEYERHOLD No.
NKVD 1 You are further accused of involvement in a counter-revolutionary conspiracy led by enemy of the people Leo Trotsky in which you planned to stage the harmful play *The Suicide* by enemy of the people Nikolai Erdman.
MEYERHOLD There was no conspiracy. *The Suicide* was a good play. A *Soviet* / play.
NKVD 1 Is it not true that you are of bourgeois, Jewish, and German origin?
MEYERHOLD My parents came from Germany, yes.
NKVD 1 And they were very well off.
MEYERHOLD My father owned a vodka distillery in Penza.
NKVD 1 And he was not a Russian citizen.
MEYERHOLD No. I took Russian citizenship myself in 1895.
NKVD 1 And before converting to Lutheranism your father was a Jew?
MEYERHOLD What has all this to do with anything?

> *NKVD 2 grabs MEYERHOLD by the hair and throws him to the floor, pulls him up and back into the chair and throws his head forward against the table. MEYERHOLD is quite shaken.*

NKVD 1 …We will give you one week to consider your confession to these crimes, at which time Comrade Kobulov will help you formulate your official statement.
MEYERHOLD Who is Comrade Kobulov?

> *But the NKVD men have left. MEYERHOLD is alone. Distraught, RAIKH lights a candle and paces at home; there is a sitting chair with a small table next to it. It is night.*

MEYERHOLD What have I done? …What have I done?
RAIKH What have I done?
MEYERHOLD It serves me right.
RAIKH I should not have written that letter.
MEYERHOLD I was too proud, too arrogant. *(slams his fist on the table)* …So: this is the way it has to be. Tell them what they want and they will let me go. Shostakovich was taken in and they let him go. …Zinochka. Write the letter, Zinochka. Everything will be alright.

NKVD 2 and 3 enter.

NKVD 2 Please come with us.
MEYERHOLD I would like to send a message to my wife.
NKVD 2 Stand up please.
MEYERHOLD Will you help me get a message to my wife?
NKVD 2 We will get a message to your wife. This way please.
RAIKH I should never have written that letter.

MEYERHOLD is led out. Silence. Two flashlight beams in the dark. The sound of something knocked over, and the flashlights go out.

RAIKH Who is that? ...Who is there?

Whispering. RAIKH sets the candle on the little table and hides behind the chair. We can see her face in the light of the candle. The NKVD men enter the room. It is very dark and we can hear them better than we can see them. RAIKH peeks from around the chair and then stands up suddenly. She starts to run. NKVD 2 grabs her and forces her into the chair where he holds her down. NKVD 1 stabs her repeatedly with a long knife. With their flashlights, NKVD 3 and 4 illuminate NKVD 1's back as well as catching the knife blade each time it rises above his head. RAIKH'S hands fumble about his face and neck but he continues to stab her until she goes limp. Flashlights out, NKVD 3 and 4 exit quietly. NKVD 1 blows out the candle.

TITLE: "July 1939"

MEYERHOLD is hauled in by NKVD 3 and 4. A chair is placed and he is roughly put into it. He looks disheveled and delirious, his shirt soaking wet and speckled with blood.

NKVD 3 You admit that you are a spy.
MEYERHOLD Yes.
NKVD 3 You confess that you willingly associated with embittered and villainous enemies of the people.
MEYERHOLD Yes.
NKVD 3 You admit to having such people to dinner at your home for the purpose of anti-Soviet discussions that undermined the Soviet system.
MEYERHOLD Yes.
NKVD 3 You admit that you are a follower of Trotsky.

MEYERHOLD Yes.
NKVD 3 And you will sign a confession to these and the other crimes charged against you.

> *No answer. NKVD 4 punches MEYERHOLD hard in the stomach. After another pause, MEYERHOLD answers vacantly.*

MEYERHOLD Yes.

> *MEYERHOLD falls off his chair to the floor.*

NKVD 4 …This is no good. He doesn't know what he is doing. We could lose him.
NKVD 3 If you refuse to write it down, we will beat you again. We will leave only your head and right hand and turn the rest of you to bloody, shapeless meat! Do you understand me?
MEYERHOLD …Yes.
NKVD 4 No. He needs to rest. He needs to go to the hospital.
NKVD 3 I think you're right. …Okay.
NKVD 4 I know, I know, more paperwork.
NKVD 3 No, it's not the paper work. I'm just tired.

> *And they have exited, taking the chair. MEYERHOLD is alone on the floor. After a moment, a title appears:*

TITLE: "August 1939"

MEYERHOLD …Yes.

TITLE: "September 1939"

MEYERHOLD …Yes.

TITLE: "October 1939"

MEYERHOLD …Yes I am a spy.

TITLE: "November 1939"

MEYERHOLD …Yes I have committed slanders. …Yes I have made mistakes. I put on: bad plays. Forgive me. …Forgive me, Zina. Zinochka. I miss you. I miss you like a blind man misses light. You are my wife, my sister, my mother, my friend, my beloved. Wait for me. Do not leave me. Nothing in the world could be more terrible than that. Rest, my beloved. Get well. And strong. Soon we will be together again. Everything will be alright. I love you. I embrace you. I kiss you. ...All my love. Vsevolod.

> TITLE: "Vsevolod Emelievich Meyerhold."

MEYERHOLD (stands) ...Yes.

> TITLE: "On this day, February 1st, 1940, you stand accused of crimes against the Soviet people."

MEYERHOLD Yes.

> TITLE: "How do you plead?"
> TITLE: "How do you plead?"

MEYERHOLD Not guilty.

> TITLE: "Then you deny the accusations made against you?"

MEYERHOLD Yes.

> TITLE: "You deny the confession that you yourself have written and signed."

MEYERHOLD Yes, I do.

> TITLE: "The court finds you guilty as charged."
> TITLE: "You are to suffer the extreme form of criminal punishment by shooting."
> TITLE: "The sentence is final and not subject to appeal."

MEYERHOLD Is it not strange that a man my age should testify not to the truth but to a lie?

> TITLE: "The sentence is final and not subject to appeal."

MEYERHOLD I lied about myself because I was beaten into it.

TITLE: "The sentence is final and not subject to appeal."

MEYERHOLD I was beaten across the bare soles of my feet. I was beaten across my back and my head. My legs were beaten with a rubber lash until they turned red and then yellow under the skin. I screamed and wept with pain. I discovered the capacity to tremble and cringe and squeal like a dog being whipped by his master. My eyes found endless streams of tears. "Death, oh surely, death is better than this!" says the prisoner to himself. I too said this! I denounced my friends. I accused myself of the most reprehensible crimes my interrogators and I could think up. And I signed my name to every last word. Well here is my confession! I am guilty of nothing. I was never a traitor. I never committed a single act against my country! I curse the Jew Trotsky! I am a Communist. I have a wife who is a communist and whom I love. I believe in the truth and not in God. I made mistakes in art and for that I was deprived of my theatre and my actors and my reputation and that is enough! I renounce the confessions that were beaten out of me! And implore you! Save me! Give me back my freedom! I love my country! And I will devote to it all the forces of my last years of life!

With NKVD 2 standing to the side, MEYERHOLD is shot in the head by NKVD 3.

Episode Fifteen – The Death of Meyerhold

MEYERHOLD bursts into tear-stung laughter. The music, which has been building, explodes. MEYERHOLD is both the director and a participant in the mayhem that swirls around him almost regardless of his presence. There is a desperate air about him throughout. Similarly, the CAST scramble to keep up, and manage to do a good job of it.

The CAST barrel through a couple of their plays from the Provinces of Episode Two.

As in Episode Three, IMPERIAL BOURGEOISIE are executed, along with the WHITE GUARD SNIPER, and Red flags are marched across the stage. Some people scatter as in the Prologue, while STANISLAVSKY crosses, shielding his eyes from the violence, and the PAPER BOY from Episode Eleven also passes by with his paper held aloft.

BABANOVA and ILINSKY charge through the major moves of their scene from The Magnanimous Cuckhold. *When THEY are done, MEYERHOLD shakes hands with ILINSKY. BABANOVA offers her hand. MEYERHOLD shakes it.*

MEYERHOLD I'm sorry.

BABANOVA and GARIN twirl about in a graceful waltz as MEYERHOLD and RAIKH meet one another for the first time. As they step nearer one another MEYERHOLD cannot hold back his tears and RAIKH reaches out to wipe them and whispers comforting words in his ear. MAYAKOVSKY and STANISLAVSKY take up positions on the stairs and enact the aim and stab from the etude, "Stab With The Dagger," their final stab coinciding with:

SHOSTAKOVICH suddenly bursts in. NKVD 1 leads NKVD 2, 3, and a BOLSHEVIK SOLDIER, rifles aimed, after SHOSTAKOVICH as he scrambles about the set as he did in Episode Twelve.

The entire CAST run onstage from all directions, joining hands and surging forward in a line to take a bow. MEYERHOLD cheers for them from the side. RAIKH steps out of the line and gestures toward MEYERHOLD. The CAST applaud him in slow motion. Still in real time himself, MEYERHOLD crosses to center, takes a bow, turns to the CAST, bows to them, then joins them in a group bow at which point their tempo immediately returns to real time as well. The CAST run offstage in all directions.

Seeing the rest have gone, MEYERHOLD turns to the audience, steps forward to take one last bow, and when he comes up NKVD 2 and 3 are in place as before, 3 with a gun to MEYERHOLD'S head. The gun goes off as before only this time MEYERHOLD falls limp to the ground in a harsh spotlight. The music is silent. The NKVD men walk away, leaving MEYERHOLD alone in the spotlight.

Blackout.

The end.

Faust Pt1

freely adapted from *Faust. Der Tragödie Erster Teil*
by Johann Wolfgang von Goethe

Faust Pt1

The world premiere of *Faust Pt1* was presented by Shotgun Players at the Ashby Stage in Berkeley, CA, on May 22, 2009. The production was co-directed by the author and Kevin Clarke, with the following cast and staff:

FAUST	Mark Jackson
WAGNER	Phil Lowery
MEPHISTOPHELES	Peter Ruocco
STUDENT / VALENTIN	Dara Yazdani
GRETCHEN	Blythe Foster
MOTHER	Zehra Berkman
Set	Nina Ball
Costumes / Props / Blood Effects	Kevin Clarke
Lights	Joan Arhelger
Sound	Matt Stines
Stage Manager	Michelle Smith

Dramatis Personae

> *Faust*
> *Wagner*
> *Mephistopheles*
> *Student*
> *Gretchen*
> *Mother*
> *Valentin*

Note

> *The play is a journey across the landscape of Faust's soul. The design and performance style should reflect this with simplicity, modernity, and theatricality – a space defined by the actors' language and physicality, by light, sound, and only the essential material objects.*
>
> *A slash in the dialogue (/) indicates that the next actor should start their line, creating overlapping speech.*

Scene One

>*FAUST alone, looking at a glass of brownish liquid on a shelf. He almost takes it down, but doesn't. Then...*

FAUST I have
studied
philosophy, law, medicine, and
even worse
theology,
with heated zeal.
I have been called Doctor and Master
by student upon scholar
upon scholar upon student
each of whom I have led by the nose
down my own
scribbled paths.
I have been translated many times,
sometimes in prose,
sometimes it rhymes.
Yet!:
here I am where I now stand
right back where I began.
And from this vantage point
I see quite clearly:
that we know
only know
can know
Nothing.
This,
Nothing,
burns
in my hollow heart.

Of course,
dear doctors, professors, writers, and priests,
of course, it is true:
I am smarter than all of you.
For I am plagued by neither scruple nor doubt.
I do not fear the Devil,
or his Hell.
Why fear Hell when one lives as
I

do:
without delight,
without knowing a thing
despite knowing everything known.
What have I to teach,
what to say,
that would better mankind in any way
whatsoever?
And, so, I have
neither money, treasure, honor,
nor pleasure,
despite having all that
and more
in abundance.
A dog would not live on such sustenance!

For a time I sought for answers
in what some call a
kind
of magic.
Night after night I shot dreams up my sleeve,
but found they were all just poppies.
Such earthly tricks one can swallow or sniff
taught me nothing,
and left my heart stiff as before.
So, now I look to the heavens,
and try to see past
those stars I have charted.
If earthly tricks can only cast spells,
what are the secrets the sky's magic tells?
I know what the men of the Scriptures would tell me.
But what would Nature's Own Spirit say?
Oh, to relieve the burden
of all I don't know!
To fall to earth on a lightning bolt,
shake with all that its strike reveals
and drop my long-winded trade!
If only I could grasp that secret force
that shepherds the world along its course!

Ah! The Moon.
It seems she has heard my clamoring
and graces me with her light touch.

How often I have waited here
'till you appeared,
Dear Moon,
to glance over my papers, notes, and books
with your gloomy, unhurried looks.
If I could only climb your beams
and perch on a mountain's peak.
There might I float
with Nature's Spirit
through caves and trees,
weave in your twilight through tall, swaying grasses
where moths and crickets gather to whisper.
There might I shake off this dust of Knowledge and
as you fade into mist
drench myself in morning's clear dew.

Ah!
Am I
in this dungeon
still?
Still a mole?
Walled up in this musty hole
where Nature's light must strain herself through glass,
dimming her beauty
for what? – not looks.
For books?
Tomes with pages gnawed at by worms and
wrapped in shrouds of dust!
Surrounded by bones and beakers of glass
that breed still
more
dust for still
more
worms!
This is the world! This!
As far as the I can see!
This is called a world!
With every scrap of insight known to man
at hand!
And still I ask
why
my heart bangs against my breast?
And why such

agony
stirs in here
instead of Nature, cruel and fair!
I know, Nature's Spirit,
that you hover near me,
keeping cleverly
just beyond reach.
Well,
If I can nightly beckon your moon,
I'll seduce you, Nature, soon enough.
You breast, you wellspring of life!
You flow and you soak!
I will not desire you in vain.
I'd brave the blast of hurricanes
to have you
hold you
in these hands!
Pound me like waves and I'd bear you no hate!
I'll give you my love when you pound at my gate!

Ah Ha! The moon is afraid, and steals away!
The stars put out their light!
The winds go silent and clouds hold still.
Dear Nature, you fear my might?
Well! Am I not a god? In His image cast?
Then I say to you, Nature, what your master should say:
that your mind,
not mine,
is closed and locked.
Your heart is dead and buried.
Open to me, and stand.
Rise, Nature, and bathe without dread
your immortal breast in your morning's red!
And if you do not I will summon your master.
And should He fail me I'll pronounce his disaster thus:
We all weave ourselves
into the whole!
And each of us lives
in the other's soul!
So don't you pretend that
YOU
rule over
ME!

My hand is your hand, God,
and I conjure thee!

Scene Two

A knock. Another. A door opens, revealing light. But: enter WAGNER.

FAUST Ah! My assistant.
WAGNER Forgive me. From down the hall I could hear the booming of your declamations. Are you practicing some Grecian tragic play?
FAUST A play. Alas, only a play. What keeps you up so late, Wagner, besides my tragic farce? I am sorry that I woke you.
WAGNER I would do well to study the Greeks. These days it comes in handy. I have often been told that an actor could instruct a politician.
FAUST Yes, when the politician is an actor, which happens from time to time.

WAGNER laughs a nervously hearty laugh. Then:

WAGNER But when one is confined to one's museum as we are, and only sees the world on holiday at a distance, how can even the finest rhetoric persuade a thing.
FAUST What you do not feel, you cannot grasp. If it does not surge from your soul with the pure energy of joy, your most attentive listener will not hear you. Go, sit down and paste your words together with syllables from this that and the other. Rehash your hashes. Draw sparks from the ashes. Children and apes will stand in awe, but not one heart will beat one beat faster if from your heart your words don't spring.
WAGNER Yet much comes from the delivery, don't you agree? And in that art I am far behind.
FAUST Search for your effects in honesty and don't be a prattling knave. When you speak from your earnest heart, do you ever hunt for words? A truthful thought needs little art. Those tinseled phrases and sequined verbs with which men gild their tongues are like the lifeless fog that old Autumn exhales to coat the dying leaves.
WAGNER I should write this down.
FAUST Is paper your inspiration then? Dry parchment your drink? Quaff a draught of your soul if you hope to quench your thirst.
WAGNER But surely you of all must understand the satisfaction it gives, to note the spirit of an ancient age, to see how wise men once thought, to take pleasure in how far we've come?

FAUST Oh yes, to the stars! And back. My friend, history is a book bound between two covers. What you call the spirit of an ancient age is but the remnants of an old scholar now dead and buried. History is misery, at best a half-told pompous and moralistic melodrama fit for a puppet stage. Learn from the sun, shining on the fields. Look at the motley crowd that gathers in the public square on Sunday afternoon. They seek sunshine to celebrate the resurrection, for they themselves are resurrected from their stifling little houses, the trades to which they've been subjected, the church's dark night from which they surge to seek the light of day. Look how they amble through gardens and splash along the river's edge in their plain, happy attire. If we were to shut our mouths we might hear the hum and bustle of those lucky people who stand on earth. They shout up to us, "Down here, I am human!" Down there. Where beauty lives.

WAGNER Well! Were you to walk among them they would no doubt stop their bustling and thank you for their beautiful humanity. Many stand there, still alive, because of your father's toiling among these very books to douse the fiery plague. And if tomorrow they soak up that warm Easter sun it is quite likely because he wrestled them from the fever's rage. And you, a young man then with life to live, made daily rounds from house to house. No matter how many corpses were carried out, still you emerged safe and well, holding the tearful living by the hand. What a feeling you must carry with you, when crowds revere you for all you are. A blessing to be so regarded, to benefit thus from all this. Fathers show you to their sons. People stand in rows as you pass. They wave and put out their hands in hope that even your sleeve will brush their fingertips as you go by. A handshake and they would faint, as if God himself had caressed them. How gratifying from all your quiet learning to hear such resounding acclaim!

FAUST It rings of mockery.

WAGNER …Sir?

FAUST Read these books, Wagner, and be content. But read my inmost soul and you would learn how little the son and father deserve the people's praise, much less thanks. My father was an honorable, dark gentleman. He studied Nature and her sacred circles with great sincerity, it's true, and chased his pursuits with a zeal by turns direct and wayward. With his coterie of devotees, he did, as you say, toil against the dreaded plague. And in his black kitchen he fused the most contrary elements into a brew. A strange red petal was mated to a lily and dipped in a pungent lukewarm bath. Then with an open fire the two were driven from bridal chamber to bridal chamber, until a young Queen with fiery cheeks was born and shone herself through the steaming glass. We called her Medicine. And though our patients died and died, nobody questioned why so few survived. And so with our hellish drink we raged across the countryside and like a rabbit leapt past the tortoise plague. And after that reptile had run its course, only then did we realize: our cure was worse. I myself fed that poison to thousands, but lived to reap their praise. So, one thing you said is partly true. No matter how many corpses were carried out, I did emerge, not safe and well, but safe in hell.

WAGNER Sir. You should not be so grieved. If in your youth you revered your father and eagerly took up his teachings, it is only natural. And if you take those teachings farther, as you have, your son can go still farther. This is progress, the very affirmation of human greatness.

FAUST Oh yes, progress. Happy is he who still hopes to emerge from that sea of wrongs. What we do not know, we need; and what we know, is needless. If knowing is progress, give me no more to know. Give me wings to lift me from this place and carry me behind the dawning sun as he journeys through the sky! If there be spirits in the air that sway between earth and Heaven, let them sweep me up in their clutches and carry me to brighter life! Let me fly with them and see the world revealed beneath my feet! I tell you: if a demon's magic cloak fell upon my shoulders from the black and glittering sky I'd not trade it for the finest clothes, no, nor even a king's mighty robes.

WAGNER Sir, do not invoke that well-known throng that festers in the misty haze. They gladly listen to your every hopeful word, but twist them into harm. They'll whisper in your ear like angels while they lie and wait for you to fall.

FAUST Forgive me, friend, it is now deep in the night. We must cut this short.

WAGNER Well, I should have liked to stay awake longer to continue our discussion. But, yes, Easter rises soon. Perhaps then we might talk more, for I still have questions. I have eagerly studied and know a great deal, it's true. But I would like to know all.

FAUST Good night.

Exit WAGNER.

Scene Three

FAUST alone.

FAUST How is it that such hope dwells only in those whose heads pack dust? They dig greedily for treasure and are delighted when they find a worm. And yet I must thank you, dim friend, of all people, for brightening somewhat my dark mood, even if only at first and fleetingly.
I
who had only just proclaimed himself the image of god,
thrown off mortality,
presumed eternal truth was in his reach;
I

greater than cherubs,
whose unbounded strength
demanded Nature course through his veins;
I
who for all my confidence
and haughty pains
summoned not thunder,
but dear mumbling Wagner:
I
cannot
measure myself
to you,
dear Spirit!
And now how I feel so small.
So light.
That you, God, Nature,
pushed me back to humankind's
most certain uncertain fate.

I am no God.
That I feel deeply.
I am but a worm; The worm for which the multitudinous Wagners dig
but crush
beneath their meandering heels.
And
worm that I am
I have fed
my life
on dust!
Must I read in a thousand books
that everywhere men have tormented themselves,
that here and there one has lived happily?
Why does the hollow skull grin so,
save that his brain,
once confused like my own,
searched
at the light of day
but with the heavy dawn
lost his way?

The Scriptures say,
as clear as confidence,
"In the beginning was the Word."

How absurd.
I cannot grant a single syllable such pre-eminence.
It must be rewritten…
"In the beginning was the Mind."
Yet is it the mind that makes all things?
Makes up dreams, to be sure.
Still there must be something more…
"In the beginning there was Power,"
for power makes the world go 'round.
Or so would little minds expound.

"In the beginning was the Act."
Yes! What Power the Mind may have to make Words
would better serve Nature her summons
with deeds!
Ha!
Take the step,
willing and glad,
though you may stand on the fiery brink of Nothing!
The time has come
to prove with action
that mortal man does not yield to God
and need not tremble before that dark hole
where fantasy condemns itself to agonies of its own devising!
Now.
Come down to me, murky crystal.
Let me lift you from your dusty porch
where last my father's hand
set you to rest.
I have not touched you since.
It seems that in the smoke of my nightly lamp
your ruddy cheeks have muddied.
What we inherit from our father's past
we must put to use in order truly to possess it.
What one does not use becomes a heavy burden.
Only the moment is useful.
And so I greet you, precious glass,
and take you up with my devotion.
In you I honor human wit and art,
making of past ends a present birth.
You distillation of slumbering juices,
you essence of all deadly powers,
you mouthful of my guilty sea,

bear me on your last remaining wave.
Carry to the shore and save
this man.
There I will stand,
and with my dignity
in my hand.
If you won't come to me,
God, Nature, Spirit, Powers,
I'll pay visit unto thee
with this dead brew of flowers.
I toast you now with these,
the last brown drops
of my father's and my deeds.
For if with words I cannot greet you,
then with my action I come to meet you.
In one swift gesture
now
I take this final drink,
and with it toss away
the last batch
of all my burden!
With all my soul
I vow to show
I say farewell
to say hello!

>   *FAUST drinks. The moon comes out. Nothing else. A dog barks in the distance, then growls. Silence.*

Scene Four

>   *MEPHISTOPHELES enters and stands next to FAUST. After a moment...*

MEPHISTO Why all the noise?

>   *FAUST looks at MEPHISTOPHELES.*

FAUST Are you a wayward scholar?
MEPHISTO Hmp!
FAUST What is your name?

MEPHISTO That question seems small for one who despises words and other outward shows, craving only Nature's silent depths. What is in a name, after all?

FAUST Who are you?

MEPHISTO A part of that power that always promises evil, and always makes good.

FAUST A riddle!

MEPHISTO I am the Spirit that negates.

FAUST Sssoo, you do as the Devil advocates?

MEPHISTO And rightly so. All that rises up deserves to return below. It would be better if nothing would begin. So it is that all that you call sin, destruction, in short, evil – that is me.

FAUST You said you were "a part." Yet here you stand in one piece whole.

MEPHISTO What I'm telling you is true. While mankind, that tiny crowd of fools, likes to think itself whole, I am a part of that part that once was everything, a part of that darkness that gave birth to light – proud light that envies mother night her ancient rank. Yet, light only shines on the bodies of men, and, though it makes them beautiful, never passes through them. Inside mankind is dark, despite the light's best efforts by which it merely stains the earth with shadows. I trust it won't be long until light dies, clinging to its pretty bodies, and follows them back into the dark dust. This bright world, this Something, confronts as foe my Nothing.

FAUST I get it. Unable to cause mass destruction you've come to pick on something small.

MEPHISTO Change one man, you change them all.

This catches FAUST'S attention, but MEPHISTOPHELES continues.

MEPHISTO Not that any One would notice. So, yes, I'll admit my accomplishments don't amount to much. I try and try but cannot put my finger on it. That cursed brood, mankind, simply won't be stifled. Think of the numbers I have buried in the ground and yet fresh blood always circles back around. And so it goes. I could rage and despair. Endless seeds will push their way up through earth, water, even air, in drought, flood, heat, or cold. Lucky I kept the fire for myself or now I'd have no hand to hold.

FAUST So, poor son of Chaos, rather than clenching your empty fist in vain, why not turn your hand to something else?

MEPHISTOPHELES looks at FAUST.

MEPHISTO It is my great hope that we will get along. For I have come to chase out your boredom, release you, free you that you may understand What

Life Is.

FAUST Oh, I wish you luck in your great quest. I am too old to merely play, too young to live without desire. What possibility can the world offer me? "Renounce! Renounce your wishes!" That is the never-ending chant that daily rants in every ear. I wake each morning with fear and clench bitter tears that I must face yet another day that cannot by nightfall grant one wish, not one!

Even the mere thought of delight is crushed by the critical light of day. My heart's eager inventions shatter between life's leering teeth. And when darkness finally comes again I lay back on my bed in fear and wait for sleep to erupt in wild unfinished dreams. And so, to me, to merely be is a burden. Death is more desirable. Life is hateful.

MEPHISTO And yet death is never entirely a welcome guest.

FAUST Just before your entrance I swallowed a stagnant poison that for twenty years had filled this innocuous glass. I had hoped to toast my final day and find myself confronting God. But my churlish drink, it seemed, had died before me. Died while it slept.

FAUST places the glass back on its shelf.

FAUST That drink I hated, now how I envy it. Forgotten and dead. What bliss. I curse all of this, all things that would feign to entertain my soul with pretentious tricks and fictions. I curse wine that mocks our reason. I curse high-minded thought, with which the mind deludes itself. I curse the spectacle of appearance that presses at our senses. I curse fine possessions that would reflect us in their sheen. I curse fame for its lies and vows. I curse hopes and dreams for their deceit! I curse love! I curse faith! And above all else I curse patience!

MEPHISTO Stop – playing games with your woes. They feed on your life like vultures. The lowest of society would call you a man among men. That's not to say that you should join that pack. I am not among the great myself; but, if you take Life's steps with me, I shall be quite happily yours. And if you like the work I do, I'll be your servant, and your slave, too.

FAUST And what must I give you in return?

MEPHISTO For that we have plenty of time.

FAUST No, no! The Devil is an egoist, and does not for God's sake so easily do things for others. State your conditions clearly: what do you want from me?

MEPHISTO I will bind myself to serve you, here and now, and will not rest if you but lift a finger. But if we meet again Beyond, then and there you will do the same for me.

FAUST Hm. Of that Beyond I can only care very little. Once we finally bash this world to rubble, let the other rise. In the meantime, from this earth spring all my joys and in this sun burn all my sorrows. I do not care to hear whether Beyond man still loves and hates. I do not care whether there exists, as on earth, a top and a bottom. Of Heaven and Hell, I do not care, I do not care.

MEPHISTO If that's the spirit then take the dare. Commit yourself and you will see such art, such life, such beauty.

FAUST Ha! What do you know of earthly, real, human yearning? What, poor Devil, do you have to offer? Show me the wild orchard with fruit that falls before it's plucked. Show me the trees that burst fresh green leaves to greet each morning. Show me Nature, pure and true.

MEPHISTO That I can do. But: the time always comes, good friend, when we wish to lay back in peace and feast on something merely tasty.

FAUST If ever I lay back in peace, you may slaughter me then and there on my bed of sloth. If ever you lure me to feed on your flatteries, or bedazzle me with pretty pleasures, let that day be my very last.

MEPHISTO Agreed.

FAUST Let me then be locked up in chains. Drag me underground, my complaint will be but to smile. Toll the bell for me three times and go about your business, free.
Let the clock stop,
let its hands drop,
let my hour come to its end –
and I'll not bend
one finger to protest.
All of this will be your prize,
if ever I have cause
to look one moment in the eyes
and say,
"Stay! You are so beautiful!"
This is the wager I offer.

MEPHISTO Consider this carefully. We will not forget it.

FAUST No, nor should you, that's your right. Trust me, I have not weighed this bargain haphazardly. As it stands I am a slave. So in the end, whether yours or whose, it makes no matter.

MEPHISTO Then, for life's sake, or death's, will you put your name to this in writing?

FAUST Ah, the pedant wants it black on white. It is not enough to speak my word. If you have no faith in my living breathing vow, how can you believe it once it has dried up on the page? A paper officially scribbled and stamped is the spectre of a promise. What would you like instead, evil spirit? Shall I give you my name with a chisel or axe, on metal, marble, granite, or wood? Take your pick. My word will be dead before it's down.

MEPHISTO Why do you heat your rhetoric until it's overripe? I don't need a word from you. A single drop of blood will do.

FAUST That will satisfy you?

MEPHISTO Blood is a very precious juice.

FAUST You need not fear that I will break this pact. My thread of thought is shredded. All knowledge is repugnant to me. Let me fall into the depths of passion. Plunge me in time's torrent and let me tumble in the senses. Let pain and joy, struggle and success, wash over me as they may. Such restless striving makes man man.

MEPHISTO Your rhetoric is flooding. Stop it with a finger prick.

FAUST Yes, my speech is overblown. Really, I'm like you. I am not concerned with pleasures. I crave painful joy, loving hatred, and sharp despair. My heart has healed from learning's wounds and beats for pain. I want to taste the grief of humankind, to savor true fate, to touch the highest and the lowest woe and feel its bliss deep in my breast, in this way to entwine my own self with mankind's and, in the end, let myself like them be shattered.

MEPHISTO Believe me – me, who for many thousand years has chewed life's tough hide – this ancient pain you sing of is made for Gods that actors play. You must content yourself with night and day.

FAUST I am determined.

MEPHISTO I hear that.

FAUST What are we if we cannot reach with all our senses for the crown of humanity?

MEPHISTO You are, in the end, what you are. You will remain, always, what you are.

FAUST I feel it. I have in vain piled up all the treasures of human intellect, and I am not one step higher for it, not one inch closer to the Infinite!

MEPHISTO You conceive of your dilemma in the dullest way! Stop dissecting your desires with blunt-edged words! You bore yourself, your students, and me! Reach into Life! Leave this torture chamber and leap with me into the teeming ocean! We all swim its currents not knowing their course. Dive in, with courage, and without remorse!

FAUST You are right. You know what I need. I'll give you my hand. Take your pick of any finger. I'm willing to bleed, and ready to stand, though my regret may forever linger.

MEPHISTOPHELES opens a blade. A knock. Then another.

FAUST Someone is here.

MEPHISTO No doubt that wayward scholar you mistook me for.

FAUST No doubt, indeed. They always come at dawn. Oh! I cannot bear to see him.

MEPHISTO Leave him to me. I'll need only a moment.
FAUST And then?
MEPHISTO We proceed.

Exit FAUST.

Scene Five

A door opens, revealing light. Enter a STUDENT.

STUDENT Pardon me. I only just arrived. I hope I'm not too early. If I am, take it as a sign of my devotion to one of whom everyone speaks with reverence.
MEPHISTO You're very courteous. But I am a man like any man. Surely you have applied to others already.
STUDENT No, not one. I beg you to take me on. I've come with courage, fresh blood, and lots of money. My mother would have preferred I stay at home, but there is so much I wish to learn and know!
MEPHISTO Once again, here we go.
STUDENT Sir?
MEPHISTO You've come to the right place if learning is what you're after.
STUDENT Oh! I hope so. Though I must admit, the halls here are rather gloomy.
MEPHISTO All the better to help one study. Believe me, you'll get more than used to it. The deeper you plunge yourself into these shelves the greater the feeling, until your lust is such that you find yourself clinging to these books like breasts, sucking with all your senses.
STUDENT Oh. How do I do that?
MEPHISTO That depends on your pursuit.
STUDENT I would like to know everything, and follow your lead from Earth to Heaven and back again.
MEPHISTO Sounds like you're on the right track. But your chosen subject is tremendous. Success will require vigilant resistance to any distraction.
STUDENT I am devoted with my heart and soul. Though, of course, some free time for summer holidays would be welcomed.
MEPHISTO Use your time well, son – it goes so fast. Let me give you some advice, to take as you see fit. Instead of encompassing Earth and Heaven, narrow your focus just a bit. Start with Logic. Study that. The web of thought appears complex, yet is as simple as a weaver's masterpiece. Look at it whole and the threads are invisible. But step closer and you may follow their thoughts,

under and over, in and around. By itself each thread has its color. But sew them together and they blend one with the other. The philosopher will try to prove a theory, that the first thread is this, the second that, the third and fourth he has down pat, and if the first and second weren't there, the third and fourth would not come to bear. This is what philosophical students believe. And yet they never learn to weave. Those who know thought and write about what's in it, are very quick to remove the spirit. The chemists call thought "the finger of nature," and fail to see how they mock their own features. Ergo, be a logician.

STUDENT I didn't quite follow you.

MEPHISTO That will improve with study. You too will soon learn to reduce and classify.

STUDENT I'm already feeling dizzy in the head.

MEPHISTO Was it something that I said?

STUDENT You want me to choose only one course of study. Well! I wouldn't know where to start! I don't care much for Law, I suppose.

MEPHISTO Oh, I hardly blame you. I'm well versed in Jurisprudence. It spreads itself like a pestilent nuisance from generation to generation, mutating according to the latest trend, yet set in stone that does not bend. Law amounts to the art of persuasion, while the rights we are born with don't affect the equation.

STUDENT You are so right. I like the Law now even less. Maybe then Theology.

MEPHISTO In that you would do well to follow what your masters tell you. Do precisely what they say is best, and you'll be sure to pass the test.

STUDENT But certainly there must be some room for thought.

MEPHISTO Nope, hatching ideas is all for nought. But, where there is a lack of ideas, words thrive. One can win any argument with enough words on hand. And words can make any old System stand.

STUDENT So many choices of where to begin. Forgive me if I ask more questions. I have so many. And God, the field is so wide! What would you say, for example, to a career in medicine?

MEPHISTO This is getting old.

STUDENT Pardon?

MEPHISTO Medicine is bold. I say pursue it.

STUDENT Really?

MEPHISTO Yes. You seem a fit young lad, confident, warm blooded – your curriculum is nearly done. A true doctor need hardly study. The best let Nature run its course. Trust yourself, and others will quickly follow. You'll rack up clients by the hundreds, and have them in and out the door before they know it. But never rush your female patient, this I strongly advise. Her groans are only cured with the careful prodding of a single spot. Bear yourself honorably and you'll have her in your hand. Then touch her tender places to understand her pulse. When it quickens, slip a hand around her waist, to see how tightly she is laced.

STUDENT That's a doctor's way of seeing? Not by books?

MEPHISTO No. By feeling. Medical theory is old and gray. It's your young throbbing finger that points the way.

STUDENT I see. You have helped me immensely. One more question before I go?

MEPHISTO What is it?

STUDENT I couldn't possibly leave without asking you to sign this copy of your book.

MEPHISTOPHELES writes in the STUDENT'S book.

STUDENT "Eritis sicut Deus, scientes bonum et malum."

MEPHISTO "You will be like God, knowing Good and Evil."

STUDENT I will be like God, knowing good and evil.

A door opens, revealing light. Exit the STUDENT into the light, reverently repeating what MEPHISTOPHELES has written.

Scene Six

Enter FAUST.

FAUST You have got to take me away from this place!

MEPHISTO Anywhere you like, but not in haste.

FAUST You saw how easily that boy was persuaded! He never even made a single rhyme! He merely proves how youth is wasted! I understand the promise of a valley ablaze with tight buds about to unleash their beauty. That boy would crush them in the dirt! As I did, in my ignorant years. Now? I would gather them up in my eyes, not pluck a single petal, and listen as they whisper Nature's secrets to the bees. Please! If you have power, as you claim, give me back my youth again. With all my years I will use it well, then gladly I will follow you straight to hell.

MEPHISTO Think now, do you really need youth for any reason? One does need youth when charging into battle, or when young girls unleash their arms with force, or to feast and drink and dance into the night. But to understand the flower and the bee, you need no special gift from me. Age does not, as they say, make us children again. It rather finds that we always were.

FAUST Enough. No more words. Let action speak. You know what I want. It's not his age or his ignorant bliss, but his zeal to scale life's precipice. I will give you my blood, but we mustn't linger. Take my hand, here, and pick a finger, do it! Take it! Do it! Take it!

> *MEPHISTOPHELES opens his blade again and gives one of FAUST'S fingers a sharp nick, then exits with the empty glass, returning with it full of clear water. MEPHISTOPHELES stirs the water with FAUST'S bloody finger, then makes FAUST suck off the bloody fingertip before doing the same himself.*

MEPHISTO The best drinks refresh the world. My congratulations, Sir. To your rebirth.

> *FAUST drinks the glass of bloody water. As the drink begins to make its way through FAUST'S body, MEPHISTOPHELES takes the glass and exits. FAUST begins to stumble with the effects of the drink. WAGNER enters and looks at him questioningly. As FAUST begins to move with increasingly drunken abandon and strength, the world opens up, WAGNER exits, and FAUST'S dance bounds across the open space. MEPHISTOPHELES watches from a distance.*

Scene Seven

> *Church bells. Enter GRETCHEN. The sight of her startles FAUST, and this in turn catches GRETCHEN'S attention. THEY stare at one another for a moment.*

FAUST My beautiful young lady, may I offer you my arm and accompany you to home?
GRETCHEN I'm neither a lady nor beautiful, nor yours, and can get home on my own.

> *Exit GRETCHEN.*

FAUST My God. She's great! Is it possible that a woman on earth could be so beautiful?
MEPHISTO I think you'll find with that drink in your belly there's a Helen of Troy in just about every woman.
FAUST I have never seen another like her, no, not even in my imagination. She's so modest and virtuous. And spirited too. Even the way she was short

with me was exquisite. The red in her lips, the light in her face, in all the days I have left on this earth I will not forget them. And that look in her eyes, so shy and smart. With that look alone she is buried in my heart. You must get that girl for me.

MEPHISTO Which girl?

FAUST The one who just went by.

MEPHISTO That one? She just came from her Priest, who told her she was free of sin. I listened from behind her chair. She's very innocent.

FAUST And fair.

MEPHISTO And, flawless as she is, went to her confession without reason. I have no power to persuade the likes of her.

FAUST But she's easily over twenty. By that age a girl knows plenty.

MEPHISTO Listen to you. You talk like Don Juan, as if every lovely flower exists for you to pluck.

FAUST I beg your pardon, Herr Righteousness, please spare me the laws of morality. I tell you, if that sweet young blood does not flow in my arms this very evening you and I will part by midnight.

MEPHISTO Think about what is possible. I would need at least a week to discern an opportunity.

FAUST If I had just an hour I wouldn't need the Devil to seduce that sweet young creature.

MEPHISTO Now you're talking like a Frenchman. Have patience. You must not wildly rush with this beautiful child. She will not be gained by storm. We must content ourselves with careful planning.

FAUST Alright then, get me something from this angel's chamber, a kerchief that has graced her breast, a garter that her leg has caressed. Better, take me directly to her chamber. No, now I have it: get me a present to give her tonight, something from me that will lean on her heart and persuade her pulse to my favor.

MEPHISTO Why tonight? Why wait? If you're really so hot, let's just give it to her straight. I will leave your gift at her open heart's gate.

FAUST And shall I see her? Have her?

MEPHISTO No. But meanwhile you can feast alone on hopes of future pleasures.

FAUST Go then. Deliver my gift.

Exit FAUST.

Scene Eight

Enter GRETCHEN.

GRETCHEN I'd give anything if I could know who that gentleman was today. He must be Somebody – that much was clear from his face alone – otherwise he could not have been so bold with me. Mother would advise me otherwise. But I felt a distant thunder in my heart when he struck my eye. What other reason could such a feeling have to storm so?

MEPHISTOPHELES moves near GRETCHEN.

GRETCHEN It's so humid here. But the weather isn't too warm. It makes me feel so – I'm not sure what.

A shudder moves through GRETCHEN like a passing quake, as MEPHISTOPHELES moves past her and off to the side.

GRETCHEN What kind of shudder, to run through my body so strangely? Now it feels cold. What does that mean? Oh! How ridiculous I am.

GRETCHEN puts a hand to her chest and feels something there, pulls a necklace that is around her neck out from under her collar and quickly removes it.

GRETCHEN My god in heaven! What is this? How did this necklace come around my neck? It's such a beautiful thing. And strange. I would not forget such a gift. How could this flaming jewel lean against my heart without my knowing, and how long has it been smoldering there? Ah! The gentleman! He must have fastened it when he brushed my shoulder. But why give such a gift to me, and why give it with such shy dexterity? Only a fine lady would wear this. How could this sparkle so fairly on the likes of me? What good is beauty and young blood? Maybe they are good and well according to men, but they always leave us in the end. Their praises are half pity – they: beauty, youth and men. They all rush and cling to gold, and we stay poor, and grow old.

Enter MOTHER in a wheelchair.

MOTHER Gretchen, I need your help.
GRETCHEN Yes mother. You're awake.

MOTHER I drank too tall a glass of milk before I fell asleep, and now I must you know what.

GRETCHEN I'll help you mother.

MOTHER What are you hiding there? What's in your hand?

GRETCHEN It's nothing. Just something I found.

MOTHER What did you find that's worth hiding behind your back.

GRETCHEN It's just a silly costume piece, I think. A necklace for a lady of the stage.

MOTHER No true Lady is of the stage, my dear. And if she lost her necklace in the street, then no doubt the street is her stage where she plays to a godless audience of one per night. Let me see this strumpet-jewel. Ah, Gretchen! It's beautiful. What fine gold. How pure these gems are. This cannot be a harlot's prop. Where did you find this Lady's treasure?

GRETCHEN In the street.

MOTHER Mm-hm! A noble lady is a careless tart, dropping fine gifts without a thought. A lady truly worthy of such a treat would never neglect it. And if she did then she must have plenty more. Yet what more did she do to deserve such a pleasure than sit on her bottom. My girl, unfair goods ensnare the soul and poison the blood. We'll give this to our Virgin Mary, who will enrich us with God's blessing. We'll make of this lady's clumsy gift a gift that's pure and true. In the meantime, we mustn't let it sit in the open. I'll take it to a hiding place, then tomorrow to our Lady of Grace. And, before I go back to sleep, you will help me with you know what?

GRETCHEN Yes mother. Go and I'll follow you.

Exit MOTHER in her wheelchair. GRETCHEN puts her fingertips to her heart.

GRETCHEN It was a gift horse, after all. But that gentleman who brought it here so carefully could not have been a godless man.

GRETCHEN stands alone, lost in her thoughts.

Scene Nine

Enter FAUST.

FAUST And how did she like my gift?

MEPHISTO She liked it well enough. Her mother liked it too.

FAUST Her mother?

MEPHISTO Of whom good Gretchen takes good care.

FAUST Then her name is Gretchen. When will I see my Gretchen again with my gift to her glistening on her breast.

MEPHISTO Never. Her mother took the necklace for a harlot's choker, then took it even farther: to a Priest. The Priest proclaimed, "You have done a proper good. Those who overcome avarice are richest in the end. But the church has a good stomach, my gracious woman, and can digest ill-gotten property without an ache. It has swallowed entire countries and never yet overeaten. I offer you Heaven's blessing, and my thanks." And so the Priest went home enriched, and the mother blessed.

FAUST And Gretchen?

MEPHISTO She stands without knowing what to do, thinks of the jewels day and night, but more of the gentleman who brought them.

FAUST Mm! My darling's grief saddens me. Go and fetch her another gift, a necklace, and this time earrings too.

MEPHISTO Easily said. To the gentleman, this is child's play.

FAUST No, better still, forget the jewels, and bring her me instead. Ah, here it is: go and give her first the present, and then her gentleman in her presence.

MEPHISTO Yes, my gracious sir, and gladly.

FAUST steps off to the side. MEPHISTOPHELES moves near GRETCHEN and drops a small ebony box into her hands.

Scene Ten

GRETCHEN faints but catches herself immediately.

GRETCHEN I thought my knees would give me away when today I found a trove of jewels. They were wonderful, and richer than the first, and lay in an ebony case on my pillow. I hid them in my closet straight away.

GRETCHEN conceals the box behind her back. MEPHISTOPHELES takes it and exits. FAUST quietly walks closer to her as she continues.

GRETCHEN This time I mustn't tell mother. She'd give them promptly to the Priest, and ask me to confess why Luck has twice granted me its treasure. I can't be seen in the streets or church with them, but must wear them only in secret. And when there is occasion, a festival or celebration, I'll bring the jewels out bit by bit. A necklace first. And then a pearl. Worn slowly, nobody may notice.

A town clock strikes three.

GRETCHEN I should get back home, before mother questions where I've been.

GRETCHEN turns and runs into FAUST, and immediately backs away and glances down, then looks back up to him.

FAUST Young Lady, do you remember me?

GRETCHEN Didn't you see? How I glanced down?

FAUST Will you forgive me the liberty I took, the insolence I gave, when you came out from the church the other day?

GRETCHEN I was appalled. Nothing like that had ever happened to me. Until then, no one could say ill of me. Has he seen something brazen or indecent in my face, I thought, that he showed no hesitation to take up the arm of a poor girl? I confess I didn't know that I had been moved already to your advantage. And I was angry with myself, that I could not be angrier with you.

FAUST My sweet love.

GRETCHEN I'm sure you're only being kind, or cruel. A well-to-do traveler is used to taking what he can find. I know too well that my poor rank could never please a gentleman for long.

FAUST One look from you, one word, gives me more pleasure than all the wisdom of this world.

GRETCHEN I'm sure that you know Ladies who are cleverer than I.

FAUST Believe me, what the world calls clever is more often vain and rash.

GRETCHEN How is that?

FAUST Oh! If only innocence and simplicity appreciated their own worth. Humility is the highest gift of loving, bountiful Nature.

GRETCHEN You mock me.

FAUST No. I worship you, and can think of nothing else this moment.

GRETCHEN You have this moment to think of me. I have plenty of time to think on you.

FAUST Are you so often alone?

GRETCHEN Yes. Our house is very small, but still it takes much looking after. We have no help, so I cook and sweep and knit, and sew and run early and late. And my mother busies herself in everything though she herself can do nothing. My brother is a soldier. My little sister died. She made my life trouble when she lived, but I'd gladly take on every burden twice over to have her back again, she was so dear to me.

FAUST An angel, if she was like you.

GRETCHEN She was born after my father died. Mother was near death herself and we thought we'd lose her as well, but very slowly she got better. Still, she couldn't even think of nursing the little mite herself, so I took care of her with milk and water and she became my own. And she adored me, too.

FAUST You must have felt the purest happiness.

GRETCHEN And many difficult hours, too. Her little cradle was beside my bed, and if she stirred even a bit I would awaken. She'd cry and I would lift her up and pace with her about the room, feed her, take her into my bed, then up again and pace again. I slept so little. I'd wash myself before sunrise, then off to the market, over the kitchen fire, and on and on, one day like the next. One doesn't always feel like smiling, Sir. But then the food tastes good, and sleep is good.

FAUST Mmm. …How did she die?

GRETCHEN The plague. Like my father. And almost my mother. My brother and I escaped – he to war, and me… here. Finally here.

FAUST moves to kiss GRETCHEN, who steps away and plucks a flower.

FAUST What is that for?
GRETCHEN A game.
FAUST What game?

GRETCHEN plucks the petals one by one.

GRETCHEN He loves me. He loves me not. He loves me. Loves me not. Loves me. Loves not. Loves. Not. …He loves me.

FAUST Yes. This sweet flower tells you the truth. He loves you. Do you understand what that means? He loves you.

GRETCHEN I'm trembling now.

FAUST Don't move even that much. Let this look, let these hands clasped tell you what is inexpressible: to give oneself entirely and feel a rapture that must last forever. Forever! The end of it would be despair. There will be no end. There will be no end!

GRETCHEN covers FAUST'S mouth gently, then removes her hand as she steps closer and looks up at him openly.

GRETCHEN Dearest man. I love you from my heart.

It seems THEY might kiss. Enter MEPHISTOPHELES. A shudder moves through GRETCHEN like a passing quake and she gently pulls away, her heart and mind mixed up together.

GRETCHEN The sky is getting dark. It will be late soon. I should go.
FAUST May I see you home?
GRETCHEN No, my mother. …Goodbye.
FAUST Must I let go?
GRETCHEN Yes! No! Yes. …Until we meet again.

Exit GRETCHEN.

Scene Eleven

FAUST I have been given all that I asked. This summation of Nature. The time to enjoy and to feel her. The chance to look into the depths of her breast as one would look into the heart of a dear friend. She works. She thinks. She feels. She struggles. She lives. She glows with the beauty of Helen and the simplicity of starlight. This is good. This is the breath of progress.

FAUST puts a hand to his heart, feeling something at first good, then disconcerting. FAUST shakes it off and breathes in deeply.

FAUST And now before my eyes the pure moon rises to reveal the silver edge of an ancient age still living. Now I should like to compare my darling to that other Nature, where the storms roar and bang in the forests, and the towering pines topple and smash their neighbor's branches, rattling the mountain with the thunder of their fall. In the safe heart of a cave I might listen to the shuddering of the earth, and the deep wonders of my own heart will open up. This would make me happy next.

MEPHISTOPHELES steps forward.

FAUST But that man is granted nothing perfect I know too well. I cannot scale the peaks alone. Even for that happiness of sweet Gretchen, which brought me closer to the gods, I suffered this companion whom I cannot do without.
MEPHISTO How much longer can this amuse you?
FAUST He stokes within my breast a wild fire that burns for every beautiful image. And so I stagger from desire to fulfillment, and in fulfillment hunger for desire.

MEPHISTO Yes, a taste of one desire and before you stomach it already you turn your tongue to another. And somehow I am to blame.

FAUST I wish you had more to do than plague me.

MEPHISTO I will gladly leave you in peace. You needn't ask in earnest. Such an unpleasant, mad, and spiteful fellow as yourself is very little to lose. What now pleases and now upsets you one can never know for sure.

FAUST That's a fine tone to moan. He wants thanks for boring me with his tedium.

MEPHISTO How would you, poor earthbound man, have found even this little happiness that you have done without me? I freed you from the confines of your dark and dim imagination. And were it not for me you would already have exited the globe and never met poor Gretchen. But now you stand here like a proud old cock and crow?

FAUST Can you possibly understand what new strength of life I feel from living near the life of this real person, and what more it stirs in me? If you could comprehend this I would think you'd be devil enough to envy me my happiness.

MEPHISTO Such happiness, yes! To kiss a young thing whose hands have aged from daily life. That done, to drop those hands and reach for the tip of a tree top where surely you will find god in yourself. And then no doubt to overflow with heated love for all things Nature, and, by girl or by tree, to finally ejaculate your greatest ambitions.

FAUST Shame!

MEPHISTO Oh, my language is too coarse for the dear Sir; he cries "Shame!" Heaven forbid one say to a chaste ear what all chaste hearts cannot wait to hear. I'll put it to you short and sweet: I will begrudge you the pleasure of your self-delusion. But it cannot last much longer. You are already over driven, and before long you will crash again. First your furious passion overflowed like a brook that had swollen with melting snow. You poured yourself into Gretchen's heart. And now that brook is dry again. You thirst instead for trees and mountain tops. Enough of that. I think, rather than play king of the forest, the great Sir might consider giving his poor young monkey a reward for her love. Your darling sits at home and waits, and everything there is oppressive and dreary to her. You are never out of her mind. She feels for you an overwhelming love. Time is unbearably long to her. She stands at the window and watches the clouds pass her by. "If only I were a bird," she sings, all day long and half the night. The other half she sleeps beneath the unfulfilling dream of her dear gentleman. For one moment she is happy, then mostly sad. One moment her tears are streaming, then she is calm – it would seem. But always in love.

FAUST You snake! Beast! Leave me alone, and never again mention that girl's name. Do not drag the lust for her sweet limbs before my half fiendish senses again!

MEPHISTO What have I said? And what should I say? She waits and thinks you have flown away. It's half true, you already have.

FAUST I will be with her always. Even if I flew ten thousand miles, I would never forget her. I would envy God each time her devoted lips touched his cross.

MEPHISTO And how I envy you, my friend, when your devoted mind kisses her breasts.

FAUST Oh fly away yourself, you pimp! You are and always will be a pervert and a liar!

MEPHISTO Yes, so long as you aren't one bit deeper. Did you not in all honor swear to poor Gretchen your deepest love?

FAUST And with all my heart.

MEPHISTO Very good. Then of eternal faithfulness and love, of a single overwhelming vow – will your good heart also swear to this?

FAUST Leave it! I say it will – I will!

MEPHISTO You rage, and I laugh. Go on! It's not to your grave I'm sending you, but into your lover's doting embrace.

FAUST Where now is the heavenly joy in her arms? I feel her woe on my back. Am I not the aimless, restless brute, raging with passion toward the black hole with you as my guide. And there she is with her lovely, childlike senses, in a home on a little Alpine meadow. Everything she needed she had in her small world until I, whom the gods hate, ruined her peace and caged her freedom. Take this sacrifice, Hell. Do what must be done. Let my fate crash together with hers. Let me burn in her breast. Take me with her underground.

MEPHISTO Oh, how you boil and burn. Where such a small mind sees no way out, he stands himself immediately at "the End." You are usually so devilish and clever. I can think of nothing worse in the world than a devil who despairs. Go, and comfort her you fool.

Exit MEPHISTOPHELES. FAUST remains in thought.

Scene Twelve

Enter GRETCHEN. She sings the following song in German. A literal English translation is in italics.

GRETCHEN Meine Ruh ist hin, *My peace is gone,*
Mein Herz ist schwer, *My heart is sore,*
Ich finde sie nimmer *I'll find it never*
Und nimmermehr. *And never more.*

Wo ich ihn nicht hab, *Where I don't have him*
Ist mir das Grab, *Is to me the grave,*
Die ganze Welt *The entire world*
Ist mir vergällt. *Is to me turned to gall*

Mein armer Kopf *My poor head*
Ist mir verrückt, *Is to me gone mad. / has gone mad*
Mein armer Sinn *My poor mind*
Ist mir zerstückt. *Is to me divided in two / is in two*

Meine Ruh ist hin, *My peace is gone,*
Mein Herz ist schwer, *My heart is sore,*
Ich finde sie nimmer *I'll find it never*
Und nimmermehr. *And never more.*

Nach ihm nur schau ich *For him only I look*
Zum Fenster hinaus, *Out the window,*
Nach ihm nur geh ich *For him only I go*
Aus dem Haus. *Out of the house.*

Sein hoher Gang, *His noble walk,*
Sein edle Gestalt, *His honorable figure,*
Seines Mundes Lächeln, *His mouth's smile,*
Seiner Augen Gewalt *His eyes' force*

Und seiner Rede *And his speech*
Zauberfluß, *A magic river,*
Sein Händedruck, *His hand's touch/clasp,*
Und, ach, sein Kuß! *And, oh, his kiss!*

Meine Ruh ist hin, *My peace is gone,*
Mein Herz ist schwer, *My heart is sore,*
Ich finde sie nimmer *I'll find it never*
Und nimmermehr. *And never more.*

Mein Busen drängt *My breast surges/urges*
Sich nach ihm hin, *Itself to him,*
Ach dürft ich fassen *Oh may I clasp/seize*
Und halten ihn *And hold him*
Und küssen ihn, *And kiss him,*
So wie ich wollt, *like how I want to.*
An seinen Küssen *On his kisses*
Vergehen sollt! *I should die / float away / pass away!*

Enter MOTHER in her wheelchair.

MOTHER Gretchen, I need your help.

GRETCHEN Yes mother.

MOTHER What was it you were singing just now?

GRETCHEN Just an old song.

MOTHER Oh, Gretchen, have you heard about young Barbara?

GRETCHEN Not a word.

MOTHER Sybil from down the road told me today. She has finally made herself a fool. That's what happens when a girl puts on airs.

GRETCHEN What happened?

MOTHER Well, it stinks. She's feeding two when she eats and drinks.

GRETCHEN Oh.

MOTHER She got what she deserves. How long did she hang on that fellow? Strolling through the village, dancing, and always the first in line, if you understand my meaning. Him always giving her presents and wine, and her always parading her fine looks. She was so brazen and had no shame. They fondled and groped, and now her little flower has been plucked by his rope.

GRETCHEN The poor thing.

MOTHER Don't feel sorry for her. When other girls were busy working or staying home at night with their mothers, she was with her sweet lover in a doorway or some dark alley. No amount of time was too long for them, I hear. Now maybe she'd like to kneel and do penance in a church.

GRETCHEN But surely he will marry her.

MOTHER He'd be a fool. Any sharp and nimble boy finds air elsewhere. He's gone already.

GRETCHEN That isn't right.

MOTHER Even if she does catch him it will be nasty. The local boys will tear her wedding bouquet from her hands and scatter the pieces at her door.

GRETCHEN What was it you wanted help with, Mother?

MOTHER Oh! I've forgotten. I'm sure it will come to me.

MOTHER does not move. Neither does GRETCHEN.

GRETCHEN You'll call me when it does.

MOTHER Oh, yes dear. I will.

Exit MOTHER in her wheelchair.

GRETCHEN How I once would bravely chide when some poor girl would slip. My tongue could not find words enough to lash her name. If it were black, I blackened it more, and to me it would never be black enough. And I would bless myself and act so proud. And now I stand naked in shadow. Yet everything that drove me here – my God! – was so good! Ah! So loving and dear!

Scene Thirteen

> *Enter FAUST. GRETCHEN looks at him and they curiously explore one another's faces with their fingertips. Then GRETCHEN enfolds herself in FAUST'S arms.*

GRETCHEN Oh Heinrich. I feel so good in your arms, so free, so yielding and warm. …There's something makes me tremble from time to time. I don't know what.
FAUST You foreboding angel, you.

> *GRETCHEN looks at FAUST.*

GRETCHEN I know it can't be you.

> *GRETCHEN embraces FAUST again, then:*

GRETCHEN But I should go.
FAUST Ah! Will I never for one short hour of peace hang on your limbs, pressing breast onto breast and soul into soul?
GRETCHEN Oh! If I only slept alone. I would gladly leave my door unlatched for you tonight. But my mother does not sleep deeply. If she found us there together, I would die on the spot.
FAUST You angel. This is no difficulty. Take this little bottle. Just three small droplets in her cup will wrap her in a deep sleep.
GRETCHEN It will not harm her?
FAUST Would I prescribe it, sweet, if it would?
GRETCHEN What would I not do that you would wish me do? When I look on you, dear man, I don't know what drives me to your will. I have already imagined doing so much for you, that almost nothing remains undone.

> *GRETCHEN touches FAUST.*

GRETCHEN Until soon.

Exit FAUST.

Scene Fourteen

MEPHISTOPHELES crosses and exits after FAUST. GRETCHEN shudders as he passes.

GRETCHEN That warm, sultry feeling runs through me. Is it my anticipation, or my foreboding? I must listen to my heart. Any girl whose name I once blackened, I did not knowing more of her than what mother and the others snickered. Poor Barbara may well have loved her boy, who shames their love for fear of shame. If they were brave they would kiss in the center of town, and marry then and there. But who can find their honest senses when all their neighbors chide over fences? Oh! Must I hate my mother to love my dear, sweet man? It can't be. She must have compassion. I know this. But will she let me go with him if I have already let myself go? Oh! Why does honest duty tear a devoted soul in two? I must do what I must, that's good and fair, to free my loving heart.

Enter MOTHER in her wheelchair.

MOTHER Gretchen, I need your help.
GRETCHEN Yes Mother.
MOTHER I don't feel well.
GRETCHEN What's the matter Mother?
MOTHER …Did you see that dog rummaging in our yard this afternoon?
GRETCHEN No, I didn't.
MOTHER That's right, you were out… Curious devil, poking about. … Gretchen, I'm so depressed tonight.
GRETCHEN What is it?
MOTHER These walls. And these windows through which the world is small. This is all I ever see. How I would love to go outside.
GRETCHEN But you do, Mother.
MOTHER Yes, the yard. With the fence. And beyond the fence, old Sybil standing guard. I haven't been outside that fence for ages. I hardly speak to anyone but Sybil, and the Priest when he comes to call. I feel trapped. Trapped, do you hear? In these walls! This yard! That fence! Sybil! The periodic priest!

This is not a life!

GRETCHEN Go to sleep, Mother. You'll feel better.

MOTHER I can't sleep, I told you, I don't feel well. Oh Gretchen, how I would love to go into town. Just once. To stroll down the boulevard. Like when I was young. Like when I was free.

GRETCHEN steps forward.

GRETCHEN What if I take you there tomorrow?

MOTHER What? What Gretchen?

GRETCHEN What if I take you into town tomorrow?

MOTHER Oh, Gretchen! Really? Don't you have work? Well, it might be cold. I haven't anything to wear. What could I wear?

GRETCHEN You can wear your Sunday clothes.

MOTHER Ah! Yes, my Sunday clothes. But they're very old. Do you think they'll look alright? Oh! Gretchen. You're so good to me. What would I do without you? Your father and sister flew away, and then your brother too. But you have always been here. Always.

GRETCHEN Go to sleep, Mother. You want to be well rested for tomorrow.

MOTHER Oh but I can't sleep. I'm too excited!

GRETCHEN Have some milk.

MEPHISTOPHELES enters and holds out for GRETCHEN a glass of milk.

MOTHER Yes, that will help. But not too much.

GRETCHEN pours three droplets from the little bottle into the milk.

MOTHER Dear Gretchen. I have always been able to count on you. You will never leave me.

GRETCHEN pours the entire bottle into the milk. A dog barks angrily in the distance.

MOTHER Oh! Gretchen! Do you hear that? It's that dog again!

GRETCHEN Drink your milk, Mother. And go to sleep.

MEPHISTOPHELES takes the milk to MOTHER and hands it to her.

The dog growls as MOTHER drinks the milk. Then, the dog is silent.

MOTHER Thank you, Gretchen. I will see you in the morning in my Sunday best.

Exit MOTHER in her wheelchair. Exit MEPHISTOPHELES after her.

Scene Fifteen

Enter FAUST. GRETCHEN looks at him, then runs and throws her arms around him.

FAUST Does your mother sleep?

GRETCHEN She does. No doubt she does.

FAUST And do you weep?

GRETCHEN To see you.

FAUST It is a happy sight I hope.

GRETCHEN More happy than I could hope. Heinrich, promise me.

FAUST Whatever I can.

GRETCHEN How is it with you – and religion? You are a kind and good man, but I don't believe you hold much faith in it.

FAUST Let that be, love. You feel that I am good. And know this: that for those I love I abandon body and blood, and would rob no one of her feelings or faith.

GRETCHEN But that is not yet right. One must believe.

FAUST Must one?

GRETCHEN Do you believe in God?

FAUST Darling, who may say "I believe in God?" Ask priests and wise men and their answers only mock the asker. Do not mistake me, fair angel. But who may name Him, and who profess "I believe in Him?" And who would dare say, "I do not believe in Him?" Does the All Embracing, All Containing not embrace and contain you, me, itself? Does the sky not arch overhead? Does the earth not lie firmly underfoot? And do the friendly, ever-blinking stars not rise to gaze upon us? Do my eyes not look deep into your eyes, and does not everything in you surge to your heart and head and weave in eternal mystery, invisible and visible around you? Let it fill your heart to bursting, and when you feel this bliss completely, then name it what you will. Happiness. Heart. Love. God. I have no name for it. Feeling is all. A name is sound and smoke clouding the heavens' glow.

GRETCHEN Do you believe in God?

FAUST Darling. Who may say "I believe in God?" Ask priests and wise men and their answers only mock the asker. Do not mistake me, fair angel. But who may name Him, and who profess "I believe in Him?" And who would dare say, "I do not believe in Him?" Does the All Embracing, All Containing not embrace and contain you, me, itself? Does the sky not arch overhead? Does the earth not lie firmly underfoot? And do the friendly, ever-blinking stars not rise to gaze upon us? Do my eyes not look deep into your eyes, and does not everything in you surge to your heart and head and weave in eternal mystery, invisible and visible around you? Let it fill your heart to bursting, and when you feel this bliss completely, then name it what you will! Happiness! Heart! Love! God! I have no name for it! Feeling is all! A name is sound and smoke clouding the heavens' glow!

GRETCHEN Do you believe in God?

FAUST Darling! Who may say "I believe in God?!" Ask priests and wise men and their answers only mock the asker! Do not mistake me, fair angel! But who may name Him, and who profess "I believe in Him?!" And who would dare say, "I do not believe in Him?!" Does the All Embracing, All Containing not embrace and contain you, me, itself?! Does the sky not arch overhead?! Does the earth not lie firmly underfoot?! And do the friendly, ever-blinking stars not rise to gaze upon us?! Do my eyes not look deep into your eyes, and does not everything in you surge to your heart and head and weave in eternal mystery, invisible and visible around you?! Let it fill your heart to bursting, and when you feel this bliss completely, then name it what you will!! Happiness!! Heart!! Love!! God!! I have no name for it!! Feeling is all!! A name is sound and smoke clouding the heavens' glow!!!

GRETCHEN Do you believe in God?

FAUST Darling!! Who may say "I believe in God?!" Hm?! Ask priests and wise men and their answers only mock the asker!! Do not mistake me, fair angel!!! But who may name Him, and who profess "I believe in Him?!" And who would dare say, "I do not believe in Him?!" Does the All Embracing, All Containing not embrace and contain you, me, itself?! Does the sky not arch overhead?! Does the earth not lie firmly underfoot?! And do the friendly, ever-blinking stars not rise to gaze upon us?! Do my eyes not look deep into your eyes, and does not everything in you surge to your heart and head and weave in eternal mystery, invisible and visible around you?! Let it fill your heart to bursting, and when you feel this bliss completely, then name it what you will!!! Happiness!!! Heart!!! Love!!! God!!! I have absolutely no name for it!!! Feeling is all!!! A name is sound and smoke clouding the heavens' glow!!!!

GRETCHEN Do you believe in God?!

FAUST Darling!!! Who may say "I believe in God?!!" Ask priests and wise men and their answers only mock the asker!!! Do not mistake me, fair angel! But who may name Him, and who profess "I believe in Him?!!" And who would dare say, "I do not believe in Him?!!" Does the All Embracing, All

Containing not embrace and contain you, me, itself?!! Does the sky not arch overhead?!! Does the earth not lie firmly underfoot?!! And do the friendly, ever-blinking stars not rise to gaze upon us?!! Do my eyes not look deep into your eyes, and does not everything in you surge to your heart and head and weave in eternal mystery, invisible and visible around you?!! Let it fill your heart to bursting, and when you feel this bliss completely, then name it what you will!!!! Happiness!!!! Heart!!!! Love!!!! God!!!! I have no name for it!!!! Feeling is all!!!! A name is sound and smoke clouding the heavens' glow!!!!!
GRETCHEN Do you believe in God?!!

FAUST does not move for a moment, then approaches GRETCHEN.

FAUST ...Darling?

That said, FAUST takes GRETCHEN in his arms and kisses her passionately on the mouth.

GRETCHEN Then you do not believe!

In what follows, GRETCHEN is distracted between her doubts and desires as FAUST continues to embrace her passionately.

FAUST I believe in you!
GRETCHEN The priest says something like what you've said, only with slightly different words.
FAUST It is said everywhere. All hearts under the heavenly day. Each in his own way. Why not I in mine?
GRETCHEN When I hear you say it, it seems reasonable to say. But something is wrong. To have no Christian faith–
FAUST Dearest child!
GRETCHEN Heinrich!

GRETCHEN catches herself and pulls away, but FAUST holds her tight.

FAUST Stay! You are so beautiful!

A beat, then GRETCHEN kisses FAUST passionately. GRETCHEN and FAUST exit kissing. Enter VALENTIN, catching sight of them as they go. Silence. MEPHISTOPHELES crosses, pushing an empty wheelchair.

Scene Sixteen

VALENTIN alone.

VALENTIN It used to be, when I would sit with drunkards in this town, and everyone started to brag and lift their glasses in proud toast to that week's favorite women, and glass after glass was drained with boasting, elbows leaning on the tables, I would sit back quietly, listening to the swaggering rabble. Then I would smile and lift my own glass and say with satisfaction, "To each his own, but does anyone know a single one who can hold a candle to my good sister Gretchen." Then clink and clank and all agreed, "He is right. The flower of all womankind." And all the braggarts went silent. And now I return to this backwater burg to bury my mother who died in her bed, only to learn I must bury my pride – in my sister, who lied in her bed. With who? That man among men, I am told. That plague pedlar, wealthy, and far too old. Accepting his gifts, and taking his kisses as well. Giving him all of herself in return. And for what? A fine place in hell. And how the neighbors love to inform me of every scarlet detail, feigning their sympathy behind clenched glee. Who comes now? Who sneaks around the house? If one of them be Gretchen's lover, I'll take him by the neck. And if he leaves this place tonight he will be carried on his back.

VALENTIN hides. Enter FAUST and MEPHISTOPHELES.

FAUST Even from here through the window of that distant sacristy I can see the flickering light of the eternal flame. It seems to lean sideways and grows slowly weaker as darkness presses in around us. I feel night falling in my heart.
MEPHISTO I feel like a cat, prowling up the fire escape and quietly hugging the wall, ready to leap in the bountiful darkness and gather its treasures in my paw!
FAUST And my treasure, still glimmering over there, will I see her again tomorrow night?
MEPHISTO As soon as you wish. You may enjoy that joy of opening your trove and breathing in the scented pleasure. I see in it a mound of treasure.
FAUST And do you see some jewelry there, a ring perhaps, to bring my sweetheart.
MEPHISTO I think I saw that sort of thing, a string of silvery pearls perhaps.
FAUST Good. I would be remiss to go to her again without a present.
MEPHISTO You shouldn't feel so badly to enjoy your treasure free of charge. Now that the heavens are filled with diamonds, which cost you nothing, you could sing her a song and she would be certain to harmonize with your arms.
FAUST Yes, she would.

Enter VALENTIN.

VALENTIN What would she, devil? I'll smash your skull no matter what you answer.

MEPHISTO What do you defend, my friend?

VALENTIN Poor wretched Gretchen. My sister slain.

FAUST She is not slain.

VALENTIN Her honor lies dead beside her hopes and trust. And if she breathes still then it is not air, but the smoke of her own hell to which you have damned her.

FAUST She loves me, sir.

VALENTIN Then she is deceived, for you repay her love with hatred.

FAUST You are mistaken. I do feel love for her.

VALENTIN Where, Doctor? Where your demons are buried? They rise and bury her!

MEPHISTO Do not give way, Herr Doktor Professor. I'll follow you closely, then you follow me.

VALENTIN attacks FAUST and they fight, but only briefly since MEPHISTOPHELES stays near and, in an opportune moment, places a knife in FAUST'S hand. FAUST and MEPHISTOPHELES exchange a glance and VALENTIN is stabbed.

VALENTIN Ah!

MEPHISTO Now the lout is tame. No need to gawk. We must leave this place. There will be an outcry soon enough.

Exit FAUST and MEPHISTOPHELES. Enter GRETCHEN.

VALENTIN Ah!

GRETCHEN Who's there?

VALENTIN Your mother's son.

GRETCHEN My God! My brother! Where have you come from?

VALENTIN I've come from war to die. It is quickly said and sooner done.

GRETCHEN What has happened to you here?

VALENTIN Come close and I'll tell you.

GRETCHEN gets close to VALENTIN and he seizes her arm forcefully, gripping her and life both.

GRETCHEN Ah!

VALENTIN My Gretchen, see me. You are still young, still not yet wary, and make of your life a horrid mess. I tell you here before the neighbors do: now you are a whore, so be one, and be nothing else.

VALENTIN pushes GRETCHEN away.

GRETCHEN My brother! God! What do you mean by this?

During the following, VALENTIN struggles to stand and then stumbles about railing at GRETCHEN.

VALENTIN Leave the Lord God out of this game! What's done is done. And how it will end, it will. You began secretly with one. That very One who deigned to step down from his palace and damn our family to his cures! That Same One who left me here for dead!

GRETCHEN What?

VALENTIN So now your gate is open. Soon more than One will come to you. And when you've had a dozen then you'll have the entire town! When Disgrace is born she slips out in careful secrecy and draws the veil of night over her head. Yes, one would love to murder her, but she grows and makes herself bigger, walking naked in the daylight, and not more beautifully than before! Even should God at last forgive her, her life on earth is stained! The more hateful her condition the more she seeks the light, until she births her guilt and treason and bares it in plain sight!

GRETCHEN No! Order your own soul to God! Would you lay such blasphemies on yourself as you die?

VALENTIN I would lay my hands on your unholy body and smash it if I could! There I would hope to find forgiveness for all my life's sins.

GRETCHEN My brother! What hell you wish upon me! It isn't fair!

VALENTIN I tell you, keep your tears in your head. When you bade your honor farewell, you gave me my sister's broken heart. I stumble to God a soldier and brave.

Exit VALENTIN, smearing his blood in his wake.

Scene Seventeen

MEPHISTOPHELES enters behind GRETCHEN.

MEPHISTO How different it was when you were still innocent and stepped before the altar, and from a well-worn little book you babbled prayers, half childish games, half God in your heart. Gretchen! What has happened to your head? What misdeeds in your heart? Whose blood is spilled on your doorstep? Do you pray for the soul of your mother that you sent through sleep to eternal pain? And beneath your heart, what now stirs and grows, frightened and frightening with its swelling presence?
GRETCHEN Oh God! The world grows narrow! Let me escape! Let me find air! Let me go! Let me go! Let me–! Let me–!

GRETCHEN goes insane and the world changes. GRETCHEN exits.

Scene Eighteen

Enter FAUST, catching sight of GRETCHEN as she exits.

FAUST In misery! Despairing! Wretchedly lost on the earth and now imprisoned in the dungeon of her horrible torments! It's come to that! To That! Treacherous, unworthy spirit! Stand there! Stand and roll your devil's eyes in your head! Stand and defy me with your unbearable presence! Imprisoned in hopeless agony! This fair unblessed creature!
MEPHISTO She is not the first.
FAUST You dog! You monster! Not the first! Grief! Grief, that no human soul can grasp, that more than one creature has sunk to the depths of such misery! That the first one did not writhe enough in the eyes of Redemption for the guilt of all the others! The misery of this one woman surges through my blood and bones, while you grin contentedly over the fate of millions!
MEPHISTO Now we are once again at the edge of our wits, where your mortal minds snap. Why do you make company with me when you cannot see it through? You would fly, but get dizzy. Did I push myself on you or you on me?
FAUST Don't bare your greedy teeth at me! It makes me sick!
MEPHISTO Are you finished?
FAUST Save her! Or woe to you! The most terrible curse on you for millennia!
MEPHISTO Save her! Who was it that sank her into ruin? Me or you?

FAUST looks around furiously.

MEPHISTO Are you reaching for thunder? Fortunate that it wasn't given to you mortals, to shatter those who innocently answer to you. That is the tyrant's way of easing his embarrassment.

FAUST Take me to her. She will be set free.

MEPHISTO And the danger you subject yourself to? The blood spread by your hand still streaks the town, and no doubt a crowd hovers over the slain man's body awaiting the murderer.

FAUST This again from you? Barking dog! Take me to her I tell you, and save her!

MEPHISTO Do I have all the power in Heaven, and on the earth? I will take you to her. That I can do. The rest good Sir I leave to you.

Exit MEPHISTOPHELES.

Scene Nineteen

MEPHISTOPHELES enters, leading GRETCHEN. FAUST watches as MEPHISTOPHELES puts makeup on GRETCHEN'S face and she sings.

GRETCHEN My mother the whore
Who killed me
My father the rogue
Who ate me
My sweet little sister
Who gathered the bones
In a cold dry place
Where I became
A beautiful forest bird
Fly away! Fly away!

MEPHISTOPHELES finishes by smearing GRETCHEN'S red lipstick with his palm.

FAUST Mankind's entire grief grips me.

GRETCHEN Oh, that mankind is so unhappy. I will say Requiems for him.

MEPHISTO You are a very kind and loving child. You ought to marry.

GRETCHEN Oh no, that would not do.

MEPHISTO If not a husband, then a lover. It is one of the greatest gifts of

Heaven to have such a dear thing in one's arms.
GRETCHEN That is not the custom here.
MEPHISTO Custom or not, it is done, my dear. …How is your heart?
GRETCHEN What do you mean, Sir?
MEPHISTO You good, innocent child. Farewell.

MEPHISTOPHELES prepares to snap GRETCHEN'S neck for mercy.

GRETCHEN Farewell.
FAUST Wait!
GRETCHEN Oh! It comes! Bitter death!
FAUST No, I come! I come, to set you free from this!
GRETCHEN You come for me in the middle of the night! If you are human, pity my distress! What have I done to you? I am still so young, very young. I was beautiful, too, and that was my mistake. My friend was so close to me. Now he is far away. The flowers are scattered at the door. I am entirely in your hands.

FAUST moves toward GRETCHEN, who reacts suddenly.

GRETCHEN Only first let me nurse my child! …I held it through the night. They took it away to make me sick, and now they say, I killed it.

MEPHISTOPHELES embraces GRETCHEN from behind, wrings her dress over her stomach, and blood soaks out. FAUST looks away in horror.

GRETCHEN An ancient fairy tale ends that way. It was cruel of people to write it.
FAUST Will I survive this grief? Gretchen. Gretchen!
GRETCHEN That was my lover's voice. Where is he? I heard him call: Gretchen! Through the howling and banging of Hell I know that sweet, that loving sound!
FAUST Gretchen, I am here!
GRETCHEN Ah! It is you – come to save me. Oh, I am saved. Where is all my torment? Already the street is there again where I saw you for the first time, and the garden beneath my window where I waited every night.
FAUST Gretchen come, come with me!
GRETCHEN Stay! You are so beautiful. I am happy where you are. Kiss me.
FAUST No, Gretchen, come, follow me, / darling–!

GRETCHEN Kiss me, Heinrich. Can you not kiss me? Are you my Heinrich and have forgotten how to kiss? Once from your words and from your eyes a whole Heaven overwhelmed me, and you would kiss me as if to smother me. Kiss me, Heinrich. Kiss me. Or I'll kiss you.

FAUST kisses GRETCHEN but she spits it away.

GRETCHEN Your lips are cold! Dead! Where is your love in them?!
FAUST No, Darling, I'll love you with a thousand passions / only come with me!
GRETCHEN And is it you?!
FAUST What?!
GRETCHEN Is it you?! / Is it really?!
FAUST Yes! Yes, it is!
GRETCHEN How is it that you do not shrink from me, Heinrich?! Do you know, my friend, whom you would set free?!
FAUST Come come come, Gretchen, I beg / of you!
GRETCHEN I killed my mother! A gift for you and me! I murdered my child! Your child, Heinrich! …Your hand, Heinrich. Wipe it off, I beg you. There is blood on it.
FAUST Leave the past in the past, God, or kill me too!
GRETCHEN No, you must live! You must arrange the graves tomorrow. Give the best place to my mother. And next to her, my brother. Me, a little to the side, only not so wide a space. And put the little one on my right breast. Nobody else would lie beside me.
FAUST Gretchen, hear me, hear me, come now, please come.
GRETCHEN Where?
FAUST With me.
GRETCHEN You are leaving? Where?
FAUST We are leaving, here!
GRETCHEN Oh, Heinrich. That I could go with you.
FAUST You can! You can!
GRETCHEN No, no, I may not go. There is no hope for me. What help is it to run away?
FAUST I can free you.
GRETCHEN I cannot be free. Wherever I might go with you, I could never leave this place.

And GRETCHEN taps his forehead lightly.

FAUST Come. Then I will carry you away.

GRETCHEN Leave me! I will not be forced! I have done everything else you asked!

FAUST Dear love! The day is breaking! Sweet angel!

GRETCHEN Day. It would be day. The last day – breaks. It was supposed to have been my wedding day. Tell nobody that you have already been with Gretchen. We will meet again. But we will not dance then. Oh Heinrich, I shudder for you. …The world is quiet.

> *GRETCHEN walks upstage and stands alone to wait for something, patiently and ready.*

FAUST Oh had I never been born.

MEPHISTO Up. Or you are lost.

FAUST That pale, beautiful child, alone in her distant place. She stands with her feet chained together, and looks much as my good Gretchen did. Those are the eyes of one already dead, which no loving hand ever closed. That is the breast that Gretchen yielded to me. That is the sweet body that I enjoyed. Oh what agony! I cannot leave her. I will save her. She will live. Gretchen! You will live!

> *GRETCHEN turns.*

GRETCHEN Judgment of God. I give myself to you.

> *GRETCHEN slits her throat and dies.*

FAUST …That this sweet throat now bears this single red necklace. My final everlasting gift. How strange it looks. And what strange beauty, that Life finds her way back into earth, seeping ever downward that Nature's every precious flower may be revived by her blood. Perhaps Nature's plagues are her revenge for the abuses we heap upon her endlessly.

MEPHISTO Nature has no feeling for us. She is not burdened by sentiment. We will die, and Nature will continue on without a thought or word on our behalf. We can flay her skin, and we'll be left exposed.

FAUST Oh that this moment would last forever. Let the great world rush onward and let me stay here in the stillness of this peace. Now what shall become of me, what greater, what more beautiful, more real, now that I've had this?

MEPHISTO There have been those who would commend thee to Heaven. And others still who would damn thee to Hell.

But tonight, I think,
neither you
nor those who would be audience to your act
will gain such relief.
Tonight you will live
to stand adjacent to your deed
that you might see and hear
these times,
perhaps.

FAUST I did find Something. Something beautiful. She was pure. And now it is over.

MEPHISTO Over? Why over?
And pure?
Over is purely nothing, and nothing is pure.
But why go on about it eternally
when in the end all comes to nothing.
It is as if it had not been,
as if nothing ever happened.
And yet
something seems to circle round,
circling
perhaps
around nothing.
"Now it is over."
What meaning can one see?
I should prefer:
eternal emptiness.

The end.

The Forest War

an ancient play for modern times

The Forest War

The Forest War was written at the Djerassi Resident Artists Program, Woodside, CA. The play subsequently received development at the American Conservatory Theater, San Francisco, CA. The world premiere of *The Forest War* was presented by Shotgun Players at the Ashby Stage, Berkeley, CA, on December 1, 2006. The production was directed by the author, with the following cast and staff:

KARUG / ZOHAK	Drew Anderson
KAIN	Kevin Clarke
KULAN	Cassidy Brown
EMA	Fontana Butterfield
ANGE	Caroline Hewitt
MAU TANT	Reid Davis
MITA	Tonya Glanz
LUNENN / MOT / KUROGO	Thu Tran
MADAM AJBI	Carla Pantoja
OLAN	Ryan Tasker
MORDUK	Richard Reinholdt
APSU	Lukas Ferreira
MADAM AJTZA	Anna Ishida
GAUT / KUROGO	Erin Stuart
MUSICIANS	Dan Bruno, Christopher Broderick
Set	Melpomene Katakolos
Costumes	Valera Coble
Lights	Heather Basarab
Props	Ambra Sultzbaugh
Stage Manager	Sarah Deutsch

Dramatis Personae

>*The Grand Lord Karug (KAH-roog)*
>*His Son, Lord Kain (cane)*

>*Lord Kulan (koo-LAHN)*
>*His wife, Ema (AIM-uh)*
>*His daughter, Ange (ahn-zhay)*

>*General Mau Tant (mow tahnt)*

Mita (MEE-tah), a courtesan of Grand Lord Karug's
Lord Lunenn (Loo-NEHN), cousin to Lord Kain

Madam Ajbi (azh-bee), a cloth maker
Her son, Olan (OH-lahn), a painter
Morduk (MORE-duhk), a sword maker
His boy apprentice, Apsu (ahp-soo)
Madam Ajtza (azh-tzah), a medicine woman

Lord Zohak (ZOH-hawk), an enemy Lord
Gaut (gowt), a soldier
Mot (mawt), a soldier

Kurogo, two onstage assistants
Musicians

Performance Note

The play is to be performed in a ritualized theatrical style. Movement and voice should be very pared down, with the upper class characters frequently oriented out toward the audience as in the Kabuki and Greek theatres, and the lower class characters played in a freer style as with traditional street theatres. Entrances and exits should not be traffic but rather embodiments of a character's given state at the beginning or end of a scene. Two Kurogo-style assistants are present to help with costumes, props, and any other necessities of the event. Musicians glue the event together throughout.

Act One
Episode One

Enter the Grand Lord KARUG, his son the Lord KAIN and nephew Lord LUNENN, Lord KULAN, his wife EMA and daughter ANGE, the General MAU TANT, and the courtesan MITA.

KARUG With this new sun, we greet a long awaited peace.
KULAN Forgive me, my Grand Lord Karug: if we now have peace, it is only because we have forgotten why for so many years we did not have peace.
KARUG Lord Kulan, I have forgotten nothing. Without the Great Forest in our hand, time would rot the beams on which our future rests. Now the ill wind of our warring neighbors The Vohakta has died, and the Great Forest is ours. But our people are weary. And I am weary. I have lost a dear brother. My nephew, Lord Lunenn, a father. Still others have lost much more. Bloodshed

drains the spirit over time, and blood spilt grows ill-natured weeds. The people no longer wish to plant flowers where their families once stood. And their trust in the wisdom of nobility has grown weaker with every new patch of earth stained by the tears of wives, daughters, sons, and brothers.

KULAN And why is it we have buried so many husbands and brothers? For what reason?

KAIN Lord Kulan. Do not play the fool. You know very well. Without the Great Forest we would have no fuel for fire, we could not build houses and boats. The sacrifice is right. And men grow far more quickly than trees.

KULAN And should they be as quickly cut down?

KAIN Your compassion would have our city crushed beneath a rotten ceiling!

KULAN And your ambition, Lord Kain, would have our foundation cracked into pieces!

> *KAIN moves suddenly as if to fight and KULAN immediately does the same.*

KARUG Be still, both of you! My son is right, Lord Kulan, the Great Forest must be kept for our own security. And, my son, Lord Kulan is also right: we must care for what we have. And if the people who must live or die by our decrees do not believe we have chosen for them wisely, then we have nothing, and the Great Forest is as useful as a field of ashes. ...And so to our purpose. Long, dark years of struggle have made victory a dim reward. I am old in a time that seeks new vision. We must win back the hearts of our people whose sacrifice of blood and bone has exhausted their spirit. Therefore, today I sheath the sword of our estate, and place it in the hands of Lord Kulan.

KAIN Ah? My Grand Lord–

KARUG You are a decisive man, my son, but too hot for weary days. Lord Kulan is well liked, and the people trust he keeps them in his sight. My Lord Kulan, I give you my sword, and my sovereignty, and so pronounce you Grand Lord Kulan.

KULAN May time and fate see fit to prove me worthy of your judgment, and your judgment right.

KARUG I have no doubt.

KAIN But my Grand Lord Karug, it is not right.

KARUG My mind is firm.

KAIN But father–!

KARUG You question my judgment.

KAIN You cannot possibly have given it proper thought.

KARUG Be silent! How dare you insult me so, you hot-blooded boy! Not given it proper thought? I have given this my thought since the day you were born. I watched as you learned to walk, and have always admired your perseverance and resolve. But there are times to hesitate, times for waiting, times when one must give careful consideration. This you do not understand. Not given it proper thought?

KAIN Forgive me, my Grand Lord.

KARUG *(laughs)* You see how quickly you forget. As of today, I am no longer your Grand Lord. But still I am your father. And that is the more important title, my son.

KAIN Yes, dear father.

KARUG And so. Enough debate. Come. We will make the announcement. The celebrations are already prepared, for you, Grand Lord Kulan, and our victory.

Exit ALL but Lord KAIN and MAU TANT.

KAIN So, my father sides against his blood. Old man, once I thought you very wise, but now I see how much the fire has faded from your brain. Promote a farmer over me? What good is a happy mob if their leader is weak? Long have I known my father's admiration for the good Lord Kulan. But too long did I wait to tarnish it. Well, I'll bide my time no longer. ...General Mau Tant!

MAU TANT My Lord Kain.

KAIN Despite the dark peace that stains this day, I trust you remain as dedicated to our countryside's betterment as am I.

MAU TANT But of course, my Lord Kain.

KAIN My father has mistakenly dropped his reign into the hands of a glorified landowner. And so our war is still not won. Kind-hearted Kulan will impress the peasants, and the significance of the Great Forest will soon be forgotten. And so the Vohakta will quietly dig their teeth back into our land like termites under a sleeping nation's foot. I will not be sated by false victory while all we've fought for is eaten away.

MAU TANT No, nor I, my Lord Kain.

KAIN And should anyone stand in our way...

MAU TANT I'll cut him into pieces!

KAIN Good. Tonight, let's leave them to their celebrations, and retire to some private place where we may twist our plot to set right this rickety time of peace.

MAU TANT Yes, my Lord Kain.

KAIN Huht!

Exit Lord KAIN, followed by MAU TANT.

Episode Two

Enter EMA and ANGE.

EMA You are the daughter of a Grand Lord, Ange. What will you do now?
ANGE I don't know mother. You are the wife of a Grand Lord. Perhaps you can give me good advice.
EMA I advise you to enjoy tonight, and think carefully tomorrow.
ANGE What do you mean?
EMA I mean that you are the daughter of a Grand Lord, and everyone who meets you will know it. Our lives have changed, though we cannot yet see precisely how.

Enter KULAN.

KULAN My Lady Ema, and Young Lady Ange.
EMA My Grand Lord Kulan.
ANGE Mother says we are to think carefully from now on, father.
KULAN Your mother is right. Though I hope you have thought carefully before today as well.
ANGE I have!
KULAN I have no doubt, my daughter.
ANGE Congratulations, Grand Lord Kulan. Only don't forget: with me you're still just father. You won't forget to be my father, will you?
KULAN When I do, I trust you will be so good to remind me.
ANGE Ah! You will not forget!
KULAN Not even the morning after my dying day.
EMA Rejoin the celebrations, Ange. Your father and I have much to discuss.

Exit ANGE.

KULAN Our daughter will make a sharp Lady someday.
EMA She is sharper already than she realizes. I too hope that you will not forget she is your daughter.
KULAN Why do you say this?
EMA I know you to be a thoughtful man, but in your own way ambitious. Your passion is great.
KULAN Are you warning me?
EMA Not a warning. But perhaps a reminder. Today we celebrate, and

tomorrow we begin the business of rebuilding the spirit of the countryside. It will not be a simple task. And I fear Lord Kain will not make it any simpler for you.

KULAN Lord Kain believes in blood. He will do as his father wishes.

EMA Lord Kain does believe in blood. …Be cautious, my husband.

KULAN I trust you will advise me in my new role as you have always done.

EMA I will. And let this be my first advice to you in this new time. Imagine tomorrow. Forget not yesterday. And see with open eyes today. For today is life, yesterday is memory, and tomorrow is yet a dream.

KULAN You speak like a holy woman. …And I thank you, my wife, my friend.

EMA And your love.

KULAN And my love.

Exit EMA.

KULAN So. Grand Lord Kulan. What will you do first?

Enter MITA.

MITA Forgive me, my Grand Lord. I did not know you were alone. …Shall I leave you to your meditations?

KULAN You did not know I was alone? And still you entered my chamber? Are you sure of what you did not know?

MITA *(looks after EMA)* I am sure… my lord.

MITA moves farther into the room. KULAN looks after EMA, then turns to MITA. They go to one another, embrace and kiss passionately.

MITA I am not your wife.

KULAN Am I to be reminded by everyone who they are and who they are not?

MITA Tell me how you love me still, or am I dying slowly each time we kiss?

KULAN Mita. You are a courtesan of the Grand Lord Karug.

MITA You are the Grand Lord, now.

KULAN Still, you do not serve me, Mita.

MITA I serve you with my love. I serve Lord Karug according to my duty.

KULAN And are you still so new to your duty that you forget it?

MITA I know my job.

KULAN You are the youngest of Lord Karug's courtesans, and as such the most vulnerable. Our secret could put you on the streets, or worse.

MITA And have you no sway over my fate? Lord Karug has given you his sword and made you Grand Lord.

KULAN That is a formality. He will remain my ultimate advisor in all things.

MITA You are too modest. Your new title makes you nervous, I think, and doubtful. Or maybe you no longer share my helpless passion.

THEY kiss again.

MITA I spoke only the truth when I told you I love you. I could never lie about that.

KULAN I believe you, my sweet Mita. But my life has been changed. And so I think we too must change.

MITA What are you saying to me?

KULAN The steps from war to peace make a dangerous path. Much remains uncertain. Our small love may be too risky for us both during the great climb ahead.

MITA Small love! You do me disrespect, Grand Lord Kulan. I am but a servant in the house of a Lord. And you may think me no more than such. But when I look at you I know what it is to love. And when you look at me I see that you know what it is to love. I am your passion. And you are mine. Without passion, yesterday tomorrow and today mean nothing. Without passion there is no time. Without love, there is no life. You know that I am right.

KULAN and MITA kiss again. KULAN stands to go.

MITA I love you, my most tender love.
KULAN I will not forget.

Exit KULAN.

MITA And woe to me that I cannot forget.

Exit MITA.

Episode Three

Enter APSU and MADAM AJBI.

MADAM AJBI Oh! Hello! Good morning young Apsu!

APSU Good morning Madam Ajbi.

MADAM AJBI Have you seen my son Olan today?

APSU Not yet, Madam Ajbi.

MADAM AJBI Out dreaming somewhere no doubt. And where is old Morduk this morning? Still drunk from last night's celebrations no doubt.

APSU He's inside. Shall I call him?

MADAM AJBI No, no, let him come to on his own. He needs his rest as much as I do, I'm sure. Oh, the day has just begun and already my bones are creaking. This is what happens when you live a long time, young Apsu. I don't recommend it.

APSU You don't recommend I live long?

MADAM AJBI No! Live long. Live very long. Just don't get old!

APSU I'll try, Madam Ajbi.

MADAM AJBI What will you do today, Apsu, now that we have a new Grand Lord.

APSU The same as yesterday, Madam Ajbi. Work.

MADAM AJBI Ha! Work! I've stuck my fingers so often sewing this damn cloth my hands are like pincushions. This is what happens when you deal in fabrics, young Apsu. I don't recommend it. Stick to your blade making. And be kind to old Morduk. He will make a fine bladesmith of you one day. At times I think I'd prefer one of his swords to one of his terrible needles.

APSU Why is that, Madam Ajbi?

MADAM AJBI A sword is big enough that I can see it coming. Needles have a way of sneaking up on you. But I should not complain. We are lucky to have chosen the trades that we did, you and I. People will always need cloth for a shirt on their back. And the world will always have Lords and scoundrels to keep you and Morduk making blades 'til doomsday.

APSU Not just Lords and scoundrels, Madam Ajbi. Everyone needs a good knife.

MADAM AJBI Knives, yes. Swords? No. A decade of war and no husband: this is what happens when men pick up swords, young Apsu. I don't recommend it.

Enter MORDUK.

MORDUK Oh! The sun is early.

MADAM AJBI You are late.

MORDUK Madam Ajbi. Just the woman I wanted to see. I need some cloth for a fresh new blanket. I seem to have misplaced mine last night.

MADAM AJBI When you've sobered up I'm sure you'll find it.
MORDUK I am sober. I think.
MADAM AJBI And what do you think of our new Grand Lord Kulan? His wife is such a handsome woman, and his daughter is a beauty. Surely they'll be in the market for some finely woven fabrics.
MORDUK Good for you, but what about me? Swords don't sell in times of peace.
MADAM AJBI You would rather have war? I'm sure you made enough money these past ten years to retire for good, you greedy man. Pass your bloody business on to Apsu and be done with it.
MORDUK And did the soldiers not buy your fabrics for their flags and uniforms?
MADAM AJBI Maybe a few yards. But it's not the same thing.
MORDUK I see. Well, I think Lord Kain would have been his father's better choice.
MADAM AJBI I gave a husband to his father's war. That family needs nothing more from me. The Grand Lord Kulan knows us well. As a boy he worked the land that he now owns. He knows what it is to be nobody special. He will put the countryside back together.
MORDUK We shall see. Until then, let us hope for prosperity.

Enter MADAM AJTZA.

MADAM AJBI Ah, Madam Ajtza. Please tend to poor Morduk. He is not well.
MADAM AJTZA What is the matter with you, dear Morduk?
MADAM AJBI He's delusional. He wants the war to come back.
MADAM AJTZA Morduk, is this true?
MORDUK Of course not. But I could use some of your medicine to soothe my head. Oh how it aches.
MADAM AJTZA From what?
MADAM AJBI Too much celebration.
MADAM AJTZA I thought so. You don't need my medicine. You need willpower. As for the countryside, we need our hope and our prayers. If you ask me, and you haven't, this Lord, that Lord, it makes no difference. It's been a long time since our new Grand Lord Kulan had his hands in the dirt. Hopefully he has not forgotten. And as for Lord Kain, he was born with dirty hands. So, either way, the hand on the hilt is dirty. We'll see what time does for us. But I best not stay and chatter. Goodbye my neighbors. Even after war, there is still much healing to be done.

Exit MADAM AJTZA.

MADAM AJBI I still say Kulan.
MORDUK Kain.
MADAM AJBI Kulan!
MORDUK …Kain.
MADAM AJBI Oh, you are impossible.
MORDUK Anything is possible, Madam Ajbi. Even me. Come Apsu, we have work to do. We must make for Madam Ajbi a sharp new set of needles so she can sew her fine fabrics for the Grand Lord's wife.
MADAM AJBI Your needles will be the end of me, old man.
MORDUK If your tongue doesn't kill me first.
MADAM AJBI Oh, you terrible man. *(laughs)*

MORDUK and APSU exit.

MADAM AJBI Oh how fast and tight-lipped the gods of time can be. When will the days slow down and tell us all their little secrets?

Enter OLAN.

MADAM AJBI Olan! Where have you been?
OLAN I am sorry mother. I stayed up with the celebrations. I hope you did not worry.
MADAM AJBI I've learned to expect anything from you, my son. Always too busy dreaming.
OLAN And what about you, always too busy selling cloth?
MADAM AJBI Something people can use, my son. Why did you never apprentice with Morduk like young Apsu? You could have learned a real skill.
OLAN I have a skill, mother. I paint.
MADAM AJBI Oh! An artist!
OLAN Morduk is an artist too, in his way.
MADAM AJBI No, Morduk is not an artist. He is an artisan. That's different. His knives may be beautiful to look at, but they are also useful.
OLAN And his swords?
MADAM AJBI At times an unfortunate necessity.
OLAN I see. I'd rather wield my paintbrushes. If Father were here he would agree with me.
MADAM AJBI Olan!

OLAN Have a good day mother!

OLAN exits.

MADAM AJBI Oh, that terrible boy. If he were not my son, I would disown him. This is what happens when you are a mother. I don't recommend it.

MADAM AJBI exits.

Episode Four

Enter KULAN, EMA, KARUG, MITA, KAIN, MAU TANT, MADAM AJTZA, and LUNENN.

KULAN The sun flies at a steady pace, and when he retires the moon takes up his task and keeps night rolling toward another day. It is time to make a memory of celebration and of war, look to today, and plan for tomorrow.
KAIN *(aside to MAU TANT)* Well said.
KULAN And so it is with great hope and eagerness that I make my first decrees. Our people are ill and tired. We must build their strength again so that together we can rebuild our countryside. Madam Ajtza.
MADAM AJTZA My Grand Lord Kulan.
KULAN I have asked for your help, as I know you to be a wise and respected woman of medicine. You shall oversee the health of our city, make inspections of the grain supplies, the waterways, and central public markets. See that they are all well-tended and free of the squalor that breeds illness.
MADAM AJTZA Yes, my Grand Lord.
KAIN My Grand Lord Kulan, the city is already inspected regularly. Why bring a medicine woman into it?
KULAN Our systems are faulty, Lord Kain. They require renovation, which I fully trust you to manage. However, Madam Ajtza's perspective will help us to improve upon the past, and fortify a vibrant city. You will be very busy rebuilding the Grand Port and central markets. I think you will find another pair of eyes will prove useful.
KAIN Yesss, My Grand Lord.
KULAN Lord Lunenn.
LUNENN My Grand Lord Kulan.
KULAN As the major landowner of the southern district, I charge you with looking after our smaller river ports there. See to it they are secure from the danger of floods, as well as the piracy and corruption bred by desperate times.

LUNENN I will do as you ask, my Grand Lord. Though my cousin, Lord Kain, has often looked after the river ports as well.

KULAN He will be very busy with these other matters. You might consult him, but I leave the river ports in your care.

LUNENN Yes, My Grand Lord.

KULAN Lady Ema.

EMA My Grand Lord Kulan.

KULAN You shall look after the welfare of those left without means by devastation and misfortune, and shall put in place systems for temporary refuge while they recoup.

EMA Yes, My Grand Lord.

KAIN You are very generous, my Grand Lord Kulan. Your charity will cost a fortune.

EMA You would prefer those whom fate deems unlucky should starve rather than contribute to the countryside. Such a waste of life can hardly help rebuild your Grand Port, Lord Kain.

KAIN So, the Grand Lord's wife answers for him, not to him.

KULAN She has said only what I would myself, Lord Kain. I ask that you respect her word.

KAIN Father! This is an outrage!

KARUG Abide the wishes of your Grand Lord, my son.

KAIN He is not my Grand Lord. I did not choose him.

KARUG That is right! I chose him!

KAIN Throwing our countryside in the hands of women! The Vohakta will rape all that we bled for and leave us whimpering like little girls!

KULAN Lord Kain! You will be silent! These days beg for compassion, and it is clear I cannot entrust that to you. Do not fear the safety of the Great Forest. General Mau Tant and his men will look after our hard won prize. And do not doubt my decrees, nor the authority of those to whom I give charge. Do you understand me, Lord Kain.

KAIN Yes, my Grand Lord.

KULAN Good. Let us all begin our work, then.

Exit ALL but KAIN and MAU TANT.

KAIN *(draws his sword and slashes the air; then)* It is unbearable. To be traipsed after by an old woman!

MAU TANT Surely the Grand Lord has employed Madam Ajtza as a spy to watch over you.

KAIN Yes, while his wife entertains the poor rabble who haven't the wits to help themselves. We see who has the Grand Lord's ear – not his councilors, but a woman. Woe to a countryside led by a wife's poppet.

MAU TANT What shall be done?

KAIN We must act quickly. Kulan is not one to waste time. On his first day he is already making decrees. We must stir the general blood against his reign. If my father will not hear my voice, then perhaps he will hear the snarling of an angry mob. On your watch, Mau Tant, walk among the people and take their pulse. Find out which way their blood flows. Meanwhile, I will study our Grand Lord Kulan carefully. The first crack I find I will fill with my sword – and break him open!

Exit KAIN and MAU TANT.

Episode Five

Enter OLAN.

OLAN Hold still, Time, while I catch you with my brushes. And one day, we may learn from this memory of you held captive by color and wrapped in lines. My mother would rather my brush was a hammer that I might beat out a living like old Morduk, making knives and needles. We each help in our own way. Ah, don't move, Time, this part's important.

Enter MORDUK and APSU.

MORDUK Olan, my young friend. Hard at work I see.

OLAN Hello Morduk. Hello Apsu.

APSU Hello Olan.

MORDUK Have you heard the news? Madam Ajtza has been enlisted to work with Lord Kain. She will surely help him bring our city back to good health. Your mother is right, the Grand Lord Kulan has not forgotten where he came from.

OLAN She will be pleased to hear it.

MORDUK And she will be pleased for me to hear it again and again. What are you painting today, Olan?

OLAN The meadow.

MORDUK Always the meadow. I see you've put a crowd of people in the meadow who are not there. Are you painting ghosts?

OLAN They are people who have passed by, or came to meditate one afternoon but did not notice me sitting here. If today another person passes by, perhaps I'll paint her too.

APSU Why is your meadow blue, Olan?

OLAN You see how the wind blows waves through the grass just like the sea. The sea and the meadow are different, but they are also the same. The night sky lifts up the sea and sprinkles it on the meadow, then calls the sun to dry the grass. The meadow grows from the sea and sun, as the color green does from blue and yellow. They are different, but they are the same.

APSU And your ghosts float in the meadow like boats?

OLAN Yes. Little boats made of thistles.

APSU What happens to our ghosts when we die?

OLAN The gods give them thistles to carry them away.

APSU Where do they go?

OLAN I don't know. Across the sea perhaps.

APSU I'd want my ghost to go to your meadow. I like your painting.

MORDUK Olan, you will lure my apprentice away from me. Then where will I be?

Enter MAU TANT. MORDUK, APSU, and OLAN all bow to him.

MAU TANT A beautiful afternoon, my friends. Soon it will be a beautiful evening.

MORDUK Very beautiful, General Mau Tant.

MAU TANT Morduk, the swordmaker, and his little helper, Apsu. I am surprised to see you away from your hammers and stone.

MORDUK I am just returning from town with some jade for the hilt of a fine new sword.

APSU It's a beautiful sword, General Mau Tant. You should see it.

MAU TANT Your tutor has taught you well, young Apsu. Tell me, good Morduk, how is business now that the war is past?

MORDUK People are always in the market for blades of all kinds. A knife to gut fish, a needle to sew cloth, an axe to chop wood. Perhaps I will make a few less swords, but those I do make will be exquisite. With less demand, I will have more time for each.

MAU TANT Well, perhaps I will have to have another of your fine swords for myself, Morduk.

MORDUK Certainly, General Mau Tant.

MAU TANT And how about you, young painter?

OLAN My name is Olan, General Mau Tant.

MAU TANT Why is your meadow blue?

OLAN That's how I see it.

MAU TANT Mmm. An unfortunate handicap for a painter.
APSU No, General Mau Tant, the meadow is like the sea. Look how the wind blows waves through the grass.
MAU TANT I see, you are right young Apsu. Tell me, painter, are people in the market for paintings these days?
OLAN Perhaps now they will be, more than before – when war made even food a costly luxury.
MAU TANT Well, now that the war is won and the Great Forest is ours, you'll never lack wood for your brushes and frames.
OLAN That's true, General Mau Tant. And if I am awoken at night by howls I will know it is the wolves and not my mother crying for her husband.
MAU TANT We all make sacrifices for the greater good. Even an artist.
OLAN And a son.
MAU TANT Perhaps your blue meadows will bring solace to somebody's wall.
OLAN The wall of the Young Lady Ange, herself, daughter of the Grand Lord Kulan, finds solace in one of my blue meadows.
MAU TANT Well. When I see Young Lady Ange again I will tell her we met.
OLAN She won't remember my name. She has many paintings, no doubt.
MORDUK General Mau Tant, forgive me. Apsu and I must be running along. And Olan, too. Your mother is expecting you.
MAU TANT Good day, my friends. I'll come tomorrow and have a look at that sword, Morduk.
MORDUK It will be my honor, General Mau Tant.
MAU TANT Goodbye, young painter, and good luck with your blue meadows.
OLAN Thank you, General Mau Tant.
MORDUK *(aside to OLAN)* Why do you taunt the General, Olan? Besides being bad for business, it's just not a good idea. You're mother would agree. Come Apsu.

Exit MORDUK and APSU.

OLAN *(aside, to himself)* I should not have mentioned Young Lady Ange. My pride is blind to sense, and may have planted seeds better swallowed than sown.

Exit OLAN.

MAU TANT The swordmaker is content in times of war and of peace. The painter does not seem as pleased. Artists are born unhappy, I think. …Who comes here now? Ah. It is the Grand Lord Kulan, walking alone. Perhaps he, too, meditates in a blue meadow. I will withdraw, and study him like the painter. Anything interesting I'll etch in my memory.

MAU TANT hides himself. Enter KULAN, alone.

KULAN How I envy the landscape. I hope one day I am as patient as the meadow, and as modest as each blade of grass. Look how they all work together, content to be nameless, happy to give us their beauty. Or perhaps they feel nothing for us. Maybe they are as selfish as we are, and grow for their own satisfaction, and care not whether we admire them or cut them down, knowing they will still be growing when we are long since buried beneath their roots. …What do I hear? Is that the breeze and grass whispering among themselves, or are they laughing at me and my ruminations?

Enter MITA. She goes immediately to KULAN. They embrace and kiss one another.

MITA When I found your blade of grass on my pillow I came at once. I could not walk fast enough, but did not run for fear my secret joy would be discovered. Our meadow always waits to harbor us.
KULAN Sometimes I come alone to hold you in my thoughts.
MITA In the long days between each silent kiss your name is always on my tongue. I have to bite it with my teeth to keep from calling you to back me.
KULAN Your poor, bitten tongue. Let me heal it with a tiny kiss.

MITA and KULAN kiss again, melting together.

KULAN I have forgotten why I called you here.
MITA Let us stay 'til you remember.
KULAN We won't stay long, then.
MITA Then forget a little longer.
KULAN I can't. My mind weighs heavily.
MITA …Why have you called me here?
KULAN It is time for us to forget our passion.
MITA If it were only passion we could learn to forget. But when passion entwines with love, we can only remember. …Why do you pull away?
KULAN I love my wife, Mita, and that I cannot forget. I love my wife. She is my confidant. She is my friend.
MITA She is not your passion.
KULAN She is more than that.
MITA Then you do not love me. …Your silence confirms it. You see only your

new sword, I think, that sword the Grand Lord Karug has lent to you.

KULAN He has bequeathed it unto me, and all the burden of power that comes with it.

MITA My poor Grand Lord Kulan, suffering from his power. How I envy your burden!

KULAN You indulge the vanity of your pain, and let it overwhelm your reason. You do not see my love for you, how I press it down and bury it beneath my heart. But I have searched my heart, and know what I must sacrifice. Our love grows ever bigger in our silence, and yet is small to the howling world. I am Grand Lord Kulan. I have a wife whom I love and respect, a daughter whom I love and respect, and a countryside whose love and respect I must keep. Our love must live in our memory, but not today, and not tomorrow. I hope that you will see I am right.

> *MITA bows her head and weeps. KULAN embraces her and she returns it fiercely.*

KULAN Goodbye, my secret love.

> *Exit KULAN. MITA loses her balance for a moment but catches it just as quickly.*

MITA Woe to this courtesan who betrayed her duty and fell in love. Woe to this careless world that grants no justice to a breaking heart. Woe to this field that does not swallow me up but only waits patiently for my bones. I leave you my hopes, dear meadow, to do with as you please.

> *Exit MITA.*

MAU TANT O, lucky day! I'll take the hopes that you so sadly leave behind, sweet courtesan – and give them to Lord Kain! Surely the Meadow has less use for them than he! *(laughs)*

> *Exit MAU TANT.*

Episode Six

> *Enter KARUG, followed closely by KAIN.*

KARUG Your barking and teeth gnashing weary me, my son. You insult me with your persistent disrespect for my wishes. Was a father ever so cursed by so adamantly unhappy a child? You are more devoted to your resentment, I think, than to me.

KAIN You chide me, father, for words that you will not hear. Even if I wrote them out you could not read them. You are deaf and blind to my good intent.

KARUG Your good intent! And what do you intend that is so good?

KAIN I intend to protect all that we have struggled to gain. As long as the Vohakta stand, the Great Forest is at risk, and the security of our countryside along with it. We can never truly rest until the Vohakta are wiped from the face of the earth. And once they are gone, there will still be other less bold neighbors gathering their courage to take action against us. But with Vohakta lands in our borders as well, father, our rule will be secured. And invincible.

KARUG How insatiable you are. You would stuff your mouth on a full stomach, my son. When will you learn to wait?

KAIN And what are we waiting for?

KARUG The Grand Lord Kulan is a great visionary.

KAIN He is a fool! He flatters the masses by giving his childhood medicine woman a job. He gives false hope to thousands by promoting one, while his wife squanders the wealth of the countryside on a pathetic rabble that doesn't have the sense of an ox to pick up a plow. While Kulan and his wife cuddle their peasants, the Vohakta spin their webs.

KARUG He will make our countryside stronger than it ever was.

KAIN By wasting your unwarranted gift?

KARUG By earning the faith of the people! ...The loss of that faith was our greatest loss in ten long years of battle. You must be patient my son. Once the countryside has finally mended its wounds, once the scars have flaked away from memory, once the people are enlivened again by pride, you will have your turn.

KAIN My turn. What do you mean?

KARUG ...You do not deserve my confidence.

KAIN thinks, then takes a submissive stance.

KARUG Kulan is a good man. And, he is not the son of a Grand Lord who dragged his people through half a generation of blood. And so he is the right man for a people reacquainting themselves to peace, hope, and prosperity. As you say, the Vohakta will spin their webs, but that will take them plenty of time. Where we lost five men, they lost twenty. Once our countryside can show the blood in its cheeks again, and walk without a crutch, Kulan will have served his time. ...Do you understand... my son?

KAIN Yes, father. ...But if the people get attached to their great visionary, that

will make things very difficult for his successor.
KARUG Ungrateful boy! I waste my time with you. You do not deserve the rights of your blood.
KAIN Father. ...I thank you for your confidence. And put my faith entirely in your wisdom. I cannot help but that I am eager.
KARUG *(laughs)* Eager. That's my son. Eager. I leave you, eager boy. ...Do not betray my confidence.

KAIN bows low in a show of devotion. Exit KARUG.

KAIN I thank you, old man. Your confidence is touching. It fills my open heart like salt. May the gods restore your sight that you may see the blindness of your great visionary, and unclog your ears that you may hear that this time of peace must march to my drum or none at all.

Enter MAU TANT.

MAU TANT My Lord Kain.
KAIN General Mau Tant.
MAU TANT I have news. But first you will want to draw your sword.
KAIN My sword?
MAU TANT For I have found the crack in our Grand Lord Kulan.
KAIN Tell me your news.
MAU TANT In the meadow just beyond the eastern Palace wall, returning again from town where as you asked I have gone to count the general pulse, I saw our young Grand Lord walking alone. But not for long. He was soon joined by Mita, your father's pretty courtesan.
KAIN The Grand Lord Kulan and Mita?
MAU TANT That is right. They had not spoken a single word before their limbs had tangled in a knot, and between stolen kisses they unraveled their amorous treason.
KAIN *(aside)* Yes. Well done, Mita. And not too late.
MAU TANT My Lord Kain?
KAIN How timely is your news, Mau Tant. My father's voice was still fading from the air when you arrived. Behind his spotty old hand he made plain the motive of his baffling abdication. He has thrown out Kulan as bait to lure back the trust of the war weary shoal. Once they are hooked, Kulan will be thrown to the fishes, and my ship will come to port.
MAU TANT Then his indiscretion is no matter.
KAIN No, Mau Tant, it is all the better. His lust will only hasten his demise.

Once the man of principle is revealed a fraud, his ship is as good as sunk, and his fleet of doting minnows will tear him up like sharks.

KAIN and MAU TANT laugh wickedly.

KAIN Come, we must carefully chart our course. This tide is ours to drag in.

Exit KAIN and MAU TANT.

Episode Seven

Enter KULAN, EMA, ANGE, KARUG, MITA, MADAM AJTZA, and LUNENN.

KARUG The countryside grows greener everyday. Already the people seem to walk with lighter step. Is that not true, my Nephew?
LUNENN It seems so, my honored Lord and uncle.
KARUG Yes, good. All is progressing well, Grand Lord Kulan.
KULAN Coming from you, that title still feels strange to me, like borrowed robes.
KARUG They are your robes now. You must wear them proudly.
EMA I assure you, he does. I know my husband well. He will not disappoint you.
KARUG I do not doubt it, Lady Ema.

Enter KAIN and MAU TANT.

KAIN My apologies, Grand Lord Kulan.
KULAN It is unlike you to be late, Lord Kain.
KAIN I have been busier than I expected.
KULAN I hope I have not overburdened you.
KAIN No. Madam Ajtza is much more clever than she looks.
MADAM AJTZA From you, Lord Kain, I will take that as a compliment.
KULAN What keeps you so busy today, Lord Kain?
KAIN Grand Lord Kulan, are you an honest man?
KULAN Why do you ask me this?
KAIN It is an honest question.
KULAN And a foolish one. For if I were not honest, I'd be a fool to admit it.
KAIN Shall I ask your wife, then?

EMA What is on your mind, Lord Kain?

KAIN …Mita!

MITA …Yes, Lord Kain.

KAIN You are fair, but are you honest?

MITA I think I am, Lord Kain.

KAIN You do not know?

MITA …I know I am, Lord Kain.

KARUG Why such an interest in honesty today, my son?

KAIN I will tell you, father, for it is twice my duty.

KARUG *Twice* your duty?

KAIN Yes, as a loyal servant to my countryside, and as your son.

KARUG You will explain yourself.

KAIN You have entrusted your sword to the hands of a lustful thief, my good father.

EMA Still clutching at your jealousy! Your father made his decision. Why must you forever stage your bitter protest?

KAIN You misinterpret me, Lady Ema.

EMA And how is that, Lord Kain?

KAIN Ask your husband.

EMA I ask you.

KAIN And I say: Ask your husband.

EMA *(looks at KULAN, then to KAIN)* I know my husband well. He is more honest a man than you could hope to be.

KAIN How can that be, when I meet your gaze while he avoids it?

EMA Look at me, husband.

A pause before KULAN looks at EMA.

EMA *(to KAIN)* There, you see?

KAIN grabs MITA by the arm and drags her forward.

KARUG My son!

KAIN Will you tell them why the Grand Lord Kulan hangs his head in shame, little Mita, or shall I?

MITA I don't know!

KAIN Mau Tant! Your news!

MAU TANT I saw them both, my honored Lord, Grand Lord Kulan and Mita, in the meadow outside the Palace wall, where it seems they've often met in secret to exchange their lewd and treacherous vows.

KULAN General Mau Tant! Lord Kain! You will not make such accusations!

KAIN Do you deny them?

KULAN You insult me to ask such a question!

KAIN You condemn yourself not to answer!

EMA Husband?

KULAN Do not doubt me, wife! You know me to be honest.

KAIN Father! Do not let this villain make a fool of you!

KULAN Lord Kain! I have for too long suffered your bitterness and unveiled hatred for me. You have used all my patience. Let me tell you once, and once only: I have never met in secret with Lord Karug's courtesan. I have made no lewd or treacherous vows. You do me unpardonable dishonor to suggest it! And you abuse my wife and daughter! And as for General Mau Tant, affection makes him false. That, too, I cannot forgive. You abuse this woman for your own vanity, and me at your own risk. As you are the son of my honored Lord Karug, you will keep your head. But do not test my will!

KAIN Father!

KULAN Silence! You have said enough.

KAIN Father.

KULAN takes a readied pose. KARUG looks away. KAIN bows obediently, and MAU TANT follows suit.

KULAN Come wife, come daughter. My honored Lord Karug, I leave you to your son. All the rest go your ways.

Exit KULAN, EMA, and ANGE. Followed by MADAM AJTZA and LUNENN.

KAIN What we've told is true, my lord.

KARUG Mita. Go before me.

MITA Yes, my honored Lord.

MITA kisses KARUG's hand, then exits. A long pause before KARUG makes his own silent exit.

KAIN Well spoken, General Mau Tant.

MAU TANT Do you think your father will take our bait?

KAIN Seeds of doubt, once planted, soon grow like weeds. This, too, will take root and fester in the old man's head. The medicine woman Ajtza will plant our news in every neighbor's ear. And my good cousin Lunenn will scatter rumors down the river. Gossip is the ally that will bring our Grand Lord Kulan to his knees. Then we: can get back to business!

> *Exit MAU TANT. KAIN brandishes his sword, menaces the audience with a long sweep of his eye, then wields his unsheathed blade in an elaborate, triumphant display before making a grand exit of victory.*

End of Act One.

Act Two
Episode Eight

> *Enter MADAM AJBI and MADAM AJTZA.*

MADAM AJBI But I can't believe it.
MADAM AJTZA I was there. Besides, we have known each other a long time, why should I lie to you?
MADAM AJBI The Grand Lord Kulan is known to have been a loyal and trustworthy man from his youth. He once plowed the fields he now owns. How many noblemen have done the same?
MADAM AJTZA The plow yields dirt, Ajbi, not honesty. The Grand Lord may once have tilled the soil like lesser men, but that was his choice, not his burden. At the end of the day he never retired to a drafty old shack. He was born of noble stock. He was never one of us.
MADAM AJBI But he remembered you. And now you mingle with nobility like a great man.
MADAM AJTZA Yes. Great men half my age. Boys in golden robes.
MADAM AJBI Then why did you accept the job?
MADAM AJTZA I am cynical, Ajbi, not stupid. I have seen enough ill souls give their bodies up to death regardless of my pains to know that life is short. Besides, I know myself, and I know that I can do some good.
MADAM AJBI And I know: The Grand Lord Kulan will still do good.

> *Enter MORDUK and APSU.*

MORDUK Hello Madam Ajbi, Madam Ajtza.
MADAM AJBI Oh Morduk, have you heard the rumor?
MORDUK Of course. Very interesting.
MADAM AJBI I can't believe it's true.

MORDUK A royal man has his way with the courtesan of another royal man, and you are surprised? It happens everyday. Besides, what does it matter what the Grand Lord Kulan does at night? Are the ports being rebuilt, or aren't they?

MADAM AJBI Oh, Morduk, not you as well. Don't listen to this terrible man, young Apsu. He deals in daggers, after all. And if Madam Ajtza ever gives you her medicine again, spit it out at once. She muddies her remedies with pessimism.

MORDUK You're thinking too much about it, Madam Ajbi.

MADAM AJTZA Or too little.

Enter OLAN.

MADAM AJBI Oh! Good Olan, my son, come help me protect young Apsu from these bitter old toads. Where are you off to?

OLAN The meadows, mother.

MADAM AJBI Always in your meadows, Olan. Will you paint nothing else?

OLAN I find them peaceful.

MADAM AJBI My poor son, wandering in your dreams and your meadows, and tracking your paint everywhere you go. Lucky for my cloth, or we'd really be in the poor house. Dreams don't bring in much money, Olan.

MADAM AJTZA Now who's the cynical one?

MADAM AJBI Oh be quiet, you terrible old woman.

OLAN Goodbye mother.

OLAN exits.

MADAM AJBI My poor son. His meadows are always blue, and his dreams I think are full of clouds.

MADAM AJTZA He has a strong heart. He will be alright.

MORDUK Yes, don't worry for him, Madam Ajbi.

APSU Madam Ajbi, your needles.

MADAM AJBI Oh, thank you, Apsu! And how much do I owe you?

MORDUK A nice piece of your cloth will do. I still can't find my blanket.

MADAM AJBI A fair trade. Come, we'll take my needles home, and pick you out a nice warm piece of cloth.

MADAM AJTZI Back to business, and all is well. Goodbye, my good neighbors.

ALL exit.

Episode Nine

Enter KARUG, KAIN, and KULAN.

KARUG It is with great conflict of mind and stones in my heart that I have asked to see you both. I will speak to you candidly, though you do not deserve such a courtesy. I was disturbed by your accusations, my son. I am also too familiar with your long history of mischief to entirely trust your motive. Lord Kulan, I have known you to be a good and passionate man of honor and integrity. That is why it was with great sorrow that I listened to Mita's confession, which she gave to me with many tears and much pleading.

KULAN My honored Lord–

KARUG Be silent. You have disgraced my reputation, soiling with your secret lust the great honor I granted to you. Over my son, who claims my sword with his blood, I gave you my countryside, my sovereignty, and my trust. And this is how you repay me, by making a whore of my courtesan, and a mockery of my good judgment.

KULAN My honored Lord–

KARUG I said be silent!

A KUROGO takes the royal sword from KULAN.

KARUG You are no longer Grand Lord Kulan. Nor will I hand my sword to you, my son.

KAIN But you said yourself it is my right!

KARUG Nor will anything I have said be spoken of outside this room. This precious time of peace is still too young and too delicate for so soon and drastic an emendation. I will serve as Grand Lord, and you, Lord Kulan…

The KUROGO returns the royal sword to KULAN.

KARUG …will mouth my decrees, until I have decided exactly how we shall proceed and when.

KAIN Father–

KARUG This is my decision. It will be respected. And when the correct path does emerge from this swamp, then I hope you will finally understand the necessity for waiting and timely hesitation.

KULAN And what is to become of young Mita, my Grand Lord Karug?

KARUG She has earned the consequence Justice owes to her disgrace.

Episode Ten

The scene transforms to a public space in the Palace. Enter EMA with ANGE; also LUNENN and MADAM AJTZA. MITA is escorted forth by MAU TANT.

MITA Please, my dear Lord Karug! Be merciful!

A rope and noose is lowered and MAU TANT places it around MITA'S neck.

KARUG My mercy is your private execution, where the public will not know the full disgrace of your deed and cannot gawk and spit at you.
MITA Kulan! My love! I was never more honest in my life than when I surrendered to my love for you. I could have lied and died slowly instead. My crime was to love you, Kulan! Why do you stand there, why do you not speak out for me?

MITA suddenly runs to KAIN and kneels at his feet, clutching his legs.

MITA Lord Kain! Save me! Do not let me die like this! You can save me! Persuade your father with what you know is true!
KAIN You made your choice!
MITA How could I know I would fall in love with him? That was not my choice!
KAIN Mau Tant!

MAU TANT drags MITA back and puts her in place.

MITA Please! ...Why does nobody help me? ...Why does a woman die while men do as they please? Why is love hanged so that cruel ambition may run free!

KAIN goes to MAU TANT and takes up the rope.

MITA No–!

KAIN yanks MITA up into the air. MITA struggles silently at the end of the rope, and dies. After a moment, KARUG exits, followed by MADAM AJTZA and LUNENN. Then KAIN and MAU TANT exit. Only KULAN, EMA, and ANGE remain.

The KUROGO lower MITA down to a kneeling position on the ground and remove the noose from her neck. They lift her head and hand her a white paper umbrella. MITA stands, holding the umbrella aloft, and makes her final exit.

Episode Eleven

KULAN, EMA, and ANGE, alone.

EMA Ange.
ANGE Yes mother.
EMA Leave your father and me to speak in private.
ANGE Yes mother.
KULAN Ange. …I hope you will forgive me.

ANGE and EMA exchange a look, and ANGE exits. EMA moves away from KULAN.

EMA You are right to ask for her forgiveness.
KULAN I hope for yours as well, and will do whatever I must to earn it.
EMA How can I say what I need from you to make up for what cannot be undone?
KULAN For my shameful bargain I am prepared to pay the price, and it is yours to name.
EMA Well you will pardon me, Kulan, but I do not know by what scale to weigh such a fee. What value shall I place on the generosity you ask of me? By what measure shall I negotiate the rates of our trade? A marriage is not so cold a business.
KULAN There are no words that describe my regret.
EMA Find them if you like. It is with your deeds that you must bear the weight of your repentance. Your words are cheap and weak from much abuse.
KULAN Then I will say nothing, and do all that I can.
EMA …Did you love her? …Did you love her?
KULAN There were times I felt I did. It would be easy to dismiss my deeds as but the reckless gesture of a transient lust. But I can't explain it with such simplicity.
EMA I see. …Your daughter will carry this deed with her name for the rest of her life. I must face the world with this shame perched like a black raven forever squalling on my shoulder. And all the good we might have done with your great office will be buried by this fitful storm of lust… or *love*…

EMA loses her footing momentarily but catches herself.

EMA Time offers no choice but to move on, dragging the past behind us. ...I will not be condemned by memory. I will keep pace with the day. And make tomorrow the fire that guides my step and burns away disgrace. I suggest you do the same.

Exit EMA.

KULAN No words for me. No prayers for Mita. No hopes but those I compel with my deeds. My time had just begun, and already I've stumbled behind. May whatever time remains see fit to teach me the meaning of my ways, of honor, and of love.

Exit KULAN.

Episode Twelve

Enter KAIN and MAU TANT.

MAU TANT Poor, pretty Mita. A fitting end to a slut seduced by love. How hopeless she must have been to cry to *you* for help. *(laughs)*
KAIN ...Yes. The desperate words of a dying whore.
MAU TANT And what is our next move, my Lord Kain?
KAIN The old man's dithering slows my ambition. The world does not wait on fear and wavering, but rolls over them. We must find a way to persuade my father to my side. Once his sword is in my hand, I'll cut the knot that binds my purpose. Until then, this waiting will gnaw my patience into scraps.
MAU TANT ...I have a suggestion, my Lord Kain.
KAIN What is it?
MAU TANT We see how quickly the fire of scandal spreads throughout the countryside. Weak minds bow gladly before rumor, and eagerly drink its bathwater. How thirsty the rabble would get if rumor delivered some truly burning message to their doorstep. When the people fear their own necks are at the stake, they'll drink whatever tonic we pour down their throats.
KAIN And what tonic do you propose?
MAU TANT ...What if: the Vohakta, moved by their hunger for revenge, are using the mask of surrender to lay low and dig beneath the tranquil surface of this happy time of peace. While we cultivate our newfound prosperity, they infiltrate the countryside like worms, laying the wick of their revenge. Then one

dark night, while we are snoring in our beds, they strike their match, surprise us in our slumber, and blow our city into bits! …Of course: this evil scheme must be prevented.

KAIN Yes, General Mau Tant, it must indeed. You are wise, my good General. Go recruit your most trusting men that they in turn may draft still more with hints and imaginings. While on their watch, perhaps their fear overcomes them, and they let slip to curious ears their suspicions of our devious neighbor's ill intent.

MAU TANT It will only take a few sparks to kindle our blaze.

KAIN Meanwhile, I'll call upon my cousin, Lord Lunenn. He has my father's ear, being the son of the old man's dear brother, lost to battle, from whom he often sought advice. Perhaps a word or two from dear nephew Lunenn describing the prevailing winds of mood that sweep the southern district he commands will tip the scales of my careful father's thinking, and bring about my swift ascent.

MAU TANT A good plan, my Lord Kain.

KAIN Let's put it to use. You: to your men, and I'll to my cousin. And let this waiting come to its end.

Exit KAIN and MAU TANT in opposite directions.

Episode Thirteen

Enter MADAM AJTZA with MORDUK.

MADAM AJTZA How you have managed to survive your trade this long I'll never know. A man who deals with such sharp things all day should not drink all night. It's a wonder you have any fingers left at all.

MORDUK Not your advice, Madam Ajtza, just your medicine.

MADAM AJTZA My advice is my medicine. The ointments and teas are only to help you swallow it. Now, hold out your hand.

MORDUK Eeeeeeeh!

MADAM AJTZA Oh! Little Apsu has a stronger stomach than you, old man. There. Hold that.

MORDUK …Tell me, when they hung the girl, was she brave?

MADAM AJTZA She was not silent, if that's what you mean.

MORDUK What did she say?

MADAM AJTZA Whatever she could. Now remember, I never said a word to you. You get your news from little birds.

MORDUK And where they fly off to I never can remember.

MADAM AJTZA Good. Drink this.

MORDUK What is it?

MADAM AJTZA It will help you forget your pain without forgetting how you got your pain, unlike your usual drink that blots out everything.

MORDUK Thank you Madam Ajtza.

MADAM AJTZA If you ask me, and you haven't, that girl should not have met her fate alone.

MORDUK You don't mean the Grand Lord Kulan should have hung himself?

MADAM AJTZA Why should she pay the full price for their crime, and he pays none?

MORDUK Who can punish a Grand Lord? He is the Grand Lord. Justice is his to deal out.

MADAM AJTZA You men, always sticking together. You don't even know why. It's just some instinct, like eating and sleeping and other things I won't bother mentioning. If you ask me, and you haven't, all Lords, Grand or not, should be made to suffer the torments they inflict on this world. If they had to live by the laws they make, things would be different.

MORDUK You are probably right. Then again, perhaps we are to blame.

MADAM AJTZA Why? What do we do?

MORDUK A very good question: what do we do? Let's see. Well, we talk a lot. Some of us more than others. For example, where is this rebellion you carry in your mouth? I never see it. It never comes. Wait! Madam Ajtza! I have a house filled with swords and daggers! We could storm the palace tonight! No, I think we're happy as we are, as long as our bellies are full. Lords make their laws. We follow them. The seasons change. If we really wanted it some other way, we'd have made it so already.

MADAM AJTZA Ajbi is right. You are a terrible man.

Enter MADAM AJBI with two soldiers, MOT and GAUT.

MADAM AJBI Madam Ajtza! This man needs your service.

MADAM AJTZA What is it?

MOT An accident at the port.

GAUT He singed his arm burning old planks.

MOT It wouldn't have happened if you hadn't distracted me.

GAUT Blame yourself, you clumsy ox.

MOT Always talking. And never working. He falls asleep on his watch, too.

GAUT That's a lie. I was praying.

MOT Oh yes, frightened by your nonsense. If you keep praying about it so much the Vohakta will hear you and think oh what a good idea.

GAUT Tssst!

MOT Madam Ajtza is the court doctor. She hears everything.

GAUT And what about her friends, you idiot.

MOT This pig gobbles up every silly rumor that drops in his trough. The Vohakta will be licking their wounds for years. We won't have to worry about them again for some time.

GAUT And you say I talk too much.

MORDUK Are the Vohakta making a plot?

MOT No!

GAUT You don't know that.

MOT I killed a hundred of them myself, without a scratch. Of course, now that the war is over I get burnt cleaning it up. Fate has a wicked sense of humor.

GAUT The Vohakta are like mice. If you see one, there are a thousand behind the wall. Waiting!

MOT Help him Madam Ajtza. His mind is filled with poison. And little else.

MADAM AJTZA Take this with you. Soak your arm again tonight and tomorrow.

MOT Thank you, Madam Ajtza. The Grand Lord Kulan made a wise decision. Much better than that other fellow – didn't care much for an ordinary soldier, and drank too much of his own medicine I think.

MADAM AJBI You will let us know if it comes time to worry.

MOT Worry about your needles, cloth maker.

MADAM AJBI Of course, if you need cloth of any kind, I will make you the best.

GAUT Everything you've heard stays in his room, or else. Do you understand?

MOT Stop beating your chest like a monkey. Don't listen to Gaut. He worries enough for the entire countryside. *(to GAUT)* Get going.

Exit GAUT and MOT.

MADAM AJBI So, the Vohakta are making plans.

MADAM AJTZA Don't believe that quivering monkey, Ajbi.

MADAM AJBI Why would he be so worked up if it weren't true?

MADAM AJTZA Who knows? Funny things happen to soldiers' brains during battle. Their heads never come back the same.

MORDUK The other one seemed confident. I'm sure there is nothing to worry about, Madam Ajbi.

MADAM AJBI The thought of ten more years. Oh! I don't even want to imagine it. I've already lost a husband. If I lost Olan as well, I'd sew myself in a bag and drop into the river. I worry about Olan. Always in his meadows.

Always buried in his thoughts. He needs a father to tell him what to do, not General Mau Tant.
MORDUK You worry too much, Madam Ajbi. The war is over.
MADAM AJBI This is what happens when you are a widow and mother, Morduk. I don't recommend it.
MADAM AJTZA If you ask me, and you haven't, Lady Ema should be Grand Lord. She's the only one in that palace with a clear head on her shoulders.
MADAM AJBI Her head must be very busy these days. And think of the poor Young Lady Ange. What must she think of all this?
MORDUK More worry. Lady Ema and Young Lady Ange have plenty of servants to help them survive.
MADAM AJBI Oh, you terrible man. If you had ever married and had children like a normal person you'd know what I mean.
MADAM AJTZA Enough of this chatter. Back to work, cloth maker. And you, less drinking with your sharp things. And when you two stop arguing and get married, let me know.
MADAM AJBI Oh! You terrible woman. *(to MORDUK)* Let go of me.

Exit ALL.

Episode Fourteen

Enter ANGE, alone in the meadow. She looks over the landscape for a long time, and follows some passing birds. Eventually she kneels, and falls deep into thought.

Enter OLAN. He watches ANGE for a long moment, then begins to paint her.

ANGE notices OLAN and stands.

ANGE How long have you been here?
OLAN These past few months. Don't move. This part's important. ...There.

ANGE and OLAN go to each other, embrace, and kiss.

OLAN The city is full of rumors.
ANGE My head is too full already to hear them. I don't know what the truth is any longer. I've always looked at your painting on my wall, and imagined the two strangers standing together were you and I. Now I'm not certain. Part of

me hates my father and Mita. But part of me understands them, because I know what it is to hide love.

OLAN Do you believe your father loved her?

ANGE I don't know. I believe she loved him. I saw it in her eyes. I heard it in her anger.

OLAN Her anger?

ANGE If she truly loved him, what did she do wrong but to let the truth be known?

OLAN Ange, your father is the Grand Lord, and she was the courtesan of the elder Grand Lord who appointed him.

ANGE But if she loved him. …I hear Mita crying out her questions in my dreams at night, and read them now in the lines of your painting which I've looked at a thousand times before and thought I knew every detail of. And I ask them now when I think of us meeting only in secret. And I ask myself: what is Justice that it does not count love among its laws? …I feel afraid for us.

OLAN We should not be afraid.

ANGE Olan, I am the daughter of the Grand Lord. You are a painter from the countryside whose mother sews cloth to sell. If our love is found out, we'll both be hanged – you by my father's hand, and me by my own.

OLAN It will not come to that. If your father loved Mita, he will understand.

ANGE And if my father loved Mita, then for my mother's sake I must hate him, and I will not have his sympathy.

OLAN Is your father really so cruel?

ANGE …I never thought the elder Lord Karug cruel until Mita told the truth.

OLAN Ange. You may think I am just a painter of strange meadows.

ANGE *(hugging him tight)* You are my poet. You are my friend. You are my pulse and my breath. You are my most precious kiss.

OLAN I am the son of a father killed by a war he believed in; who fought with a sword made by his neighbor; who died despite the medicine administered to him by an old friend, and the endless streams of prayer shed over him by a loving wife. I paint the meadow as I see it, because I see the world for what it is. And the world cares not a bit for us. We have no choice but to imagine something different. How else can we hope to change our ways?

ANGE And what should we imagine?

OLAN I painted us in the meadow, and here we are.

ANGE Then paint me in your arms. And paint our families all around us. Paint your father on a white star watching over us. And paint Mita, seated on a passing cloud, so she may see that the truth is not told for nothing.

OLAN I will do it. I will paint it all. I will paint everything.

OLAN and ANGE kiss, part, and back away from one another, exiting in opposite directions.

Episode Fifteen

Enter KARUG and LUNENN.

KARUG My doubt runs deep, nephew. I wish your father were still alive. My brother's counsel always brought me great confidence. His death was an unspeakable loss. Had I known it would happen, I would have stopped the war long before.
LUNENN My father would have chided you, dear uncle. The Great Forest bears the roots of our future. The trees grip the land with strong fingers, and bind prosperity to our countryside. It's vital that we keep The Forest whole. My father would agree.
KARUG And what would your father have to say about our Grand Lord Kulan?
LUNENN That I do not know. But if I may be so bold…
KARUG Yes, nephew.
LUNENN It is not my place to speak, but I feel I must.
KARUG What is it?
LUNENN …The Grand Lord Kulan held your sword with a benevolent hand. He gave confidence to a people exhausted by years of war. He made them feel well cared for. But now there are doubts. The truth about the courtesan's death has got about. And the Grand Lord's honesty is questioned. The people ask, if he would betray the elder Grand Lord himself, and so close on the heels of his establishment, why not us as well?
KARUG You have heard these rumors yourself?
LUNENN I speak only for the southern district under my command. But the river ports are a great meeting place. And I think the doubt is wide spread. Also, there is great fear the Vohakta are plotting their revenge.
KARUG Yes, I know. It is a concern.
LUNENN Even Mau Tant's soldiers keep a nervous watch. And they know the Grand Lord Kulan is *not* a soldier. If something were to happen…
KARUG If something were to happen…?
LUNENN If the Vohakta waged their rumored vengeance, and Kulan was still Grand Lord, I think the soldiers might not rally to his call. A fatal doubt would rapidly entrench itself throughout the countryside. And the people would not stand to bear a second war, regardless of Necessity.
KARUG I see.

LUNENN …I think my father would agree.

Episode Sixteen

> *The scene transforms. LUNENN bows his head and backs away. Enter KULAN, EMA, ANGE, KAIN, MAU TANT, MADAM AJTZA.*

KARUG In times of strife, we must have trust. In times of healing, we must have faith. The people look to us to guide and to protect them. They are the blood that fills the bones of our countryside. It is not wise to give them reason to doubt our strength of mind, or steadiness of hand. …Grand Lord Kulan.
KULAN My honored Lord.
KARUG You have cast doubt on my judgment, and shamed the title of Grand Lord. The people look to you now with uncertainty. The good work you have done for them will remain in place, and your lands you will keep. But my sword, and the honor it commands, I ask you to relinquish.

> *EMA and ANGE brace themselves and KULAN.*

KULAN …As you wish, my honored Lord.

> *A KUROGO takes the royal sword from KULAN.*

KARUG Lord Kain – my son.
KAIN Yes, my Grand Lord and father.
KARUG With my Most… Careful… Trust… I grant you your blood's right. I give to you my sword, and my sovereignty, and so pronounce you Grand Lord Kain.

> *The KUROGO hands the royal sword to KAIN, who takes it with barely concealed lust.*

KAIN I will not disgrace you. I accept the rights that my blood affords me, and immediately I do make my first decree. It is well known The Vohakta do not lie in slumber, but rather dig the trenches of their bloody retribution. We will not dally in a false peace while they advance on our wellbeing. We must take up the sword, and cut them down once and for all before they have the chance to lay their traps.
EMA No! This is too rash! The sword is barely warm in his hand!
KAIN Lord Kulan! You will silence your wife! Or did pretty Mita's death

relieve her of her duty to obey?

> *KULAN takes a step, reaching for his sword that is not there, and EMA braces him.*

KAIN My Lords and subjects hear me: the countryside will be protected! And for that protection we will shed more blood if need be. Time is a decisive God, and does not wait on hesitation. Let there be no question: there are two sides to this war. And those who stand against our will shall taste our blades with their throats!

> *Exit ALL but KULAN, EMA, and ANGE.*

EMA You see what your deeds have wrought? A wife may one day forgive a husband his disloyalty. But history does not forgive those who betray its trust, and will not forget.
KULAN May I live to earn your love again, and let history do what it must.
EMA I fear the Grand Lord Kain, and suspect his purpose. Attend his actions, my husband. Discern their truth, and bring it to light for all to see. In this way, you shall make your amends. And may Time see fit to grant you forgiveness… and love.

> *Exit EMA. ANGE touches KULAN'S hand. Exit KULAN. ANGE stands alone for a moment. Exit ANGE.*

End of Act Two.

Act Three
Episode Seventeen

> *Enter MORDUK, APSU, and MADAM AJBI.*

MADAM AJBI Morduk! Apsu! Have you heard the news?
MORDUK I've heard so much I can't keep track.
MADAM AJBI The soldiers are in dissent. They fear their numbers, and Lord Kain has called upon all young men throughout the countryside to be prepared if need be to join the ranks of his campaign. My nightmare is coming true. If Olan is sent off to join his father, I don't know how I'll live.
MORDUK Madam Ajbi, do not worry. It won't come to that. Don't let your mind run away from you.

MADAM AJBI Oh, where is Madam Ajtza?

MORDUK She would tell you the same thing.

APSU Don't worry, Madam Ajbi. Olan will be alright.

MORDUK If Grand Lord Kain's skirmish actually comes to pass, it will be sharp and swift. He'll have no need of Olan.

Enter OLAN.

OLAN Mother.

MADAM AJBI Olan! There you are! Where have you been? Don't ever leave my sight you terrible boy.

OLAN I'm afraid I might.

MADAM AJBI What do you mean?

OLAN It has been commanded by the Grand Lord Kain. The decree was posted in the center of town today. All young men must report to the Palace and General Mau Tant within the week.

MADAM AJBI *(grabbing OLAN)* No! Morduk! Give me one of your swords! General Mau Tant will have to cut through me if he wants to uproot what remains of my tiny family!

OLAN Mother, I'm only to report myself. It may not come to anything more.

MORDUK You see, Madam Ajbi. It's just a precaution.

MADAM AJBI Grand Lord Kain's plans are already exacting their fee. The farmers are charging double for a sack of grain. I will have to raise the price of my cloth because the dye maker has raised his for fear of need. Not one soldier has yet unsheathed his sword in the field, but in town: people are already piling their stocks of gold and grain.

MORDUK They waste their peace of mind to panic so soon.

MADAM AJBI No one has forgotten the signs. This is how war begins. And it will never end. Peace is just a moment's pause for aim.

OLAN We will not repeat our past mistakes, mother. We will find another way. This time it will be different.

MADAM AJBI Oh! I hope you are right, my dear son.

OLAN I will go to the Palace as the Grand Lord Kain commands, and put my name in General Mau Tant's ledger. Go home, mother, and weave your cloth with sturdy hope. We will change these times with our bare hands, and our will.

Exit ALL.

Episode Eighteen

Enter KAIN and MAU TANT.

KAIN From this remote place we can see the entire countryside at once. The Great Forest to the north, the city to the south. How quiet they both seem from here.
MAU TANT It is the quiet of readiness, my Grand Lord.
KAIN Have the people taken up our call, General Mau Tant?
MAU TANT They have.
KAIN Has there been much dissent?
MAU TANT I guarantee you: those who lack conviction will be persuaded. And those who would stubbornly cling to fear will be put at ease without delay.
KAIN Good. Go now, and wait for me at the city gate. This ridge affords a great perspective. I will stay a moment to reflect on it.
MAU TANT Yes, my Grand Lord Kain.

Exit MAU TANT.

KAIN The merchants are making their final sales. The customers carry their goods through the streets to home. The farmers herd in their oxen. Soon they will all meet around their fires and whisper through the smoke, then fall fast asleep.

Enter ZOHAK.

KAIN Who comes?
ZOHAK It is me, Zohak.
KAIN Ah, Lord Zohak. How considerate of you not to keep me waiting long.
ZOHAK Dressed in these ragged clothes I was able to move quickly. Your soldiers took me for a peasant. Are you alone?
KAIN General Mau Tant just left. Things seem to be proceeding well. I only await your decision.
ZOHAK If I wished to refuse you, I would not have come.
KAIN I knew you would accept my proposal. Your poor Grand Lord Mizhaktu *(meez-HAWK-too)* can't be paying you much these days.
ZOHAK It will take another ten years for the Vohakta to gain back their strength. My loyalty is not that patient. Besides, the old man blames everyone but himself for our loss. I never enjoyed his trust as I deserved, and with his renewed commitment to suspicion he has further earned my disdain, and my

treachery.

KAIN Does he not have reason to suspect you?

ZOHAK Of course. But why trifle over details?

KAIN And other than his suspicions, on what else does his mind gnash its teeth?

ZOHAK He feigns arrogance like a timid boy, guarding against all contradiction his ridiculous fantasy that what's left of his ragged little army will one day soon rise up to reclaim the Great Forest, and with it his own pathetic grandeur. Day and night he busies himself in futile preparations.

KAIN Well, how unwittingly then he betrays himself. His futile preparations will serve only to lend weight to the whispy rumors I have blown through our city streets. Preoccupied with his own schemes, he'll not see me coming. My thanks, Lord Zohak. You will keep me apprised of your Grand Lord's plans. And when your countrymen have all been cleansed away, you will have my thanks in deed and not just word.

ZOHAK Our agreement remains as we discussed?

KAIN You will govern the former Vohakta lands as our northern district, and there enjoy the full rights of a Lord's title.

ZOHAK And your General Mau Tant. Will he not be jealous?

KAIN Leave him to me. I'll not burden him with our bargain until the time is due. And if he complains: he can join your Grand Lord Mizhaktu in Hell's bitter exile.

ZOHAK And how do I know you will not betray me as well?

KAIN You don't. But why trifle over details? Go, Lord Zohak, we will talk again.

Exit ZOHAK. KAIN steps forward and surveys his city, then exits.

Episode Nineteen

Enter ANGE. Moments later, enter OLAN. They go to one another.

ANGE When I saw you outside the Palace gates today, it was all I could do to keep from calling your name and running to you just like this.

OLAN I was afraid I wouldn't find you here.

ANGE You took a risk in trusting that soldier with your note.

OLAN Trust for such a favor is easily bought these days. Had he not agreed he would have one less jug of wine to calm his nerves tonight. The threats of war grow louder every day.

ANGE I will talk to my father. I will ask him to have your name struck from

General Mau Tant's list.

OLAN And how will you explain such sympathy for a poor young painter from the edge of town?

ANGE By telling him the truth.

OLAN No, Ange, you don't know what he would do.

ANGE You asked me did I think my father would be cruel if we ever told him of our love. At first I was certain he'd have you put to death at once. But I see now how he looks at my mother. I can't explain what happened between him and Mita. But I have always known him to be an honest man. If I explained to him how much I love you, I know he could not look me in the eye and judge me harshly. He *would* understand. And he would help us.

OLAN You want to believe that's true.

ANGE Yes. You told me we have no choice but to imagine something different, and you were right.

Enter KAIN and MAU TANT, unseen.

OLAN Your father might be honest, but he also must be proud. He was shamed by Mita's death. He was shamed when he was so early stripped of his newly won title. Would he now stand the shame of his daughter's unworthy love?

ANGE It is not unworthy! You do us shame to say so!

OLAN Ange. We must hesitate. We will find a way. ...When General Mau Tant calls my name to join his ranks, I will bundle my clothes, bid goodbye to my mother, and meet you here again. We will escape in the night and live unknown in some far off countryside.

ANGE Let's go tonight. Why should we wait? Time is only growing darker with each passing day. The Grand Lord Kain makes certain of that. We will leave tonight!

OLAN But, what about my mother?

ANGE Go and say goodbye to her, gather your things. I'll go too and make my own preparations. Just before dawn we'll meet again, then disappear over the ridge into the Great Forest.

ANGE and OLAN stare at one another, tense with fear and excitement, then embrace.

OLAN Are we thinking too little, or too much?

ANGE Life is hopeless here, Olan. The Grand Lord Kain will have his war, and you will be marched to your death.

OLAN But you will leave behind every comfort you've ever known.
ANGE Yes. Except you.

ANGE kisses OLAN.

ANGE Go. We'll meet again, at dawn.
OLAN At dawn.
ANGE It seems a hundred years 'til then.

Exit ANGE.

OLAN What rash and sudden plans are these. But Ange's haste is right. The less time to think, the easier it is to do what I know we must. I will go to my mother, and bid her farewell. She will understand in time: an absent son is more easily missed than one in his grave.

KAIN and MAU TANT step forward.

KAIN I am afraid your mother will have to sacrifice her fond farewell.
OLAN My Grand lord Kain!
KAIN Treasonous boy. You would run from your duty. And with the Lord Kulan's daughter, no less.
MAU TANT A double treachery.
KAIN Young Lady Ange has learned well from her father. Or do deceit, weakness, and lust simply run in their family blood? What have you to say for yourself?
OLAN Nothing, my Grand Lord Kain, but to hope you will grant us your mercy.

KAIN leaps toward OLAN threateningly.

KAIN …What is that in your hand? A paintbrush. *(laughs)* The vain weapon of cowards and egoists. Of course our first deserter would be an artiste. … General Mau Tant, the young painter wishes his name to be struck from your list. Shall I oblige him now?
MAU TANT By all means, my Grand Lord.

KAIN stabs OLAN through the gut with his sword.

KAIN There! Young Traitor! You have your wish! You are released from your duty. I will leave you to share this news with your beloved Young Lady Ange.

KAIN pulls his sword from OLAN'S side. KAIN and MAU TANT exit.

OLAN Ange. We are betrayed.

OLAN scrapes something in the ground with the wooden end of a paintbrush.

OLAN I'll greet you at dawn with my unhappy news.

OLAN dies. Night passes. Dawn approaches. Enter ANGE with a bundle and small lantern.

ANGE How quickly these past few hours have gone, and yet how tedious the wait. I could not run here fast enough. Along the way I heard Olan's voice calling to me through the dark, heartening my anxious steps. Oh! He's here already. He sleeps, waiting for me. Olan, my love, wake up, before the restless sun betrays our flight. Oh! …Dead! Who has done this? Wake up, Olan! *(shaking him)* Tell me who has done this to you?
OLAN *(barely a breath)* Ange…
ANGE Olan? You said my name. I heard you say my name. Did you say my name! Say it **again**! *(pulling at him and clutching him to her)* Say my name, Olan! Say my name, Olan! Olan, who has done this to you? *(sees his fallen brush)* …Something is scratched in the earth. What does it say? *(with her lantern)* "Fight, don't weep." …Oh! Now I understand. A treason against our love! …I will obey you, my dear Olan. And from your wooden brush I'll carve a dagger to paint the meadow red! Goodbye, my tender love. This lantern will see me home. And there may it light the face of he whose wretched villainy ensures my own. Oh gods of Fate, give me your pity! Woe to one so young as I who trades her love for hatred!

Exit ANGE.

OLAN sits up. The KUROGO hand him a white paper umbrella. OLAN stands, holding the umbrella aloft, and makes his final exit.

Episode Twenty

Enter MADAM AJBI, who joins MORDUK and APSU.

MADAM AJBI Morduk! Apsu! Have you seen Olan?
MORDUK Not today, Madam Ajbi.
MADAM AJBI He was not in his bed last night. And this morning came the news! General Mau Tant has called his list early. The Grand Lord Kain has declared his second war on the Vohakta.
MORDUK Already.
MADAM AJBI Olan would not have left without saying goodbye. I know him. He must have caught wind and is making other preparations. Maybe he's hiding.
APSU Will Olan go to war?
MADAM AJBI Not if I can help it. We'll flee this wretched countryside before I send my Olan off in his father's footsteps.

Enter MADAM AJTZA.

MADAM AJTZA The day is come, my friends. The Grand Lord Kain couldn't wait a moment longer.
MORDUK Madam Ajbi has just told us the news.
MADAM AJTZA I am surprised you sound surprised, Morduk. What did you expect?
MORDUK A few more months or weeks, at least.
MADAM AJTZA If the Grand Lord Kain had had his way, the war would not have broken for breath until every last Vohakta lay quiet in their graves. He is a very determined man.
MADAM AJBI Madam Ajtza, have you seen Olan? He did not come home last night.
MADAM AJTZA I haven't seen him. I will pass through the meadow on route to the Palace, and if I see him there, I will tell him you are anxious for him to come home.
MADAM AJBI Thank you. And tell him what a terrible boy he is to worry his mother like this.
MADAM AJTZA He would know you'd said so, but I will tell him. Goodbye my friends.
MORDUK Madam Ajtza, you will let us know the latest news from the Palace when you return?
MADAM AJTZA Yes. ...But in the meantime, I suggest you pray the gods

for yourselves and us all. And take care to lay your plans well. These times may seem familiar to us, but I fear they are something quite new.

Exit MADAM AJTZA.

APSU Madam Ajtza is afraid.
MADAM AJBI We are all afraid, young Apsu. Oh, my Olan, where are you hiding? If you're off painting your meadow I'll tear your canvas into bits.

Exit MADAM AJBI.

APSU Morduk? Will General Mau Tant call us to fight?
MORDUK No, Apsu. He has no use for an old goat like me. Or a young fellow like you, either. We will be safe – with our swords and our knives. *(steps forward and surveys the landscape)*
APSU …What are you looking for, Morduk?
MORDUK I don't know, young Apsu.

Exit MORDUK with APSU by the hand.

Episode Twenty-one

Enter KAIN and MAU TANT.

MAU TANT The soldiers are gathered, my Grand Lord Kain. Young men from across the countryside have come to join their ranks. But it seems the Young Lady Ange and her painter were not alone in their disloyalty. My men have already caught dozens, some with their families, fleeing across the borders, and no doubt others have slipped under their noses.
KAIN Let those who are caught be sent to keep pretty Ange's young painter company. Can your men be ready tonight?
MAU TANT Yes, my Grand Lord.
KAIN Then tonight we launch our first attack. I will not make time for cowards who would cool our heated purpose.

Enter KULAN and EMA.

KULAN Grand Lord Kain! This call to arms is too sudden. You're early battle cry only serves to fan the people's doubts.

EMA Those who do not hide in their homes have already fled the countryside. And those who have 'til now stood in solidarity with your cause are made doubtful by those who flee.

KAIN So: conviction triumphs over shame, I see, uniting divided lovers arm in arm once more.

KULAN You are careless with the people's trust. Your haste will tear the countryside to shreds and wreck the peace we traded ten long years to gain.

KAIN You have always been naive, Lord Kulan. Wars are not waged for peace. For ten long years we fought for that Great Forest that gives our countryside a strength unmatched by any other. Our comfort and our prosperity are upheld in her mighty branches.

EMA You would cut those branches into coffins for mothers to bury their sons.

KAIN Good Lady Ema, I will not stand for treasonous contradiction.

EMA So it is treason now to contradict the Grand Lord's judgment.

> *KAIN puts his hand on his sword with a threatening gesture and KULAN steps in front of EMA.*

KAIN Lord Kulan, I suggest you reconsider the counsel you have given me. You will stand with me, or suffer the consequences of your betrayal. Go home, and take your faithful wife with you.

KULAN You will not dismiss us, Grand Lord Kain.

KAIN Your pathetic family is a joke. Your blood flows with weakness and deception.

KULAN You will not insult my family for the deceit that is mine.

KAIN ...Where was your daughter last night?

KULAN ...In bed.

MAU TANT *(laughs with KAIN)* You were right, Grand Lord Kain: the daughter has indeed learned well from her father, to catch him with his own tricks.

KULAN Why do you speak of our daughter?

KAIN Ask her yourself. Who am I to betray a child's little secrets?

> *Enter GAUT and MOT, with ZOHAK in their custody.*

MOT My Grand Lord Kain. General Mau Tant. We caught this swine at the border escaping in instead of out.

MAU TANT Too much to drink, careless traitor?

GAUT This cloak is a disguise. He is a Vohakta spy.

MAU TANT A Vohakta spy? *(drawing his sword)* Then why have you let him live this long? *(pulls off ZOHAK'S cloak)* Zohak! Mizhaktu has demoted you to his footman, I see. I am glad my soldiers did not slit your throat. I have longed for that privilege myself. My Grand Lord Kain, look what a fine catch my men have brought us?

ZOHAK My Grand Lord–!

MAU TANT Your Grand Lord can't hear you now.

ZOHAK My Grand Lord Kain!

MAU TANT Be silent! You will not speak to him. *(to KAIN)* He seeks to flatter you with false familiarity. Shall I kill him now? Or better yet: drag him to the public square for all to see! Behold! The rumors are true! The Vohakta snakes are crawling beneath our floorboards to strangle us in our beds!

ZOHAK My Grand Lord Kain, I can still help you! There is much I can do!

MAU TANT Don't beg, you pathetic dog.

ZOHAK Do not betray me! We had a bargain!

> *KAIN leaps with his sword to ZOHAK and sticks him in the side before just as suddenly slitting his throat.*

KAIN My apologies, General Mau Tant. I know you wanted that pleasure for yourself. But I could not stand to hear his sniveling any longer. And I will not bargain with petty villains. Lord Kulan. You see what happens to my enemies. I suggest you do not join them.

> *Exit KAIN.*

EMA What was that about a bargain.

MAU TANT Desperate men say what they must.

EMA Why did the Grand Lord Kain kill him so suddenly.

MAU TANT Why do you think? Zohak is an enemy Lord.

KULAN "I can still help you," he said. What did he mean by that?

MAU TANT You will not make such intimations.

EMA "I can still help you. There is much I can do. We had a bargain."

MAU TANT You risk your neck to suggest such treason.

KULAN The Grand Lord Kain would do anything to have his aim met. Why not take in the enemy!

MAU TANT He would not take such measures without my council!

EMA You flatter yourself General Mau Tant. What are you to him but his dog?

> *MAU TANT draws his sword and pushes EMA down. KULAN steps*

forward but is held back by GAUT and MOT.

KULAN General Mau Tant!
MAU TANT You are a traitor to your countryside! You spit on the Grand Lord Kain with outrageous slander! Dare you accuse your Grand Lord of conspiring with our most wretched enemy?
EMA Why do you trust a man so blindly who is driven by such ambition?
MAU TANT Hold your tongue or I will cut it from your mouth!
KULAN General Mau Tant! Put down your sword!
EMA Why are you so enraged? Why are you so afraid?

MAU TANT sticks EMA through the back. EMA stumbles to her feet and staggers for balance.

EMA I am killed. I am killed. This rash and bloody deed confirms our suspicions, my husband. Do not let me die for nothing. Fight. Fight.

EMA collapses and dies.

KULAN You. Murdering. Villain. You cowardly and wretched dog.
MAU TANT Do not taunt this angry dog. He will bite out your throat.
KULAN Your Grand Lord Kain has betrayed you. He has conspired with the very enemy he trains you to hate! And he will be done with you just as quickly when you too have worn out your use!

MAU TANT stabs KULAN in the gut. GAUT and MOT release their grip on KULAN and stumble away. KULAN grabs MAU TANT'S blade that is stuck in his gut.

KULAN You think the truth weighs so little that you can toss it to the air. It will rain down on you in bloody sheets, and the blood will be your own.
MAU TANT Go! Join your wife! I'll fetch your daughter and send her after you!

KULAN braces his grip on MAU TANT'S blade, forces MAU TANT to the ground and pushes him back several steps. KULAN heaves MAU TANT's sword from his belly, then collapses to his knees beside EMA.

KULAN Forgive me, my beloved wife, my dearest friend, and love. I wasted… so much… Time.

KULAN dies.

MAU TANT There. Dead, both of you. Let the gods do with you what they will.
MOT General Mau Tant. Could what they said be true?
MAU TANT Not you as well.
GAUT "I can still help you. There is much I can do. We had a bargain." He did say those things.
MAU TANT Now you listen to me! Clean up this mess. Then say goodbye to your mothers, and nothing else. You go tonight to fight for their safety, and the safety of your countryside.
MOT & GAUT Yes, General Mau Tant.
MAU TANT Not one word of Zohak's leaves this place. Do you understand?
MOT & GAUT Yes, General Mau Tant.
MAU TANT Good. To your business. Huht!

Exit MAU TANT. GAUT and MOT look over the bodies.

GAUT Let's abandon this place. I fear the Grand Lord Kain leads us to our deaths.
MOT We will take these bodies to their proper place. They deserve that much. Then let's go to our mothers as General Mau Tant advised, and join the peasants who flee under the moon's watchful eye.

GAUT and MOT administer the white umbrellas, first to ZOHAK who then exits, then to EMA, who does not make a full exit but waits upstage, and finally to KULAN, who begins his exit but stops when he sees EMA waiting. They exchange a look that is filled with feeling. EMA exits. KULAN exits.

Episode Twenty-two

Enter KAIN and MAU TANT with torches, swords drawn, and bloodied.

KAIN The fighting is fierce. Who would have guessed the beleaguered Vohakta still had such determination in their bones. Even from high on this ridge we can hear the clamor of battle rising up from the Great Forest below. How do your men stand, General Mau Tant? …General Mau Tant!
MAU TANT Those who remain fight valiantly, my Grand Lord.

KAIN Have we suffered many losses, then?

MAU TANT And many deserters.

KAIN Cowards! Fear poisons their resolve.

MAU TANT If my Grand Lord will permit my advice, I suggest we withdraw tonight and lay plans for a second, less sudden attack. With more warning and preparation, our men will fight more bravely. It would also give us time to dispel the fears that vie for their zeal, and their trust.

KAIN You are right. Boldness is braced by strategy. I have in fact long since already laid plans to bolster the countryside's support for our cause.

MAU TANT *Already* laid plans. And what are they?

KAIN You see the lights still glowing in the central markets, the Grand Port – both placed under my supervision for restoration by the former Grand Lord Kulan. Between them I had my men submerge small streams of powder, anchored at either end by enough barrels to blow them both to bits. The rumors of Vohakta snakes slithering beneath our floorboards will indeed have come to pass, and the people will rally to our cause. Tonight's retreat may even serve to further square their sentiments in our favor, since pride has always disliked the taste of defeat.

MAU TANT You would destroy the markets and port you have worked so long at rebuilding?

KAIN The Great Forest will provide us with a hundred ports and markets.

MAU TANT Why did you not share this plan with me before?

KAIN Don't be offended, General Mau Tant. As we have often agreed, such drastic measures are best kept quiet.

MAU TANT And when the war is done, what then?

KAIN When the parades have passed, the clean up will begin.

MAU TANT …Why did Lord Zohak say he could still help you?

KAIN *(turns slowly; then)* So, the plague of doubt infects you as well, my General.

MAU TANT Why did he mention a bargain?

KAIN Do not insult me, General Mau Tant.

MAU TANT And just before you strung up the courtesan Mita by the neck, she begged you to save her, she begged you to persuade your father with the truth. What was the truth?

KAIN I would not take such questions from Kulan and his nagging wife, and I will not take them from you.

MAU TANT Your secret plan to destroy the central markets and Grand Port is grotesque. How do you think you could get away with such a monstrous deed? Time would surely discover it.

KAIN Are you deserting me as well, General Mau Tant!

MAU TANT As your General, I ask that you tell me the truth.

KAIN And as my General you will do as you are told.

MAU TANT No, my Grand Lord!

KAIN Return to your men and order the retreat.

MAU TANT Not until my questions are answered!

KAIN Ask again and I'll answer with my sword.

MAU TANT Why do you give me reason to doubt you?

KAIN You will obey me, Mau Tant! Order your men to retreat!

MAU TANT *(a pause; then, toward the Great Forest)* Treason! We fight for treason! Save yourselves! Retreat men! Retreat!

KAIN cuts MAU TANT open in a few quick stabs. MAU TANT staggers forward, brandishing his sword and torch.

MAU TANT Retreat!

KAIN manages to take MAU TANT'S sword from him. MAU TANT collapses and dies, leaving his torch on the ground beside him. The KUROGO administer the white umbrella. KAIN watches as MAU TANT make his final exit.

KAIN You abandon me, General Mau Tant. *(stumbles in place.)* Now I am alone.

A flood of panic and rage wells up and comes out KAIN'S mouth in screams and through his two swords slashing at the air. The fit subsides.

KAIN I will order the army to retreat. Once the wind of this night's squall has died away, I'll prepare them for the battle that will dictate to Fate. All I have fought for will not be lost to traitors and cowards.

Enter ANGE. KAIN does not notice her.

ANGE My Grand Lord Kain.

KAIN turns to ANGE suddenly.

KAIN Ah. Young Lady Ange. Have you come to join the fight? Or is your heart still filled with your family's blood?

ANGE My heart is filled with hate. It is my eyes that are filled with blood, and tears.

KAIN Wipe your tears, and leave your blood to me.

ANGE You've had enough of my blood already. You murdered my mother and father.

KAIN All liars murder themselves on the edge of their own deceit.

ANGE You murdered the beautiful man who would have been my husband.

KAIN A paint-stained boy who would have been his countryside's traitor.

ANGE You murdered Mita for telling the truth.

KAIN *(laughs)* You give your father's whore too much credit. Mita was a master at her craft. She knew what she was doing when she agreed to seduce your weak-kneed father.

ANGE Agreed…!

KAIN Money buys anything. Even love. As it came to pass, my amorous little plot did not unfold as I had expected, but rather better. I should have given Mita something extra for a job well done. Alas, she died before I had the chance. And if she really did love him as she said, then she deserved her fate all the more. A whore deserves a whore's justice.

KAIN takes up MAU TANT'S torch and looks out over the countryside, his back to ANGE.

KAIN Look over this countryside, my sweet Young Lady. See all the lights that still glow in the windows. Whores staying up to count their gold. They'll do whatever they need to keep what they have, and will gladly sin for more.

ANGE fights back tears.

KAIN Poor sad Ange. *(back still turned, lifting his sword)* What can I do to relieve you of your sorrow?

ANGE Accept this gift I bring to you.

KAIN A gift.

ANGE When you took Olan's life, you forgot to take this.

ANGE pulls out OLAN's wooden brush, sharpened to a point, and stabs KAIN repeatedly in the back. KAIN staggers backwards as ANGE continues to stab him. ANGE pulls away as KAIN slashes with his sword and waves his torch, still stumbling. He collapses to the ground, seated. A moment's stillness. Just as suddenly as he collapsed, KAIN stands and staggers forward, slashing with his sword, only to collapse again.

KAIN Fight.

Again KAIN stands, staggering backward, slashing, only this time when he stops he manages to remain standing.

KAIN We must... fight!

The KUROGO exchange KAIN'S sword for a black umbrella. KAIN falls backwards over the ridge, plunging into the Great Forest. His torch flies through the air and is lost in the branches below. As ANGE speaks, the flickering of flames soon begins to glow over the ridge.

ANGE He is gone. But he was standing there just moments ago. Oh! Benevolent Time! God of speed! How quickly we forget your wrath. Kain's torch spreads fire through the branches of the Great Forest. They yield and fall! One day they will grow again, forgetting all that we've done in their name. The wind rushes the fire toward me. The flames will carry me on their waves to my father, my mother, Mita, and into the arms of my Olan. *(holding up OLAN's brush)* I add this terrible deed to my fistful of tears, and mourn the death of love!

ANGE steps forward and kneels to await the approaching flames, which the musicians have brought to a roar.

Enter MADAM AJTZA, MADAM AJBI, MORDUK, and APSU clutching bundles and one another's hands.

MADAM AJTZA We must hurry my friends! The flames are rapidly climbing!
MADAM AJBI We will die on this ridge! We must turn back!
MORDUK No! We will escape to the west! We will be safe there! Keep running!
MADAM AJBI We are running from everything we have ever known!
MADAM AJTZA Everything you know will burn to the ground if the Grand Lord has not butchered it already! Go Ajbi! Go! Run!

Exit MADAM AJBI, MADAM AJTZA, APSU, and MORDUK, all looking back at the countryside as they go, and none of them noticing ANGE.

The flames rush up over the ridge, a sea of red umbrellas spinning and bellowing, all carried by the CAST. ANGE closes her eyes and remains untouched as the fire rages and then eventually dies around her.

Everything is still and quiet. ANGE remains seated, eyes closed.

The KUROGO step through the corpses, collecting the red umbrellas and exchanging them for white umbrellas. ANGE opens her eyes and watches. KAIN is the last to receive an umbrella, and it is black. Stillness again. Then all the umbrellas open at once. All the ROYALS but KAIN rise and gather side-by-side in a line upstage. Then the PEASANTS all rise and gather in a line upstage, kneeling just downstage of the Royals. Then KAIN rises and joins the ROYAL line upstage.

The KUROGO now take kneeling positions at a distance on either side of ANGE, and await her need. ANGE looks at the KUROGO as they do this. ANGE looks out at the horizon.

The end.

I Am Hamlet

as written and performed by Hamlet

I Am Hamlet

The world premiere of *I Am Hamlet* was presented by Art Street Theatre at EXIT Stage Left, San Francisco, CA, on March 8, 2002. The production was directed by Kevin Clarke, with the following cast and staff:

HAMLET   Mark Jackson
OPHELIA   Temple Crocker

Set   Kevin Clarke and Mark Jackson
Costumes / Props   Temple Crocker
Lighting   Jason Ries
Sound   Jake Rodriguez
Stage Manager   Lorraine Olsen

Note

> *I AM HAMLET is to be performed by one actor in the role of Hamlet, who in turn plays all the other roles, until Ophelia's entrance at the end of the play. He should never leave the stage until the end of the play.*
>
> *Necessary props include a chair, a hardback copy of HAMLET, a ghost light, and Yorick's skull. Everything else can and should be mimed.*

Preshow

> *As the audience enters, restless classical music is playing. HAMLET is unobtrusively present onstage – stretching, reading a hardback copy of his play, thinking. There is a chair, a ghost light, and Yorick's skull. One wall is covered with tick marks in the classic clusters of five, such as those one might expect to find on a prison wall.*

PROLOGUE

> *Quite suddenly, music of grand, romantic proportions fills the theatre. A wash of colored light hits HAMLET who was kneeling USC reading his book. He looks up at the light, then out at the audience. At once he springs into action, setting his book upright on the chair, then rolling the ghost light over to the SL wall before returning to USC to find his first mark, back turned to the audience. Lights change suddenly to bright white, the music ends, and HAMLET spins to face the audience. After a*

moment a sly smile creeps across his face and, quite deliberately, he takes a very Shakespearean pose for:

HAMLET   To be, or–?

Waits for the audience to fill in the remainder of this infamous sound bite. Once they catch on, he continues:

HAMLET   that is the question:
Whether 'tis nobler in the mind to suffer
The slings and arrows of outrageous fortune,
Or to take arms against a sea of troubles
And by opposing end them. To die – to sleep,
No more; and by a sleep to say we end
The heart-ache and the thousand natural shocks
That flesh is heir to: 'tis a consummation
Devoutly to be wish'd. To die, to sleep;
To sleep, perchance to dream – ay, there's the rub:
For in that sleep of death what dreams may come,
When we have shuffled off this mortal coil,
Must give us pause – there's the respect
That makes calamity of so long life.
For who would bear the whips and scorns of time,
Th' oppressor's wrong, the proud man's contumely,
The pangs of dispriz'd love, the law's delay,
The insolence of office, and the spurns
That patient merit of th' unworthy takes,
When he himself might his quietus make
With a bare bodkin? Who would fardels bear,
To grunt and sweat under a weary life,
But that the dread of something after death,
The undiscover'd country, from whose bourn
No traveller returns, puzzles the will,
And makes us rather bear those ills we have
Than fly to others that we know not of?
Thus conscience does make cowards of us all,
And thus the native hue of resolution
Is sicklied o'er with the pale cast of thought,
And enterprises of great pitch and moment
With this regard their currents turn awry
And lose the name of action.
    So. Now that we've got *that* one out of the way. We can enjoy ourselves.

Let's to the play, shall we!

Ah. But, being the good host, I should first introduce myself. I am: Hamlet. Actor. Director. Critic. Comedian. Dramatist. Philosopher. Adventurer. Lover. Son. Nephew. Prince. Hero. And villain. I am Hamlet.

But where's the rest of the cast? Where is the set? Why am I talking this way? What about Shakespeare? What about the Wooden O and Kristin Linklater and Kenneth Brannagh? Perhaps you have come here tonight specifically to see *Hamlet*. Well: I am:

> *HAMLET executes a series of gestures and poses indicating the many sides of:*

HAMLET Hamlet.

And I am fated, it seems, to walk the night, as my father did before me, for having at my plot's end been snuffed out unaneled, no reck'ning made, sent to my account with all my crimes on my head, and therefore denied entrance through Heaven's gate. A questionable policy of bad timing, to say the least, of which I'll be certain to ask Saint Peter should we ever finally be introduced.

My Hell, as it turns out, is two fold. First, I am doomed to house and feed generations of academics who have built a dubious industry on the analysis of this Quarto and that Folio – rumor mongers with nothing better to do than reduce my life to a dry heap of words to be poked and prodded like the carcass of some fantastical dead beast, once so full of life and kicking, now packed in ice, sliced up, and divvied out to any soft set of hands in need of highbrow gesticulation.

Secondly, I have been made to stand idly by whilst various actors and directors take their stabs at me, dissecting William's loving and passionate rendition of my life and times and refashioning it to suit their own. Which I haven't anything against, per se. It's all very fascinating, and flattering, really, that so many people would care to tell and sit through my bio time and time again. I should be grateful. I've been played Elizabethan. I've been played uptown Manhattan. I've been played Weimar Republic. I've been played Imperial Japan. I've been played Cold War Poland. I've been played post-modern, whatever the hell that means. In short, my fifteen minutes have been wrapped around thousands of wrists, counted out in every language at every hour on the hour somewhere in the world at any given time. Never has anyone but Jesus had to listen to his story told more than I. Resurrected at regular intervals in the likes of Sarah Bernhardt, Sir Lawrence, Ethan Hawke, and endless others, I have watched my life paraded before me in various states of dress by these countless players.

But when *they* take their final bow and disappear behind that great curtain where they may rest in the warm glory of their deeds, I am left onstage, hung up in darkness, a thing of memory, until the next batch of patrons arrives to call forth the players once again.

For these many hundred years I have lived at the mercy of actors and PhDs. Lived, yes, but on borrowed blood.

So, I have decided to be a bit more proactive in regard to my Fate. And to that end I have devised for you this evening. From the horse's mouth, so to speak, I shall feed to your open ears my perspective on my life. To tell what happened as I first saw it, heard it, and felt it, and as I now see hear and feel it over and over again whilst others perform it night after night, season upon season, or grind it into dust beneath the pressure of their critical quills. Illumination is my aim! And, therefore, here we are again. In! The theatre!

Audience… Stage… Actor… Aaaaaand Curtain!

ACT 1, SCENE 2

> *Lights shift. Baroque or some such music. HAMLET, alone in the crowd, at Claudius' official gathering. He looks very much the Melancholy Dane. HAMLET's solitude is interrupted by a guest on his left who offers condolences, then another on his right, who offers congratulations.*

HAMLET By this time, the play has already begun. Unless it's one of those painfully faithful productions we're about five minutes into it by now as I make my first appearance, watching mine uncle, Claudius, now my father and King of Denmark, as he addresses the crowd at a rather confusing event. Is this an official gathering of the heads of state? A wedding reception? Or a funeral? Though I am of course inclined toward the latter, it *is*, methinks, a tidy and convenient hodgepodge of all three. Whatever it is, with my smiling mother's hand in his sweaty palm, his stomach no doubt freshly filled with chops of baby lamb washed down by goblets of my father's sweetest wine, King Claudius of Denmark looks out over his newly acquired subjects.

God! That it should come to this! That *my mother* would hang her lips evermore on that garbage, as if increase of appetite had grown by what it fed on, and my father but two months dead – nay, not so much, not two – A month! A little month! O most wicked speed! To post with such dexterity to incestuous sheets! Frailty, thy name is woman. A beast that wants discourse of reason would have mourn'd longer than *she* now hitch'd to my father's brother, and he no more like my father that I to Hercules. It is not, nor it can not come to good. …Nevertheless, there he stands: fed, wed, and peacock-like, and in this fattened and contented state, he now so solemnly coos:

CLAUDIUS Though yet of Hamlet our dear brother's death
The memory be green, and that it is befitted
To bear our hearts in grief, and our whole kingdom

To be contracted in one brow of woe,
Yet so far hath discretion fought with nature
That we with wisest sorrow think on him
Together with remembrance of ourselves.
Therefore our sometime sister, now our queen,
Have we, as 'twere with a defeated joy,
With an auspicious and a dropping eye,
With mirth in funeral and with dirge in marriage,
In equal scale weighing delight and dole,
Taken to wife. Nor have we herein barr'd
Your better wisdoms, which have freely gone
With this affair along. For all, our thanks.

Applause. CLAUDIUS takes a swig of wine and tosses the glass.

HAMLET   And yes of course everybody applauds. Wholeheartedly no less. For they would prefer to remain standing on whatever rung it is they're clinging to these days, and complimenting the new King's sudden marriage to a hot corpse's wife surely helps to ease those uneasy pangs of fear that accompany such a quick change of power.

Claudius goes on to chatter about the young Prince Fortinbras of Norway who has plans to march on Denmark and take her lands by force, and who nobody really cares about, but he's got to come on at the end and say a few words to wrap things up since everybody else of royal note is dead by that point; so we must plant his seed now, mention him periodically over the course of the evening, and then in the end pretend he's not an anti-climax.

So, after a few military dispatches on the matter of this impending Fortinbras, and some other banter with Laertes, brother of my– *dear* Ophelia, in which Claudius grants the lad permission to go romp about in France, my kind Uncle Father then turns the eyes of the entire room on me. Thank you Claudius. He says:

CLAUDIUS   But now, my cousin Hamlet, and my son–
HAMLET   A little more than kin, and less than kind.
CLAUDIUS   How is it that the clouds still hang on you?
HAMLET   How is it? How is't? What, have you not read the script? Are you that lazy you bloated sandbox villain? Adulterate beast! Traitorous thieving prick!

But of course I don't say that. Instead, I say something like, no, the clouds aren't hanging over my head. Rather, I am too much in the sun. Get it? Son? A little play on words? I would rather not *be* your son and therefore I stand too much *in the sun*? Entire books have been written about that line you idiotic fraud! Do I have to draw you a diagram? My father did just *die* yuh know! So

I'm not feeling particularly social at the moment! Please do not direct the light of all eyes unto me when I would much prefer my privacy!

Of course I don't say that either. I stand still, not unlike: this, whilst my lipsticked hair-done strapless silver-sequined garter-underneath no-panties mother offers her comforting hand and loving plea:

GERTRUDE Good Hamlet, cast thy nighted colour off,
And let thine eyes look like a friend on Denmark.

HAMLET Meaning *him*. As if so small a man could embody so great a thing as nations. She goes on:

GERTRUDE Do not forever with thy vailed lids
Seek for thy noble father in the dust.
Thou know'st 'tis common: all that lives must die,
Passing through nature to eternity.

HAMLET Ay, madam, it is common… Like your impatient lust. Like your wanton hunger for this foul meat. You who but one month ago cried like Niobe as you followed my poor father's body draped in the black regalia of mourning. I should commend you for your political proficiency. Tears are good politics indeed when the king your husband lies warm in his cold new womb that never will bare fruit but for worms and maggots!

But it is too early in the play for such an outburst as this. Therefore:

Ay, madam, it is common.

GERTRUDE If it be,
Why seems it so particular with thee?

HAMLET Seems, madam? Nay, it is. I know not 'seems'.
'Tis not alone my inky cloak, good mother,
Nor customary suits of solemn black,
Nor windy suspirations of forc'd breath,
No, nor the fruitful river in the eye,
Together with all forms, moods, shapes of grief,
That can denote me truly. These indeed seem,
For they are actions that a man might play;
But I have that within which passes show,
These but the trappings and the suits of woe.

What I am saying is so transparent. That Gertrude and Claudius cannot hear it for the accusation it is is testament to the depths of their imbecility. Or their self control. For of course at this point in the play their taking full note of my sordid implications would behoove neither them nor the plot. And therefore they remain conveniently dumb. And you, the audience, are at once made my sole conspirator. Shhhh. So, whilst Claudius then prattles on, offering me his advice and sympathies and bad breath, I can hear only the hissing of steam as it shoots from my heart like a jet stream straight to my head. Luckily this unbearable scene is now over. The room clears before I must suffer any more toxic gas from rank mouths, or the sore eyeful of my mother so stupidly grinning at that man's side and no longer the mother whose bossom I once clung to and fed at and cried on and felt safe against. That's all over now. She is a living example of Bertolt Brecht's "Alienation Effect." She has become strange. She has married another and therefore is no longer My Mother but a woman.

And now I: am alone…

O that this too too solid flesh would melt,
Thaw and resolve itself into a dew,
Or that the Everlasting had not fix'd
His canon 'gainst self-slaughter. O God! God!
How weary, stale, flat, and unprofitable
Seem to me all the uses of this world.

Or so they did until what happens next! Enter Horatio. My good and dear friend. Perhaps the most perfect friend that History has ever seen. Always ready with a laugh for my jokes, a patient sponge for my thoughts, a hand-on-the-shoulder-squeeze for my woes. A bit boring. But steeped in his endless devotion to me. Friend. Horatio. Now he comes to, one: give me my purpose, and two: kick this play into gear.

HORATIO I think I saw him yesternight.

HAMLET he says. "Saw? Who?" I ask.

HORATIO The king, your father.

HAMLET Ah! What?! The king my father? For god's love let me hear!

Horatio explains how he and two secondaries, Marcellus and Bernardo, did see the apparition of my father walk in solemn march upon the platform where in the dead and middle of the night they did make their watch. And! And! Apparently this was fast becoming a regular habit of my father's, given that he'd been seen thus marching twice already, his face pale, a countenance more in sorrow than in anger, and arm'd from tip to toe. To which I said, "That's strange. *(snaps)* I would that I had been there. I will watch tonight. For perchance 'twill walk again."

ACT I, SCENE V

HAMLET So, that night, hoping for a glimpse of the miracle described unto me, I hurry myself to the platform to wait in biting cold.

Staring into the black night, my breath billowing from my lips like the coattails of ascending spirits, I only half listen to the obligatory banter between myself Horatio and Marcellus… In the distance can be heard the carousing of the new king, his widow-wife, and selected guests as they drain their draughts of Rhenish, swagger about in dance, and sound the trumpets in triumph of their conjugal pledge. 'Tis a foul Danish custom, this bawdy post-nuptial drunkenness. Pfff!

HAMLET shakes his head and looks away from the distant carousing. Quite suddenly he is the GHOST of his father and an ominous chord of music strikes the air. Then as HAMLET:

HAMLET Ah! Look, it comes!

The GHOST again for a moment. Then again as HAMLET:

HAMLET Angels and ministers of grace defend me! It is the king! My father!

The GHOST reaches out and beckons HAMLET to follow. HAMLET then says:

HAMLET Look with what courteous action it beckons me to go away with it!
HORATIO But do not go with it, my lord, do not!
HAMLET Yea but I will! What have I to fear? I do not set my life at a pin's fee! Though Hell itself should gape I'll follow it!

A bit impatient now, the GHOST beckons HAMLET once again to follow.

HAMLET It waves me forth again. Go on, spirit, I'll follow thee!
     And so I do. Now, different productions handle this next and most quick transition in various ways. Most often, however, in order to denote the change of location, I am simply made to run off in one direction, and, within a handful of lines from Horatio and Marcellus, must scramble through the backstage clutter and re-enter on the opposite side of the stage. Like this.

HAMLET demonstrates.

HAMLET And now we're off in the woods someplace where the Ghost and I may talk in private, and he says:
GHOST Mark me.
HAMLET O but I will. I will.
GHOST The hour is almost come
When I to sulph'rous and tormenting flames
Must render up myself.
HAMLET O, Alas, poor ghost–!
GHOST Pity me not, but lend thy serious hearing

To what I shall unfold.
HAMLET   And then he drops the bomb.
GHOST   'Tis given out that, while sleeping in my orchard,
A serpent stung me – so the whole ear of Denmark
Is by a forged process of my death
Rankly adus'd – but know, thou noble youth,
The serpent that did sting thy father's life
Now wears his crown!
HAMLET   Ah-HA! I knew it! O my prophetic soul! My uncle!
GHOST   If thou didst ever thy dear father love
Revenge his foul and most unnatural murder.
HAMLET   O Murder!
GHOST   Yes Murder. Murder most foul.
If thou hast nature in thee, bear it not.
Let not the royal bed of Denmark be
A couch for luxury and damned incest.

A cock crows in the distance. The GHOST appears startled.

GHOST   Adieu. Adieu. Adieu. Remember me.
HAMLET   Remember thee?
Yea, from the table of my memory
I'll wipe away all trivial fond records,
All saws of books, all forms, all pressures past
That youth and observation copied there,
And thy commandment all alone shall live
Within the book and volume of my brain,
Unmix'd with baser matter! Yes, by heaven!
I swear it will be so!
GHOST   Very well.

Exit GHOST.

HAMLET   Bye dad!
O villain, villain, smiling damned villain!
That one may smile, and smile, and be a villain!
At least I am sure it may be so in Denmark.
So, uncle, there you are. Now to my word.
I have sworn it. Rest, rest, perturbed spirit.
But how am I to do't? This broken heart
Is called upon to beat with even pulse,

And this distracted globe t' arrive at quick
Decision; this half paralyz'd sinew
To nerve itself to action. And what if
This spirit be a devil that hath pow'r
T'assume a pleasing shape, yea, and perhaps,
Out of my weakness and my melancholy,
Abuses me to damn me?
The time is out of joint. O cursed spite,
That ever I was born to set it right.

HAMLET thinks hard on't. Then:

HAMLET Ah! Never speak of this I now impart,
Never, so help you mercy, no matter
How strange or odd some 'er I bear myself –
As I perchance hereafter shall think meet
To put an antic disposition on.
And you, at such time seeing, never shall give out
That you know aught of me – this do swear.

When they do, HAMLET gives a thumbs up and darts away, stops suddenly and turns with a thought:

HAMLET There are more things in heaven and earth, dear friends, than are dreamt of in our philosophy.
    Or in the theatre, for that matter.
    What you don't see in William's play are the sleepless nights that follow. Sleep?! After that? Not a chance. Not a wink. I'm a Wittenberg lad, you know: to my study I dutifully fly to seek out every word written on the spirits, every syllable detailing the plight of souls caught betwixt Hell and Heaven. Mine eyes made eager slits by dying candles, my head do I fill with images of mine uncle and his little vial of poison, my mother slicked by his sweat on a bed of tangled sheets, my father at the moment of his untimely demise and now toiling amidst the unimaginable. Images too horrible for weak words! But: I should have no need of words. For now I have my purpose. Uh? Now I have: my Super Objective, as comrade Stanislavsky would say. To expose Claudius. No, not just expose. Murder. Assassinate. Kill. …So what do I do?

ACT II, SCENE I

HAMLET I go visit my girlfriend. This Shakespeare also does not let you see, but rather takes the more ambiguous route by having Ophelia describe our meeting, and my bizarre behavior therein, in tormented detail to her father, Polonius, my Uncle King's right hand man. This way, by denying direct witness to the curious event itself, Shakespeare forces you to wonder at Ophelia's words what my true intentions are – thus providing the subject for tens of thousands of Masters Faeces– *theses*. Am I mad indeed, mad in craft knowing that Ophelia will run to Polonius to set my public lunacy in motion, or am I bidding a final farewell to my first love since I now have a greater purpose in life that requires my full attention?

> *HAMLET shrugs, then smiles knowingly at the audience for a moment. Then...*

HAMLET So, Ophelia– …Ophelia describes to Polonius how I came to her in her chamber. You've heard it before. How I was disheveled. How I held her by the wrist, perused her face at length, and raised a sigh so piteous and profound, and how with my head famously o'er my shoulder turn'd I seem'd to find my way without my eyes as I left the room. "Oh what does it mean?" Quick: propose a theory, write a book, scrunch brow, squeeze pen, pour like a flood over analyses past. "What is Hamlet doing?" The actor must decide. Mad indeed? Mad in craft? Bye-bye Love? What's it going to be? These are the choices the actor must make. It's theatre. It's all about Making Choices! This is the actor's craft, you see. The actor must do on stage what we cannot do in life: make a decision! Not always an easy thing to do. To commit to one's actions? In public? Yes, commitment makes the actor vulnerable to critique. "Oh please, dahling, did you learn nothing at A.C.T.?" Perhaps this is why the theatre is so well stocked with neurotics clutching at their cigarettes and suckling from mugs of toxic caffeine, people who seem to lack a protective layer of skin to defend their nerves from the outside world constantly staring, judging, probing, pawing, stabbing, grinding them down. The stage exposes the actor with its proscenium lens and we who sit comfortably in the dark are faced with the fact that we are all but mediocre. That we are but men and women…

Well. Man delights not me. Mm-mm. No, nor woman neither. In which case, what need have I for theatre, the subject of which *is* man and woman as they toil between earth and Heaven? I somewhat resent the theatre, actually. Not only for being my monument *and* my hell. But for the implication. All these actors doing extraordinary things, brimming with wit that one can never achieve in daily life. Must we pedestrians be expected to look and sound on a daily basis as they do? We haven't the means. They have costume designers, vocal coaches. They've spent tens of thousands of dollars at Yale practicing spontaneity. They're not actually that witty. Some penniless writer pushed out that wit like a constipated turd over the course of weeks, months. That can't be easy. But on stage it must look: effortless.

A brief ballet in which HAMLET stabs his victim multiple times and with exquisit grace. Then...

HAMLET Yet why is it that we cannot bring ourselves in life to utter what these actors mutter so easily, to do the things they do that we only dare achieve vicariously through them? Is it not monstrous that a player, here, but in a fiction, in a dream of passion, can force his soul so to his own conceit that from her working all his visage wanns, tears in his eyes, distraction in his aspect, a broken voice, and his whole function suiting with forms to his conceit? And all for what? For nothing. What could he do had he the motive and cue for passion that I have, for example? Why he would drown the stage with tears, cleave the general ear with horrid speech, make mad the guilty and appall the free, confound the ignorant, and amaze indeed the very faculties of eyes and ears... Yet I, a dull and muddy-mettled rascal, do nothing. No matter how many cuts they make, now matter how they dress me up, I never really get to Act Five any differently. Always the same string of soliloquies unwinding around the globe over and over and over. Oh, this is most brave, that I, the son of a dear father murder'd, prompted to my revenge by heaven and hell, must like a whore be made to unpack my heart time and again with *words!*

What am I waiting for?! "Do it! Do it Hamlet! Expose the villain! Draw your dagger and carve him open ear to ear! Fill his head with your venom as he did fill your father! Purge the pestilence for us all! Unlock the prison gates of Denmark and free us from our rotten mediocrity! O vengeance!" Sounds good. So, what, do I simply accuse him over dinner? Huh? "Uncle, could please pass the peas? Thank you. Oh and by the way, I happen to know that *you killed my father you dirty bastard! Take this!*" And shove a breadstick through his head?

How will I do it? Ah! I'll put an antic disposition on. Yes, that will buy me some time, madness providing license for all sorts of odd behavior whilst I put my dead father's allegation to the test. Can't be too careful now can we. Yes, I'll shake them, slowly. I'll have my fun with them all whilst I drum up the what, *courage?!*

ACT II, SCENE II.

HAMLET So, look you now, here comes Polonius, flush with Ophelia's news of my madness and eager to see for himself. I'll try out my new mental state on him.
POLONIUS How does my good Lord Hamlet?
HAMLET Pretending to read a prop book, I proceed to befuddle Polonius with words, words, words. Words like Conception. Honest. Slanders. Purging. And other such pungent clues that I know the tedious old fart will never sniff

out.

POLONIUS Oh, ehm, heh, what is the matter, my lord?

HAMLET Between who?

POLONIUS I mean the matter that you read, my lord?

HAMLET Oh… I then banter a bit about witless old men to which he says, aside,

POLONIUS How pregnant sometimes his replies are. Though this be madness, yet there is method in't. I will leave him and contrive a means of meeting between him and my daughter. My lord, I will take my leave of you.

HAMLET Fine. To which I reply, "You cannot, sir, take from me anything that I will not more willingly part withal – except my life."

POLONIUS does not appear to get it.

HAMLET "Except my life!" …Except my life.

We hear a drop of water fall.

HAMLET I am then informed that a travelling troupe of players has arrived and will perform for the court a play of any sort we like. Hmm.
  Hmm!
  I have heard
That guilty creatures sitting at a play
Have, by the very cunning of the scene,
Been struck so to the soul that presently
They have proclaim'd their malefactions.
And murder, though it have no tongue, will speak
With most miraculous organ. I'll have these players
Play something like the murder of my father
Before mine uncle. I'll observe his looks;
I'll tent him to the quick. If a do blanch,
I know my course. The play's the thing
Wherein I'll catch the conscience of the King!

ACT III, SCENE I

HAMLET Ha! I took Intro to Playwriting at Wittenberg. I can knock off a little drama cleverly echoing the events of my father's murder. It doesn't have to be that good, really. It's agitprop.
  Now. Polonius and Claudius at this point drag Ophelia deeper into the

swamp of their intrigues. They instruct her to return old love letters to me in the hopes that I'll flip out and give 'em a show like the one she described a few scenes back. They want proof, with their own eyes, since Ophelia is just a silly girl and her good word not good enough.

Now, Ophelia– …Ophelia has very little stage time for a character of her renown. Her story is very… Well, books have been written about *her* as well. And songs. And many a painter has described her plight. Yet she isn't given much chance to speak for herself. This is Shakespeare's choice.

Though dramaturgically it does make sense, you know, because I am so preoccupied with my super objective, and it is, after all, my play…

At any rate. There I am, lost in thought, thinking about my new play, contemplating life's mysteries, to be or not to be, that sort of thing. Claudius and Polonius have hid behind a curtain or, depending on the production, a see-through mirror. And in walks: Ophelia.

> *HAMLET gestures toward Ophelia's "entrance" through the curtains USC, though he does not embody her as he has other characters. "They" counter one another slowly.*

HAMLET …We talk. I uh– by her nervous behavior I catch on that she is– in cahoots with Claudius and Polonius. "Et tu, Ophelia? Whom I did love once? You are capable of treachery as well. Frailty thy name is once again woman." This was my thinking. *Is* my thinking, in the play. And so I berate her soundly for being of the sex of sirens, command that she "get thee to a nunnery" rather than pollute the world with more toxic humanity, and leave her bobbing in the wake of my wrath. And that's that.

ACT III, SCENE II

HAMLET From there I run off to direct the players in my new play since it must needs be ready by this evening.

Now, Shakespeare gives me a long passage to them that begins famously with "Speak the speech, I pray you," and goes on with what we presume are his thoughts about actors and acting. Why would I lecture a troupe of actors about basic acting techniques as Shakespeare has me do? They're not undergrads. They're professionals. They're on constant tour. They're giving a command performance before the king and queen for god's sake. They know what they're doing. I prefer the productions that cut this bit. It's rather embarrassing.

So, curtain time approaches. My audience is finding their seats. I grab Horatio by the arm and tell him:
There is a play tonight before the King;
One scene of it comes near the circumstance

Which I have told thee of my father's death.
I prithee, when thou seest that act afoot,
Observe my uncle. Give him heedful note.
HORATIO Yes my lord,
HAMLET etcetera, and off he goes to find his seat as the lobby lights blink.

I call the play: *The Mousetrap*. 'Tis a knavish piece of work, but what o' that? Claudius must be pinned, and I intend catch him and stick him until he squeals. I have already, and continue to do so e'en in this scene, used my counterfeit madness to slip all sorts of needles into his ear and those of his willing and/or unknowing cohorts: Polonius, Ophelia, my Mother, other sundry members of the court sent to spy on me morning noon and night! O God let this play be the final act that nails that thief to the stage where he trods beneath his stolen crown.

Sound of applause...

HAMLET And so it begins.

Now, Claudius is not entirely an idiot. Like a good politician-actor he has studied his craft. He may lack any integrity whatsoever but he did manage to plot his bum square on the throne without too much trouble. When the critical scene of my little drama unfolds, he's not going to stand up and
CLAUDIUS Ho bloody fuck Hamlet knows what I– *(covers mouth)*
HAMLET Not at all. He's no Iago, but he is a general. He's not going to AAGH! and soil his knickers. So: when the crucial moment arrives and the players begin to enact the poisoning, I watch... Horatio watches... And Claudius...

HAMLET demonstrates CLAUDIUS reacting to the unfolding scene.

HAMLET And then, when the prop vile of green food coloring finally tips and spatters into the player king's ear, Claudius:

CLAUDIUS stands.

HAMLET Me: Ah HA! ...Gertrude:
GERTRUDE How fares my lord?
CLAUDIUS Give me some light. Away.

CLAUDIUS turns and leaves.

HAMLET Horatio! O good Horatio, I'll take the ghost's word for a thousand

pound. Didst percieve? Upon the talk of the poisoning?
HORATIO Very well, my lord.
HAMLET But no sooner have I popped that stinking boil and exploded with victorious glee then Claudius has set upon me Rosencrantz and Guildenstern, two old friends of mine now tugged by Herr Uncle's golden strings. One of them says – which one doesn't matter –
ROSENCRANTZ OR GUILDENSTERN The Queen your mother desires to speak with you, my lord.
HAMLET Good. Then I know *she* watched the play as well. *(to Ros or Guild)* I will come to my mother by and by! Exeunt all but Hamlet!

Exit Rosencrantz and Guildenstern.

HAMLET 'Tis now the very witching time of night,
When churchyards yawn and hell itself breathes out
Contagion to this world. Now could I drink hot blood,
And do such bitter business as the day
Would quake to look on!
But soft, what light through yonder window–!
Wait, wrong play. Damn those summer reps. Ah:
And do such bitter business as the day
Would quake to look on! Soft, now to my mother.

ACT III, SCENE III

> *HAMLET storms through the halls toward the Queen's closet. He notices something through an open doorway and stops suddenly, pressing his back to the wall. He peeks around the open door into the room. His eyes widen. He mouths to us, "Claudius," pointing, then mocks Claudius praying. CLAUDIUS must have moved, for HAMLET ducks away. He peeks around the doorway again and becomes more focused.*

HAMLET Now might I do it pat, now a is a-praying.

> *HAMLET looks down the hall in both directions, then carefully steps into the doorway.*

HAMLET And now I'll do't.

> *HAMLET draws his sword and begins to creep toward CLAUDIUS.*

HAMLET And so a goes to heaven;
And so I am reveng'd!

> *HAMLET stabs CLAUDIUS viciously. CLAUDIUS resists. HAMLET does not relent. But at the peak of his victory his expression suddenly changes and he stops cold.*

HAMLET Now wait a second:
A villain kills my father, and for that
I, his sole son, do this same villain send
To heaven.
Why, this is hire and salary, not revenge.
A took my father grossly, full of bread,
With all his crimes broad blown, as flush as May;
And how his audit stands who knows save heaven?
But in our circumstance and course of thought
'Tis heavy with him. And am I then reveng'd,
To take him in the purging of his soul,
When he is fit and season'd for his passage?
No.
Up, sword, and know thou a more horrid hent:
When he is drunk asleep, or in his rage,
Or in th' incestuous pleasure of his bed,
Or any act that hath no relish of salvation in't,
Then trip him, that his heels may kick at heaven
And that his soul may be as damn'd and black
As hell, whereto it goes. My mother waits.

ACT III, SCENE IV

> *HAMLET continues down the hall. Stops. Almost goes back.*

HAMLET No. Mother. Keep your mind on the mother. Mother! Mother!
  Now, in my Mother's chambers, a very famous scene, Polonius has been instructing her as to how to deal with me:
POLONIUS Tell him his pranks have been too bold to bear
And that your Grace hath stood between
Much heat and him. I'll silence me e'en here.
Pray you be round with him.
GERTRUDE I warrant you, fear me not.

HAMLET Mother! Mother!
GERTRUDE Ah! Withdraw, I hear him coming!

> *POLONIUS hides behind a curtain. GERTRUDE attempts a casual air. HAMLET storms toward the bed chambers and enters:*

HAMLET Mother! Mother!
Now, mother, what's the matter?
GERTRUDE Hamlet, thou hast thy father much offended.
HAMLET Mother you have my father much offended!
GERTRUDE Come, come, you answer with an idle tongue.
HAMLET Go to, you question with a wicked tongue.
GERTRUDE Why, how now, Hamlet? Have you forgot me?
HAMLET No, by the rood, not so.
You are the Queen, your husband's brother's wife,
And, would it were not so, you are my mother.
GERTRUDE Nay, then I'll set those to you that can speak.
HAMLET Come, come, and sit you down.
You go not till I set you up a glass
Where you may see the inmost part of you!
GERTRUDE What wilt thou do? Thou wilt not murder me?
Help, help!

> *Behind his curtain, POLONIUS listens to the commotion in distress. He tries to get the attention of someone far off and in doing so makes a bit of noise. HAMLET stops whatever he's doing to GERTRUDE. He's heard something. GERTRUDE looks guilty. HAMLET gestures for GERTRUDE to stay silent. HAMLET draws his sword and carefully stabs his way along the curtain, closer and closer to POLONIUS, who stands still and mortified. When HAMLET hits home, POLONIUS squeals. HAMLET drives the sword in deeper, then rips it out. He beholds the bloody blade and wipes it off with his hand. He's done it!*

GERTRUDE O me, what hast thou done?
HAMLET Nay, I know not. Is it the King?
GERTRUDE O what a rash and bloody deed is this!
HAMLET Almost as bad, good mother,
As kill a king and marry with his brother?!
GERTRUDE As kill a king?
HAMLET Ay, lady, it was my word.

> *HAMLET rips open the curtain triumphantly but is terribly disappointed to see that it's only POLONIUS.*

HAMLET Thou wretched, rash, intruding fool. Farewell.
I took thee for thy better. Take thy fortune:
Thou find'st to be too busy is some danger…

> *He closes the curtain again. He looks at the blood on his hands, wipes it off on his shirt. Then looks at GERTRUDE.*

HAMLET Leave wringing of your hands
And let me wring your heart; for so I shall
If it be made of penetrable stuff.
GERTRUDE What have I done, that thou dar'st wag thy tongue
In noise so rude against me?
HAMLET Such an act
That blurs the grace and blush of modesty,
Calls virtue hypocrite, takes off the rose
From the fair forehead of an innocent love
And sets a blister there!
GERTRUDE Ay me, what act?!
HAMLET Now, there are many ways to do this next bit: in which I show Gertrude a picture of my Father and a picture of Claudius so as to compare the one man 'gainst the other. Numerous ways to go about it. I've seen 'em all. I could have a locket strung around my neck with my father's picture inside, and Gertrude one with a picture of Claudius. A very common solution. And then we fumble about with these bitty little props that can't be seen past the first few rows – though of course in this theatre that wouldn't matter so much.[1] But over at the *Geary*[2] you get subscribers toward the back saying "What's he doing to her now, Martha?" …Or, I could have Dad tattooed on my arm, and Claudius on Gertrude's butt. Then of course we'd have to look at Gertrude's butt. Keep it simple. Two paintings hung on either wall.
Look here upon this picture, and on this,
The counterfeit presentment of two brothers.
See what a grace was seated on this brow,
Hyperion's curls, the front of Jove himself,
An eye like Mars to threaten and command,
A combination and a form indeed

---

[1] *This line assumes the performance is being given in a modest venue.*
[2] *The name of the largest local theatre may be substituted.*

Where every god did seem to set his seal
To give the world assurance of a man.
This was your husband. Look you now what follows.
Here is your husband, like a mildew'd ear
Blasting his wholesome brother. Have you eyes?
Could you on this fair mountain leave to feed
And fatten on this moor? Ha? Have you eyes?
You cannot call this love; for at your age
The heyday in the blood is tame, it's humble,
And waits upon the judgement, and what judgment
Would steps from this to this?!
GERTRUDE O Hamlet, speak no more.
Thou turn'st my eyes into my very soul–
HAMLET Nay, but to live
In the rank sweat of an enseamed bed,
Stew'd in corruption, honeying and making love
Over the nasty sty!
GERTRUDE O speak no more.
These words like daggers enter in my ears.
No more, sweet Hamlet.
HAMLET A murderer and a villain,
A slave that is not twentieth part the tithe
Of your precedent lord! A cut purse of the empire
That from a shelf the precious diadem stole
And put it in his pocket–
GERTRUDE No more!
HAMLET A king of *shreds and patches!*

The GHOST appears! HAMLET is startled.

HAMLET Ah! Look!
GERTRUDE O! What! What! What!
HAMLET Look there!

A moment of the GHOST.

HAMLET Oh! Dear Father.
   Now of course Gertrude cannot see the ghost. It is for my eyes only. And my reaction only serves to fortify in her mind my madness.
GERTRUDE Alas, he is mad.
HAMLET See what I mean? I spot Dad and immediately assume I'm in

trouble.
Dear Father!
Do you not come your tardy son to chide
That, laps'd in time and passion, let go by
Th' important acting of your dread command?
GHOST Do not forget. This visitation
Is but to whet thy almost blunted purpose.
But look, amazement on thy mother sits.

GERTRUDE looks amazed.

GHOST Come, step between her and her fighting soul.
Speak to her, Hamlet.
HAMLET Okay.
How is it with you, lady?
GERTRUDE How is it with you
That you do bend your eyes on vacancy
And with th' incorporal air do hold discourse?
Where on do you look?
HAMLET On him, on him! Do you see nothing?
GERTRUDE Nothing at all; yet all there is I see.

The GHOST exits.

HAMLET Why, look you there, look how he steals away!
    And the ghost is gone. Gertrude:
GERTRUDE This is the very coinage of your brain–
HAMLET Me:
It is not madness
that I have utter'd, Mother. For love of grace,
Lay not that flattering unction to your soul
That not your trespass but my madness speaks.
GERTRUDE What shall I do?
HAMLET Not this, by no means, that I bid you do:
Let the bloat king tempt you again to bed,
Call you his mouse, pinch wanton on your cheek–
GERTRUDE Hamlet!
HAMLET And let him, for a pair of reechy kisses,
Make you to ravel all this matter out
That I essentially am not in madness,
But mad in craft.

GERTRUDE Be thou assur'd, if words are made of breath,
And breath of life, I have no life to breathe
What thou hast said to me.
HAMLET Well, 'twere good you let him know. And as for him,
This man shall set me packing.
I'll lug these guts into the neighbor room.
Mother, good night indeed.
Come, sir, to draw toward an end with you.

> *HAMLET begins to drag POLONIUS.*

HAMLET Good night, mother.

> *And HAMLET drags POLONIUS away. The old man is very heavy and HAMLET struggles at it for a while before collapsing to the floor on his bum, exhausted. He looks at the audience.*

HAMLET This is exhausting… You know there comes a point in every one-person show when you just wish another actor would come out and share the load.

> *HAMLET looks upstage at the curtains. Nobody arrives.*

HAMLET But, even with a full cast, Shakespeare's little skit *always* feels like a one-man show. There is no one – not my mother, nor my old school chums Rosencrantz and Guildenstern, no nor even my once true love Ophelia – to help me toward mine end. Horatio is always there and that's nice. But he's just so damned agreeable all the time. Nothing to play against. Nope: just "the empty space" as Monsieur Brook would say. And I thought Denmark was a prison.

> *HAMLET looks upstage at the curtains again. Still nobody. We hear a drop of water fall.*

ACT IV, SCENE III

HAMLET At any rate. So. Now. Claudius. Is pissed.
CLAUDIUS Where is Polonius?! *(slaps HAMLET)*
HAMLET He demands. To which I retort "At supper."
CLAUDIUS Oh, at supper? Where?

HAMLET Not where he eats, but where he is eaten. A certain convocation of politic worms are eating at him. Yuh know, a man may fish with a worm that hath eat of a king, and eat of the fish that hath fed on that worm. But to your question–

CLAUDIUS Where is Polonius?! *(slaps HAMLET)*

HAMLET In heaven. And if your messenger find him not there, go seek him i' th' other place yourself. And if indeed you find him not within this month, you shall *(sniff)* nose him as you go up the stairs into the lobby.

CLAUDIUS Syrah, go seek him there.

HAMLET A will stay till you come.

CLAUDIUS Hamlet, this deed, for thine especial safety
must we send thee hence
With fiery quickness. Therefore prepare thyself.
The boat is ready, and the wind at help,
And everything is bent for England.

HAMLET For England?

CLAUDIUS For England.

HAMLET Good. For England. Farewell, dear mother.

CLAUDIUS Thy loving father, Hamlet.

HAMLET Ehp! Father and mother is man and wife, man and wife is of one flesh; so my mother.

HAMLET's hands are forcefully handcuffed behind his back.

HAMLET Come, for England!

HAMLET is hauled away.

ACT IV, SCENE IV

HAMLET Damn! Exiled to England unavenged and now out o' the reach of my purpose. I should have stuck it to Claudius while I had the chance, prayers or no prayers. Saint Peter, if he hath yet to give *me* the pearly key, could not possibly have admitted Claudius, that stinking heap of hypocrisy. Well, for the moment: Polonius' gore will have to do. For now I am sent to England. Production After Production, I am Sent to England. It is rather amazing how time and time again all occasions do inform against me,
And spur my dull revenge. How stand I then,
That hath a father kill'd, a mother stain'd,
Excitements of my reason and my blood,
And still I let all sleep?

Sure He that made us with such large discourse,
Looking before and after, gave us not
That capability and godlike reason
To fust in us unus'd. I do not know
Why yet I live to say this thing's to do,
Since I have cause, and will, and strength, and means
To do't!
"From this time forth
My thoughts be bloody or be nothing worth!"

Anyway. So. Claudius sends Rosencrantz and Guildenstern as my escorts to England, and in their pockets an order to relieve me of my life. He would have done well to solicit brighter spies than Roz and Guild. For: in the blindness of their sleep, I steal the letter that damns me to the guillotine, pocket it as future Exhibit A, then substitute for it, in fonts carefully construed to mock the pen of yee old King, fresh commandments ordering the deaths of my traitorous old chums. So, yes, Rosencrantz and Guildenstern are dead. And no they are not near my conscience, but two more notches on the belt of my swelling villainies. All justified mind you by honor and right. Or as it is often called: just revenge. Such an odd agreement we make, that blood endorse blood, that a hero may be a villain to be a hero. "I *must* be cruel, only to be kind." And I am certain, loving audience, that you will excuse my villainies still, as you so graciously have these four centuries past, as I am your hero for the evening, and vicarious avenger of all your daily angst, hate, resentment, perceived injustice. True, I haven't killed Claudius. Yet. But oh how sweet that red rush of blood that unfurled like victorious flags from the guts of my surrogate success: old Polonius. I slay my grand Shakespearean adversaries as *you* would your quotidian foes: your far too fashionable friends, jaded government employees, nagging telemarketers, fellow public transit patrons whose cell-phone chatter *cuts* through your ear! "Kill them all, Hamlet! And thank you! For by your efforts and the price of admission we are – for the moment – avenged." I: am your: Polonius.

ACT V, SCENE I

HAMLET Following my clever twisting of Rosencrantz and Guildenstern's plot, my boat is conveniently intercepted by pirates, with whom I exhibit much dueling prowess, add a few more stripes of blood to my credit, yet: fail to escape. Luckily they deal with me like thieves of mercy, and in exchange for the promise of future favors, set me free minus my belongings up the shore from Denmark. All of this, of course, transpiring off stage – budgets being what they are.

So, having narrowly undone designs on my life, and now with a handful of lives upon my back, I meander my way home to Elsinor.

Faithful Horatio meets me at the docks. And it is with him that on the outskirts of Elsinor I happen upon a gravedigger deep in his trade, bones scattered about him, and where we have come at last to Yorick, the best-known skull in all the world, who for some reason, though he is but a skull like any skull, has occasioned more sappiness in the history of *Hamlet* criticism than any other figure in Will's play, myself included. I loved him in my childhood when he lived. He was a fine fellow, I admit, and full of infinite jest, etcetera. But the academics wrap Yorick in flags of sentimentality, and dwell intolerably on his fineness. To which I say, pah! Is he so fine as to revise "To be or not to be" and obliterate entirely from my epitaph the shrewd observation: that paradise on earth is never more than an unweeded garden? I think not...

There is nothing sentimental in Death. Death is unlike anything that comes before it, always unprepared for, and ugly. Like Yorick. With his dirt-filled eyes, his mocking half grin, his fatal stink, no matter how sweet or clever he once was.

There's more of his like 'neath the earth than on't,
And less of us above the ground than in't.

Might this not be the pate of a politician? It might. Or of a courtesan, which could say "Good morrow, sweet lord. How dost thou, sweet lord?" Why, may not this be the skull of a lawyer? Where be his cases now, his tenures, and his tricks? This fellow might in's time be a great buyer of land, with his fines and his recoveries. Is this the fine of his fines and the recovery of his recoveries, to have his fine pate full of fine dirt?

Ladies, though you may paint an inch thick, to this favour you must come. Gentlemen, bred to conquer the world, dost thou think the great Alexander looked o' this fashion i' th' earth? E'en so.

Alexander died, Alexander was buried, Alexander returneth to dust, the dust is earth, of earth we make clay; and why of that clay whereto he was converted might we not stop a hole to keep the wind away? O that that earth that kept the world in awe should patch a wall t'expel the winter's flaw.

A chorus is heard singing afar off.

HAMLET But soft, here comes the King, the queen, and– that is Laertes returned from France, all with flickering lamps glowing at arms length as courtiers float a silent pine box through the dark. Who is this they follow so silent and yet so far removed from royal tombs? Such maimed rites doth betoken the corpse they carry did with desp'rate hand fordo its own life...

I'll not pretend ignorance. The dying candles they bare they do so to light the way for fair Ophelia...

Ophelia's light glows from above, circles slowly around HAMLET from left to right and then from upstage. His back to the audience, he raises his hand to the blinding light before it settles in the earth upstage and glows there quietly on the horizon. HAMLET walks closer to it, then turns to look out at the audience as the chorus finishes its song.

HAMLET Horatio and I remain hidden out of view. When the churlish priest refuses to profane the service of the dead by administ'ring full rites to one released by her own hand, Laertes grows indignant at his sister's o'er-simplified burial, and with bold brotherly love he bellows:

In a terribly overdone French accent...

LAERTES O treble woe
Fall ten times treble on that cursed head –
HAMLET Meaning mine
LAERTES –Whose wicked deeds her most ingenious sense
Depriv'd her of. Hold off the earth a while,
Till I have caught her once more in my arms!
HAMLET And leaps into her grave! *Leaps into* her grave! O, the bravery of this grief does put me into a tow'ring passion and I step forward to say Hey:
What is he whose grief
Bears such an emphasis? Dost thou come to
To outface me with leaping in her grave?
I lov'd Ophelia! Forty thousand brothers
Could not with all their quantity of love
Make up my sum!
  And we struggle and we make threats and we use strong words, mine better crafted that his, and we are quite thoroughly men before *pfft* going our separate ways, he with the pedestrian:
LAERTES The devil take thy soul!
HAMLET And I with yet another origin of daily expression:
Let Hercules himself do what he may,
The cat will mew, and dog will have his day.

ACT V, SCENE II

HAMLET Act Five, Scene Two. The final leg of Shakespeare's course.

We hear a drop of water fall.

HAMLET Claudius, his English plot 'gainst my life having been tangled, and now without his right arm, Polonius, doth take up that right arm's right heir, Laertes, coaches the lad to o'erflex the burning muscle of his hate for me, and squeezes out a hot steaming plot to void that guilt that stains the lining of his conscience:

He shall wager – wink wink – that in a dozen passes between myself and Laertes the latter shall not exceed me three hits. Tired from my journey, becalmed by time away, and thinking not much of it though I should know better given this is Shakespeare, I agree to play their game. Unbeknownst to me this plot *is* foul and Laertes' sword envenomed. And should he miss his mark, Claudius sports a poisoned pearl to plop into the cup of wine he shall offer me once I am parched from swordplay and in need of drink. Why do people keep such things around the house? It's just askin' for trouble.

So, the plot is laid. I have in perfect ignorance taken up my part in't. And with a mighty flourish the crowd of lords, ladies, Laertes, Horatio, the King, the Queen, and the swords are all brought forth.

Now. Oh let's see. Many characters at once.

Claudius… The Queen, my mother… Laertes… Horatio… Lords… Ladies…

Oh, and one lord in particular, he who shall judge our match, Osric.

OSRIC, in secret, applies poison to the tip of one sword, then places it in the rack. OSRIC wheels forth the rack of swords.

OSRIC Gentlemen, come, the foils.
HAMLET We pick them out.
This likes me well.
LAERTES This one is – how you say? – too heavy. Let me see another.
Ah, oui bon, this one suits me well.
HAMLET I'll be your foil, Laertes. In mine ignorance
Your skill shall like a star i' th' darkest night
Stick fiery off indeed.
LAERTES You mock me, monsieur?
HAMLET No, by this hand… Sheesh.
CLAUDIUS If Hamlet give the first or second hit
The King shall drink to Hamlet's better breath,
And in the cup a union shall he throw
Richer than that which four successive kings
In Denmark's crown have worn – Come, begin.
HAMLET Come, Laertes.
LAERTES Come, my lord.
GERTRUDE Go Hamlet!

HAMLET Thanks mum.

They play. HAMLET strikes LAERTES.

HAMLET Judgment!
OSRIC A hit, a very palpable hit.
CLAUDIUS Hamlet this pearl is thine.
Here's to thy health.

CLAUDIUS drinks, then makes a show of dropping the pearl in the cup. There is an amplified sound of the poisoned pearl hitting the wine with a plop and fizz trailed by a dark and ominous chord. CLAUDIUS offers the cup to HAMLET.

HAMLET Nay, I'll play this next bout first. Set it by awhile.
Come, Laertes.

CLAUDIUS steps away, clearly displeased. The dark chord fades.

HAMLET Come, Laertes.

They play. Very quickly, another hit.

HAMLET Another hit. What say you?
LAERTES Oui, a touch, I do confess't.
CLAUDIUS Gertrude, our son shall win.
GERTRUDE The Queen carouses to thy fortune Hamlet.

GERTRUDE has taken the poisoned cup of wine.

CLAUDIUS Gertrude! …Do not drink.
GERTRUDE I will, my lord, I pray you pardon me.

GERTRUDE drinks.

CLAUDIUS *(aside)* It is the poison'd cup. It is too late.
GERTRUDE Come, Hamlet, let me sate thy thirst.
HAMLET I dare not drink yet, madam – by and by.
LAERTES My lord, I'll hit him now.

CLAUDIUS I do not think't.

> *GERTRUDE returns to her seat, a bit wobbly, and sets down the cup.*

HAMLET Come for the third, Laertes. You do but dally.
I pray you pass your best violence.
I am afeard you make a wanton of me.

> *LAERTES lunges forward and slices HAMLET deep across the arm. HAMLET will have none of that and goes on the offensive.*

CLAUDIUS Part them, they are incensed.

> *In the fighting, HAMLET manages to get hold of LAERTES' sword and stabs him fatally with both of them at once.*

HAMLET Gertrude:

> *GERTRUDE begins to swoon and topples over in her chair. Another dark chord slips into the air.*

HAMLET Osric:
OSRIC Look to the Queen there, ho!
HAMLET Horatio:
HORATIO They bleed on both sides. How does lord Hamlet?
HAMLET Osric:
OSRIC How is't, Laertes?
HAMLET Me: Nay, how does the Queen? Claudius:
CLAUDIUS She swoons to see them bleed!
HAMLET Gertrude:
GERTRUDE No, no, the drink, the drink! O my dear Hamlet! It is the drink! I am poison'd.

> *GERTRUDE dies, pointing at CLAUDIUS as she goes.*

HAMLET Me: O villainy! Ho! Let the doors be lock'd!
Treachery! Seek it out! Laertes:
LAERTES It is here, Hamlet. Hamlet, thou art slain.
No med'cine in the world can do thee good.

Nay, not thee, thou bloody, bawdy villain!
Remorseless, treacherous, lecherous, kindless villain!
He who kill'd my father, whor'd my mother–

HAMLET Sister! No– Wait– Uh– That's, uh, earlier. That's *me*. Hih. Now, *now*, Laertes, he says:

LAERTES But I, who have a noble father lost,
A sister driven into desp'rate terms,
Excitements of my reason and my blood–

HAMLET …I'm sorry. Actually. Laertes is dying. He has forgiven me. He *forgives* me! He says, uh– Hamlet:

LAERTES In thee there is not half an hour's life.
The treacherous instrument is in thy hand,
Unblunted and envenom'd. This foul practice
Hath turn'd itself on me. It is the King.
The King's to blame!

HAMLET What say you?
The point envenom'd too! Then, venom, to thy work!

HAMLET runs CLAUDIUS through!

CLAUDIUS O yet defend me friends! I am but hurt!

HAMLET Here, thou incestuous, murd'rous, damned Dane,
Drink off this poison. Is thy union here?
Follow my mother!

CLAUDIUS dies terribly. HAMLET arises from the performing of it a bit distracted:

HAMLET If it be now 'tis not to come if it be not to come it will be now. If it be not now, Hamlet… Hamlet? …Hamlet! Yes! Laertes!

LAERTES Exchange forgiveness with me, noble Hamlet.
Mine and my father's death come not upon thee,
Nor thine on me…?

LAERTES dies, eyes open. HAMLET closes them.

HAMLET Heaven make thee free of it. I follow thee. *(winces at the wound in his arm. Claudius:)* And thee. *(Gertrude:)* And thee. *(Rosencrantz and Guildenstern:)* And they. *(Polonius:)* And he. *(Ophelia:)* And she.
   Had I but time – As this fell sergeant, Death,
Is strict in his arrest – O, I could tell you–

But– heh, but you see – and it *is* well documented – my time is: out of– joint– out of my hands! My objective is written. I cannot help but that I Am Hamlet. And that which fills this mortal sack that is nor water nor blood, nor ink, is but ego and ego: is who we are. Ego: is individuality. Give up on individuality and rather than ideas we get ideology. We get– culture that glimpses no horizon. We get that bland modern pride known as "political correctness" with its presumption that we might one day become creatures unable to give offense.

To be honest, the more I consider my life the less I understand it and now despair of ever meeting with any critique that will reconcile these endless and perplexing inconsistencies. At times I seem a bundle of Elizabethan cliches! Other times a rack of fashionable fetishes wrapped up in Freudian chatter. Herr von Goethe's condescending sentimentality would have mine be the story of "a great deed imposed upon a soul unequal to zeh performance of it." Mister T.S. Eliot went so far as to declare me an "artistic failure" on the grounds that I am dominated "by an emotion in excess of the facts as they appear." Did he read the play? Mine is a play of stunningly murky questions. The light of these infinite answers grows evermore dim beneath my legendary shadow now stretched into yet another century of scrutiny.

"Action! Action! Why doesn't he take Action?" Well, let me tell you: my *Action* could never change anything in the eternal nature of things. This I know. It is ridiculous and humiliating that I should be asked to set right a world so far out of joint, when, all said and done, it is but to this *(Yorick's skull)* favor that I must come.

But: hih-hih, this is the curse of Knowing. Knowledge exposes action. Knowledge murders action. Action needs the veils of illusion. Action must see through a blind eye. My problem isn't too much reflection. My problem isn't an excess of possibility. My problem isn't that I think too much. It's that I think too well! Insight into the horrible truth, *this* outweighs any motive for action. This is your infamous ambiguity that every patron, critic, academician, actor, director has climbed aboard and made love to. I have been made the tart of world drama. Pimped out as promiscuously as the alphabet!

You think it's easy being Hamlet? Shakespeare put me on the map, yes, but across these centuries I have o'erwhelmed that terrain. Hamlet: *is*. With or without *The Tragedy of Hamlet, Prince of Denmark, by William Shakespeare*. Mine is a life that hath risen off the page. A life beyond the proscenium. A life in the very language. A life of the world. Can you imagine? *The* life. And yet: no life. I have at last become what I have fought to escape: thoughts! Words! I am but Horatio to countless Lit Crit Hamlets who would be Hamlet if only they had time and means to do't *but* they do not. I do. Why? Because I am well-crafted. An author's dream. A fiction: terminally immortal. Life: will never pass me by! This: empty space! This: is not life! This Is Art! I: Am–!

Epiphany. A complete change of tone.

HAMLET …I am very sorry that to Laertes I did forget myself;
For by the image of my cause I see
The portraiture of his.
Hath he not a father slain? A sister stain'd?
Excitements of his reason and his blood?
He was a very noble youth who to
His own self was true.
How many out of us can claim as much?
Your pardon, sir.
    Wretched Queen, adieu. Goodbye, good lady.
Farewell, dear mother.
    And for Ophelia… I do regret… I have no art to reckon my groans. But that I lov'd her best, O most best… Believe it.
    God, what a wounded name I leave behind me,
Of carnal, bloody, and unnatural acts,
Of accidental judgments, casual slaughters,
Of deaths put on by cunning and forc'd cause,
And, in this upshot, purposes mistook,
Fall'n on th'inventors' heads. All this did I
Truly deliver.
    What piece of work is a man, how noble in reason, how infinite in faculties, in form and moving how express and admirable, in action how like an angel, in apprehension how like a god. The beauty of the world, the paragon of animals – and yet, to me, what is this quintessence of dust?
    There's a divinity that shapes our ends,
Rough-hew them how we will. That is most certain.
The rest is silence.
    Let be.
    Let be.
    Let be.

> *HAMLET looks at the wall of tick marks. He walks up to it, pulls a piece of chalk from his pocket, and adds one more tick mark to the wall. He steps back and takes in the wall, then turns to the audience and bows. In the applause, HAMLET picks up the copy of his play as, upstage, OPHELIA steps out from the curtains. HAMLET notices a change in the audience's attention. If they happen to stop applauding, he says, a bit incredulously:*

HAMLET What?

Otherwise, he looks upstage and is stunned to see OPHELIA. He slowly approaches her and reaches out to touch her but OPHELIA steps away. There is a gentle underscoring of water droplets falling one by one as OPHELIA begins to enact the events of her demise: her picking and weaving of flowers into a garland that she places on her head, her climbing the willow and, at the top, reaching for a flower at the end of a branch, and her fall into the water below. She enacts the drowning for a moment, then looks at HAMLET. HAMLET turns to the audience and relays OPHELIA's fate. It is a difficult speech for HAMLET to deliver.

HAMLET There is a willow grows askant the brook
That shows his hoary leaves in the glassy stream.
Therewith fantastic garlands did she make
Of crow-flowers, nettles, daisies, and long purples.
There on the pendent boughs, her crownet weeds
Clamb'ring to hang, an envious sliver broke,
When down her weedy trophies and herself
Fell in the weeping brook. Her clothes spread wide,
And mermaid-like awhile they bore her up,
Which time she chanted snatches of old songs
As one incapable of her own distress.
But long it could not be
Till that her garments, heavy with their drink,
Pull'd the poor wretch from her melodious lay
To muddy death.

HAMLET kneels beside OPHELIA and she touches him tenderly. After a moment, she walks upstage and stands waiting just within the curtains. HAMLET stands. He looks around at the theatre one last time, sets his play down on the chair, and goes to OPHELIA, but hesitates. OPHELIA offers her hand. HAMLET takes it and steps through the curtains and offstage.

The end.

little extremes

a tragicomedy in one act

little extremes

The world premiere of *little extremes* was presented by Art Street Theatre at the 450 Geary Studio Theatre, San Francisco, CA, during EXIT Theatre's San Francisco Fringe Festival, on September 8, 1995. The production was directed by the author, with the following cast and staff:

ELDERLY WOMAN / HUSBAND / FATHER / POLICEMAN	Frank Torrano
MAN / HASTY / SON	Jake Rodriguez
WOMAN / HOPE / CALM	Gillian Brecker
WIFE / NEUROTIC	Caroline Ford
Technical Design	Andrew Sproule
Stage Manager	Lisa Maher

Note

> The play benefits from a stripped down, actor-centric approach. Only the minimum props need be used, including toy cap gun pistols rather than more realistic looking guns.
>
> Though the actors say "bang" when firing their guns, caps should still be used. For the final round of gunshots in the last scene, nobody should say "bang."
>
> A slash in the dialogue (/) indicates that the next actor should start their line, creating overlapping speech.

Cast

> Actor 1, young – Man / Hasty / Son
> Actress 1, young – Woman / Hope / Calm
> Actor 2, middle aged – Elderly Woman / Husband / Father / Policeman
> Actress 2, middle aged – Wife / Neurotic

Scene One

> A bus stop. A MAN and WOMAN on a bench made of three chairs. Sound of a bus braking, stopping, then leaving. An ELDERLY WOMAN runs past, dropping her purse.

ELDERLY WOMAN Hold! Bus! Wait! Please wait! Bus! etc...

ELDERLY WOMAN exits. MAN notices purse and picks it up.

MAN *(to himself)* She dropped her purse. *(beat)* Ma'am? Ma'am! You dropped your– Ma'am! *(to WOMAN)* She dropped her purse. But she's gone now.
WOMAN That bus stopped for her?
MAN Yes.
WOMAN Well we must return it to her. Look inside for an address or phone number.

MAN does. He finds a plump white envelope.

MAN Hello. What's this?
WOMAN What's that?
MAN I don't know, I'll look.
WOMAN No, it's none of our business.
MAN It's money!
WOMAN Money?!
MAN There's about ten thousand dollars here!
WOMAN Oh my goodness! Who is she? Find some identification.
MAN Ten thousand dollars!
WOMAN Find some identification.
MAN *(searches)* Nothing. Nothing but this.
WOMAN Oh my goodness. Well we've got to return it. We'll take it to the police, she's bound to want it back.
MAN What if she stole it?
WOMAN Stole it?
MAN Stole it.
WOMAN Her? She was an elderly woman. Elderly women don't steal.
MAN Ha! That's what folks like us think, and that's why they get away with it. She must have stolen this!
WOMAN Well then we must turn it in.
MAN *(beat)* We could keep it!
WOMAN Keep it?
MAN Keep it! For ourselves. It's already stolen anyway.
WOMAN But that's illegal.
MAN *She* stole it. So she's certainly not going to go to the police.
WOMAN That's true.

MAN And you can't tell me ten grand wouldn't be of any use to you.
WOMAN That's true.
MAN Then we'll keep it.
WOMAN *(takes purse)* Yes, we'll keep it. But we must use it.
MAN Certainly.
WOMAN We must use it to better our world. We must donate it to charity, to save the rain forest, to help find cures for disease. We could feed the homeless, calm the incessant rumbling of children's stomachs in Africa, in Europe, in America. We could buy clothing for the poor, shelter for their families, hats for the bald monkeys of Brazil. We could save eagles from hunters, whales from harpoons, and dolphins from nets. We could make our world a better place for our children, and *their* children! A beautiful world of peace and love, where each man and woman can be proud to stand tall and say, "This is my home! This is my earth, that I cherish and love with all my heart! and all my soul!" That's what we can do with this fortune! That's what we can do for our fellow man!! That's what we can do!!!

Having been quite still throughout WOMAN'S speech, MAN pulls a gun out and shoots her dead.

MAN BANG!!!

MAN takes the money from the purse, looks out, then exits.

Scene Two

A family room. Enter a HUSBAND with his newspaper. He notices the body of the WOMAN, stops, steps around it, then sits to read his newspaper. Enter a WIFE with two cups of coffee. She, too, steps around the body, pretending not to notice. She sets both cups of coffee on a little table and sits down in her own chair. Silence. WIFE and HUSBAND both reach for their coffee cups, freeze and stare at one another. HUSBAND vanishes behind his paper with his coffee and WIFE holds hers with both hands. HUSBAND takes a sip and sets his cup down, remains hidden. Silence.

HUSBAND …Darling?
WIFE Yes Dear?

Significant pause.

HUSBAND I meant to thank you.
WIFE Yes?
HUSBAND For the coffee.
WIFE …You're welcome.

Silence. HUSBAND appears nervous, agitated. WIFE appears concerned, staring out. Finally:

HUSBAND Darling?
WIFE Yes Dear?
HUSBAND *(beat)* Darling?
WIFE Yes?
HUSBAND Well– Do I have to spell it out for you?!
WIFE Yes!
HUSBAND For Christ's sake, she's been lying there for over two weeks now!
WIFE I know! Don't you think I know?!
HUSBAND Well aren't you going to do anything?
WIFE Why haven't you done anything?
HUSBAND She's your daughter!
WIFE Oh! What, do you think I conceived all by myself?
HUSBAND Alright.
WIFE Or did I hire some gigolo from down town?
HUSBAND Okay.
WIFE Maybe I went to a sperm bank because you can't–
HUSBAND Alright! Look we– At least let's, throw a blanket over her or *something.*
WIFE We should have done something the moment we first found her. Our child. Our only child. How could it have happened?
HUSBAND *(eyes locked on body)* We did the best we could.
WIFE We gave her everything she wanted. We enrolled her in the best schools, the best summer camps. I told her about boys and what happens when you kiss them.
HUSBAND We did just fine. She was defective. She didn't listen.
WIFE We kept her away from the neighbor children who might put ideas in her head. We let her know the virtuous route to Heaven.
HUSBAND We did just fine.
WIFE We made sure she thought like we do, so that she could grow up to be a great big, healthy little girl. Mommy's little girl. God will provide.
HUSBAND Just fine…

WIFE But then she started to rebel. She started to rebel and do things, do things for herself. She *kissed* that boy! She tried to get that job so she could move away. She can't move away. I thought, where did we go wrong. What did we do wrong? We did everything for her. *(pause)* Yet, to be honest, to be fair, maybe we *were* too–

HUSBAND "Maybe we" nothing! We did just fine! If anything she smothered to death under your hovering.

WIFE My hovering? I protected her from evils! You know that!

HUSBAND *(mournfully)* Daddy's princess.

WIFE I made sure she was safe! She didn't have to work for herself! She didn't have to do her homework for herself! She didn't have to find respectable young men for herself! She didn't have to think! I gave her everything!

HUSBAND You! You! YOU! What about me? I'm the bank around here! I put the food on the table! I'm the man!

WIFE That is not fair! You do not say that to me!

HUSBAND *(kneeling, sad again)* And I come home one day, and find my daughter is dead. My beautiful little girl is dead.

WIFE I told you, God will forgive.

HUSBAND Her perfect little face, frozen. Her beautiful eyes, glazed over and cold.

WIFE God will forgive!

HUSBAND I'm away at work, seven days a week, fourteen, fifteen hours a day, never home, all for *you,* making money for *you!* And I come home and my daughter is dead, smothered to death by *you!*

WIFE *(sets down cup)* Oh!!!

HUSBAND And I never even knew her name.

WIFE God will forgive!!! *(pulls a gun and shoots him dead)* BANG!!! I told you I didn't kill her! I didn't kill her! She just wouldn't listen! She never listened! You never listen!

> WIFE *looks out, then moves to pick up the cups, looks out again, and exits.*

Scene Three

> *An apartment with a couch. A young woman, HOPE, lying asleep on the ground. She is like a girl. A young man, HASTY, enters, pulling off an old woman's wig. He is like a boy. He tiptoes into the room and makes a loud sound on purpose. HOPE wakes up.*

HOPE Oh, you startled me.

HASTY Sorry.

HOPE Where are we?

HASTY My place. Best place to hide. Ten thousand bucks Angel! Ten thousand bucks! We did it! *(kisses her)*

HOPE *(hugs him sincerely)* Now everything is perfect.

HASTY We'll just give it a few days and go.

HOPE *(excited)* Where will we go first?

HASTY Uh, I don't know, where do you want to go?

HOPE Let's go to Disneyland! I've always wanted to go to Disneyland!

HASTY Okay! We'll go to Disneyland! And while we're there we'll go to Hollywood, and go to that mountain that has "HOLLYWOOD" written in big letters on it, and stand on the "H". And we'll walk down that street with all the stars on the sidewalk, and see Graumann's Chinese Theatre! How 'bout that?

HOPE Mm, perfect!

HASTY And then we'll go to the ocean and lay in the warm sand. We'll see wonderful places.

HOPE Romantic places.

HASTY Then we'll just drive on. Anywhere. Just drive away down a yellow brick road and live happily ever after.

> *HASTY kisses her hair. They stare out happily, HOPE nestled into HASTY on the floor. They look very sweet and tender. Long pause.*

HOPE …Hey.

HASTY Hm?

HOPE At the bank… If you had had to… Would you actually have shot anyone?

HASTY I don't like to think about that.

HOPE But would you have? Really?

HASTY I suppose if I had to.

HOPE You would have?

HASTY Well, if I had to but I didn't so let's not worry about it okay?

HOPE *(pause)* I had that dream again.

HASTY You did?

HOPE Yeah… Only this time I never got up. I just laid there on the floor, and it was as if I wasn't just pretending to be dead this time, I was really dead, and *I* was someone else, like a fly on the wall or something, and I just watched my mother and father arguing, and myself lying there. And this time when Mom shot Dad, I didn't do anything to stop her. I didn't get up or call out or anything.

HASTY Hmm.

HOPE And what's the weirdest thing is I didn't even want to. Or I just didn't think to. It was like I just didn't care anymore.

HASTY That is weird.

HOPE It's scary, the things that can happen. How people change. Become so different. *(pause)* Promise me we'll never become like that.

HASTY I promise.

HOPE No promise me–

HASTY I promise.

HOPE –Because I wouldn't be able to stand it, not one minute of it. I just want to escape and go to Disneyland, ride the Peter Pan ride and It's A Small World, and then drive away, far far away! Leave all this behind and escape! I want to be free! Promise me we'll be free.

HASTY I promise.

HOPE Promise we'll always be together.

HASTY I promise.

HOPE Promise?

HASTY Yes, I do…

HOPE hugs HASTY, tight.

HOPE I love you… Do you love me?

HASTY *(beat)* Yes.

HOPE Say it. I need to hear you say it.

HASTY …I love you, I promise.

Suddenly an unseen voice cracks over a megaphone and a red light flashes, as from a police car.

POLICEMAN *(voice)* Alright! This is the police! We know you're in there! Come out with your hands up and get *down* on the pavement! / No one will get hurt!

HOPE Oh my God!

HASTY Police! How did they find us?

HOPE What are we going to do?

POLICEMAN Give us a sign that you understand! Come out with your hands in the air!

HOPE What are we going to do?

HASTY I don't know. *(digs out his gun)*

HOPE You said they wouldn't find us! You said it was fool proof!

HASTY I know, shut up a second!

POLICEMAN Come out with your hands up!

HOPE *(beat)* Let's just turn ourselves in!

HASTY What?

HOPE Let's just turn ourselves in! We'll say we're sorry and maybe they'll go easy on us!

HASTY They'll *throw* us in jail! I'm *not* going to jail!

HOPE I'm scared! I'm frightened! I knew it my dream was a bad omen please let's just turn ourselves in!

HASTY No! What are you talking about?

POLICEMAN I'm going to count to three!

HASTY What about our plans?

HOPE For God's sake they're right there! The police are right outside! They're going to catch us!

HASTY No they're not!

HOPE Please–

HASTY We're not going anywhere!! We're *going* to Disneyland!

POLICEMAN One!

HOPE I said I'd follow you to the end of the world but please, if we don't turn ourselves in it'll be worse! We'll never be free, never! And at least this way we might get off easier!

HASTY I told you no!

POLICEMAN Two!

HOPE I don't want to go to jail for the rest of my life! I want to turn myself in!

HASTY What do I have to say to you?!

HOPE …I'm going out there!

HASTY Sit down!

HOPE No I'm going out there!

POLICEMAN Three!

HASTY Sit *down!*

HOPE I'm going! It's the best thing we can do!!! We'll never be together if we don't! I'm going for us!! I'm doing it for us!!!

HASTY shoots HOPE dead!

HASTY BANG!!!

At once the POLICEMAN'S voice begins to holler hysterically through the megaphone and HASTY realizes what he has done.

POLICEMAN Get down! Get down! Get ready! Inside, put the gun down! Come out with your hands in the air and put the gun on the ground! If you don't come out with your hands in the air we will come in! If you do not come out, we will come in! We've surrounded the building! You are entirely surrounded! There is no escape! You have no choice but to surrender! Put your gun down and surrender! If you do not surrender we will open fire! We will open fire!
HASTY *(to the "window")* I'm turning / myself in-
POLICEMAN Get down! Look out!

We hear a multitude of guns thunder off–

POLICEMAN BANG!!! BANG!!! BANG!!! BANG!!! BANG!!!

–and HASTY falls to the ground. Silence. Pause. Black out.

Scene Four

A candle is lit. In the light of the candle we see a FATHER'S face.

FATHER I can't sleep lately. I tell people, "I can't sleep lately." They say "Oh…" They don't know quite what to say. Some of them follow it up by asking why. That's usually what they do is ask why. "I don't know," I say. "I'm not sure." And I'm not.
   But I have an idea.
   I don't know if it's the news, or the stress at work, or just stress… But you know you watch the news. It's just one dreadful thing after another. They tell you all the terrible things, all the murders and fires, children in trash bins, it's just overkill. But they never show the good things. Sometimes, I mean, yeah, there'll be the token nice story at the end, something about ducks or an elderly woman in Nebraska who runs a small farm. Nice stories. And the anchor man he smiles and says good night. But when they say, "Hey, thirty people died in an earthquake today," why don't they also say, "And some other people were okay. It's alright. It's bad right now but things are going to be okay." No one ever mentions that part!
   Maybe they don't think it will be. Maybe they don't want us to think it will be, because then nobody would watch their program.
   I've often thought, maybe people should be like bears, and chase their young off into the woods when it's time. The image of that makes me laugh. Of

course, you'd raise them first, raise them well, but then– chase 'em off. Make'm go. For their own good.

I was thinking about this, you see… Well it's, you know, it's my lack of sleep I was telling you about.

The real reason I think is that I've been having this dream. I know, haven't we all. We all have dreams. But… Well I'll just tell you…

My wife– In the dream –My wife and I are sitting in our living room. And we're drinking coffee, just relaxing, trying to relax. Only our daughter is lying on the floor dead. And the idea is that we've killed her. O-or I don't know if we killed her. But she's dead and the cause of death is killing, and there my wife and I are feeling guilty, and so I figure it's because one of us killed her.

This is only a dream now. You know, just so you don't, you know…

Anyway. So we're drinking joe and she's dead. And uh, my wife and I start to argue about it, about who did it, sort of. And the arguing gets worse… and worse… And she pulled a gun on me. She was going to shoot me. She was actually going to shoot me.

In the dream.

But she didn't.

I always wake up. It's very convenient.

A friend of mind suggested I try to continue the dream, that if I try not to wake up but instead try to continue the dream, I might work out whatever it is that's bugging me…

I don't know. Some dreams are just meant to be dreamt…

Besides, what if I did continue the dream and found out that the ending was: she shot me. That wouldn't be any good. I'd rather not know…

Yeah, maybe we should be like bears, chase'm off…

Maybe if I continue my dream, I should try to revive my daughter… or something. Ask her who killed her, what went wrong.

Scene Five

> *A porch. Late summer evening. We can hear evening noises such as soft crickets, a distant dog barking or a passing car. A FATHER sitting with a lit candle. His SON enters and joins him.*

SON Dad?
FATHER Oh. Hey there. *(blows out candle)* What are you doing up?
SON I was going to ask you. What are you out here on the porch for?
FATHER Couldn't sleep.
SON Still, huh?

FATHER Thought listening to the wind rustling in the trees might help. Might put me to sleep.
SON Mom inside?
FATHER Yup, like a lamb. *(pause)* Nice out, huh?
SON Yeah. Pretty.
FATHER *(pause)* Nice bright moon. Nice sky.
SON Mm-hm.
FATHER Look at that moon, son. It's far away. Farther than the sky. It's so quiet up there.
SON *(pause)* I'm sorry Dad.
FATHER I know you are. No use saying again… Be glad *you're* not dead.
SON *(pause)* Do you understand that it was an accident?
FATHER *(quickly, but calm)* No I don't understand. I don't understand.

> FATHER looks away again. Long pause.

FATHER You're sister, uh… You're sister tells us she's leaving now. She tell you that? That she's moving away?
SON Uh-uh…
FATHER She should. Good for her. She'll be just fine.
SON I should probably go too… sometime… you think?
FATHER Sure. It'd be good for you. Long as you do it right this time. Not running, I mean. But legitimate.
SON *(Sighs shortly, then, almost inaudibly)* I know…

> Long pause. They stare out…

SON I was thinking I might go to school. I figure I better learn something if I'm going to try to live on my own. I better know how to do something, right? *(pause)* I thought maybe business, accounting maybe. Or I sort of like architecture maybe I'll build things how 'bout that, huh? Come back and build you and Mom a big house? *(long pause)* Yeah so I figured I'd go to school.
FATHER That's good. Good start.
SON *(pause)* I'm gonna leave in a few months. It's funny you mention sis.
FATHER She's going next Sunday. Your Mother'll be upset to see her go.
SON *(pause)* Oh, you know, I found that ball you gave me. Long time ago? The baseball? I was seven, or six? It was in the back of my closet. I thought I lost that a *long* time ago…
FATHER I gave that to you?

SON Yeah.
FATHER I don't remember.
SON Yeah, it was… …

> *Pause. FATHER looks up at the sky. SON notices and does the same.*

SON See that star there? And those? That's Ursa Major. That's the bear.
FATHER *(looking)* It's a big sky up there. Goes on a long ways.

> *In the distance we hear a police siren, very faintly. FATHER looks off in the direction of the siren, then out at the evening. Lights out.*

Scene Six

> *Lights up. Bright, sunny day. A park with bench. A CALM woman sitting quietly, happily. She looks housewife-like with a plain scarf around her head. Enter a NEUROTIC woman with clear intent and wearing an old hat. She sits on the bench. Loooooonnnng pause…*

NEUROTIC W'll that's no way to start a conversation.
CALM Pardon?
NEUROTIC Aren't you going to ask me about my day? I mean I'm sitting here. Here I am. Aren't you going to ask me?
CALM I hadn't thought about it, no.
NEUROTIC *(under her breath)* Bitch…

> *Long pause. Eventually NEUROTIC stares at CALM, waiting to be asked. CALM notices and stares back, wondering why she is being stared upon. Finally…*

CALM How was your day?
NEUROTIC Great! Great! Just peachy! What a swell day.
CALM Why don't I believe you?
NEUROTIC Because I'm utilizing irony. It's been a terrible day.

> *Pause. NEUROTIC looks sharply to CALM.*

CALM Uh– Why is that?
NEUROTIC You know sometimes you just have to get away. Just get away. Get

out of the house, get away from the office, don't type, don't clean, just get away and sit, you know? Like we are now. *(beat)* What are you getting away from?
CALM Nothing. I'm just sitting here. Enjoying the scenery.
NEUROTIC Just sitting here. Very pretty. Pretty scenery. Guess you came to the right place, everywhere you look there's scenery.

Again NEUROTIC waits but CALM is quicker to pick up on her cue this time.

CALM You came to get away?
NEUROTIC Yeah! You need some pretty scenery every once in a while to calm the nerves. *(beat)* You know sometimes I have these impulses, I have these daydreams, I imagine myself lashing out, just lashing out, picking up the typewriter and knocking that Brickman across the head. And everyone would yell "What's that noise? What's that noise?" And I'd say "that's the sound of Mister Brickman's split head shattering beneath my dancing feet!" *(beat)* I imagine that sometimes.
CALM *(pulls her purse closer)* That's quite an imagination.
NEUROTIC I would never do it though. I'm too sweet. God will provide, I always remind myself. …God will provide. …My therapist says I need to let people know the burning rage and resentment that I bottle up inside, otherwise one day I *will* explode. It's very difficult.
CALM Yes.
NEUROTIC Maybe John Bradshaw is right. Maybe I've just got to get a hold of my inner child, write a letter to my parents telling them what I needed. But I think if I wrote a letter I would end up ranting and swearing, I'd get caught up in the moment. The typing it out would remind me of work and Mister Brickman and I'd end up dancing on his cracked skull. And if I ever found my inner child I'd probably kill it on accident anyway. Maybe that's why I never try those things.
CALM Well, it sounds like you haven't given them a chance, have you?

NEUROTIC looks at CALM suddenly, warily. Pause. Then looks away.

NEUROTIC I keep having this dream in which I finally break and act on my impulses. My husband accuses me of killing our daughter – which *I didn't* do – and I get fed up and shoot him, right in the head! Bang! Only I don't dance on it though. The dream ends before I see how I feel. Which is sort of disappointing because I'd like to know what it's like in the case that I ever actually do try it. You know? …I mean, you know?
CALM *(beat)* No, actually. No. I don't know. I don't know a single thing about

what you're saying. This is completely foreign to me. I don't know what your therapist is doing but it doesn't sound like much. I think you're sick. You strike me as dangerous. I don't think any of these thoughts you have are healthy at all. And I think you will explode. I think maybe you have already and just deny it, that these aren't dreams at all. For all I know you did shoot your husband, and probably your daughter too. And for all I know that Mister Brickman's head is cracked open right this very minute, you could have just fled the scene and come straight here. So that now I'm sitting beside a murderer who just killed her family *and* her boss.

NEUROTIC Pardon me, I think you've lost a hold on your senses. Do you hear yourself?

CALM Yes I do. Very clearly. I came to this park to escape too, just like you did. Only I came here for peace, for quiet and tranquility. You came here for the sole purpose of haunting me, to let out all your aggression on some stranger whom you could care less about because you're never going to see her again. Do you think that's okay? Do you think that when we leave here everything will be okay, that you will have purged your frustrations and I'll be that happy stranger who listened in your time of need? That's not it at all. I'm disturbed now. I have to be disturbed for the rest of my day because you came here and told me all these terrible things. This pretty scenery might as well be a manure pile now for all I care! That's how much good it's done me after listening to you! You have ruined my day! Do you understand? You have absolutely ruined my otherwise perfect day!

NEUROTIC Excuse me, I did not mean to upset you. If I had thought that–

CALM Oh! God! "If you had thought" nothing. You didn't think at all! If you *had* thought then you wouldn't have emptied all that garbage out of your mind and on to me! I'm tainted now! I'm disheveled! And I blame you!!

NEUROTIC *(matter-o'-factly)* You're co-dependent.

CALM pulls her gun and shoots NEUROTIC dead.

CALM BANG!!!

The sound of the gun is followed by the crashing finale of "O Fortuna," an extreme bit from Carmina Burana, *as NEUROTIC'S body flies ungracefully to the ground. Beat. CALM looks out into the audience with an urgent and surprised expression. Blackout, save the flashing red police light.*

Lights up to reveal the MAN standing above WOMAN with gun in hand, as in Scene One. Beat. Blackout as before.

Lights up to reveal WIFE standing above HUSBAND with gun in hand, as in Scene Two. Beat. Blackout as before.

Lights up to reveal HASTY and HOPE on the floor, the red light flashing, as in Scene Three. Beat. Blackout as before.

Lights up to reveal FATHER and SON sitting on their porch, as in Scene Five. Beat. Blackout as before.

Lights up on CALM holding her gun and NEUROTIC dead, as in moments ago. CALM pierces us with her urgent glare. Beat. Blackout. The loud music ends.

Scene Seven

Lights up immediately. The stage is bare. The actors are scattered about, all facing the audience. The scene moves quickly and though they may at times be speaking to each other, the actors do not necessarily need to make eye contact.

NEUROTIC Sometimes I have these impulses, I have these daydreams, I imagine myself lashing out.
FATHER I can't sleep lately. I tell people, "I can't sleep lately." They say, "Oh." They don't know quite what to say.
HOPE It's scary, the things that can happen. People change. Become different. Promise me we'll never become like that.
SON I figure I better learn something if I'm going to try to live on my own.
HOPE Promise me.
SON I better know how to do something, right?
NEUROTIC What do I gotta do, spell it out?
FATHER Maybe I *should* continue the dream and turn it around.
SON I can't just sit around and wait.
FATHER I've got to do something.
NEUROTIC When I dream about violence it scares me. But when I actually do it, it doesn't. Why is that? You would think it would be the other way around.
CALM Maybe when you actually do it you aren't thinking. Maybe you're really asleep.
FATHER Maybe I'll grab the gun from her hand and get her first.

WIFE Maybe I'll crush your head!
SON Something.
NEUROTIC Kill! Kill! Kill'm all!
FATHER Just turn things upside down, just turn the tables!
CALM At any rate it's ruined my day!
SON Gotta look out for myself!
NEUROTIC Gotta kill'm! Kill'm dead!
CALM & HOPE I wish I had stayed home!
SON And saved myself.
FATHER Then I'd be okay.
NEUROTIC *(determined)* Sometimes I have these impulses, I have these day dreams, and I imagine myself lashing out!
FATHER *(determined)* I can't sleep lately! I tell people, "I can't sleep lately!" They say, "Oh!" They don't know quite what to say!
HOPE *(desperate)* It's scary, the things that can happen. People change! Become different! Promise me we'll never become like that!
SON *(ironic)* "I've gotta learn something if I'm going to live on my own!"

Blackout. Immediately followed by a special up on NEUROTIC.

NEUROTIC *(sincerely)* I have this dream, in which I've killed my daughter, and kill my husband. It scares me. It frightens me very much. And I'm not sure what to do. When I wake up, my daughter is in her room, and my husband is beside me. And I'm not sure I know either one of them.

Special down on NEUROTIC and up on FATHER.

FATHER *(sincerely)* I have this dream, in which my daughter is dead, and my wife attempts to kill me. I'm not sure who killed my daughter, I think it was my wife. *I* couldn't have done it, I'm never around. It's terrifying. But then I wake up, my daughter is in her room, and my wife is beside me. And I'm not sure I know either one of them.

Special down on FATHER and up on SON.

SON *(sincerely)* I have this dream, that I make it on my own. And life is pretty good. But the trouble is other people always get in the way. And I'm not sure what to do. Because nobody listens anymore. They're all too afraid. And I'm not sure what to do, except look out for myself.

Special down on SON and up on HOPE.

HOPE *(sincerely)* I have this dream, that we go to Disneyland, we ride the Peter Pan ride and It's A Small World. And everything is okay. Only then I realize that nobody has been listening to each other. We've been having all this fun but not *with* anyone. They're all too afraid... Promise me we'll never become like that.

Special up on SON.

SON *(hesitant)* I promise.
HOPE Promise me we'll always be together.

Special up on FATHER.

FATHER I...
HOPE Promise me you love me.

Special up on NEUROTIC. Beat. She says nothing.

HOPE Promise me. *(beat. Then directly to SON.)* I love you. Promise me.

SON looks at her, torn. Beat. NEUROTIC and FATHER look at each other, tense and wary. Beat. SON turns away and pulls a gun, aims it straight at the audience. The others notice and do the same, first NEUROTIC, then FATHER, then finally HOPE. They all hesitate nervously. Then SON cocks his gun. The others do the same. At the sound of a loud collective bang, blackout. In darkness we hear:

HOPE I love you. Do you love me?
SON Yes.
HOPE I need to hear you say it.
SON ...I love you.
NEUROTIC I've been having this dream!
FATHER ...I know. So have I.

Music in darkness. Lights up. Bows.

The end.

Messenger #1

a new ancient greek tragedy

Messenger #1

The world premiere of *Messenger #1* was presented by Art Street Theatre at EXIT Stage Left, San Francisco, CA, on March 10, 2000. The production was directed by the author, with the following cast and staff:

MESSENGER #1	Karl Ramsey
MESSENGER #2	David Babich
MESSENGER #3	Beth Wilmurt
TROJAN MAIDEN / IPHIGENIA / ELECTRA	Gillian Chadsey
AGAMEMNON / ORESTES / EXECUTIONER	Kevin Clarke
TROJAN MAIDEN / CLYTEMNESTRA / THE FURIES / ATHENA	Michelle Talgarow

Set	Mark Jackson
Costumes	Elizabeth Spreen
Lights	Jason Ries
Sound	Jake Rodriguez
Stage Manager	Kathryn Clark

Dramatis Personae

Messenger #1, recently returned from the Trojan War.
Messenger #2, a man with a plan.
Messenger #3, recently discovered the world around her.
THE ROYAL CHORUS:
    1. Agamemnon, Orestes, The Royal Executioner.
    2. Trojan Maiden, Iphigenia, Electra.
    3. Trojan Maiden, Clytemnestra, The Furies, Athena.

Note

Though on its surface, the language of the play might at times suggest parody, it is important that the tragedy be played as seriously as the comedy is played for laughs. The one is the swinging door to the other, and the shifts between comedy and tragedy can be played as abruptly or as gradually as they appear to be on the page.

Scene One – Iphigenia in Aulis

In darkness, a match is struck. It is IPHIGENIA kneeling alone and lighting a candle. She stands and crosses slowly downstage. Behind her, a curtain parts suddenly. It is AGAMEMNON. He moves behind IPHIGENIA, drawing a knife with one hand and taking her by the shoulder with the other. CLYTEMNESTRA enters and crosses swiftly downstage to imagine in her mind's eye what she cannot see. A trio of MESSENGERS spray across the stage. MESSENGER #1 takes up his position on AGAMEMNON's ship, bound for Troy. MESSENGER #2 perches atop the House of Atreus. MESSENGER #3, dressed as a slave girl, hides off to the side. IPHIGENIA pleads for her life. MESSENGERS #1 and #3 sneak a final farewell. Tormented, AGAMEMNON finally does the deed, stabbing his daughter several times and viciously. CLYTEMNESTRA reacts from where she stands with an overwhelming grief as IPHIGENIA gasps her last breaths and falls dead. AGAMEMNON boards his ship.

Scene Two – Agamemnon

Paying close attention, but still hiding, MESSENGER #3 sneaks off and makes herself boyish, dressing in the uniform of the Messengers. MESSENGER #2 relays the following message and we are allowed to see much of what he describes.

MESS #2 Across the raging sea to Troy sails King Agamemnon and ten thousand Argive heroes to be! Cries of war burn their lungs and bait their breath! With bitter spats of vengeance they drench the name of Paris!

AGAMEMNON and MESSENGERS #1 and #2 all spit.

MESS #2 Paris! That two-faced guest in our House of Atreus. That bastard Trojan bum who, in swiping our Helen, shattered international laws of hospitality. For broken trust and swindled goods we fight. For Helen, Hope and Right did King Agamemnon sacrifice His Own Young Miss, Princess Iphigenia: daughter of his wife our queen Clytemnestra who now governs our fair state in her dear hubby's absence. A noble sacrifice – which, I hear it said, the young and supple girl did proudly bear like silver scars of war. On demand of that great Goddess Artemis, for fair winds to Troy did Agamemnon sacrifice his Baby Girl. For honor and country did our right and royal leader smear with red those pale and lovely limbs. For the righting of wrongs did he steep his hands in family blood! …It's a good thing! And oh the glory of battle! The glory of a thousand Argive ships ramming Trojan soil! Blades clamor for blades, spears pierce, shields crack on shields as Argive arrows split Trojan hearts, limbs, names, blood, battle, women, Helen, history! Let might be right and oh boy what a show!

We are witness to a few brief moments of the war in Troy, culminating in the point-blank execution of two TROJAN MAIDENS by AGAMEMNON's bow and arrow. Then...

MESS #2   And all this while I man the home front, serve my country perched atop the House of Atreus awaiting even one glimmer of conquest, one distant raging fire on yonder mountain peak, the blazing fruit of our victory gardens, the signal that triumph is ours. Against cold winds I pace. Under blazing summers I sweat. Dog-like I await my master's return no matter how many years it takes... And then: today. Atop that distant crag the curves of which my peepers have traced a thousand times and again: a ball of flames unfurls, a proud and orange flower to light up the night! Citizens! Queen Clytemnestra! Gods above! It is my proud honor and duty to inform you that Troy Is Wasted, the battle won, and Agamemnon is come back to us chest held peacock high and backed by row after row of Argive hero! Scars! Spears! Helmets under arms! Pucker up gals our boys are comin' home! God bless Argos! and the House! of Atreus!!

Silence. CLYTEMNESTRA and MESSENGER #2 are alone in the royal palace at Argos. CLYTEMNESTRA's silence clearly unnerves MESSENGER #2.

MESS #2   So... Pretty good news eh? ...Eh?
CLYTEMNESTRA   Agamemnon murdered Iphigenia. My husband murdered my daughter. For Helen.
MESS #2   Uhm. *(swallows audibly)* If you'd like to send a reply I have the forms.
CLYTEMNESTRA   Do you have children?
MESS #2   Nnnno but I have reply forms.
CLYTEMNESTRA   Do you have a daughter?
MESS #2   No, ma'am, I'm a messenger.
CLYTEMNESTRA   You cannot imagine. So much blood on such a face.
MESS #2   Yes. I mean no I– ...So. About that reply.
CLYTEMNESTRA   ...Tell Agamemnon: I eagerly await his return...
MESS #2   Gotcha. Right away. Thank you.

MESSENGER #2 hurries out and approaches MESSENGER #1. At first they are excited to see one another again, but quickly snap into a professional mode.

MESS #2   Hey how yuh doin'?

MESS #1 Good good.

MESS #2 Eh-hem! A message please, for King Agamemnon, from the queen his wife Clytemnestra. *(embellishing)* She joyously awaits his return with the love of a thousand wives; all the suppliants of Mount Olympus do not love their gods more than Clytemnestra loves her beefy war torn hubby, such is her love for him.

MESS #1 Jesus. Uh–, thank you. I will deliver your message... Sir–! Sir. If you please, a message from the queen your wife Clytemnestra.

AGAMEMNON Speak, herald.

MESS #1 It is told me: that Clytemnestra joyously awaits your return with the love of a thousand wives; all the suppliants of Mount Olympus do not love their gods more than Clytemnestra loves her beefy war torn hubby, such is her love for him. You.

AGAMEMNON Ah! To return from ten years' battle to such a loving welcome is more than mortal man can hope for. See to it that he who heralded these sweet tidings from my dear wife is richly rewarded for his pains.

AGAMEMNON hands MESSENGER #1 a bag of coins.

MESS #1 Sir.

AGAMEMNON And herald, see too that my concubines are well tended. Leave me now. I must prepare for my loving wife's welcome. No doubt she craves me. If you know what I mean. And I think you do.

MESS #1 Sir.

Scene Three – Homecoming

MESSENGER #1 takes his leave of AGAMEMNON and speaks to the audience. MESSENGER #3 watches from the side, still hiding.

MESS #1 And leave him I did! My duties done. Assignment complete. My war time dues paid in full. Back on Argive soil I stand and never happier!

MESS #2 *(enters)* Hey hey, there he is the big palooka!

MESS #1 *(to audience)* My old pal from days gone by! *(to MESS #2)* Hey buddy boy!

MESS #2 They make a man out of you or are yuh still that little snapper I used to whip on Sundays? Com'ere I'll give you a clobberin'!

THEY lurch into a loud and back-smacking embrace that eventually goes sincere.

MESS #2 How yuh doin' friend?

MESS #1 Oh I missed yuh old boy. I missed everything.

MESS #2 Wash your mouth out. You don't know a-b-c, pal. I'm the one who missed his chance. …So? …How was it?

MESS #1 What?

MESS #2 Don't play dumb how was it? The Trojan Damn War!

MESS #1 I was a messenger.

MESS #2 Did you kill anybody?

MESS #1 …I was a messenger.

MESS #2 Well don't leave me hangin' here like damp laundry, gimme the scoop, what happened? Did you see Helen? I mean: did yuh see 'er? Ooo! An' how 'bout them Trojan gals I hear they're the cat's meow; did yuh bag one o' them?

MESS #1 No sir.

MESS #2 Well come on wha'd you do over there in Troy?

MESS #1 I did my job if you really want to know what's what. For ten years I heralded this and messengered that for Agamemnon's Operation Helen. *(to the audience)* Helen! That stolen wench and fine-thighed woman, that infamous hotty, envy of a thousand shipfuls of drooling post-pubescent eyes who traded their youth for sword play, glory, and the hope of glimpsing Helen's wondrous hooters. Or at least of plastering their fantasy of that ship-launching face over the grimaces of those poor Trojan maidens who lost their childhood as spoils of war, and drank the bad breath of soldier after Argive soldier fumbling his way up his first skirt. And I ain't whistlin' Dixie. Believe you me, a boom of Trojan/Argive half breeds in patched-up knickers will soon be playing kick the can on Troy's shattered landscape. The war won, victory ours, and the salacious celebrations commenced, I fell back in the warm and bloody Trojan sands and wept and drank the sky above me, vowed no more talk of war, and sang to drown out the grunts of newly made men and the sobbing of their pre-teen conquests. I wept for my childhood lost in battle. I wept for my strange journey to manhood and the years sluiced down the drain in bloody spurts. I wept for the million messages I carried, the endless lists of sons and husbands now sucked at by new Trojan flowers. No I did not pop the cork of victory. …Now back to him. *(to MESS #2)* What did I do you ask?

MESS #2 I'm askin'!

MESS #1 Well I'll tell yuh. I fell back and I searched the clouds for my lovely's face.

MESS #2 Your what?

MESS #1 My girl back home! And as the clouds formed her face and the stars became her eyes and the moon shone down on her cumulus hair, I held tight my hands and prayed for that moment I hold her again. To her heavenly being I sang and sang and wept and sang!

MESS #2 Hey hey hey, keep it down will yuh. You're still workin' for the House of Atreus you know. No carryin' torches, remember?

MESS #1 Is that a fact. Ten years of ten thousand men at war for one woman and still no love allowed? So what else is new around here?

MESS #2 Plenty. But a messenger is still a messenger.

MESS #1 *(to audience)* The swells get the goods and all the riff raff gets is stories to tell if they're lucky, and their sons brothers and hubbies traded for names engraved in stone if their luck runs out.

MESS #2 Glory, pal, you get glory. And respect. You fought the big fight. You're on a page of History.

MESS #1 *(to audience)* All I did was wait to come back to my lovely.

MESS #2 Hey. I just saw yuh get off the boat so I know you didn't miss it.

MESS #1 Don't yuh see? It was her that kept my head above water. The thought of her wrapped around me and my hands in her golden hair. Her face. Her belly. Her small of her back. Her laughing in my ear and in my head her voice teaching me what daylight means.

MESS #2 You don't even know her anymore.

MESS #1 Oh I know her alright. I know her up and down.

MESS #2 You don't think ten years can change a gal's direction?

MESS #1 For ten years I've skirted Trojan arrows to make my way back to her loveliness. That windy day I set sail for Troy, that day Iphigenia gave her young limbs for a "page of history," on that morning my sweet love and I made a date to rendezvous in secret in the fields outside Argos on the eve of my return. If love is what I think it is, she'll be there tonight and that war will have meant something if only to make waiting to kiss her nose again more worth the waiting for.

MESS #2 Jeez Louise, zip it will yuh? Was it with cupid's arrows the Trojan brutes did wage their defense? I don't think so. War it seems has made not a man of you but a sap. You know the rules. Or did some Trojan torpedo give your block a knocking? You are a mess-en-ger. No steadies, no wives, no pitter patter of little feet. They up the insurance rates, buddy boy, rules are rules, and a messenger ain't worth more than food-for-one in their eyes. And worse than that now. That overseas skirmish wasn't cheap. You've been eatin' on the military's dollar for ten years but you're on civilian land again pal o' mine, and the price of beans ain't what it used to be. The cost o' living is gonna cost yuh. We got a good gig, you an I: The House of Damn Atreus! Ain't no ladder higher than that. Only Mercury's got it better. And a pink slip is your ticket back to slavery. So don't you blow it for some sheba.

MESS #1 Oh, I almost forgot! *(hands MESS #2 the coins)* Thanks, from Agamemnon, for your pains.

MESS #2 *(to audience)* Hot dog! I love this job!
MESS #1 *(to audience)* He loves this job.

> As MESSENGER #2 goes on and on, MESSENGER #1 eventually plugs his ears, singing, and leaves with MESSENGER #2 calling after him.

MESS #2 Oh go ahead, make fun. Sure we sweat and scramble, darting hither and yon to make a deadline, beat a rumor, –no: enlighten the uninformed. We get the exercise a body needs as we make sure the truth be told and the people in the know are in the know. A King can kill a princess his daughter but what's the difference if nobody hears about it? We're not just some cog in a machine. The swells may press the buttons, yes, but we are the energy that dashes from cause to effect. We're the blood in the veins that moves the nation. We spread the words that make History happen!

Scene Four – History 1A

> MESSENGER #3, who has been eavesdropping all this time, pops out to put in her two cents.

MESS #3 Yeah. Never mind our feet smashed to a pulp as we pound across endless wastelands of rock. Never mind our skin made leather by the hateful sun as we stand ready to faint while blurting out between gasps for breath some message to some Queen only half listening from beneath her slave-held parasol. Never mind our legs sliced to shreds as we hop through mine fields of thorny weeds to pass on a sprig of gossip for some doughy princess contemplating revenge for the smirks thrown her way by jealous debutantes at last night's society soirée. Never mind that we live in daily fear of royal whims to "kill the messenger" should we be unlucky enough to bear bad press, brewed by some pedestaled gent, who never knew us from Adam, nor never would launch a thousand ships to avenge our loss of face!

MESS #2 Yeah yeah yeah, on your way comrade! He'd do good to get wise before he rigs himself a noose with that talk. Success in the field means makin' the most of it. Travel! That's what it is! And adventure! A dollar earned by the grease of an honest elbow – and room to grow, if you're wily!

> The three MESSENGERS each dash forward in turn to speak to the audience, then dash off on their duties when they're done.

MESS #1 To pound out my angst on the sandy dunes or leap with my joy through soft grassy fields as I go about my duties. I'm unknown, unencumbered, unimportant. Perfect. I had my fill of purpose on the sands of Troy. I used to give a damn about the perils of my job description, but back then: I hadn't seen nothin' yet. Now I've peeked into Hell and delivered royal news with fierce Trojan arrows at my back like packs of hornets. The plight of the messenger here on Argive soil is as a jog to my years spent sprinting past the sting of death in bloody Troy. I'll take my civilian plight and I'll like it, for I've seen death in the flesh. And if to live long I have to button my lip, slap on a pair of rose-colored spectacles and blow secret kisses to my sweet and lovely lady: then that's just what I'm a'gonna do. Call me Joe Blow and forget my name as I run off into the sunset.

MESS #2 I got plans, yuh see. I have come to recognize that the message is the wave of the future. There's more gold to be mined from messenging than the occasional gratuity. Today, yes, we blister our toes to spread the news. But I say we grab the reins, clandestine like, with each passing year make the news more widely known and ourselves that much more central. I say we give our dogs a rest and put parchment to use, dole out the day's events to passersby on every main drag in every city. And that's just for starters. One day, news will pour in rivers through a thousand channels from town to town and house to house. And one day soon thereafter shall we spread the word on waves of air rippling across the heavens over oceans deep and mountains high. We'll cast our net over great Gaia's earth and for the right price no one will be left alone, not one person deprived of knowing what's what. The world will turn on the messenger's word and the swells' plump lives will be but meat for us to grind up and dish out to that hungry drooling populace half dead from boredom by their own daily grind. That's the day I'm livin' for. Until then, what good is it to bite the hand that feeds? Take it, shake it, and pull yourself up old boy. I got plans, yuh see.

MESS #3 Twenty and a handful years ago I slipped out the sulfurous pit of my ma, a bastard bundle of joy spawned of a messenger pop and the concubine dame he managed to corner in a beer-soaked moment. Orphan they called me and dumped me off at the National Slave Administration; said they had found me wailing in a trash bin on the side of the Road to Nowhere. And once I'd grown big enough to hoist a fan, for the next ten summers I fanned the likes of Princess Iphigenia and Princess Electra at the House of Atreus. For ten winters I stoked fires to warm their toes, never knowing there was more to womanhood than two kinds of woman: one made of gold and the other dirt, each doomed to a woman's life in Argos. Then. One fine day. I met a messenger boy, who, like my messenger pop, being a messenger, couldn't love me out loud. Our snuggles were secret but warm and wondrous. In his eyes I found out who I was and he found his who reflected in me. We shared our first malt and held our first hands and trembled together during our first fumble in the dark – after which he did not deposit me on a beer stained floor, but rather held me tight and told me I was his blood and bones and reason for living. And when woman-like he cried before my very eyes I believed his words and knew I'd found the light of day. Then suddenly comes the news: Iphigenia has given life and limb for her country and our great goddess Artemis reinstated the draft on Agamemnon's behalf. That windswept day my dear messenger boy set sail for Troy I felt my body torn in two. I stood on the shore and watched him disappear across the sea. And when those thousand black ships finally slipped over the horizon, I turned back to Argos and saw, clear as crystal, my lot in life, to which I said: "No thank you, I've had enough." Then, quicker than a blind eye can blink, I slipped away amongst the weeping throngs who'd gathered at the docks to wave farewell to our nation's boys. I chopped my hair and traded my skirts for knickers. Now I deliver the dirt my sweet boy once carried, and somehow I feel next to him as I race along the pathways once traced by him. I've seen corners of the world my woman's feet would never have touched. The slop I eat is by my own earnings bought, not tossed by some royal hash slinger to my corner of the dungeon. And between bouts of love-aches for my boy-off-to-war, my horizons widen as I take note of the state of Argos in King Agamemnon's absence. Word gets around. Quite often: I'm the one who gets it there. And I've spied a few cracks in this House of Atreus:

CLYTEMNESTRA enters, alone.

CLYTEMNESTRA   When my husband sailed for Troy I lost a daughter. When he returns, I shall lose a kingdom.

MESSENGER #2 enters CLYTEMNESTRA'S chamber.

MESS #2   I beg your pardon, Queen Clytemnestra. But I come bearing– …news– of your two sweet children Electra and Orestes.
CLYTEMNESTRA   What of them, my herald?
MESS #2   Before I relay this message, I'd just like to remind your highness that the content of the messages assigned to a particular messenger do not necessarily reflect the actions, opinions, or views of the messenger himself.
CLYTEMNESTRA   What of my children?
MESS #2   I'm just doin' my job.
CLYTEMNESTRA   Speak, herald, if you value your life.
MESS #2   Cutting to the chase then: I regret to inform you that officials at the National Slave Administration tell me that Electra and Orestes, those sweetest bundles of giggling offspring joy– …have been auctioned and sold, and that they now toil in the fields outside Corinth.
CLYTEMNESTRA   …Thank you, herald.
MESS #2   I'm so sorry your highness they were such good kids–

CLYTEMNESTRA Thank you, herald. You may leave me to my grief.
MESS #2 I can? I mean I will! Thank you, sorry for your loss, bye.

> *MESSENGER #2 hurries away. Once alone, CLYTEMNESTRA's sighing subsides and her habitually solemn expression morphs into a huge grin. She gives the audience a sudden thumbs-up gesture, then returns to her solemnity.*

Scene Five – Rendezvous

> *MESSENGER #1 en route to the fields outside Argos to meet his lovely.*

MESS #1 Hopping for joy I make my way to the fields outside Argos to meet my love. The years seem to roll back at the thought of her and I am a pimple-pocked boy once again, my stomach a swarm of flaming butterflies and my hands all sweaty from their heat. Will she recognize me? How's my hair? Will my musk still give her goose bumps? Or has war fouled my scent and hardship drained my fun factor? I'm fit. I'm trim. I've still got the odd joke up my sleeve to make her belly ache from laughing into the wee night hours. And I've learned a thing or two. I've got more living under my belt, more to offer a girl than chatter about the latest ditty on the pop charts. *(Pause. A realization:)* I'm different now.
CLYTEMNESTRA For ten years have I awaited this day. Agamemnon left Argos my husband, returns my husband, and as such will he go hence.
MESS #1 Perhaps she will not be herself. That self I once waved farewell to on the docks, I mean. Or, rather, will she be more herself and now grown too big for the confines of our childhood romance?

> *Enter AGAMEMNON, somewhere in the palace.*

AGAMEMNON Was it only yesterday I bade farewell to my sweet and weeping wife?
CLYTEMNESTRA Was it only yesterday I lost a daughter, and gained a crown?
MESS #1 Will we again be love at first sight? Or have I lost more at war than fellow soldiers?
AGAMEMNON To return at last to the arms of my Clytemnestra have I waited too long. Nights spent sweating amongst the limbs of concubines is one thing. But a man's wife is the ground beneath his feet.

> *AGAMEMNON and CLYTEMNESTRA's eyes meet. THEY exit together,*

the happy royal couple.

MESS #1 Have we been too long away? And yet I have ten years of questions to ask her! Ten years of stories to tell! I've dreamt this day ten million times with me the rain drenching her in kisses and words and laughing and she the earth to soak me up and give me her new spring flowers, all her beauty, her smells, her wishes. …Her Life Story… I've worked so hard to remember her just the way she was. Though of course we all know in ten years a girl's bound to change a bit. It's just that sometimes we forget.

MESSENGER #3 appears in the field and looks at MESSENGER #1.

MESS #3 …Hello.

A very long pause as they stare at one another for the first time in ten years. Eventually, MESSENGER #3 remembers she is wearing a cap and takes it off, releasing her hidden hair. Another pause. Then…

MESS #3 …How are you?
MESS #1 Good.
MESS #3 …How was Troy?
MESS #1 Not so good… You?
MESS #3 I'm a messenger now.
MESS #1 I see that. How?
MESS #3 I ran off the day you left, laid low. Then came back like this and asked for a job. They think I'm a boy. Guess I'm not pretty enough to get caught… You look good.
MESS #1 You look beautiful.
MESS #3 You look beautiful.
MESS #1 Thank you. You look beautiful too.
MESS #3 Thank you… I watched yuh get off the boat today. It was all I could do to keep from calling out.
MESS #1 …Uh… Y-you been keepin' busy?
MESS #3 Messenging. Like you. It's a step up from slaving, believe me. I've seen so many things. And realized so many things. We deserve so much more. We're all just struggling to be mortal yet somehow I wonder if the swells tend to confuse themselves with the gods. It's not right. You shouldn't have had to sail to Troy for Helen's sake. A messenger shouldn't have to live in daily fear of hanging for delivering someone else's bad news. We shouldn't have to hide out here in a field to maintain their insurance rates. I didn't realize this before when

my only view of the world was the back of Princess Electra and Iphigenia's heads. I didn't know anything. But on my messenger's journeys I've now seen the world for what it is. And it's not right. ...What do you think?

> MESSENGER #1 *now reaches out and touches* MESSENGER #3's *hair. Then a kiss. The kiss is a precious thing, backed up by a ten-year wait.*

MESS #3   Oh I've missed you.
MESS #1   I dreamt of you every day.
MESS #3   Did you?
MESS #1   Did I?

> MESSENGER #1 *takes* MESSENGER #3's *hat from her hands and tosses it to the side. He faces her and puts out his left hand. She looks at it, then at him. Smiling.*

MESS #3   What are you doing?
MESS #1   Take it.

> MESSENGER #3 *takes* MESSENGER #1's *hand. The smiles fade. He slowly steps closer and puts his right hand on her waist. Her left hand moves slowly to his shoulder. Music bursts into the air. Etta James. "At Last." Very romantic.* MESSENGERS #1 *and* #3 *begin to dance. Meanwhile,* CLYTEMNESTRA *welcomes* AGAMEMNON *into her bedchambers.* AGAMEMNON *prepares for some heavy petting.* CLYTEMNESTRA *stabs him repeatedly until he is dead and the* MESSENGERS' *dance climaxes.* CLYTEMNESTRA *removes her wedding ring and then exits as* MESSENGERS #1 *and* #3 *twirl about the stage.*

Scene Six – Extra! Extra!

> *The song scratches to a halt as* MESSENGER #2 *bursts through the fields.* MESSENGER #3 *quickly dons her cap.*

MESS #2   Hey guys! Big news! You'll never guess what happened! ...What are you doing? ...You're kidding. You're kidding! That dream girl that had you saluting during wartime is him?!
MESS #1   It's not what you think.
MESS #2   So it's true what they say about men packed in boats.

MESS #3 I'm not a boy.
MESS #2 Not a boy!

> *MESSENGER #2 feels MESSENGER #3's chest. He is startled by what he finds there and jerks his hand away. He reaches out slowly with one finger, amazed, to touch her again but she slaps it down.*

MESS #2 I've wondered why you always use the stalls! I just thought you were shy. You're not shy, you're a girl!
MESS #3 Yes I am.
MESS #1 It's okay.
MESS #2 It's illegal! That's what it is!
MESS #3 The Trojan War was illegal.
MESS #2 Hey watch it, sister, that man's a veteran yuh know. Show some respect!
MESS #1 Say, what's that big news?
MESS #2 What?
MESS #1 That big news you were so excited about.
MESS #2 Oh! That's right! Clytemnestra killed Agamemnon!

> *AGAMEMNON stands and exits to the afterlife.*

MESS #1 & #3 What?!
MESS #2 It's the crime of the century! *(to himself)* What am I gonna do? Everything's about to change.
MESS #1 We should tell the people.
MESS #2 Okay but what exactly do we tell them?
MESS #3 Someone has to tell Electra and Orestes.
MESS #2 They were sold into slavery. They're not royalty anymore.
MESS #3 Their mother killed their father.
MESS #2 They're slaves.
MESS #1 No time for politics, folks, we've got news to deliver.
MESS #3 This news is politics!
MESS #1 *(quick kiss)* Time to go to work.
MESS #3 What about us?
MESS #1 Us? We have a lifetime ahead of us.
MESS #2 If you were smart you'd make like you'd never met.
MESS #1 Well… we've never been the sharpest tools in the shed, now have we?

MESS #2 She's a girl! Messengers are men! It's the law!

MESS #1 But what's the difference if nobody hears about it? …Right?

MESS #2 Listen pal, I could get in big trouble for this. Before I didn't know. Now I know. That changes everything. I'm a third party. It's illegal!

MESS #1 And we've got bigger news to bear so get moving!

MESS #3 Everything is about to change.

The MESSENGERS burst into work mode.

MESS #2 People of Argos, I come bearing news to burst your hearts! Agamemnon our king is dead! Chaos rules in Argos! She who has ruled our land since Agamemnon first set sail for victory in Troy ten long years ago, she, our queen, his wife, Clytemnestra–

CLYTEMNESTRA enters. MESSENGER #2 has a light-bulb, and his tone transmutes into that of a happy introduction.

MESS #2 Clytemnestra… now takes the throne. Therefore fear not, good people. For our dear queen, despite her own great suffering, will heal this wound that bleeds the heart of Argos. We are lucky, indeed, for her strength. Long live Queen Clytemnestra and The House of Atreus.

Sound of applause. MESSENGER #2 steps to the side graciously as CLYTEMNESTRA moves forward to address the people of Argos. All three MESSENGERS stand at attention during their Queen's speech.

CLYTEMNESTRA My fellow Argives. Neither I nor the greatest poets of our land can express in words the agony I suffer today. Who would have expected such misery would come to us on this joyous day of celebration. Agamemnon's Trojan wounds were deeper than reported, and he clung to his life but long enough to touch Argos soil once more before sighing his last. That's what happened. Let us not ask why. It is not for us to understand the dictates of Fate. Let's just drop it, and move on, shall we? And pray to the gods that our nation's suffering ends here with this our final sacrifice. Good night, and long live the House of Atreus.

Applause swells. CLYTEMNESTRA exits feigning solemnity. Applause fades away. The MESSENGERS remain where they are, standing at attention.

MESS #3 That was the most heinous display I have ever seen.

MESS #2 Don't bite the hand that feeds you.
MESS #3 That hand would ring your neck for so much as a stutter.
MESS #2 Exactly my point!
MESS #1 It's not our business.
MESS #3 It is our business.
MESS #1 This is a family drama and we are not family. We are employees.
MESS #2 Amen, brother.
MESS #3 How can you say that?
MESS #1 I am not your brother.
MESS #3 How can you say that?
MESS #2 What do you mean you're not my brother, we're eye-to-eye on this are we not?
MESS #1 No we are not.
MESS #2 But you just said–
MESS #1 Cork it, pal. I love yuh but you're a sucked-up idiot with a brown schnozz. Fact is, Helen did not launch a thousand ships. Agamemnon launched a thousand ships. It was not Helen's hips that grounded half the men of Argos. Agamemnon's war cry managed that well enough! Ah! But I have done with talk of that. I'm a messenger, that's that, the war is over and we're free of it.
MESS #3 We're none of us free. We're slaves to the tyrannical whims of the House of Atreus.
MESS #2 Would you shut up!
MESS #3 They drag us on their ego trips and bid us do their dirty work. We didn't go to Troy because Paris broke "international laws of hospitality," please! We went to Troy for Agamemnon's pride. And if Helen had been saggy and pear-shaped like a real woman, and not silicon-pumped with hips sliced off at ten thousand smackers a pop, then Agamemnon would never have been so proud.
MESS #2 You have a death wish.
MESS #1 Can't we talk about something else?
MESS #3 I am going to Corinth to tell Orestes and Electra. They have a right to know their father has been murdered.
MESS #1 Clytemnestra would have you flogged with vipers. It's the curse on the House of Atreus, stay out of it. It's a family thing.
MESS #3 That family does not share my values.
MESS #2 Oh god, bravo, clever comeback. They may not be the model family but they do pay your rent. Besides he's right: their House is cursed, ever since that business with old man Atreus and his brother. They've got homicide in their blood. There's nothing you can do about it.
MESS #1 It's their fight, not yours.

MESS #3 You did go away to war... I will to Corinth to give Orestes and Electra the gift of truth. They deserve to know their father shall not come free them from Clytemnestra's tyranny... Goodbye... ...?
MESS #1 ...Goodbye.

Scene Seven – The Royal Tots in Exile

ORESTES and ELECTRA toil in the fields of Corinth.

ELECTRA Where is the garden of velvet moss that once cooled my feet? Where the loving arms of a father and mother to quiet my cries in the dark?
ORESTES Where is the house with beams tall and strong? Where the walls that shielded me from the daggers of winter winds and cruel branding of summer's vengeful sun?
ELECTRA Where the tenderness?
ORESTES Where comfort?
ELECTRA We've come a long way from home.
ORESTES Now there is but blasting heat and blisters underfoot.
ELECTRA My hands rough like the backs of desert lizards.
ORESTES My spine a low and crooked branch that begs mercy.
ELECTRA My eyes bleary and tear stung.
ORESTES Sold into slavery by our mother. That venomous viper.
ELECTRA Sulfurous pit.
ORESTES Gold digging hag.
ELECTRA Penis envying crock for spew.
ORESTES Fie, Fie, and fuck her!
ELECTRA Cunt bitch shit for brains and fatherland fucker!
ORESTES I hope she goes mad from syphilis and blisters in the heat of ten thousand sweltering plagues!
ELECTRA I hope a swarm of flies infects her stinking crack with maggots!
ORESTES I hope a dozen writhing cobras suck the toxic milk from those sagging bags men once called boobs!
ELECTRA I hope a fleet of drunken sailors drops anchor in her ass, and stuffs her mouth full o' shit!
ELECTRA / ORESTES I hope she dies!!!

A pause. Sometime soon, MESSENGER #3 enters unnoticed.

ORESTES ...I hate her.

ELECTRA …I hate her too.

ORESTES Let's hate her together.

ELECTRA Brother you can say that twice.

ORESTES Let's hate her together.

ELECTRA One more time.

ORESTES Let's hate her together.

ELECTRA Say it like you mean it!

ORESTES Let's hate her together!

ELECTRA Say it to the gods!

ORESTES Let's hate her together!

ELECTRA Say it!

ORESTES I hate her!

ELECTRA Hate! her!

ORESTES Hate!

ELECTRA Hate!

ORESTES / ELECTRA Hate!

MESS #3 Hey there! …I come bearing news from Argos.

ORESTES Who art thou?

MESS #3 I am a messenger from the House of Atreus, your home.

ELECTRA You mean our mother's home. Come you from her to mock our misery?

MESS #3 I come of my own accord.

ORESTES Have you come then to free us from exile?

MESS #3 No. Worse.

ELECTRA Huh. What could be worse than the life of a slave?

MESS #3 …I wouldn't know, Princess.

ORESTES Tell us your news, quickly, lest our new masters find you here and hang us all.

MESS #3 Agamemnon, your father, has returned from Troy.

ELECTRA Oh! At last the day has come!

ORESTES We are rescued!

ORESTES and ELECTRA embrace, laughing joyfully.

MESS #3 But no sooner did he greet your mother, the queen, then she did stab and kill him.

A Pause. Then…

ELECTRA That fucking bitch!

ORESTES She killed him!?

MESS #3 Yes.

ELECTRA Well that's just great!

ORESTES Now what are we gonna do?!

ELECTRA I told you she was a bitch! We're screwed! We're so fucking screwed! I hate this shit! I hate it! *(breaking down)* I can't take it. I'm a princess goddamn it. I'm a princess.

MESS #3 I-I'm sorry for your loss. I thought you should know. If Clytemnestra knew I was here she would have me hanged.

ELECTRA What shall become of us, Orestes?

ORESTES We will die as slaves.

MESS #3 I'm sorry to be so brief, but–

ELECTRA No. We will not die as slaves!

ORESTES But whatever shall we do? Father is dead and our mother his reaper! We are all alone in the world.

ELECTRA We'll think of something.

MESS #3 …So, at any rate, goodbye… …Glad I could be of help.

ORESTES and ELECTRA remain in an embrace, not paying one iota of attention to MESSENGER #3, who finally leaves a bit perturbed. ORESTES and ELECTRA remain in their tight embrace as they speak.

ORESTES I could just kill somebody right now.

ELECTRA My sentiment exactly.

ORESTES Are you thinking what I'm thinking?

ELECTRA I think so.

ORESTES But how is't to be done?

ELECTRA When all the house is asleep, and we slaves condemned to our chambers, the gatekeepers shall I with wine so convince that memory shall be but a fume. And when in swinish sleep the drunken bums lie as in a death, at that dark hour shall we slip between the moonlight's slivers and wend our way back to Argos.

ORESTES If we should fail?

ELECTRA Fail? But screw your courage to the sticking place and we'll be just fine. Think of Argos. And her.

ORESTES Oh, I hate her.

ELECTRA I hate her too.

ORESTES Murderess of our homeland.
ELECTRA Thief of our birthright.
ORESTES It is for Argos, after all, that we now toil in Corinth.
ELECTRA As it will be for Argos that we return.

Beat. Then giddy giggles, which ORESTES suddenly halts with:

ORESTES Oh, and to avenge our dear Father's blood.
ELECTRA Oh yes, that too.
ORESTES Come, let's away. And thank the gods above for this so foul and fair weathered day.
ELECTRA Fuckin' A.

THEY high-five.

Scene Eight – While On Assignment…

A sharp thunderclap and trailing rumble. The MESSENGERS all monologue about the current state of affairs while on their separate assignments.

MESS #1 Such news! And who would have guessed it? A return fit for a king now curdled in the blood of the habits of Atreus. As I pass the official version of the story from noble to noble, I contemplate my own recent reunion – also cut short in the midst by Clytemnestra's death blow. …Say, she's one tough cookie, that woman of mine. A woman indeed. No twittering girl, her, no! And yet her question rings in my ears. "What about us?" she asked, "What about us?" …Well, what about us? That's what I'd like to know, and what I still wonder as I dash from dune to dune on these my hotly charged duties of historical proportion. I might love her all the more. If I knew who she was.

MESS #3 How do you like that? Thankless brats whose sweaty brows I once did fan, whose stinking feet I once laced in fine slippers to keep their soft toes soft, me, a child their age yet twice as old from carrying the burden of their royal adolescent whimsies. Here I deliver them the truth, that will not be shared with the general public for at least a few hundred years, at which time some red-taped ninny will release a file all streaked with black marker, revealing just enough juice for the poets to dip their pens into and scribble a rendering of these days then safely gone by. And who will care in those hundreds of years from now but fresh college grads and tenured academic twits who feed on this schlock we call history. "Leave it to history to tell." Well let me remind you that, outside the memory of those who were there, history is something bought and paid for and not by you and the likes of I. It's a couple o' swells like Orestes and Electra who make history happen.

MESS #2 Get the message, deliver the message, get the message, deliver the message. A system that works. And look how I change the course of Argos, just me and my buzz words. All I have to do is turn a phrase and everything's different. After all, the news is as it is told. Maybe when the royals do kill us for bearing their bad press it's because they recognize the power of our mouths to render their days dark and spin their world in new directions. They need us and they know it. Best not to remind them too often, though. Let them think they make news. A system that works. Why mess with it?

MESS #1 I returned from Troy to be done with carnage and here my first civilian assignment is the gory end of that selfsame King who dragged me down his bloody path to manhood.

MESS #2 You think you know a guy,

MESS #1 Not the path I'd have chosen myself.

MESS #2 and then he turns out to be a girl with a thing for anarchy

MESS #3 Filthy rich-kid snots!

MESS #2 and wrapped around the heart o' your best pal.

MESS #1 Argos is promising to be as gut-strewn as the Trojan shores

MESS #2 It's dangerous I tell yuh!

MESS #1 and if that's the case I wish my woman was a girl again, and me her gangly boy, and neither of us ever awakened to the wicked ways of this our homeland.

MESS #3 But wait!

MESS #2 And I wish to Zeus I'd never busted in on that damned "secret rendezvous."

MESS #3 In all my fuming I've misplaced thoughts of my recently returned boy.

MESS #2 A good case of what I didn't know didn't hurt me.

MESS #3 What about us, I asked.

MESS #2 But, too late now!

MESS #1 What about us.

MESS #3 And glad I was that news of Clytemnestra's reptilian crime broke our love spell. Is that not strange? Glad I was. Relieved, even! If the truth be known I'm afraid I may love him still, and willingly hopped aboard the excuse of our sudden messenger's duties to make an exit. For what will become of me if I must play the woman's part again? I cannot deny the world I've come to know, my new life, the knowledge that we who inform the world can change the world. It's our duty. Somehow. We can make things happen.

MESS #1 Think about her later old boy.

MESS #2 There's work to be done.

MESS #3 It's just that sometimes we forget.

Scene Nine – The Libation Bearers.

It is night. ELECTRA and ORESTES sneak up to the House of Atreus.

ELECTRA The evening's feasts are done. Soon the House prepares to sleep. When all are to their beds and dreaming, then shall we strike.
ORESTES What of the guards?
ELECTRA Guards are guards. That which freed us from Corinth will just as easily open the gates of this our former home. A glimpse of thigh and a couple o' swigs of vino will take care of them. Then: in you go.
ORESTES Me? What about you?
ELECTRA Someone has to make sure the coast stays clear.
ORESTES No. We will proceed no further in this business.
ELECTRA Excuse me?
ORESTES A son to kill his mother? A prince his queen?
ELECTRA …Happens all the time.
ORESTES I will be hated by the people of Argos. What good is royalty then?
ELECTRA Better to be hated by men than by the gods. If we do not avenge our father's murder it will be as a black hole in heaven. Apollo will plague our days and nights with rabid hell hounds and other weird voodoo shit.
ORESTES We can pray at his temple, offer sacrifices. Sheep!
ELECTRA Think of our dear father, slain by that woman's ungrateful hands. Shall we doom him to roll forever in his grave? We must wash away his blood with the blood of Clytemnestra lest our father's eternal restlessness break open the earth beneath our feet.
ORESTES And once our hands are dipped in her red venom, who then shall come to wipe us from the earth?
ELECTRA …These are the Laws of Blood. It is our duty to kill Clytemnestra. It is our right. She wears your crown. She dwells in our house. We are the heirs of Agamemnon. We pulse with the blood of kings. She's just some hussy who got lucky. A murderess. A wicked siren who lured our father to untimely death.
ORESTES Right.
ELECTRA So you go in there, and you do what's right.
ORESTES Right.
ELECTRA Do it for the gods.
ORESTES The gods.
ELECTRA Do it for history.
ORESTES History.

ELECTRA Do it for your father!
ORESTES My Father!

CLYTEMNESTRA enters, though she does not yet see her children.

ELECTRA Go get'm, Tiger!
ORESTES ARRR! Oh! There she is!
ELECTRA Oh! Quick! Hide hide hide hide!

ORESTES and ELECTRA scatter and hide.

CLYTEMNESTRA Herald! I have a message for thee!

MESSENGER #2 pops in obediently.

MESS #2 At your service, my Queen.
CLYTEMNESTRA You are the swiftest of my messengers.
MESS #2 Thank you.
CLYTEMNESTRA And the most loyal.
MESS #2 I'm so glad you think so.
CLYTEMNESTRA I have a message of great import that needs the fire of your feet.
MESS #2 Lay it on me. …My queen.
CLYTEMNESTRA I have been reviewing the books, and have composed a new law which I expect to be enacted by morning. From this day forth, before going to market all harvests shall pass through the House of Atreus for purposes of health and safe-handling inspection. The House shall retain its usual share plus additional sums to compensate for the added cost of inspection, red tape, and whatnot. It is for the good of our people's health. Deliver this news, herald, to the Royal Agriculture Administration. I will expect a full report as to their reply and progress before the night is through.
MESS #2 I'll get right on it.
CLYTEMNESTRA Leave me now. I must continue my lamentations for my dear husband's untimely death.
MESS #2 Right.

MESSENGER #2 slips away. CLYTEMNESTRA grins and chuckles with self satisfaction. ELECTRA shoves ORESTES into view. ORESTES hides again, shoving ELECTRA into view. ELECTRA hides again, shoving ORESTES back into view.

CLYTEMNESTRA My son!

ORESTES My father's son.

CLYTEMNESTRA What are you doing here? Oh–! Uh, how I have worried about you so! Where have you been?

ORESTES You know right well where I have been! In Corinth, a slave in the fields by order of the queen, Clytemnestra!

CLYTEMNESTRA …Who has fed you such lies?

ORESTES You killed our father for the key to the House of Atreus!

CLYTEMNESTRA More lies.

ORESTES You swept your children under the rug for the throne of Argos.

CLYTEMNESTRA If I rule now over Argos, Destiny made it so.

ORESTES Then your Destiny ends tonight.

CLYTEMNESTRA Ah! You would take my life when I gave life to you?

ORESTES You abandoned motherhood when you sold your children. You gave me only birth and misery.

CLYTEMNESTRA I never abandoned you. F-fearing retributions from Troy, I I I sent you to the house of allies in Corinth. I never meant for you to be sold a slave.

ORESTES Oh what was it? A type-o?

CLYTEMNESTRA Yes, a type-o.

ORESTES Stupid woman! Drenched in lies and vice!

CLYTEMNESTRA You might speak of your father's vice.

ORESTES Dare you insult his name? My father was a hero. Your husband was a god!

CLYTEMNESTRA He was a man! And a soldier, I'll grant him, with a soldier's lust! No doubt the shores of Troy are strewn with your half brothers and half sisters and their deflowered twelve-ear-old mothers, disgraced and forever unwed.

ORESTES My father would not do such things.

CLYTEMNESTRA Oh, off to war for ten years and not one cherry popped? I don't think so. Soldiers are drawn to virgin blood as their daggers are to those virgins' brothers.

ORESTES And who are you to moralize?

CLYTEMNESTRA It is hard for a woman to be kept from her husband, and kept by him, for so long.

ORESTES It was his labor that gave you this House in which you keep.

CLYTEMNESTRA Labor? Don't you mean lineage?

ORESTES *(draws his dagger)* I mean to end your tyranny.

CLYTEMNESTRA You mean to kill your mother!

ORESTES You are your own killer, not I.

CLYTEMNESTRA Then beware a mother's curse!

ORESTES I have suffered your curses for too long already!

CLYTEMNESTRA To think that I suckled this serpent. That I gave it life. No! What you are doing?! Please! My son!

> *ELECTRA watches, wild eyed, as ORESTES stabs CLYTEMNESTRA viciously and SHE struggles to get at him before finally collapsing to the ground, dead. The MESSENGERS burst forth with the news. ORESTES and ELECTRA stand staring at CLYTEMNESTRA's body.*

MESS #1 Noble Gentlemen! I come bearing horror to pile on horror! With three swift blows has Orestes, son of our late king Agamemnon, slain his mother the queen. Will the endless curse on the House of Atreus forever unfold?

> *MESSENGER #2 yanks MESSENGER #1 away and tells a different story.*

MESS #2 Noble gentry of the House of Atreus. It is my duty to inform you that Clytemnestra, that coiled viperess, who, but freshly squeezed into the throne, had promptly readied herself to wield her husband's scepter like a crimson sickle over your land and reap the wealth of all Argos, this same queen has met the fate of her deceit. Agamemnon's hasty demise hard upon his return from glorious victory at Troy left us in the hands of this fiendish queen whom we trusted. Now, the gallant young Orestes, Prince of Argos, son of our former great king, has freed us from impending tyranny before it had chance to strike. In other words: Hot dog! We're in good hands now!

MESS #3 Murder follows murder! And murderers rule again in the House of Atreus–!

MESS #2 Your highness! Anything that you'd like me to tell the people? ...No? Alright. Well, when you're ready, just you remember: I'm your *(partly to MESSENGER #3:)* man.

ORESTES ...Look at all the blood.

ELECTRA We did it. Shit. You're the king now. You're the king of Argos. ...What do we do first?

ORESTES Well... We should probably tell somebody.

MESS #2 Already taken care of! I took the liberty, uh, well, best not to let rumors get started, so, I went ahead and told the gentry, uh, that she was bad and that you're good and so everything's good. You're set. The people will demand to know more so we'll have to figure out how you wanna phrase it and–

ORESTES Beware a mother's curse, she said.

ELECTRA Sh-she was desperate. You did the right thing. You only followed the dictates of blood. It's the law of heaven. Apollo supports reparations; he demands them. Apollo will protect you. It was right, Orestes. *(takes a step away)* And you did it.

ORESTES You told me to do it!

ELECTRA Well if I told you to jump off Mount Olympus would you do that too?!

ORESTES Electra!

ELECTRA Okay I'm sorry! We did it! We did it! ...And now we rule over Argos. ...?

ORESTES Yes. Yes we do.

CLYTEMNESTRA stands and exits to the afterlife.

Scene Ten – Rendezvous, Part II

As MESSENGER #1 mentions them, each character exits and we return to the fields outside Argos.

MESS #1 So: whilst my pal, as it seems, is yet again wedging himself into the good graces of this the latest king, and that gutter-mouthed sister of his, I and my sweet lovely run our separate ways to rendezvous again in the fields outside Argos. Again my gut rumbles with butterflies that roar like lions. Again I arrive sweating and not just from the jog, my anticipation swelling like a flood and me a bobbing drift of wood swept along for the ride. And once again our fondness is kept hidden from the world by the dark of night. But not for long if I can help it.

MESS #3 Hey there.

MESS #1 So the world has up and changed once again. You told Orestes and Electra the truth.

MESS #3 Tsch. Spoiled urchins barely noticed I had taken the trouble.

MESS #1 What do you mean?

MESS #3 I risked life and limb to tell them what's what and they promptly forgot I was there, too packed with their own importance to so much as thank the messenger.

MESS #1 Did you really stick your neck out for a thank you card from them?

MESS #3 I was their slave for ten years, you'd think they'd recognize me.

MESS #1 Did they?

MESS #3 *(insulted by the fact)* No.

MESS #1 Then you're lucky.

MESSENGER #3 looks at #1, then clasps her hands to her head.

MESS #3   …Oh! My mind is like a twister inside. I can't stop thinking about you, really, I can't. And then suddenly I do – when Argos comes flooding in. It's our home too. It belongs to all of us, not just the swells with their royal bloodlines like reins and us their tethered donkeys. Argos is our home.

MESS #1   Then let's run away.

MESS #3   …Run away?

MESS #1   From home. Let's leave this place, all this blood and bowing and our secret smooching under cover of darkness. Kisses need sunlight lest they whither and die.

MESS #3   You are my knight in shining armor, you are.

MESSENGER #1 kisses #3. Pause.

MESS #3   Did you kill anyone in Troy?

MESS #1   …I wasn't a soldier. That wasn't my job.

MESS #3   But did you? It's okay to tell me, isn't it?

MESS #1   I don't want to think about The War.

MESS #3   But you do think about it.

MESS #1   But I don't want to!

MESS #3   I think about it. All the time. It seems I can only think about the war. And you. And somehow I think you became for me the tomb of the unknown soldier.

MESS #1   How romantic.

MESS #3   Your name engraved on every monument and your face carved on every rusting statue tucked away in every city park in the nation. And I wanted you to come back to life.

MESS #1   And come back I have! Which makes you my life!

MESS #3   …I can't leave Argos.

MESS #1   Oh!

MESS #3   We can't leave.

MESS #1   Why! Why! Why!

MESS #3   We have a duty. It's our job. And we can make a difference. It's our responsibility.

MESS #1   My responsibility is to deliver messages for congenitally wealthy bastards, and if the world happens to up and change in the process well that's none of my business. They make history, dog gone it! We just talk about it! How are you going to change their world with words when they've got daggers?

MESS #3   I love you. I love you. I love you.

MESS #1 *(still mad)* ...I love you.
MESS #3 I love you too.
MESS #1 Then come away with me.
MESS #3 But I'm not finished here yet.
MESS #1 Well... Do you know when you might wrap things up?
MESS #3 I don't think it's a package deal.
MESS #1 What?
MESS #3 Love.
MESS #1 Love and what? What else is there?
MESS #3 Satisfaction.
MESS #1 ...Sounds like you've been shakin' the wrong packages.

Scene Eleven – The Furies

> *ORESTES bursts into the fields and MESSENGER #1 and #3 quickly hide on opposite sides of the stage.*

ORESTES AAAAH! No more noise! Please! My head pounds with the drumming of blood! My eyes are drenched with memories that my hands cannot close out! My fingers spread in horror and cannot seize the reins! ...But before I go totally insane, know this dear heavens above: that I killed my mother with the law of blood standing at my side, and that the law has a name, and that name is Apollo. Had I failed, who knows what terrible evils would have befallen me? No number of daggers could do worse than to let such a crime as Clytemnestra's against my Father go unavenged. Apollo declares it so. What I did was right. The world must be kept in balance! ...Oh what am I talking about, I'm doomed. I can't rule over Argos. I'm not my father. ...I'm not fit. ...And I'm not safe. I must run. Run from the blood I spilled. Run from my own blood. Outrun the memories which howl in my head, the bloodlines in my veins, the history that is my family. Into the desert plains of exile go I with only my fear to protect me. The House of Atreus promises me no shelter from this storm, for in life as in death my name will always be remembered for this. And this. And this. ...Apollo is my only hope.

> *MESSENGER #2 bursts in.*

MESS #2 Your highness! Your High–
ORESTES Ah-aah-uh...!
MESS #2 Oh, there you are! Your Highness!
ORESTES Do not soil the titles of royalty by draping them upon my back. I

am stooped for prayer, not coronation.

MESS #2 But I come baring news from the oracles of Apollo.

ORESTES Wha'd they say! Tell me everything!

MESS #2 You are to make for the city of Athena, show her suppliance, fall at her idol's feet, sing hymnals in praise of her loving arms, and there Apollo will defend you from Clytemnestra's curse.

ORESTES I'll do it. I'll leave right now. Beware a mother's curse, she said. What form will that mother's curse take?

> *ORESTES turns to go. Just then, the FURIES appear. ORESTES points in horror.*

ORESTES AAH!

MESS #2 Oh my god!

> *The FURIES resemble Clytemnestra, a gorilla, and a ferocious hound of hell all in one. Blood leaks from her eyes. During the scene, MESSENGER #2 tries to keep ORESTES between he and the hideous FURIES, but ORESTES does the same and eventually ORESTES succeeds.*

FURIES A mother's curse, you ask? Well, ask and yee shall receive. We are the Nameless Ones, the Dread Ones, Sentinels of law and blood. We are the Furies. Here to avenge most wrongful death. Feel the blast of our reeking breath. Curdle in the heat of our glare. We will swallow you whole and burn you alive in the flaming cistern of our belly – then shit you out our puckered asshole you stinking turd!

ORESTES Please don't.

FURIES We are come to grind you into pulp, you mother killer.

ORESTES Clytemnestra deserved her fate!

FURIES She was your mother.

ORESTES She was a murdering tyrannical woman!

FURIES And you that woman's son.

ORESTES Apollo will protect me!

FURIES Oh come on! Who got you into this mess in the first place? Apollo! Who wrote the laws of blood which now condemn you to madness? Apollo. You would trust a god who brought you to this moment? Look at me. I am your just reward. I am the crown you killed for. I am the fury. Your mother's curse.

ORESTES Stop it, stop it, you're driving me crazy!

FURIES That's the idea. Did you or did you not kill your own flesh and blood?

ORESTES I did.
FURIES Are you or are you not the most heinously ungrateful child ever to crawl the earth?
ORESTES I am not.
FURIES Liar!
ORESTES Be quiet.
FURIES Matricide!
ORESTES Stop it!
FURIES Cowardly boy!
ORESTES I can't take it anymore. Apollo! Defend me! Athena! Protect me in your arms!
FURIES You can run but you can't hide.
ORESTES *(looks at her, beat, then:)* AAAAAAAH!

ORESTES runs around the stage, pursued closely by the FURIES, and then off stage entirely. The FURIES run off with him. Silence. MESSENGER #2 stands up, looking after them in disbelief.

MESS #2 Mercy.

ORESTES bursts in from another direction, screaming, still pursued by the FURIES, runs about and off again. And again, silence.

MESS #1 They're gone.
MESS #2 AAH! Oh, Jeez Louise, it's you. What are you doing out here?
MESS #3 What was that?
MESS #2 AAH! Oh I see how it is. Another secret rendezvous. I'm sorry if we interrupted your make-out session with our historical events?
MESS #3 Our?
MESS #2 Yes. Our. Yours too, Messenger Boy.
MESS #1 Now now.
MESS #2 Were you two here that whole time? You're lucky we didn't get caught.
MESS #3 We, huh? That would make you a third wheel.
MESS #1 Never mind that. Question is, what do we do now? Are you gonna tell Electra about Orestes makin' a run for Athens?
MESS #2 Me? Noooo sir. That Electra's one wild card. She needs Orestes to be king and she knows it. I'm not droppin' this bomb. She'd have my neck for sure.
MESS #3 I'll do it.

MESS #1 & #2 What?

MESS #3 I'll tell Electra.

MESS #2 You like delivering messages to her don't you? Are you a lesbian?

MESS #3 No. Are you?

MESS #2 Maybe!

MESS #1 Can it, both o' yuh. Now listen, the Furies are chasing Orestes across the desert to Athens. They'll pluck him from Athena's arms and tear him to bits and yet another domino will have fallen in the House of Atreus. It's never going to stop. Please, let's just leave, tonight.

MESS #2 Are you two skippin' town?

MESS #3 No. Not yet.

MESS #1 Not yet?

MESS #3 Not now.

MESS #1 Then later. Soon.

MESS #3 I have to tell Electra this news. It's my job. *(to MESS #2)* Our job.

MESS #1 He's right about her, though. Maybe you shouldn't. And what if she recognizes you this time?

MESS #3 …I'll come back. Wait here for me.

Kiss. MESSENGER #3 leaves.

MESS #2 Well I will say one thing for her, the girl's got guts. …Say, I'm pretty tight with the royals. I'll follow her and wait outside. Alright?

MESS #1 Thank you.

MESS #2 It'll all work out.

MESSENGER #2 slaps MESSENGER #1's shoulder unconvincingly, then exits.

Scene Twelve – Womanhood Becomes Electra

ELECTRA in her royal bedchambers. She walks downstage center with a lit candle and kneels. MESSENGER #3 enters, but stays hidden in the background, having caught ELECTRA in the midst of a prayer. ELECTRA is very sincere and in earnest throughout.

ELECTRA Agamemnon, my father slain and doomed to walk the night, we have finally given you peace that you may lay down to rest. …Well, Orestes did it. …But I helped. And now he will be King. He is tortured by what he has done though Apollo proclaims it right, and has kept to himself. Please whisper from your heavenly seat words of solace in his ear that he may cease his torment. Then we can get this show on the road. ...I love you Father. I will always miss you. ...I hope that you believe me...

MESS #3 *(clears throat)* Princess Electra.

ELECTRA *(stands)* Yes. What is the news?

MESS #3 It is news indeed.

ELECTRA Your looks are grave. Out with it.

MESS #3 I– I come with a message concerning the newly crowned King, your brother, Orestes.

ELECTRA A message from Orestes? Why does he treat me so formally, delivering his words through a Messenger's mouth?

MESS #3 They are not his words, Princess.

ELECTRA Then whose are they? You try my patience.

MESS #3 They are my own words, Princess.

ELECTRA ...Okay, and? ...What has happened?

MESS #3 Orestes has fled Argos for Athens. He is chased there by the Furies. In Athens he will seek out the protection promised him by Apollo.

ELECTRA He's gone? He left? Then I'm alone. He left me all alone. Shit. What am I gonna to do?!

MESS #3 You will be Queen, then, won't you?

ELECTRA No they'll kill me! I'm the sister; I'm a woman and neither wife nor mother! I'll be the scapegoat for their anger! They'll hang me for Clytemnestra's murder!

MESS #3 Who will?

ELECTRA They! They! Other people! The gentry! The people of Argos! They'll want a benevolent King to follow their former deadly Queen! Without Orestes I'm just a woman and screwed don't you get it you stupid boy?!

MESS #3 Yes and don't call me a stupid boy.

ELECTRA turns on MESSENGER #3 with livid eyes and MESSENGER #3 quickly removes her cap.

MESS #3 I'm not a boy.

ELECTRA stares at MESSENGER #3 for a long time, then points, then speaks...

ELECTRA I know you.

MESS #3 Yes.

ELECTRA You came to Corinth and told Orestes and I about our Father.

MESS #3 Yes I did.

ELECTRA Is that where I've seen you before? Your face?

MESSENGER #3 begins to sing the lullaby she used to sing to ELECTRA. Soon ELECTRA covers her mouth, then sings along, then gushes:

ELECTRA You were my slave girl! Oh my gosh! What happened to you?

MESS #3 I grew up.

ELECTRA You disappeared, I was so upset! I just assumed you must have done something and somebody had put to you to death!

MESS #3 No. I escaped. The day your Father set sail for Troy. The day your sister was killed.

ELECTRA *(her expression goes cold)* Sacrificed.

MESS #3 ...Sacrificed–

ELECTRA –It was the right thing. Artemis demanded the oldest daughter. It was Iphigenia's duty.

MESS #3 Yes it was.

ELECTRA ...Do you remember when you used to comb my hair?

MESS #3 Yes I do.

ELECTRA ...Me too. ...Now you're a messenger? But you're a woman.

MESS #3 Yes. Just like you.

ELECTRA Huh! Like me? You're a slave. An escaped slave, it seems, masquerading as a messenger.

MESS #3 You'll have me killed, then?

ELECTRA If I want to.

MESS #3 I sang you to sleep when you couldn't. And you'll have me killed. I washed your back every morning and you'll have me killed.

ELECTRA How have you gotten away with this for so long?

MESS #3 I'm good at it, I'm fast, and I'm smart.

ELECTRA Oh, you think so.

MESS #3 I did it, didn't I? I wanted a life, not a woman's life. I escaped and now I have it.

ELECTRA Unless I say otherwise.

MESS #3 I came here on my own. Nobody sent me. I went to Corinth on my own. Nobody sent me. I did this because I thought you had a right to know what others would not have told you.

ELECTRA Why? You're my slave. Why do you give a shit about helping me? It can't be because we grew up together.

MESS #3 Of course not, we didn't grow up together. I grew up.

ELECTRA ...You're a bitch.

> *ELECTRA has begun to cry and covers her face with her hands. The tears leak out despite her fierce struggle to contain them.*

ELECTRA Stop it. Stop crying.

> *She gains enough control to be still. She looks out...*

ELECTRA Both my parents are dead.

> *Tears well up quietly, but ELECTRA does not move. MESSENGER #3 clearly feels awkward.*

MESS #3 ...Shall I go?
ELECTRA ...Yes. *(looks at her)* Thank you.
MESS #3 ...You're welcome.

> *After another awkward pause, MESSENGER #3 leaves. ELECTRA sings a bit of the lullaby. When she stops, her expression changes, and a bitter crust comes across her face.*

ELECTRA ...Herald. Herald come in, I say!

> *MESSENGER #2 steps in.*

MESS #2 Yes, my Princess.
ELECTRA That Messenger Boy who just came and went.
MESS #2 Yes, Princess.
ELECTRA He has told me troubling things which I did not like, and do not appreciate. A Princess should not be made to suffer such words. Please see to it that he is relieved of her life. Do you understand?
MESS #2 Yes, Princess.
ELECTRA I'll expect you to deliver a report from the Royal Executioner when the matter is done.
MESS #2 ...Yes Pr–
ELECTRA –Leave now.

> *MESSENGER #2 does.*

Scene Thirteen – Bad News

In the fields outside Argos, MESSENGER #1 springs to his feet as MESSENGER #2 approaches.

MESS #1 Well? Where is she? What happened? Did she do it?
MESS #2 I have to deliver a message. It's not for you.
MESS #1 Okay. Where is she?
MESS #2 I don't know.
MESS #1 You followed her didn't you?
MESS #2 She hasn't come back here?
MESS #1 No. What's going on?
MESS #2 Yes, she told Electra about Orestes.
MESS #1 And?
MESS #2 Electra– …Princess Electra has asked me to deliver an order to the Royal Executioner to have her killed. I'm to bring the Princess word of the execution when it's done.
MESS #1 You didn't deliver the message.
MESS #2 I thought you should know.
MESS #1 You can't deliver that message.
MESS #2 I have to, it's my job.
MESS #1 Your job?
MESS #2 Electra will have me killed if I don't do it, you know that.
MESS #1 Do you hear what you're saying?
MESS #2 You're playing the game too, buddy pal, in your own way! You made your bets. I can't help it if you're losing this round.
MESS #1 How can you say that?
MESS #2 She knew she was taking a risk! I'm not gonna get myself killed for her, you can't ask me to do that! I could lose my head for telling you what I have already! I shouldn't even be here! But I thought you should know! You're my pal! …I'm sorry, but you know how the world works. It's Fate, that's what it is. So yuh have to do what yuh have to do and that's that. And that's what I'm doing. So. I'm sorry but, …goodbye.

Pause. MESSENGER #2 leaves and is gone.

Scene Fourteen – Pre-trial Deliberations.

Split scene. ORESTES in Athens. MESSENGER #1 remains paralyzed in the fields outside Argos. ELECTRA waits for word from Orestes, Agamemnon, and Messenger #2. MESSENGERS #2 and #3 are nowhere to be seen.

ORESTES O majestic mistress of wisdom. Lady of all light. Great goddess of Athens, Athena.

ATHENA Yes?

ORESTES Worm-like I crawl to thy feet and praise thy mighty and malevolent name.

ATHENA Wherefore do you so?

ORESTES Forgive me Athena, for I may have sinned. My hands do stick at present with the blood of mine own.

FURIES Murdering stinking ungrateful son of a bitch! Thou hast skinned thine own flesh.

ATHENA Oh yes, Orestes: he that hath killed his mother.

ORESTES Electra told me to do it. She said it was the law of blood. The law of Apollo.

FURIES Clytemnestra gave you life, you butcherous ninny!

ATHENA Clytemnestra did give you life, Orestes.

ORESTES As did my father, Agamemnon, whose life that wicked viperess did viciously swipe hard upon his return from most gallant victory at Troy.

FURIES Most grave rampage, you mean.

ORESTES That woman killed my father and as his son I am bound by duty to avenge his murder.

FURIES Clytemnestra shares not the blood of Agamemnon, the man who killed her daughter. Your very veins pulse with the blood of Clytemnestra. It's different!

ORESTES Blood demands blood, that's my story and I'm stickin' to it!

ATHENA Yes, well, this is quite the complicated situation then isn't it.

MESSENGER #3 is shoved into view, her hands shackled behind her back.

FURIES I don't know, seems pretty straight forward if you ask me.

MESSENGER #2 steps into view and stands at attention.

ORESTES Please, dear Athena, you must help me.

ATHENA I will help you, Orestes.

FURIES Oh! Doesn't that figure! The goddess helps the rich kid!

ATHENA I will help you, Orestes, and fairly so.
FURIES Huh!
ORESTES Please do!
ATHENA However, it is not for I to preside over such a tangled case as this.
FURIES Tangled? He confessed it! He admits to the deed! He claims not innocence!
ORESTES I did what I must! I claim only that!
FURIES You must claim your guilt!
ORESTES I won't do it I tell yuh!
MESS #1 He can't deliver that message.
ATHENA Revenge sets the world aright, yet makes not the heavens light. Hmm. And it seems you both would rather be deemed just than act justly.

The FURIES folds her arms in a pout and looks straight ahead.

ATHENA For this reason, retire we now to my temple, where a dozen wrinkled old and impartial men sit ready to weigh each side of this most torrid tale. That done, by show of hands shall they decide your fate, Orestes. And by their verdict these bloody trials which have plagued the House of Atreus will finally reach an end.
ORESTES But–!
FURIES But–!
ATHENA Do not worry. It will aaall work out in the end. *(dryly)* Trust me.

ATHENA gives ORESTES a raised brow. Dangerous music. ORESTES understands and smiles. His mind whirling, MESSENGER #1 leaves the fields for Argos. ATHENA leads ORESTES into the temple, stops, and beckons the FURIES to follow.

ATHENA Come along.

With a pouty sneer, the FURIES do.

Scene Fifteen – Fate

Split scene. MESSENGER #2 walks a bit downstage, holding his hat in his hands. MESSENGER #1 and The Royal EXECUTIONER step into view simultaneously. The Royal EXECUTIONER gives MESSENGER #3 a shove forward and she stumbles to her knees, and MESSENGER #1 grabs MESSENGER #2 from behind. MESSENGER #3 is clearly afraid.

ELECTRA still waits.

MESS #2 Hey hey–! Oh, Jeez Louise, it's you. What are you doing?
MESS #3 Please. You mustn't do this.
MESS #2 Buddy. Pal, what are you doing?
MESS #3 *(asking herself)* O god what have I done?
MESS #2 Listen, I only do what I do to make things better in the long run. I really do hate them yuh know. I've spent my whole life hating them, just like you.
MESS #1 *(bitterly)* Where would we be without the people we hate? Sometimes I think we wouldn't know who we are.
MESS #2 Well that's a strange thing to say.
MESS #1 It is strange. And I'm sorry to have to do what I have to do.
MESS #2 Do what? What are you doing?

EXECUTIONER prepares to kill MESSENGER #3. ELECTRA stands.

MESS #3 Please! No!
MESS #2 What are you doing?
MESS #3 I was trying to do the right thing!
MESS #1 I'm making a life for myself.
MESS #3 Don't do this!
MESS #2 Buddy old pal, hold on a second–!
MESS #3 They need to know what they do to people!
MESS #2 For god's sake–!
MESS #3 I needed her to look me in the eye!
MESS #2 Look at me will yuh!
MESS #3 I waited my entire life for it!
MESS #2 I'm your oldest pal!
MESS #1 I know exactly who you are!
MESS #3 Please–!
MESS #2 Wait a second!
MESS #1 I've been waiting for ten years!
MESS #3 I didn't do anything!
MESS #2 Buddy!
MESS #3 Wait!
MESS #2 Pal!
MESS #3 No!

The EXECUTIONER stabs and kills MESSENGER #3 as MESSENGER #1 stabs and kills MESSENGER #2. Then…

MESS #2 I already delivered the message.

MESSENGER #2 dies.

MESS #1 What?

Scene Sixteen – Deus Ex Machina

Music. An old, bittersweet song of love lost. MESSENGER #3 stands and takes her place in the afterlife, still on stage. ATHENA and ORESTES emerge from the Temple, beaming. ELECTRA runs to ORESTES excitedly but he brushes her aside.

ORESTES Oh glorious day!
ATHENA The City of Athens shall be known by this moment for all eternity. And all people will forever uphold and fear this mighty court we have established here today.
ORESTES You have saved my name, Athena, and returned to me the home I was denied!
ATHENA What else could I do, when those dozen votes were tied, but cast the final word and split that knot.
ORESTES I am eternally grateful.
ATHENA How grateful?
ORESTES Uh: in return for the freedom granted me, I hereby commit the armies of Argos to forever defend your land and bind the name Athena to the lips of History for all time.
ATHENA It's a deal.
ORESTES *(to MESS #1)* Herald, relay to the people of Argos this great news. Their King is coming home.
MESS #3 They say that we essentially know everything already. There is nothing new in the universe. Love. War. Agony. Joy. History. Progress. Compassion. And that at any moment everything is about to change. It's just that sometimes we forget.

Brief pause while we hear a bit of the old song and ORESTES dances with ATHENA. Then…

MESS #1 People of Argos. It is my duty to inform you that Orestes, our new king, has been formally forgiven for his crimes. That a history of chaos has finally been disrupted by a new civic order, and the Law of Blood replaced by a Law of Reason. They call it Justice.

The old song explodes into something dramatic, climactic, and classical. The Royal CHORUS and MESSENGER #2 each enact both sides of every murder that has ever taken place in Argive history, like some strange dance to death. MESSENGER #3 stands in the afterlife looking over to MESSENGER #1, who remains downstage, looking at her and also the spectacle going on between them. When the music ends we hear the static of an old record turning while the dance continues forever. MESSENGER #1 turns out to face the audience. Slow fade to black. Silence.

The end.

R&J

based on the characters and text by
William Shakespeare

R&J

The world premiere of *R&J* was presented by Art Street Theatre at the 450 Geary Studio Theatre, San Francisco, CA, during EXIT Theatre's San Francisco Fringe Festival, on September 5, 1996. The production was directed by the author, with the following cast and staff:

JULIET	Beth Wilmurt
ENSEMBLE	Gillian Brecker, Mark Jackson, Bricine Mitchell, Jake Rodriguez

Costumes	Tammy Bates
Dramaturg	Derek Mutch
Stage Manager	Ryan Hodgkin

R&J was subsequently presented by Art Street Theatre at the 450 Geary Studio Theatre, San Francisco, CA, for a full-length run opening September 18, 1997. The production was directed by the author, with the following cast and staff:

JULIET	Beth Wilmurt
ENSEMBLE	Gillian Brecker, Mark Jackson, Bricine Mitchell, Jake Rodriguez

Costumes	Tammy Bates
Lights	Christie Gilmore
Stage Manager	Kathryn Clark

NOTE

> R&J requires a five-member ensemble comprised of three women and two men. One actor plays Juliet, while the other four each portray several characters. Notice that each character's name is preceded by an initial. Example, "W-JUL" for Juliet. The initial is in reference to the names of the original cast members of Art Street Theatre's production. These initials have been retained in the script so as to distinguish which actor is to speak which lines.
>
> An open stage, three chairs, a violin and a small paperback copy of Romeo & Juliet constituted the set and prop list for the original production. All other props were mimed and costumes kept simple. Though other productions need not take this approach, the script benefits from a physical, actor-centric approach.

Dialogue indented at the speaker's name is spoken simultaneously with the dialogue or action directly following until the point indicated by ***.

A single * indicates a consciousness of being Juliet's manipulative subconscious, her dream machine operator. Otherwise, the character indicated is to be played as such. In other words, even fragments are to be spoken as if in context unless otherwise indicated.

Scene One – The Pearly Gates

Music. In darkness we hear Juliet's tear-stained voice.

W-JUL Thy lips are warm!

A flash of lightning reveals bodies in the space, with W-JUL kneeling center.

W-JUL Yea, noise? Then I'll be brief. O happy dagger! This is thy sheath; there rest, and let me die!

Music thunders and in a circle of light we see W-JUL stabbing herself. The music ends and the CAST move slowly from US to DS, moving only when speaking:

M-CHOR Two households,
J-PRINCE Where be these enemies?
M-CHOR   both alike in dignity,
J-PRINCE   Capulet, Montague,
B-JUL   Come,
G-JUL Shall I speak ill of him that is my husband?
M-CHOR In fair Verona,
B-JUL   civil night,
G-JUL Ah,
J-PRINCE See what a scourge is laid
G-JUL   poor my lord,
M-CHOR   where we lay our scene,
J-PRINCE   upon your hate,
B-JUL Hood my unmann'd blood,
M-CHOR From ancient grudge

G-JUL What tongue shall smooth thy name
B-JUL   bating in my cheeks,
J-PRINCE That heaven
B-JUL With thy black mantle;
J-PRINCE   finds means to kill
G-JUL When I,
M-CHOR   break
J-PRINCE   your joys with love!
B-JUL   till strange love,
G-JUL   thy three-hours wife,
M-CHOR   to new mutiny,
G-JUL   have mangled it?
J-PRINCE And I
B-JUL   grown bold,
M-CHOR Where
J-PRINCE   for winking at your
M-CHOR   civil blood makes
J-PRINCE   discords
M-CHOR   civil hands
G-JUL But wherefore, villain,
M-CHOR   unclean.
G-JUL   didst thou
B-JUL Think true love acted simple modesty.
G-JUL   kill my cousin?
J-PRINCE   too
Have lost a brace of kinsmen.
G-JUL That villain cousin would have killed my husband.
B-JUL Come,
G-JUL Back,
B-JUL   gentle night,
G-JUL   foolish tears,
B-JUL   come,
M-CHOR From forth the fatal loins of these two foes
J-PRINCE   All are punish'd.
B-JUL   Romeo;
G-JUL   back to your native spring!
B-JUL   Come thou day in night;
M-CHOR A pair of star-cross'd lovers

B-JUL	For
J-PRINCE	A glooming peace
M-CHOR	take their life,
B-JUL	thou wilt lie upon
J-PRINCE	this morning with it brings.
B-JUL	the wings of night
G-JUL	Your tributary drops belong to woe,
M-CHOR	Whose misadventur'd piteous overthrows
J-PRINCE	The sun for sorrow
B-JUL	Whiter than new snow upon a raven's back.
J-PRINCE	will not show his head.
B-JUL	Come,
M-CHOR	Doth with their death bury their
B-JUL	gentle night; come,
M-CHOR	parents' strife.
G-JUL	Which you, mistaking,
B-JUL	loving,
G-JUL	offer up to joy.
B-JUL	black-brow'd night;

Give me my Romeo; and, when I shall die,
Take him

J-PRINCE	Go hence,
M-CHOR	The fearful passage of their death-mark'd
B-JUL	and cut him out
M-CHOR	love
J-PRINCE	and have more talk of these sad things;
M-CHOR	And the continuance
J-PRINCE	Some shall be pardon'd,
M-CHOR	of their parents' rage
G-JUL	My husband lives that Tybalt would have slain;

And Tybalt's dead that would have slain my husband.

J-PRINCE	and some punished;
M-CHOR	Which, but their childrens' end,
B-JUL	in little stars

And he will make the face of heaven

M-CHOR	naught
B-JUL	so
M-CHOR	could
B-JUL	fine

M-CHOR	remove
G-JUL All this is comfort; wherefore weep I then?	
M-CHOR Is now the one hours' traffic of our stage,	
The which if you with patient ears attend,	
What here shall miss,	
G-JUL Some word there was, worser than Tybalt's death,	
B-JUL That all the world will be in love	
M-CHOR	our toil
B-JUL	with night
M-CHOR	shall strive to mend.
B-JUL And pay no worship to	
J-PRINCE For never was a story of more woe	
G-JUL That murd'red me.	
J-PRINCE Than this of Juliet	
B-JUL	the garish sun.
J-PRINCE	and her Romeo.

Scene Two – Nightmare

> *Crazy music erupts. Juliet hallucinates harried images from the last week of her life. The following speech is delivered beneath the chaos, or rather as an element of it.*

M-CHOR Two households, both alike in dignity,
In fair Verona, where we lay our scene,
From ancient grudge break to new mutiny,
Where civil blood makes civil hands unclean.
From forth the fatal loins of these two foes
A pair of star-cross'd lovers take their life
Whose misadventur'd piteous overthrows
Doth with their death bury their parent's strife.
The fearful passage of their death-mark'd love
And the continuance of their parents' rage
Which, but their children's end, naught could remove,
Is now the one hour's traffic of our stage,
The which if you with patient ears attend,
What here shall miss, our toil shall strive to mend.

> *The fit ends as suddenly as it began, and with W-JUL alone center stage and the OTHERS out at the edges.*

Scene Three – Love at First Sight

> *The tinkle of softer crazy music. W-JUL'S head aches. She touches it, and then her stomach. No knife wound? She picks up the dagger and tries stabbing her stomach repeatedly. Nothing. She tries slitting her wrists. Nothing. She jabs at her skull. Nothing. She sets the dagger down. The CAST – Juliet's memory and her subconscious – float slowly back into view. It is as if the blur is coming into focus.*

G-NURSE　　　　　What, lamb! what, ladybird!
O God forbid! Where's the girl? What, Juliet!
W-JUL *(headache)* How now? Who calls?
B-LDYCAP Your mother.
G-NURSE Juuuuliet!
M-CAP My child is yet a stranger in the world.
B-LDYCAP Younger than she are happy mothers made.
J-ROM I dreamt a dream tonight.
W-JUL Romeo!
M-FRIAR On Thursday, Sir? The time is very short.
It is so very very late that we
May call it early.
J-ROM Things have fall'n out, sir.
G-LDYCAP *(aside)* Love is a smoke rais'd with the fume of sighs.
B-LDYCAP* *(aside)*　　　　　　A madness most discreet.
J-ROM Is the day so young?
G-NURSE Juuuuliet!
B-LDYCAP　　　　Tell me, daughter Juliet,
how stands your disposition to be marri'd?
W-JUL It i–
G-JUL It is an honor I dream not of.
M-CAP Disobedient wretch!
B-LDYCAP The valient Paris seeks you for his love.
J-PAR Happily met, my lady and my wife!
Do not deny that you love me.
G-JUL I will confess; what must be shall be.
M-CAP Out, you baggage!
　　　　　Get thee to a church a Thursday
Or never after look me in the face!
B-LDYCAP Can you like of Paris' love?
G-JUL I'll look to like, if looking liking move.

M-CAP we shall come too late.
J-ROM I fear, too early; for my mind misgives
some consequence, yet hanging in the stars,
shall bitterly begin his fearful date
with this night's revels and expire the term
of a despised life
by some vile forfeit of untimely death.

The music cuts off abruptly.

G-NURSE / B-NURSE Juuuuuuliet?
M-CAP Welcome, gentlemen! Ah ha, my mistresses! More light, you knaves! Come, musicians, play! Give room, give room! and foot it, girls.

Dance music is played. The CAST assume the role of revelers at the Capulet's masquerade banquet. W-JUL is danced about a bit, somewhat by force. She is manipulated* into a position to watch the scene, and in doing so, the CAST have suddenly isolated B-JUL and J-ROM – Romeo seeing Juliet for the first time. G-JUL uncaps the Friar's vile of poison and freezes.

M-ROM O, she doth teach the torches to burn bright!
It seems she hangs upon the cheek of night
Like a rich jewel in an Ethiop's ear–
Beauty too rich for use, for earth too dear!

G-JUL takes the poison.

W-JUL Romeo!
M-ROM The measure done, I'll watch her place of stand
And, touching hers, make blessed my rude hand.

G-JUL drops the vile of poison.

M-ROM Did my heart love till now? Forswear it, sight!
For I ne'er saw true beauty till this night.

M-TYB prowls* the scene. W-JUL runs up to M-TYB assuming him to still be Romeo, and is confused by the change. J-ROM approaches B-JUL. G-JUL has moved* on and soon fades into the NURSE.

J-ROM If I profane with my unworthiest hand
This holy shrine, the gentle fine is this:
My lips, two blushing pilgrims, ready stand
To smooth that rough touch with a tender kiss.
B-JUL Good pilgrim, you do wrong your hand too much,
Which mannerly devotion shows in this;
For saints have hands that pilgrims' hands do touch,
And palm to palm is holy palmer's kiss.
J-ROM Have not saints lips, and holy palmers too?
M-TYB This, by his voice, should be a Montague.
B-JUL Ay, pilgrim, lips that they must use in prayer.
M-TYB What, dares the slave
Come hither,
To fleer and scorn at our solemnity?
J-ROM Oh, then, dear saint, let lips do what hands do!
They pray;
G-NURSE Why, how now, kinsman? Wherefore storm you so?
J-ROM grant thou, lest faith turn to despair.
M-TYB Madam, this is a Montague, our foe;
B-JUL Saints do not move,
M-TYB A villain, that is hither come in spite
To scorn at our solemnity this night.
B-JUL though grant for prayer's sake.
J-ROM Then move not while my prayer's effect I take.
G-NURSE Young Romeo is it?
J-ROM Thus from my lips, by thine my sin is purg'd.

J-ROM kisses B-JUL.

M-TYB 'Tis he, that villain Romeo.
B-JUL Then have my lips the sin that they have took.
J-ROM Sin from my lips? O trespass sweetly urg'd!
Give me my sin again.

J-ROM kisses B-JUL. M-TYB grabs the hilt of his sword and G-NURSE stays him.

B-JUL You kiss by the book.

B-JUL kisses J-ROM big time. G-NURSE pulls B-JUL away.

G-NURSE Madam, your mother craves a word with you.
J-ROM What is her mother?
G-NURSE *(clandestinely)* Marry, bachelor
Her mother is the lady of the house.
And a good lady, and a wise and virtuous.
I nurs'd her daughter that you talk'd withal.
I tell you, he that can lay hold of her
Shall have the chinks.
J-ROM Is she a Capulet?
O dear account! my life is my foe's dept.
B-JUL *(to W-JUL)* Come, Nurse, what is yond gentleman?
Go ask his name.
W-JUL His name is Romeo,
G-NURSE* and a Montague,
The only son of your great enemy.
W-JUL …my great enemy…
B-JUL My only love, sprung from my only hate!
Too early seen unknown,
M-FRI On Thursday, sir?
B-JUL and known too late!
M-FRI The time is very short.
B-JUL Prodigious birth of love it is to me
That I must love a loathed enemy.

Things start to shift.

M-CAP More light, you knaves!
And quench the fire, the room has grown too hot!
J-ROM Give me a torch!
B-JUL More light and light– more dark and dark our woes!
G-FRI They stumble that run fast.
B-JUL therefore pardon me,
And not impute this yielding to light love,
Which the dark night hath so discovered.
M-FRI The grey-eyed morn smiles on the frowning night,
Chequ'ring the Eastern clouds with streaks of light;
G-JUL Although I joy in thee,
I have no joy of this contract tonight.

It is too rash, too unadvis'd, too sudd'n;
Too like the lightning, which doth cease to be
Ere one can say "It lightens."
J-ROM How oft when men are at the point of death
Have they been merry! which their keepers call
A lightning before death.
W-JUL Romeo!
J-ROM But soft, what light through yonder window breaks?

J-ROM* does a quick take to the audience in acknowledgment of having delivered this famous line.

J-ROM It is the East, and Juliet is the sun!
Arise, fair sun, and kill the envious moon
Who is already sick and pale with grief
That thou her maid art far more fair than she.
W-JUL O! Romeo, Romeo–

G* snaps at W-JUL to shut her trap.

J-ROM She speaks, yet she* *(i.e. W-JUL)* says nothing.
M-ROM*   What of that?
W-JUL   –Ay me!
J-ROM* *(To W, indicating B-JUL)*   *She* speaks.
B-JUL   –Ay me!
J-ROM   She speaks.
O speak again, bright angel! for thou art
As glorious to this night, being o'er my head,
As is a winged messenger of heaven
Unto the white-upturned wond'ring eyes
Of mortals that fall back to gaze on him,
When he bestrides the lazy puffing clouds
And sails upon the bosom of the air.

ALL suck in a much needed breath.

W-JUL O Romeo–
B-JUL   Romeo, wherefore art thou Romeo?
Deny thy father and refuse thy name;
Or, if thou wilt not, be but sworn my love,

And I'll no longer be a Capulet.
'Tis but thy name that is my enemy.
Thou art thyself, though not a Montague.
What's Montague? It is nor hand nor foot,
Nor arm nor face, nor any other part
Belonging to a man. O, be some other name!
What's in a name? That which we call a rose
By any other word would smell as sweet;
So Romeo would, were he not Romeo call'd.
           Romeo, doff thy name,
And for thy name, which is no part of thee,
Take all myself.
J-ROM   I take thee at thy word.
Call me but love, and I'll be new baptiz'd;
Henceforth I never will be Romeo.

W-JUL has moved into the audience to watch.

B-JUL What man art thou that, thus bescreen'd in night,
So stumblest on my counsel?
J-ROM   By a name
I know not how to tell thee who I am.
My name, dear saint, is hateful to myself,
Because it is an enemy to thee.
Had I it written, I would tear the word.
B-JUL My ears have not yet drunk a hundred words
Of that tongue's utterance, yet I know that sound.
Art thou not Romeo?
G-JUL*   and a Montague?

W-JUL gestures for G to can it.

J-ROM Neither, fair saint, if either thee dislike.
B-JUL How camest thou hither, tell me, and wherefore?
The orchard walls are high and hard to climb,
And the place death, considering who thou art,
If any of my kinsman find thee here.
J-ROM With love's light wings did I o'erperch these walls;
For stony limits cannot hold love out,
And what love can do, that dares love attempt.
Therefore thy kinsmen are no let to me.

G-JUL* If they do see thee, they will murder thee.

> *W-JUL throws a crumpled program at G.*

B-JUL I would not for the world they saw thee here.
J-ROM I have night's cloak to hide me from their sight;
And but thou love me, let them find me here.
           J-ROM My life were better ended by their hate
           Than death prorogued, wanting of thy love.
M-PROF *(writing on chalk board)* My life were better ended by their hate
Than death prorogued, wanting of thy love.
***

> *G soon fades into Nurse.*

B-JUL Dost thou love me?
W-JUL   I know he wilt say "Ay;"
J-ROM Lady, by yonder blessed moon I vow,
That tips with silver all these fruit-tree tops–
G-NURSE Juuuliet?

> *W-JUL gestures "damn it!"*

B-JUL   Dear love, adieu!
Anon, good nurse! Sweet Montague, be true.
Stay but a little, I will come again.

> *B-JUL moves away. W-JUL makes a 2nd balcony for her elsewhere on the stage.*

J-ROM O blessed, blessed night! I am afeard,
Being in night, all this is but a dream,
Too flattering-sweet to be substantial.

> *B-JUL "appears" again on the new balcony.*

B-JUL Three words, dear Romeo,
G-JUL*   and then good night indeed.
B-JUL If thy bent of love be honorable,

Thy purpose marriage, send me word tomorrow,
Where and what time thou wilt perform the rite;
And all my fortunes at thy foot I'll lay
And follow thee my love throughout the world.

G-NURSE *(off stage)* Madam!

B-JUL I come, anon!

G-NURSE *(now where the 1st balcony was)* Madam!

W-JUL By-and-by I come!

B-JUL Tomorrow will I send.

J-ROM   So thrive my soul!

B-JUL This bud of love, by summer's rip'ning breath,
May prove a beauteous flow'r when next we meet.

G-NURSE O God forbid! Where's the girl?

B-JUL A thousand times good night!

W-JUL rushes B-JUL around to a 3rd balcony.

J-ROM A thousand times the worse, to want thy light!
Love goes from love as schoolboys to their books;

W-JUL Romeo!

J-ROM   My sweet?

B-JUL   What o'clock tomorrow
Shall I send to thee?

M-CAP A Thursday let it be– a Thursday, tell her,
that she shall marry noble Paris.

J-ROM   By the hour of nine.

G-CAP 'Tis very late;

B-JUL I will not fail. *(pause)* 'Tis twenty years till then.

M-CAP* *(to W)* Do you like this haste?

B-JUL I have forgot why I did call thee back.

J-ROM Let me stand here till thou remember it.

B-JUL I shall forget, to have thee still stand there,
Rememb'ring how I love thy company.

J-ROM And I'll stay, to have thee still forget,
Forgetting any other home but this.

B-JUL 'Tis almost morning. I would have thee gone–
And yet no farther than a wanton's bird,
That lets it hop a little from her hand,
Like a poor prisoner in his twisted gyves,
And with a silk thread plucks it back again,

So loving-jealous of his liberty.
J-ROM I would I were thy bird.
B-JUL   Sweet, so would I.
Yet I should kill thee with much cherishing.

> *W-JUL looks to B-JUL; G and M to W-JUL.*

B-JUL Good night, good night! Parting is such sweet sorrow,
That I shall say good night till it be morrow.

> *B-JUL takes J-ROM'S face in her hands and kisses him tenderly.*

J-ROM Sleep dwell upon thine eyes, peace in thy breast!
Would I were sleep and peace, so sweet to rest!

> *B-JUL and J-ROM kiss again. B-JUL leaves to be married at Friar Laurence's cell.*

Scene Four – The Capulet / Montague Quarrel

> *Suddenly, things shift and W-JUL finds herself caught amidst a brewing spat. During the following, B-JUL travels slowly to Friar Laurence's cell.*

M-ABR Do you bite your thumb at us, sir?
J-SAMP I do bite my thumb, sir.
M-ABR Do you bite your thumb at us, sir?
J-SAMP Is the law on our side if I say ay?
G-GREG No.
J-SAMP No, sir, I do not bite my thumb at you, sir;
but I bite my thumb, sir.
G-GREG Do you Quarrel, sir?
M-TYB Quarrel, Sir? Ay, sir.
W-JUL No!
B-JUL Or, if thou wilt not, be but sworn my love,
And I'll no longer be a Capulet.
J-SAMP Then if you do, sir, I am for you. I serve as good a man as you.
M-TYB No better?
G-GREG Say "better!"
J-SAMP Yes, better, sir!

W-JUL O Lord, they fight! Sirs, hold thy desperate hands!
M-TYB You lie! Art thou not Romeo, *(draws sword)* and a Montague?
G-FRI Wisely, and slow. They stumble that run fast.
M-TYB Will you be ready? Do you like this haste?
J-SAMP Have at thee, coward!
B-JUL What's in a name?
W-JUL   No, no! Will they not hear?
G-GREG Ha!

> *Impulsively, G-GREG draws a sword and M-TYB readies himself. There is a startled vocal burst! In the same instant, J converts to the PRINCE and halts the explosion.*

J-PRINCE Where be these enemies? Capulet, Montague,

> *M and G snap to attention.*

J-PRINCE That quench the fire of your pernicious rage
With purple fountains issuing from your veins,
Three civil brawls, bred of an airy word,
Have thrice disturb'd the quiet of our streets.
If ever you disturb our streets again,
Your lives shall pay the forfeit of the peace.
For this time all the rest depart away.
Once more, on pain of death, all men depart.

> *There is a sudden and then slow motion stabbing, G and M to J. It is ugly.*

Scene Five – The Wedding

> *B-JUL circles the stage slowly. M-FRIAR enters his cell to perform the marriage rites. G-JUL and J-ROM enter Friar Laurence's cell to be married. W-JUL watches from the aisle. A marriage ritual is played out, with singing and gesture.*

Scene Six – Juliet versus Capulet

> *Things melt into what smells like a courtroom. B-LDYCAP is seated like a stenographer reading a script of Shakespeare's play. J-PRINCE is UL looking very much the judge. G-JUL sits CS as the accused on the stand.*

W-JUL is her defense lawyer at center aisle. And M-CRITIC/CAP is the Prosecution.

M-CRITIC Romeo and Juliet – is justly famed for the quality of its lyric poetry, but is no less extraordinary for its sophisticated organizational devices, which enhance its vivid evocation of a world of love and death. Shakespeare achieved a new success in R&J, which was immediately popular on its first appearance; from that day to this it has been seen constantly in the theatre, though not always in the precise form in which Shakespeare wrote it. The text of R&J presents complicated problems that offer no easy solution. The love–

This words sticks in M-CRITIC'S throat and he becomes Capulet.

M-CAP –that Romeo and Juliet display is of the idealistic type that comes with the suddenness and the devastating effect of a stroke of lightning. The force of an overwhelming love is the dominant theme of the play, and for more than three and a half centuries sentiments in this play have exerted a romantic influence upon countless readers. The probability is that it has subtly affected the attitude toward love of the entire English-speaking world.
J-PRINCE Seal up the mouth of outrage for a while,
Till we can clear these ambiguities.
B-LADYCAP I will be brief, for my short date of breath
is not so long as is a tedious tale.
Romeo, my lord, was husband to that Juliet;
And she, there dead, that Romeo's faithful wife.
M-CAP Disobedient wretch!
B-LADYCAP Tybalt is dead, and Romeo banished;
Romeo that kill'd him, he is banished.
J-PRINCE Now, say at once what thou dost know of this.
M-CAP Why, how now, Juliet?
G-JUL *(suspicious)*   Dear Sir, I am not well.
M-CAP Evermore weeping for your cousin's death?
                    Tell me, daughter Juliet,
How stands your disposition to be marri'd?
G-JUL It is an honor that I dream not of.
M-CAP Speak briefly, can you like of Paris' love.
G-JUL I'll look to like, if looking liking move.
But no more deep will I endart mine eye
Than your consent gives strength to make it fly.
M-CAP Well, then Wednesday is too soon.
A Thursday let it be– a Thursday, daughter,

You shall be married to this noble Earl.
Will you be ready? Do you like this haste?
             Tybalt being slain so late.
W-JUL   There's no trust,
No faith, no honesty in men!

M-CAP Exaggeration, we might easily guess... Romeo commits himself to the full gamut of romantic folderol as seen through the eyes of a dramatic fourteen-year-old, and the catastrophe is under way... If he had had the rational plan of trying to work a marriage settlement in an aboveboard fashion to the advantage of everyone, he abandoned it. For if romantic little Juliet wants secret messages, and clandestine words, and even an exciting forbidden marriage– then she shall have them.

G-JUL Thou canst not speak of that thou dost not feel.
Wert thou as young as I, Romeo thy love,
An hour but marri'd, Tybalt murdered,
Doting like me, and like him banished,
Then mightst thou speak.

M-CAP How, how, how, how, choplogic? What is this?
(to W) Speak not.
(to G) You fettle your fine joints 'gainst Thursday next
To go with Paris to Saint Peter's Church,
Or I will drag thee on a hurdle thither.

W-JUL Good Prince, I do beseech you on my knees,
Hear me with patience but to speak a word.

M-CAP Hang thee, young baggage! disobedient wretch!
I tell thee what– get thee to a church a Thursday
Or never after look me in the face.
             Wife, we scarce thought us blest
That God had lent us but this only child;
But now I see this one is one too much,
And that we have a curse in having her.

W-JUL You are to blame, my lord, to rate her so.

M-CAP   Hold your tongue,
Good Prudence. Smatter with your blather, go!

W-JUL I speak no treason.

M-CAP   Peace, you mumbling fool!

G-JUL Is there no pity sitting in the clouds
That sees into the bottom of my grief?
O sweet my mother, counsil me, I pray!

B-LDYCAP Talk not to me, for I'll not speak a word.
Do as thou wilt, for I have done with thee.

G-JUL *(to W)* Good nurse, how shall this be prevented?

W-JUL embraces G-JUL.

Alack, alack, that heaven should practice strategems
Upon so small a subject as myself!
M-CAP   I do not use to jest.
Thursday is near; lay hand on your heart, advise:
An you be mine, I'll give you to my friend;
An you be not, hang, beg, starve, die in the streets,
For, by my soul, I'll ne'er acknowledge thee.
W-JUL   Heaven and yourself
Had part in this fair maid! Now heaven hath all,
And all the better it is for the maid.
The most you sought was her promotion,
For 'twas your heaven she should be advanc'd;
Well, in that love, you love your child so ill
That you run mad.
M-CAP Can you like of Paris' love?
G-JUL It shall be Romeo, whom you know I love,
Rather than Paris.
M-CAP Shame come to Romeo!
G-JUL *(breaks from W, startling even her)* Blister'd be thy tongue
For such a wish! He was not born to shame.
Upon his brow shame is asham'd to sit;
For 'tis a throne where honor may be crown'd
Sole monarch of the universal earth.
M-CAP Will you speak well of him that kill'd your cousin?
G-JUL Shall I speak ill of him that is my husband?
M-CAP Did Romeo's hand shed Tybalt's blood?!

Sudden shift. G-JUL in her own world. W-JUL clasps G-JUL.

G-JUL Ah, poor my lord, what tongue shall smooth thy name
When I, thy three-hours' wife, have mangled it?
But wherefore, villain, didst thou kill my cousin?
That villain cousin would have kill'd my husband.
Back, foolish tears, back to your native spring!
Your tributary drops belong to woe,
Which you, mistaking, offer up to joy.
My husband lives, that Tybalt would have slain;
And Tybalt's dead, that would have slain my husband.

All this is comfort; wherefore weep I then?
Some word there was, worser than Tybalt's death,
That murd'red me.

G-JUL* looks at W-JUL.

Scene Seven – Tybalt & Mercutio's Deaths

B-BEN   Come, shall we go?

J-MER   What care have I to go?

B-BEN   I pray thee, good Mercutio, let's retire.
The day is hot, the Capulets abroad,
And if we meet, we shall not scape a brawl
For now, these hot days, is the mad blood stirring.

J-MER   Thou! Why, thou wilt quarrel with a man for cracking nuts, having no other reason but because thou hast hazel eyes. Thou hast quarrell'd with a man for coughing in the street. Thy head is as full of quarrels as an egg is full of meat; and yet thou wilt tutor me from quarreling.

G-BEN   By my head, here come the Capulets.

J-MER   By my heel, I care not.

M-TYB   Gentlemen, good den. A word with one of you.

J-MER   And but one word with one of us?
Couple it with something; make it a word and a blow.

M-TYB   You shall find me apt enough for that, sir, an you will give me occasion.

J-MER   Could you not take some occasion without giving?

M-TYB   Mercutio, thou consortest with Romeo–

J-MER   Consort? What, dost thou make us minstrels? An thou make minstrels of us, look to hear nothing but discords. Here's my fiddlestick; here's that shall make you dance!

G-BEN   We talk here in the public haunt of men.
Either withdraw unto some private place
And reason coldly of your grievances,
Or else depart. Here all eyes gaze on us.

J-MER   Men's eyes were made to look, and let them gaze.
I will not budge for no man's pleasure, I.

W-JUL steps in to stop potential violence. M-TYB relates to her as Romeo.

M-TYB Well, peace be with you, sir. Here comes my man.
Romeo, the love I bear thee can afford
No better term than this: thou art a villain.
W-JUL Tybalt, the reason I have to love thee
Doth much excuse the appertaining rage
To such a greeting. Villain am I none.
Therefore farewell. I see thou knowst me not.
M-TYB Boy, this shall not excuse the injuries
That thou hast done me.
W-JUL I do protest I never injur'd thee,
But love thee better than thou canst devise,
Till thou shalt know the reason of my love;
And so, good Capulet, which name I tender
As dearly as mine own, be satisfi'd.
J-MER O calm, dishonorable, vile submission!
Tybalt, you ratcatcher, will you walk?
M-TYB What wouldst thou have with me?
J-MER Good King of Cats, nothing but one of your nine lives. Make haste, lest my sword be about your ears ere yours' be out.
W-JUL Gentle Mercutio, put thy rapier up.
J-MER Come, Sir, I am for you.

> *M-TYB and J-MER have drawn swords and they begin to fight. B-JUL hides behind her monologue as the scene continues.*

      B-JUL   Come, civil night,
    Hood my unmann'd blood, bating in my cheeks,
    With thy black mantle; till strange love, grown bold,
    Think true love acted simple modesty.
    Come, night; come, Romeo; come, thou day in night;
    For thou wilt lie upon the wings of night
    Whiter than new snow upon a raven's back.
    Come, gentle night; come, loving, black-brow'd night;
    Give me my Romeo; and, when I shall die,
    Take him and cut him out in little stars,
    And he will make the face of heaven so fine
    That all the world will be in love with night
    And pay no worship to the garish sun.

W-JUL Draw, Benvolio; beat down their weapons.
Gentlemen, for shame! forbear this outrage!
Tybalt, Mercutio, the Prince expressly hath
Forbid this bandying in Verona streets.

Hold, Tybalt! Good Mercutio!

> *M-TYB, under W-JUL's arm, thrusts J-MER in and looks quite surprised. Time seems to suspend.*

J-MER   I am hurt.
A plague o' both your houses! I am sped.
G-BEN   What, art thou hurt?
J-MER Ay, ay, a scratch, a scratch. Marry, 'tis enough.
***

J-ROM Ah, soft; what light; breaks?
It is my lady; O, it is my love!
W-JUL What's here?
J-ROM Juliet! If my heart's dear love–
W-JUL Romeo?
J-MER Ay, ay; Why the devil came you between us? I was hurt under your arm.
W-JUL I thought all for the best.
J-MER Ask for me tomorrow and you shall find me a grave man.
O Romeo, Romeo, brave Mercutio's dead! *(now ROM)* Sin from my lips?

> *J-ROM dies.*

W-JUL Romeo? Romeo?
G-NURSE* *(whispers)* Romeo is banisht.
W-JUL Now, Tybalt, take that "villain" back again
That late thou gavest me, for Romeo's soul
Is but a little way above our heads,
Staying for thine to keep him company!
B-JUL All slain, all dead.

> *W-JUL picks up J-MER's sword.*

W-JUL This shall determine that!

> *W-JUL thrusts M-TYB through. Music explodes.*

Scene Eight – Dance of the Hourglass

> *M-TYB is stuck in a cycle of being stabbed and released from W-JUL's blade as the CAST wind up into a frantic series of panic and time related movements. W-JUL finds herself caught amidst this frenzy and often yanked* by the CAST into the swirl. Key text is poured into W-JUL's ears in whispers. Halfway through the music, M-TYB collapses for the last time and his life is allowed to move out of the death loop as he struggles to stay on his feet, pull out his own sword, and get a hold on W-JUL, which he finally does! M-TYB runs her through twice and she gasps, though strangely does not feel the pain. M-TYB staggers back a few steps, in a harsh whisper says*

M-TYB Romeo is banisht!

> *then turns, is stabbed again as before, and collapses dead for the last time calling*

M-TYB Juliet!

> *as he hits the stage. The music climaxes ...Silence.*

Scene Nine – Romeo & Juliet's last rendezvous

> *M-ROM and B-JUL meet in secret for the last time before Romeo is to flee Verona. M-ROM enters B-JUL's chambers. Music plays. THEY slowly move in on one another with a mix of tenderness, longing, and passion. At the end of the sequence there is something that subtly acknowledges death, leaving B-JUL on the floor and M-ROM kneeling over her tenderly. The music ends. J-ROM stands, staring at W-JUL expectantly. W-JUL steps cautiously toward the stage.*

W-JUL What man art thou?
J-ROM My name, dear saint, is hateful to myself,
Because it is an enemy to thee.
W-JUL Art thou not Romeo?
J-ROM   And a Montague.
W-JUL If you should deal double with me, truly it were an ill thing.
J-ROM Dear love, what shall I swear by?
W-JUL No, do not swear at all, for, if thou swear'st

Thou mayest prove false.
J-ROM I do beseach you, love, have patience.
Your looks are pale and wild.
W-JUL   I long to die
If what thou speak'st speak not of remedy.
Where is my Romeo?
J-ROM   Lady, I am here.
W-JUL If thou dost love pronounce it faithfully.
But if thou mean'st not well, I do beseach thee
To cease thy strife, and leave me to my grief.
Dost thou love me?
J-ROM   I do with all my heart.
In truth, fair Capulet, I am too fond,
And therefore thou mayest think my behavior light,
But trust me, Juliet, I'll prove more true
Than those that have more cunning to be strange.
Let me be taken, let me be put to death,
I am content, so thou wilt have it so.
Look thou but soft and I am proof against
All enmity. …My heart's dear love–

W-JUL is convinced. She rushes to J-ROM and hugs him fast. J-ROM eyes* the audience subtly.

W-JUL Love give me strength and I believe thee.

W-JUL kisses J-ROM feverishly. THEY kneel together and sit on the floor in an embrace. G-NURSE approaches very slowly during the following.

W-JUL Things have fall'n out so unluckily
That we have had no time to woo.
J-ROM These times of woe afford no time to woo.
W-JUL   I lov'd my cousin Tybalt dearly;
Is love a tender thing? It is too rough,
Too rude, too boist'rous, and it pricks like thorn.
          Well, we were born to die.
J-ROM I have more care to stay than will to go.
But now it is so very very late
That we may call it early. List, the lark.
W-JUL Wilt thou be gone? It is not yet near day.
It was the nightingale, and not the lark,

That pierc'd the fearful hollow of thine ear.
J-ROM It was the lark, the herald of the morn;
No nightingale. Look, love, what envious streaks
Do lace the severing clouds in yonder East.
Night's candle's are burnt out.
I must be gone and live, or stay and die.
W-JUL Yond light is not daylight; I know it, I.
It is some meteor that the sun exhales
To be to thee this night a torchbearer
And light thee on thy way to Mantua.
Therefore stay yet; thou needst not to be gone.
G-NURSE *(faintly)* Juuuuliet.
J-ROM I must be gone. More light and light it grows.
More light and light, more dark and dark our woes.

> *With a quick kiss, and a brief look*, J-ROM exits Juliet's chamber. B-JUL appears to still be dead, and M-ROM remains kneeling over her body, staring down. W-JUL is left a bit stunned by this sudden farewell.*

W-JUL Farewell! O Fortune, Fortune, be fickle Fortune:
For then I hope thou wilt not keep him long.

> *W-JUL glances about at the others.*

W-JUL Or am I Fortune's fool? I am afeard,
Being in night, all this is but a dream.

Scene Ten – Dreams and Poison

G-JUL *(enters the chamber)* I dreamt a dream tonight.
W-JUL And so did I.
G-JUL Well, what was yours?
W-JUL That dreamers often lie.
G-JUL In bed asleep, while they do dream things true.
W-JUL They are the children of an idle brain,
Begot of nothing but vain fantasy;
Which is as thin of substance as the air,
And more inconstant than the wind.
G-JUL Tybalt is gone, and Romeo banished;
Romeo that kill'd him, he is banished,

        and all the world to nothing
That he dares ne'er come back to challenge you;
And, since the case so stands as now it doth,
I think it best you marri'd with the County.

> *In his kneeling position, M-ROM is stabbed and freezes, not unlike how M-TYB was stabbed.*

G-JUL O, he's a lovely gentleman.
Romeo's a dishclout to him.

> *The sword is ripped from M-ROM's gut; freeze again.*

G-JUL   An eagle, madam,
Hath not so green, so quick, so fair an eye
As Paris hath. Beshrew my very heart,
I think you are happy in this second match.
W-JUL Speakst thou this from thy heart?
G-JUL And from my soul too.
M-ROM I dreamt my lady came and found me dead
And breath'd such life with kisses in my lips
That I reviv'd and was an emperor.
Ah me! how sweet is love itself possess'd
When but love's shadows are so rich in joy!
W-JUL Well, thou hast comforted me marvelous much.
Go in;

> *Things start to shift. Ominous music sneaks into the air.*

W-JUL and tell my mother I am gone,
Having displeas'd my father, to Laurence's cell,
To make confession and to be absolv'd.
B-JUL If all else fail, myself have pow'r to die.
J-ROM* Romeo is banisht.
G-JUL All slain, all dead.
M-FRI Romeo is exil'd.
B-JUL Romeo is banisht.

> *Beat, then M-FRI gets a sharp chill and clasps head.*

J-ROM 'Tis torture, and not mercy. Heaven is here,
Where Juliet lives; Do not say "banishment."
Thou cuttst my head off with a golden axe
And smil'st upon the stroke that murders me.

M-FRI If thou hast strength of will to slay thyself
Then it is likely thou wilt undertake
A thing like death to chide away this shame.

G-JUL Yea, is the worst well?

All three JULIETS enact the poisoning in unison.

M-FRI Take thou this vial, being when alone,
And this distilled liquor drink thou off;

B-JUL How if, when I am laid into the tomb,
I wake before the time that Romeo
Come to redeem me?

G-JUL There's a fearful point!

M-FRI When presently through all thy veins shall run
A cold and drowsy humor.
No warmth, no breath, shall testify thou livest;

B-JUL O, if I wake, shall I not be distraught,
Entomb'd with all these hideous fears?

M-FRI In the mean time, before thou shalt awake,
Shall Romeo by my letters know our drift;
And hither shall he come to bear thee hence.

G-JUL All this is comfort; wherefore weep I then?

B and G look to W, and all three down the drink. The music climaxes. Silence.

Scene Eleven – Discomfort + Time = Life

B-JUL moves slowly, clasping her head, and G-JUL mirrors the image on the opposite side of the stage. Arriving in their new places, THEY stab their stomachs and sink down into corpses, still clutching daggers in their guts. Simultaneously, M and J melt down into two ancient Capulets long-since buried. W-JUL remains standing center. Seeing the others, SHE realizes:

W-JUL It is the vault, the ancient receptacle
Where for this many hundred years the bones

Of all my buri'd ancestors are pack'd.
O friar Laurence! Where is my lord?

> *W-JUL searches the bodies.*

W-JUL I do remember well where I should be,
And here I am. Where is my Romeo?

> *J-ROM enters the vault but sees only B-JUL.*

W-JUL Romeo!
J-ROM Is it e'en so? A grave? O, no, a lantern is't,
For here lies Juliet and her beauty makes
This vault a feasting presence full of light.
How oft when men are at the point of death
Have they been merry! which their keepers call
A lightning before death. But how may I
Call this a lightning! O my love! my wife!
Death, that hath suck'd the honey of thy breath,
Hath had no power yet upon thy beauty.
Thou art not conquer'd. Beauty's ensign yet
Is crimson in thy lips and in thy cheeks,
And death's pale flag is not advanced there.
Can I go forward when my heart is here?
If dead, why art thou yet so fair? O, here
Will I set up my everlasting rest
And shake the yoke of inauspicious stars
From this world-wearied flesh.
W-JUL O, no.
J-ROM Such mortal drugs I have, of lightning speed,
As will disperse itself through all the veins
That the life-weary taker may fall dead.
W-JUL No;
This is too rash, to unadvis'd, too sudd'n,

> *M and G slowly rise* to standing.*

W-JUL Too like the lightning, which doth cease to be–
J-ROM   Eyes, look your last!

> *W-JUL gets an idea: enact the past.*

W-JUL This bud of love, by summer's rip'ning breath,
May prove a beauteous flow'r when next we meet.
J-ROM Arms, take your last embrace!
W-JUL Wilt thou be gone? It is not yet near day.
It was the nightingale, and not the lark,
That pierc'd the fearful hollow of thine ear.
Therefore stay yet; thou needst not to be gone!
J-ROM   And, lips, seal with a righteous kiss
A dateless bargain to engrossing death!
And death, not Juliet, be my loving wife.
W-JUL Good pilgrim, you do wrong your hand too much,
Which mannerly devotion shows in this;
For saints have hands that pilgrims hands do touch,
And palm to palm is holy palmer's kiss!
J-ROM Farewell! God knows when we shall meet again.
Here's to my love!
W-JUL I do remember well where I should be,
And here I am! Where is my Romeo?

    J-ROM drinks.

W-JUL O–!
J-ROM   O true apothecary!
Thy drugs are quick. Thus with a kiss I die.

    But W-JUL grabs J-ROM and takes the kiss desperately. J-ROM goes limp in her hands and dies.

W-JUL No, no! Is there no pity in the clouds?!
G-NURSE   What, lamb! what, ladybird!
O God forbid! Where's the girl? What, Juliet!
M-CAP* Do you like this haste?
G-NURSE* …Juliet?
M-CAP Why, how now, Juliet? ;*we were born to die.
G-BEN* Wisely, and slow. They stumble that run fast.
M-FRI On Thursday, sir? The time is very short.
G-JUL   Although I joy in thee,
I have no joy in this contract tonight.
M-JUL* Yea, is the worst well? All this is comfort;

G-JUL It is too rash, too unadvis'd, too sudd'n;
M-JUL   wherefore weep I then?
G-JUL Too like the lightning, which doth cease to be
Ere one can say "It lightens."
W-JUL   all this is but a dream.
M-ROM Is love a tender thing?
W-JUL   all this is but a dream.
G-JUL I dreamt a dream tonight.
M-MER*   That dreamers often lie.
G-JUL If all else fail, myself have pow'r to die!
M-CAP   Tybalt being slain so late!
              W-JUL All this is but a dream.
                  G-JUL But wherefore villain didst thou kill my cousin?
                      M-CAP Did Romeo's hand shed Tybalt's blood!
                          W-JUL All this is but a dream!
         ***

B-JUL *(dying)* I have forgot why I did call thee back.
J-ROM *(alive, comforting her)* Let me stand here till thou remember it.
B-JUL I shall forget, to have thee still stand there,
Rememb'ring how I love thy company.
J-ROM And I'll stay, to have thee still forget,
Forgetting any other home but this.
B-JUL 'Tis almost morning. I would have thee gone–
And yet no farther than a wanton's bird,
That lets it hop a little from her hand,
Like a poor prisoner in his twisted gyves,
And with a silk thread plucks it back again,
So loving-jealous of his liberty.
J-ROM I would I were thy bird.
B-JUL   Sweet, so would I.
Yet I should kill thee with much cherishing.
Good night, good night! Parting is such sweet sorrow,
That I shall say good night till it be morrow.

   B-JUL dies. Music.

J-ROM Sleep dwell upon thine eyes, peace in thy breast!
Would I were sleep and peace, so sweet to rest!

   …We hear a moment of the music. Then…

J-ROM Where be these enemies? Capulet, Montague,
See what a scourge is laid upon your hate,
That heaven finds means to kill your joys with love!
And I, for winking at your discords, too
Have lost a brace of kinsmen. All are punish'd

> ...short pause. Music still plays...

W-JUL Said he not so? Or did I dream it so?
Here's much to do with hate, but more with love.
"Wisely, and slow. They stumble that run fast."
M-CAP* Do you like this haste?
W-JUL   Time is very short.
"All this is comfort; wherefore weep I then?"

> We hear the music as M and G move in to flank W-JUL, who looks at them, then to J-ROM as he speaks.

J-ROM A glooming peace this morning with it brings.
The sun for sorrow will not show his head.
Go hence, to have more talk of these sad things;
Some shall be pardon'd, and some punished;
For never was a story of more woe
Than this of Juliet and her Romeo.
        ...Juliet and her Romeo.

> J-ROM stands, lifting B-JUL to her feet. J, B, M, and G all back up slowly to the positions where they began at the top of the show, and W-JUL is left center stage, watching them. She turns around and faces the audience and the music cuts off abruptly. W-JUL looks straight out at Heaven in the silence. Blackout.

The end.

Notes on the Plays

American $uicide

Lisa Steindler, artistic director of both Encore Theatre Company and Z Space Studio, commissioned *American $uicide* after three years of our batting various ideas around over various beers. This is the one that finally stuck.

During my work on *The Death of Meyerhold* I'd come to know Nikolai Erdman's 1928 Soviet satire, *The Suicide* – by many reports the funniest Soviet satire of its day, and also one of the most infamous given the fact that it was banned and that Meyerhold's attempt to produce it appeared on the list of "crimes against the Soviet people" for which he was eventually executed. Originally I thought I'd transplant Erdman's basic premise to America in the Great Depression, a time close to Erdman's own when Americans were desperate and a number of them contemplated Communism as a viable solution to our nation's problems. It seemed a good way to convert Erdman's very Soviet Russian material into something that Americans could better relate to. But Lisa was interested in something more contemporary. At first I was hesitant, since I was excited to try my hand at something Kaufman-and-Hart-*ish*. But the more I thought about it, the more I saw how much better it would be to set the play in the exact present moment. Soviet Communism may be dead, but greed and opportunism sure aren't, nor are celebrity, media, pop culture, capitalism, and our shared responsibility for the global impact of these things.

So I wrote the play for today, and even included a few lines that are to change according to the latest headlines. Something of the initial impulse to set the play in the Great Depression remains in the flavor of the dialogue and situations. *American $uicide* evolves in style from bright screwball comedy at the top of the show to a darker expressionism by the end. As Sam gets closer to his grand finale, the world around him grows stranger and more theatrical.

Some critics saw this as a flaw, as if I'd lost track in Act Two of what I'd set up in Act One. They didn't recognize the thematic gesture of the play's shifting form. I actually think many American critics don't look to form for content, which is bizarre – as if content is the sole province of the spoken word. Enough people got it, though, I'm glad to say, that we eventually had cause to add extra performances to the run. I was most pleased by the woman who came up to me and said that she was seeing the play for the second time, and that both times she belly laughed in Act One, felt queasy in Act Two, and cried in the end. Perfect.

BANG!

BANG! was at least in part a response to *Brave*, which was a rather politically minded play and off the beaten dramaturgical path – at the time, at least. With *BANG!* I wanted to poke fun at the Fringe theatre pool in which I was swimming, laugh at myself and my friends, make a few points aloud that I'd made twice too often in imaginary conversations in my head, and in particular to throw a punch or two below the belt of that multi-faced *prima dona* mentality that always struck me as so out of place on the Fringe, where artists break their backs for neither money nor recognition of any consequence. Why become self-important in any way when you're carrying your own props and scenery to and from rehearsal on public transportation, sweating late into the night after eight hours of day job and jockeying for space in whatever closet is substituting for a proper dressing room? Doing theatre on the Fringe is like camping – just get down to earth and enjoy the dirt, and if you don't like getting dirty then stay home.

So, I thought I'd make a little Fringe farce about Fringe theatre. As farce it was funny but at times also borderline painful in its high-octane rage. (I liked the way actress Beth Wilmurt's brother described it: "That was an 80-mile-an-hour play delivered at 120-miles-an-hour.") And as it turned out, Fringe theatre was really only a metaphor for a far more universal struggle – to make that decision that may very well change your life. It's this that audiences responded to. And so it was from them that halfway through the original production's run I learned I hadn't actually written a Fringe farce. I'd actually written a play about commitment.

Brave

Brave is about pre-millennial angst, and America as a land of young orphans and runaways still looking for a place to feel at home. It's a funny play, but also turned out to be a very emotional piece. At the time (1998) some people were thrown by some of the more theatrical dramaturgy, while others said it was the best work Art Street Theatre had produced thus far. So the reviews were mixed. But in the end we played to sold-out houses, got a lot of curtain calls and even some standing ovations, so something was working. What still surprises me today is the lump I get in my throat during the final moments. I know it's not cool to be moved by your own work. But these characters, their search for certainty and a sense of self, touch me deeply.

I wrote the script, but it is what it is because of Jordon Flato, who conceived it with me, and Kathryn Clark, first our dramaturg and then our stage manager. Andre's obsession with new physics theory and theological predictions comes from Jordon. Ana, the single mom with an unwanted child conceived in some devastating sexual encounter, was Kathryn's idea. She thought being a single mom was a brave thing to do. Jordon thought that a serious confrontation with the radical ideas proposed by new physics was brave. My girlfriend's sister had recently moved to Scotland, where she knew nobody. We thought that was brave and so we had another character, Annie, move to Scotland. I'd recently seen a documentary about Noam Chomsky, and his tenacity struck me as brave. Chomsky made me think about politicians and how, despite my mixed feelings regarding the art of politicking, it seemed brave to take a public stand for ones beliefs. And so I ransacked various political magazines and books to find the voices of our soapbox adversaries, Anne and Andrew. Then a friend who was both a priest and a sharp shooter said, "Being brave is *this* close to being stupid." So we decided that all our characters would fail to be brave, and we would watch them struggle in the wake of their stupid decisions.

Eventually we realized that "brave" is an adjective bestowed on one by others. People who get dubbed "brave" usually say they didn't feel brave at all. Usually they felt scared, desperate, or that they simply did what they needed to do in the moment and had they actually thought more about it they might not have been so stupid as to be so "brave."

Written under the looming shadow of the millennium, *Brave* is an exploration of these contradictions and of our country's generally anxious pre-millennial mindset. Once Y2K came and went without a hitch, I figured *Brave* had become a period piece. But a presentation of the play during PCPA Theaterfest's 2003 festival of new plays revealed that after September 11, 2001, the play's bomb threats, tense airport scenes, and mood of uneasy anticipation had a new context. I was glad the play had meaning beyond its premiere, but also sad. It would be nice if we could find our peace, and render the play irrelevant.

The Death of Meyerhold

In 1998 an actor friend, Gillian Chadsey, introduced me to Meyerhold's physical acting system, Biomechanics. She'd just studied for two weeks in Seattle with a Russian master of the technique, Gennadi Bogdanov. I was immediately struck by the work and began to gather as much written material on it as I could. With Chadsey's help, I also tried to experiment with the technique a bit in *Messenger #1*, in which I'd cast her as Electra. That same year (2000) I had the opportunity to study with Bogdanov myself, and it was at that point that my serious pursuit of the work began.

I had by then read a great deal of biographical information on Meyerhold, and I thought that doing a play about him might be a great way to explore his work even further. Instinct told me that such a play, given its subject, would be larger than my own little company could afford, so I approached Patrick Dooley, the Artistic Director of Shotgun Players in Berkeley, CA. He told me to start writing. I delved deeper into the biographies I'd collected, but soon realized there was a great deal about Meyerhold that I could not grasp given my limited understanding of his era. So I started to read about Russian history between 1900 and 1940.

Three years, twenty-four books, and a handful of additional workshops with Bogdanov later, *The Death of Meyerhold* premiered. Shotgun was producing it during the Christmas season, and we wondered how a play about the Soviet revolution with "death" and a strange Russian name in the title would sell. It sold exceptionally well, and eventually moved from a 150-seat house to a 350-seat house. Audiences seemed to connect to this relatively unknown figure from the distant Russian past. The play demands a strong physical, almost musical approach to performance and people liked that too. Even the play's epic length seemed to contribute to its appeal. I was delighted by those who grumbled when they were told the play ran three hours, and then came out afterward amazed by how fast the time went!

That contemporary American audiences were getting caught up in the personal, artistic and political struggles of Vsevolod Meyerhold and his comrades, among them Mayakovsky, Shostakovich and Stanislavsky, was an exciting surprise. I think this happened because, really, the play is not about Soviet Russia in the early twentieth century. It's about the death of freethinking in politically ambiguous times. You don't have to be a Red to connect with that.

Although – funny story – I was cornered after one performance by an older woman who literally screamed at me for ten minutes about how I was blaspheming Comrade Stalin's name, how ungrateful I was to the thousands of Soviet soldiers who died to make America great, and how the entire third act of my play was a pack of lies. I didn't think any American Stalinist's still existed. (Berkeley!) Contrast her with a Russian family who expressed amazement at how accurately the play conveyed the feeling of their country's history, or the Hungarian woman who told me the play perfectly captured the ambiguity of life under Communism.

In the end, what most pleased me about *The Death of Meyerhold* was how it was precisely its odd features – long running time, distant historical figures, scenes departing radically from time and place, grotesque mix of performance styles – that combined to speak to people. The play demonstrated that Meyerhold was right: audiences do want to think while they're being entertained. They do want to be challenged. They do want to argue with a production, as many did with ours. Meyerhold's art, life and era provide just such an opportunity, bound together as they are by such striking contradictions. The details may be different, but aren't our current lives and era also riddled with contradictions – on the news, on the streets, and at the kitchen table, every day?

Faust Pt1

In an 1806 conversation, two years prior to the publication of *Faust Part 1*, historian Heinrich Luden asked Goethe, "What is the central idea of Faust," to which Goethe replied, "How should I know? I wrote the play." It was a comment typical of Goethe's insistence on multiplicity of meaning and interpretation. Goethe was also an advocate of borrowing good ideas from other artists, of liberally mixing styles and genres, and of trusting passions over logic. The result was a lot of brilliant and lasting work on his part, and over two hundred years of passionately mixed criticism from others.

Goethe often chided his countrymen for their intellectual seriousness, and preferred to lean into a more kinesthetic sense of language and of showmanship. He reveled in human complexity. And so with regard to the frequent charge that his work was too ambiguous and contradictory, Goethe stated that, "The more incomprehensible for the understanding a poetic creation may be, the better," preferring that his work "remain an evident riddle, delight men on and on, and give them something to work on."

Back in 1992 I wrote a quite different adaptation of *Faust* as a college class project. Though I never did anything with it, this early attempt planted a fertile seed, and in 2007 the time seemed right to give it another go. I saw in our shifting world Goethe's theme of the struggle between desire and responsibility, and his important question as to how deeply we are willing to consider the ways in which our personal actions impact the world outside ourselves.

The only thing I salvaged from my 1992 script was the notion to pare Goethe's sprawling epic down to the triangle between Faust, Mephistopheles and Gretchen, and to bring onstage the character of Gretchen's mother. Though not at all true to the letter of Goethe, I was keen to remain faithful to his impulse. Goethe created a brilliant conundrum of a play, full of tantalizing contradictions. Stripped of Goethe's fabulous excesses, this adaptation runs several hours shorter than the original. But hopefully the characters are no less full, their actions just as confounding as they've always been. I think their story is ultimately a kind of existential comedy that turns tragic when desire confronts responsibility, but I know it's many other things as well.

I've been asked a few times if I plan to write *Part 2*. But my hope, fulfilled by the Shotgun Players world premiere, is that audiences in their own subsequent thoughts and conversations effectively write *Part 2*. I agree with Goethe about the necessity in art for challenges, gaps and loose threads. If we, the artists, were to greedily answer every question a play asks, there'd be no reason to perform it. Room must be left for the audience to participate. Their work completes the performance. *Faust Pt1* is a good example of how and why this is so. I credit Goethe for this quality that, luckily, it seems I didn't manage to cut in cutting so much else!

The Forest War

I wrote *The Forest War* in June 2003 when I was a playwright in residence at the Djerassi Resident Artists Program, situated on a gorgeous, 600-acre landscape near the central California Pacific coast. Out my window there was a sweeping field of tall grass. A hidden stream ran through it and the grass ranged in color from brown to green to maroon to blue to white. When the wind blew across it the field looked like a fretful sea. Sometimes the fog would roll through the morning sun or little thistles would float above the field like tiny white paper umbrellas and the beauty of all this was breathtaking and exquisitely peaceful.

Each night at dinner, the seven other artists and I would gather around the table to eat, drink and talk. At this point in history the Iraq War was officially "over," according to King Bush II, and the irony that more soldiers had died after the war than during was not lost on anyone. Needless to say, gather a bunch of artists around a table during the time of a questionable war and they're likely to discuss it in a manner that leans to the left. Nevertheless I was struck by the diversity of points of view at our table, and the contradictions at work – such as the young painter who drove to and from a "no blood for oil" rally in her gas-guzzling SUV.

On the bookshelf in the living room of the Djerassi writer's house I found a large book on world mythology. Its pages were filled with striking images of stone and wooden icons of various ancient deities from Asia, Central America, the Middle East and Europe. Their names were foreign to me and strange, and their stories were filled with danger, revenge, lust, love, power, adventure and hope.

I had been thinking about *King Lear* around this time. Watching Akira Kurosawa's great film adaptation of the play, *Ran*, I was struck by the simple, very direct yet poetic quality of the English subtitles, of all things.

All of these influences converged into what became *The Forest War*. Taking my cue from Brecht, who took his cue from Shakespeare, I invented a distant time and place in order to deal with contemporary, and unfortunately timeless, issues of war and justice. I cobbled together a nomenclature from Chinese, Japanese, Indian, Aztec, Toltec, and Persian mythologies. My love of showmanship and high theatricality intermingled with the barest bones of American history between the Clinton years and the then-current state of the Bush regime, resulting in a melodramatic tale of war and political intrigue. I also found myself writing a story of husbands and wives, children and parents, artists and merchants, as well as heroes and villains.

By drawing on multiple influences from multiple cultures and eras, the form of the play acknowledges the perpetual universality of history's basic building block: war. When I now consider what the play is really "about," there are two lines of dialogue that stand out for me. They are both from the same character, Ange, who grows from obedient daughter to avenging hero over the course of the play. At one point, sitting alone in a meadow with her lover, the young peasant and painter Olan, Ange asks herself, "What is justice that it does not count love among its laws?" At the end of the play, after she has killed the villain who murdered her family, she holds up her dead lover's paintbrush, which she had sharpened to a point in order to exact her revenge, and cries out, "I add this deed to my fistful of tears, and mourn the death of love!" From these two lines, which had always struck me instinctively as the heart of the play, I realized over time that *The Forest War* is about compassion. When Ange speaks of love, what she is talking about is the compassion one has for one's fellow human beings, be they family, friends, lovers, neighbors, or strangers. To her mind, justice should not exclude compassion from its consideration, nor should law be so cold a business as to forgo it – ever. Violence is an act of hatred that cuts down our capacity to love, and true love is no more or less than unyielding compassion.

Rhonda Perr, the make-up designer for the Shotgun Players production, asked me one night why *everyone* has to die in the play. I laughed at first, but recognized her question as a very good one. I hadn't thought about it so consciously. And so I did, right then and there as we were driving home after that night's dress rehearsal. The deaths that climb rapidly in number as the play reaches its end are a way of depicting the floodgate of violence, how violence only and always begets more violence. It is an ancient idea – not even an "idea," but an apparent fact – that remains ever contemporary. To be honest, I do not have much faith in humankind's ability to change its nature. But I do believe each individual human being has it within herself to change. Maybe this is why I ended the play with the entire countryside scorched clean by fire and just one person left alive, accompanied only by the fates. If not a final note of hope, it is at least one of possibility. And I think the existence of possibility itself does offer some hope. And maybe this lone survivor is a young woman because the world has been run primarily by old men. If we're going to scrape the dirty world clean and start anew, we might as well go for it fully.

Of course, in addition to all of this, the play is also about the fun of showmanship and the beauty of that which is particular to the theatre – presence, music, movement, language, a bare artificiality with which the audience participates through their imagination, and in which we hope to recognize something true.

I Am Hamlet

At this point in history we have long since figured out what William Shakespeare's *Hamlet* is. There are no more secrets to unearth. We know where the ambiguities lie and where the certainties stand. Innumerable stage productions, films, articles, critical essays and books have picked apart each letter of Shakespeare's play, so that now the experience of seeing *Hamlet* performed has a bit less to do with what *Hamlet* is than how the actors, director and designers will do it. It is a testament to what Shakespeare wrote that the vast sea of past and present explorations does not diminish one's own personal voyage with the play. Somehow *Hamlet* has remained thrilling, provocative and mysterious despite the deluge of criticism that still pours out of academia, coupled with countless annual performances around the globe.

And yet, like its loving cousin *Romeo & Juliet*, *Hamlet* suffers from our familiarity with it. Expectation has built walls so thick that when the curtain rises many of us out there in the dark can't see a thing past the perfect productions locked in our heads. Reading the play and various critical essays about it in 2001, I marveled at the sheer amount of writing devoted to *Hamlet*, and wondered what Hamlet himself might think of all that scrutiny, all the attention and analysis he has received for hundreds of years. This curiosity awoke the playwright in me who set to work contemplating a show in which Hamlet, fed up after centuries of watching his life interpreted by various actors, directors and philosophers, finally hops up on stage and has a go at it himself.

I Am Hamlet is the story of a young man who has been waiting in the wings four hundred years to act. His act is his own play. And we see that these words, "act" and "play," not unlike *Hamlet,* have many meanings. This is their value. It is this value, this multiplicity, which Hamlet begins to understand in acting out all the characters that he thought he'd figured out long ago. And it is his unresolved relationship with Ophelia in particular that finally pulls him off the stage and out of his four-century theatrical purgatory, his play.

And yet the play's the thing, as the line goes, and the multitudinous questions *Hamlet* asks of us must give us pause. Is it the pause, or the action that follows, wherein we find our purpose?

little extremes

I wrote and directed *little extremes* in 1993 while I was attending San Francisco State University, where the Theatre Arts Department has a great class called Brown Bag. Brown Bag is an entirely student-run theatre company that operates in semester-long shifts. Each semester a new set of directors audition a new company of actors and each week they put up another hour-long play. During my semester in Brown Bag I ran tech for a musical, acted in a play a classmate wrote, and myself directed Steven Berkoff's *Greek* and my own *little extremes*. In many respects the Brown Bag experience established certain ways of doing things that stuck with me for many years. Aesthetically, *little extremes*, with its economy and non-linear, non-literal dramaturgy, was a key experience in this regard.

I directed the play again as the first production of Art Street Theatre, the company I established in 1995 with the participation of several fellow SF State alumni. The production went off quite well as an offering in that year's San Francisco Fringe Festival. We packed'm in and felt proud.

Though it is a rather small play in terms of its overall scope, I have a great fondness for it. It's very much the work of a young fellow in his early twenties, with its impulsive violence, its earnestness, a sweetness that risks sentimentality, its absurdist flair, and the characters' frequently expressed need for verbal reassurance. And yet I wonder if I do the play a disservice by relegating it to the "early work" heap. Today I might express myself differently than I did when I wrote *little extremes*, but I still look at the world and see people making impulsively violent decisions, failing to communicate clearly with one another, desperate for reassurances, wishing for deeper relationships but too scared to take the necessary vulnerable steps. The little extremes many people are willing to go to in order to avoid emotional vulnerability add up to a culture of weird extremes, strange murders, lasting social fissions and profound misunderstandings. At times it all does seem quite absurd and disjointed, funny in one sense and very sad in another. So, maybe there still is room in the theatre for small plays like *little extremes*.

Messenger #1

I think I could spend the rest of my life working on Aeschylus' *Oresteia* and never run out of ways or reasons to do it. After 2500 years, you'd think we'd learn its lessons about the nature of justice and revenge. But no such luck.

With *Messenger #1* I took a tragicomic approach. I wanted to telescope the entire *Oresteia* trilogy into one evening, and use the messengers as an opportunity to critique this ancient masterpiece of political and social argument. So, the familiar story is told from the point of view of the various messengers who deliver the news and sometimes get crushed between the pages of history that their work writes.

In order to convey the disparity between rich and poor, I used a language style that combined a pseudo-Shakespearean vernacular with a jargon reminiscent of Clifford Odets. Aeschylus' royal family took on the bulk of the former, while my invented working class messengers spoke mostly the latter. Though on its surface the language and style of *Messenger #1* might appear to suggest parody, it is important that the tragedy be played as seriously as the comedy is played for laughs. The one is the swinging door to the other, and the shifts the script makes between comedy and tragedy can be played as abruptly or as gradually as they appear to be on the page.

That's regarding form. As for the matter of that form's content, we know that justice and revenge figure into the heart of it. But also in that heart flows the blood of time and the fact that what Aeschylus wrote remains sadly contemporary. In this regard I think of the title character's final message, delivered after he's lost his innocence to war, his love to the law, and his ethics to his own rage. "It is my duty to inform you," he says to the audience, "that Orestes, our new king, has been formally forgiven for his crimes, that a history of chaos has finally been disrupted by a new civic order, and the Law of Blood replaced by a Law of

Reason. They call it Justice."

R&J

This one-hour, five-actor adaptation of Shakespeare's love/hate story came about for a couple of reasons. I wanted to do a production of *Romeo & Juliet* with Art Street Theatre, but we didn't have the money at the time for a large cast. Also, I wasn't interested in doing anything straightforward with the play. *Romeo & Juliet* is so ultra familiar that people who haven't ever seen or read it know the story and can likely quote lines from it. At this point, we all may even be born with the play in our bloodstreams. When a play has become that familiar it's a blessing and a curse. The curse is the accumulation of expectation, preconception and habit – three enemies of art and life both. The blessing is that one can play upon familiarity to make the thing unfamiliar and catch fire again.

That's what four other actors and I wanted to do. So we stuck Shakespeare's play in a blender without the cap on and let the shards splatter about. For two months we met three times a week and improvised physically on characters and themes. During that time I'd go home and write based on what we were improvising. Then for another five or six weeks we rehearsed before premiering the piece under the umbrella of the 1996 San Francisco Fringe Festival. The response was so strong we produced the show again a year later for a full-length run. This gave me a chance to make a few rewrites for the better – an experience that forever sold me on second productions being infinitely superior to premieres in terms of new work development.

R&J is a highly physical meditation on the pressures time can put on one's emotions and personal judgment. Time in *Romeo & Juliet* gradually ticks faster and faster, and haste makes a lot of waste by the end. By giving Juliet a chance to review the last week of her life as it flashes before her eyes in a brain spasm after she's just killed herself, we captured the essence of Shakespeare's script in all its playfulness, violence and passion.

I say "we" because although I penned the adaptation, it is really the result of a lot of work by five actors – myself, Gillian Brecker, Bricine Mitchell, Jake Rodriguez and Beth Wilmurt. Their initials remain imprinted in the text. And without their sweat it wouldn't be what it is.

It takes actors with muscle, imagination, passion, and the means to use them, to carry off a play like this. Otherwise it might be merely arty. It can't just be spoken, but must also be set in motion. We did it with our bodies, a chair, a violin, an old paperback copy of Shakespeare's play and a bare stage. But I think it's open to all sorts of angles. Fragmented as it is, it's still Shakespeare, and what Robert Wilson once said about *Hamlet* holds true for *Romeo & Juliet* as well – it's a rock that can't be destroyed.

Unless one does it straight up, perhaps! Since performing this production, my partner Beth Wilmurt and I have "collected" productions of *Romeo & Juliet*, and by that I mean we see them whenever we get the opportunity. Inevitably it is the productions that take chances with the text, and even axes to it, that capture the passion and vibrancy of the play, while the more traditionally faithful productions rarely do more than sputter. By all reports, *R&J* gave its audience a smack of passion between the eyes that reached down to their hearts and stirred their adrenal glands to boot. I remain quite proud of it, as you can tell.

Other Plays By Mark Jackson
not included in this collection

Don Juan
Originally developed in a workshop co-produced by Art Street Theatre and EXIT Theatre in March and April 2003. Further developed in a workshop produced by the Playwrights Foundation in May 2004. The world premiere of *Don Juan* was produced by the San Francisco State University Theatre Arts Department on March 6, 2008.

Cast 5 Men, 2 Women
Single multi-functional set
Running time 2 hours

This adaptation draws on both the Moliere and Pushkin renditions of the Don Juan legend, and was initially developed with a team of actors and designers during a lengthy process involving full costumes, lighting and scenery, prior to the formal writing of the text. The result is a dark, comedic, and decidedly theatrical perspective of *Don Juan* fitted to our age – an age in which seduction and hypocrisy collaborate to get under our skins, sell us their ideologies and take from us what they like.

The Inspector
An adaptation of Gogol's *Revizor*.

Cast 13M, 4W – with doubling and some reversed-gender casting, this cast size may be reduced
Multiple sets, or a single multi-functional set
Running time approximately 2 hours, 45 minutes

When the officials of a provincial Russian town mistake a lowly con man for a government official, their fears and desires are painfully revealed, and the con man gets away with not just their money but something of their souls as well. Drawing on elements of Vsevolod Meyerhold's famous 1926 production, this adaptation of Gogol's classic satire brings out the darkness Gogol famously complained was missing in productions of the play. *The Inspector* remains an unfortunately timely critique of a corrupt society's narcissism, greed and spiritual bankruptcy.

Io Princess of Argos
Music Marci Karr
Book Mark Jackson
Lyrics Mark Jackson and Marci Karr

The world premiere of *Io Princess of Argos* was presented by Art Street Theatre at EXIT Stage Left, San Francisco, CA, on March 9, 2001. The production was nominated for five Bay Area Theatre Critics Circle Awards, winning "Best Original Score." This production was revived in May 2002 by Encore Theatre Company at Thick House, San Francisco, CA.

Cast 2 Men, 2 Women, 2-3 Musicians
Single set
Running time 75 minutes

Seduced by Zeus, transformed into a cow by Hera, with a stinging fly locked in her head, and wandering mad across the desert, Io, Princess of Argos, stumbles into a hallucinated cabaret in her own head where she sings her life story, backed up by her own singing and dancing Greek chorus. *Io Princess of Argos* blends the classic American musical with ancient Greek tragedy and several shots of bourbon. The ancient tale of Io remains a timely story of a young everywoman's personal and political awakening, and her struggle with the eternal question, "Why?"

Mary Stuart

An adaptation of Friedrich Schiller's *Maria Stuart*, commissioned by Shotgun Players, Berkeley, CA. At the time of this publication the premiere was scheduled for October 6, 2010.

Cast 6 Men, 2 Women
Multiple locations
Running time approximately 1 hour 50 minutes

This adaptation streamlines Schiller's original text, rendering it the taught political thriller it always was but with a contemporary momentum. Schiller's drama of two powerful women caught within the machinations of a largely male political system remains a timely, potent and surprisingly personal warning about the abuses of justice in the face of national anxieties over security, terrorism and the potential for war. What do we do when our system of justice and our sense of morality don't meet eye to eye?

Megan and the Magic Compass

Megan and the Magic Compass was commissioned by Il Teatro 450, San Francisco, CA, and had its world premiere there on December 3, 1999.

Cast 3 Men, 3 Women
Multiple locations
Running time 55 minutes

Megan and the Magic Compass is a fairytale play for young audiences, performed by actors and puppets. It tells the story of Megan, a young girl who wakes up one morning to the rumble of an earthquake and discovers that her parents are missing, time has stopped, and a large crack has opened up in the earth, rendering the path from her rural home into town impassable. A strange old woman emerges from the forest and gives Megan and her mischievous friend, Zak, a magic compass with which to navigate as they search for their parents and for the cause of the mysterious, time-stopping earthquake. Megan and Zak's subsequent adventure takes them to the ocean, the desert, and the mountains, where they encounter a variety of wild creatures in need of help. Eventually Megan and Zak are reunited with their parents, having discovered the confidence within themselves to navigate life's sudden obstacles.

Megan's Baby

Megan's Baby was given a development workshop and staged reading in December 2005 as a part of the New Voices West program at Magic Theatre, San Francisco, CA. *Megan's Baby* was further developed in a workshop and staged reading in June 2008 at Capital Stage, Sacramento, CA.

Cast 2 Men, 2 Women
Multiple locations done on a spare set
Running time approximately 70 minutes

Megan's Baby is a contemporary comedy about grief and our desire to believe in something greater in life than ourselves. At an upscale private hospital frequented by the rich and famous, Megan tells a prominent doctor, Karl, that she is pregnant with God's baby. When he hesitates to help her, Megan blackmails him with her knowledge that he is having an affair. Karl is up for a major promotion, and his wife's father sits on the hospital's board, so this news will surely have repercussions. The woman Karl is having an affair with is Karen, Megan's high-strung best friend, whose own marriage to a quiet fellow named Tom is unraveling. The lies thicken as events unfold, and all four characters stumble more and more as they search for something to make their small lives meaningful.

About The Author

Mark Jackson is an award-winning playwright, director and performer. He was Artistic Director of Art Street Theatre, San Francisco, from 1995 to 2004, during which time he wrote, directed, and performed in numerous productions for the company. Mark's work has also been seen at Aurora Theatre Company, Encore Theatre Company, EXIT Theatre, Potrzebie Dance Project, San Francisco International Arts Festival, Shotgun Players, and The Studio Theatre (Washington D.C.), among others; as well as internationally at Arts International Festival IV (Japan), Edinburgh Festival Fringe (UK), and Deutsches Theater Berlin (Germany). His plays have been developed at American Conservatory Theater, Capital Stage, EXIT Theatre, Playwrights Foundation, Magic Theatre, and Z Space Studio.

In June 2003, Mark was the resident playwright of the Djerassi Resident Artists Program, where he was awarded the William and Flora Hewlett Foundation Honorary Fellowship. He is a 2005 German Chancellor Fellow of the Alexander von Humboldt Foundation, which took him to Berlin, Germany, for the 04/05 season to work with Mime Centrum Berlin, a practical research center for physical theatre. Mark was named "Best Director" by the *East Bay Express* in 2009 and 2004, "Best Theatrical Auteur" by the *SF Weekly* in 2007, and one of the "Top 100 Bay Area Artists" by *San Francisco Magazine* in 2002. Other awards and honors include two Bay Area Theatre Critics Circle Awards, three *San Francisco Bay Guardian* Upstage/Downstage Awards, two Theatre Bay Area CA$H Grants, and a Magic Theatre / Z Space New Works Initiative commission. Mark's writing has benefited three times from the generosity of the Tournesol Project, a granting program for the development of new work.

Mark is a graduate of the San Francisco State University Theatre Arts Department. He lives in San Francisco with his talented and beautiful actor/singer gal pal, Beth Wilmurt. They have no pets, but did recently buy a new rug that they pet all the time.

www.ingramcontent.com/pod-product-compliance
Lightning Source LLC
Chambersburg PA
CBHW031558110426
42742CB00036B/116